The Hadza

D1206608

ORIGINS OF HUMAN BEHAVIOR AND CULTURE

Edited by Monique Borgerhoff Mulder and Joe Henrich

1. *Behavioral Ecology and the Transition to Agriculture*, edited by Douglas J. Kennett and Bruce Winterhalder

2. *Pattern and Process in Cultural Evolution*, edited by Stephen Shennan

3. *The Hadza: Hunter-Gatherers of Tanzania*, by Frank W. Marlowe

4. *Life Histories of the Dobe !Kung: Food, Fatness, and Well-being over the Life Span*, by Nancy Howell

The Hadza

Hunter-Gatherers of Tanzania

Frank W. Marlowe

UNIVERSITY OF CALIFORNIA PRESS
Berkeley · Los Angeles · London

University of California Press, one of the most distinguished university presses in the United States, enriches
lives around the world by advancing scholarship in the
humanities, social sciences, and natural sciences. Its
activities are supported by the UC Press Foundation and
by philanthropic contributions from individuals and in-
stitutions. For more information, visit www.ucpress.edu.

Origins of Human Behavior and Culture, No. 3

University of California Press
Berkeley and Los Angeles, California

University of California Press, Ltd.
London, England

© 2010 by The Regents of the University of California

Library of Congress Cataloging-in-Publication Data

Marlowe, Frank, 1954-
    The Hadza : hunter-gatherers of Tanzania / Frank
W. Marlowe.
        p.   cm. — (Origins of human behavior and culture)
    Includes bibliographical references and index.
    ISBN 978-0-520-25341-4 (cloth : alk. paper) — ISBN
978-0-520-25342-1 (pbk. : alk. paper)
    1. Hatsa (African people)—Hunting.   2. Hatsa
(African people)—Food.   3. Hatsa (African people)—
Social life and customs.   4. Hunting and gathering
societies—Tanzania.   5. Social ecology—Tanzania.
6. Social evolution—Tanzania.   7. Tanzania—Social
life and customs.   I. Title.
    DT443.3.H37M37   2010
    305.896'1—dc22   2009033727

16   15   14   13   12   11   10
10   9   8   7   6   5   4   3   2   1

∞

Cover photograph: A Hadza man shoots an arrow at an
animal in the trees. Photo by the author.

I dedicate this book to the Hadza, the fantastic, wonderful Hadza, and to my adviser and mentor, Professor Nicholas Blurton Jones, who introduced me to the Hadza. Nick was simply the greatest adviser one could ever have.

Contents

Acknowledgments   ix

1. The Hadza and Evolutionary Theory:
   An Introduction   1
2. Habitat and History   11
3. Social Organization, Beliefs, and Practices   39
4. Material Culture   69
5. Foraging   101
6. Life History   133
7. Mating   165
8. Parenting   195
9. Cooperation and Food-Sharing   225
10. The Median Foragers: Humans in
    Cross-Species Perspective   255
    Afterword: The Hadza Present and Future   285

References   291

Index   319

Acknowledgments

I thank the following: Audax Mabulla for assistance in Tanzania with permissions, advice, field assistants, and many enjoyable discussions. Col. Dr. Yadon M. Kohi, Director General of the Tanzanian Commission for Science and Technology (COSTECH) for permission to conduct research, and the many officials at the regional, district, and ward levels of government. Johannes Kleppe, Lene Kleppe, David Bygott, and Jeannette Hanby, as well as Christian and Nani Smelling, for invaluable help and hospitality in Tanzania. Daudi Peterson, Thad Peterson, and Michael Peterson and their wives for so much help, advice, and good times in Tanzania. Roger Swagler for editorial help. Colette Berbesque for fieldwork, help with images, figures, data collection, analysis, and discussions of evolutionary theory and the Hadza. Peter Gray for help with FA research. Brian Wood for sharing some of his hard-won data. Coren Apicella for so much coauthoring and Figure 7.5, along with Tony Little. Alyssa Crittenden and Claire Porter for being the best fieldworkers to oversee my site while I am gone. Help with experiments and comments on papers from Elizabeth Cashdan. My many Tanzanian assistants—Pastory Bushozi, Revocatus Bugumba, Hokki Manonga, Happy Msofe, Danny Ngumbuke, Golden Ngumbuke, and Ephraim Mutakyahwa—for their long hours of difficult fieldwork. Kirk Miller and Bonny Sands for linguistic information. James Woodburn for invaluable information and good times in the field and the UK. Lars Smith for sharing data and his knowledge of the Hadza in the bush and for hospitality in transit. Bruce Winterhalder and Eric Smith for making many helpful suggestions on an early rough draft of this book. Kristen Hawkes and James O'Connell for ideas and discussions. Nannette Bailey for encouragement and moral support. My sister Julia Marlowe Swagler for always being supportive. I thank Geoffrey Thomas for making Figure 3.3. National Science Foundation for financial support via grants #0544751, #0242455, #0136761, #9976681, and #9529278, as well as William F. Milton Fund, MacArthur Foundation, Leakey Foundation, Jim Turner and UCLA Graduate Division, UCLA Department of Anthropology, Harvard Department of Anthropology, and Florida State University Department of Anthropology. Blake Edgar at UC Press for taking on this project and providing valuable feedback, the art editors for handling so many images, and Deborah Masi for her skillful production editing. Nicholas Blurton Jones for his mentoring. And most of all the Hadza, particularly Gudo Bala, for answering so many questions.

CHAPTER I

The Hadza and Evolutionary Theory

An Introduction

The Hadza of Tanzania are one of the very few societies anywhere in the world who still live by hunting and gathering. Hunter-gatherers are people who forage for wild foods, practicing no cultivation or animal husbandry. The fact that the Hadza are still foraging makes them invaluable to researchers interested in the lifestyle of our ancestors before agriculture so greatly altered human societies. The Hadza happen to live in East Africa, an area rich in hominin fossils (Figure 1.1). Hominins are all those species (*Australopithecus afarensis, Paranthropus boisei, Homo erectus*, etc.) that share with us a common ancestor that diverged from the ancestor of our closest living relatives, chimpanzees and bonobos, 6–7 million years ago (mya). Today, we humans are the sole surviving hominin. Humans and their hominin ancestors have occupied East Africa for as long as they have existed. For testing evolutionary hypotheses about past ecological influences and outcomes, it would be difficult to find a living society more relevant than the Hadza. They have been studied extensively, but surprisingly no English-language anthropological book has been published until now.[1]

I began my research with the Hadza in 1995 when I was working on my Ph.D. at UCLA. Since then, I have been back 15 times for a total of about 4 years altogether. Even so, I speak only a little bit of the Hadza

1. In 1958 Kohl-Larsen wrote a book in German, but it has not been translated.

Figure 1.1. Map of East Africa, showing Hadza area in relation to the locations of hominin fossil sites. Inset shows Hadzaland (inside shaded ring) with key locations in a small font and names of neighboring ethnic groups in a large font.

language (Hadzane) because I can communicate with the Hadza in Kiswahili, their second language. My research entails behavioral sampling, measurement of food acquisition and consumption, skills, preferences, anthropometry, demography, and a variety of topics using experiments and interviews. All of this research involves evolutionary theory as a guide to hypothesis testing. I intend this book to serve as a general ethnography of the Hadza, but I also hope to persuade the uninitiated that an evolutionary view is essential for understanding humans. I therefore aim to make the book accessible to readers with little familiarity with evolutionary theory.

Natural selection explains how and why evolution occurs (Darwin 1859). Individuals with certain traits survive and reproduce more successfully than individuals with other traits. The genes involved in producing those successful traits are passed on to the next generation in greater numbers. Darwin did not know about genes, but he knew traits were inherited; the modern theory of selection had to await the rediscovery of Mendelian genetics and the synthesis of Mendel's laws with Darwin's theory by early population geneticists (Fisher 1930, Haldane 1932, Wright 1931). Natural selection leads to adaptation. Genes that promote more optimal use of resources in an environment result in enhanced survival and reproduction of their carriers, and consequently each successive generation becomes more adapted to the environment. When the environment changes, the population will eventually track the changes or go extinct. The environment includes everything: climate, flora and fauna, predators, parasites, and members of one's own species (conspecifics). Conspecifics are especially important among social animals like us because kin and potential rivals, allies, and mates have a strong impact on an individual's reproductive success (RS).

Our bodies and behavior have been shaped by competition between individuals in the past, and we all have inherited our genes from the winners of that competition. Sexual selection is the component of natural selection that deals with reproduction (Darwin 1871). Ultimately, greater RS matters more than longevity because no one lives forever. Even if one lived to be a thousand years old, without reproducing, one's own genes would not be passed on, so one's personal (or direct) fitness would be zero. We can see, therefore, why selection should commonly favor individuals who selfishly exploit resources for their own reproductive benefit (individual selection).

Our understanding of how evolution works greatly expanded when William Hamilton (1964) explained why, despite individual selection, we observe seemingly altruistic behavior in many species. Hamilton's formula tells us when selection should favor one individual helping another. The formula can be expressed as $C < Br$, where C equals the cost to the helper, B equals the benefit to the beneficiary, and r equals the degree of relatedness between helper and beneficiary. When the helper and beneficiary are related by 50%, as full siblings are on average, as long as the benefit is more than twice the cost (e.g., benefit = 2.1 and cost = 1), it will pay one sibling to help the other because $0.5 * 2.1 = 1.05 > 1$. More precisely, there is positive selection for a gene that promotes helping relatives (nepotism). Hamilton (1964) thus introduced the concept of inclusive fitness. An individual's inclusive fitness includes the person's own RS (direct fitness) plus his or her effect on others who carry the same alleles by common descent, weighted by the degree of relatedness between them (indirect fitness) (Creel 1991, Hamilton 1964, Lucas, Creel, and Waser 1996).

The reason Hamilton's paper was such a profound development was that it explained seemingly altruistic behavior without invoking group selection. One proponent of group selection, Wynne-Edwards (1962) had suggested that a population of birds restrains its reproduction to avoid overexploitation of resources and to prevent group extinction. But David Lack's (1966) experiments had already shown that optimal clutch size, rather than maximum clutch size, was favored because a female who laid too many eggs fledged fewer chicks than when she laid the optimal number. G. C. Williams (1966) made the case that Lack's explanation of reproductive restraint was more consistent with basic Darwinian theory because restraint increased the individual mother's RS.

Darwin's natural selection was fundamentally about individuals competing for resources and turning them into more offspring than their rivals had (individual selection). Nonetheless, before Hamilton's seminal paper, one commonly heard group selection arguments like "subordinates defer to dominant individuals" or "the slowest animal gets eaten by the predator" because it is "for the good of the species." Even Darwin himself invoked group selection to explain behavior seen in warfare, saying that those who were bravest, risking death to save their group, would make the best warriors and that self-sacrificing behavior would evolve from their defeating other groups (Darwin 1871). On the other hand, he had no explanation for the existence of sterile castes within bees, wasps, and ants, but recognized that their inability to reproduce posed a potentially fatal blow to his theory of natural selection that depended on reproduction. Hamilton's formula provided an explanation: The sterile workers helped the queen make more sisters for them because given their haplo-diploid genetic system they were more closely related to their sisters ($r = 75\%$). This explanation highlighted that it is the gene, not the group or the individual, that is selected. Because genes behave as if they are selfish, individuals sometimes behave unselfishly (Dawkins 1976).

No one ever puzzled over why a mother was willing to risk her life to protect her offspring; they are her genes' vehicles into the future. Helping other kinds of kin can be favored for the same reason, even though the path to the next generation is less direct. Hamilton's rule tells us that even a mother will sometimes fail to help her offspring. Her interests and those of her offspring do not overlap perfectly because she shares only

50% of her genes with each one. She should weigh the gains of helping one offspring against the costs to her future offspring. In other words, we can expect parent-offspring conflict (Trivers 1974). A mother shares 50% of her genes with each of her two children, so she wants to help both equally. On the other hand, the child shares 50% of its genes with its full sib, which is only half of the 100% in its own genome. The child will prefer to get more help from mother than is in the mother's best interest or the interest of the other sib. The ages of individuals will also affect the calculus because a very young sib may not be capable of helping its older sib, while the elder may be able to help the younger.

It is inclusive fitness that determines a gene's success in succeeding populations, more precisely, the success of particular variants of the genes called alleles. There may be a brown or blue allele occupying the site of the gene coding for eye color. Often one allele is so successful that it spreads throughout the population and replaces all alternatives, at which point it is "fixed." By influencing the individual's behavior in ways that cause them to get passed on, genes affect their own representation in the gene pool. From the perspective of the allele, any behavior that helps make copies in others is advantageous, even if it causes its host to behave in an unselfish, even self-destructive way, so long as this leaves the greatest number of copies in the next generation. However, since genes in the individual's genome share their fate and will all die together, they tend to work well together; otherwise they are less likely to be passed on. For this reason, genes tend to promote a considerable degree of self-regarding behavior in individuals. Dawkins (1976) used the metaphor of rowers in a boat; they go nowhere if they do not paddle in concert and in the same direction.

How animals meet their energetic and nutritional requirements is the focus of optimal foraging theory (OFT). OFT assumes that individuals will seek to minimize costs and maximize benefits in their foraging behavior. That means they will usually not waste time or energy going after low-yield foods when higher-yield foods are available. They should be efficient in harvesting energy, and energy is used as a proxy for fitness. However, the individual always faces many constraints. The first constraint is the diet itself; committed carnivores cannot live on plant foods and herbivores on meat. Other important questions include the proper currency to use (kilocalories vs. protein) and the primary goal (maximize average rate of energy intake vs. minimize risk of shortfall) (Stephens and Krebs 1986). OFT models, like models of morphological evolution, are essentially engineering problems. With a given availability

TABLE 1.1. PAYOFF MATRIX FOR
HAWK-DOVE GAME

	H	D
H	(prob. win * value of food) + (prob. lose * cost of injury) (0.5 * 50) + (0.5 * −100) = 25 − 50 = −25	(prob. win * value of food) (1 * 50) = 50
D	(prob. win * value of food) (0 * 50) = 0	(prob. win * value of food) + (prob. lose * cost of display) (0.5) * (50 − 10) + (0.5) * (−10) = 20 − 5 = 15

NOTE: Payoffs shown are for the player listed in the row.

of food A and food B, each with a different nutritional value and a required search and handling time, how much of A vs. B should a forager take? But in life there are always competitors, and we need to consider their effect. Game theory is ideally suited for this.

Game theory treats individuals as different strategies, lets them play against each other in a game with specified payoffs for certain outcomes, and then sees which strategy wins. In the hawk-dove game, two strategies are employed with regard to a food source. A hawk is willing to fight and risk injury to get the food. A dove only displays, which goes on a while against another dove, but gives up quickly against a hawk. When dove meets dove, each gets the food half the time. If the value of the food is worth a gain of 50 points, the cost of a dove's long display is a loss of 10 points, and the cost of injury in a fight is a loss of 100 points, we can calculate the outcome (Table 1.1). When doves meet, each has a 50-50 chance of getting the food, so each receives an average of 25 minus the cost of display (25 − 10 = 15). When a hawk meets a dove, hawk gets the food and 50 points. When two hawks meet, they each have the same chance of winning their fight and getting the food but also the same chance of being injured. That gives each an average of 25 for getting the food and −50 for getting injured; thus their average payoff is −25.

In each instance, the hawk beats the dove, which means hawks can always invade a population of doves and do very well (+50). However, when there are too many hawks, they do poorly (−25). Doves do better against each other (+15); even against a hawk, doves get 0, which is better than two hawks against each other (−25). This means that no pure strategy is stable. With the payoffs specified here, there will be a mixed strategy with an equilibrium frequency of 0.58 hawk and 0.42 dove. This might consist of a population of 58% hawks and 42% doves, or individuals who play the hawk strategy 58% of the time and the dove strategy 42% of the time. The strategy that does best against other strategies and against itself, and therefore cannot be invaded by other strategies, is called an evolutionarily stable strategy (ESS) (Maynard Smith 1982). A strategy called "bourgeois," in which one defends food if there first or if closest to the food, is an ESS because it avoids fights against other bourgeois by using a simple, salient rule—proximity or priority—yet does not cause one to relinquish food like a dove does against a hawk (Maynard Smith 1982).

Genetic selection leads to adaptive behavior across environments, but because optimal solutions vary in different environments and different circumstances (different games), so too does behavior. Although we do not know precisely how alleles at genetic loci translate into specific behaviors, we can assume behavioral strategies, or decision rules (which do not imply conscious decisions), have been favored by selection to create adaptive phenotypes. This assumption of a link between heritability and phenotype, known as the phenotypic gambit (Grafen 1984, Smith and Winterhalder 1992), allows us to make predictions about behavioral outcomes. That is, we expect to see individuals modify their behavior in ways that tend to enhance their inclusive fitness. Just as our bodies tell us to seek water to quench our thirst, so our emotions tell us to flee an enemy, recruit allies, or seek a mate. Behavioral ecologists tend to measure behavior directly to test predictions about fitness outcomes. For this reason, they have mostly studied simpler societies (Borgerhoff Mulder 1988a, Winterhalder and Smith 2000), not necessarily foragers, but at least natural fertility (non-contracepting) societies, where there is still a direct link between behavior and RS.

Evolutionary psychology focuses on the mind and the mechanisms that selection has favored to execute adaptive behavior (Hagen 2003). Such mechanisms are assumed to be universal across humans, by and large. This means humans anywhere are appropriate subjects. Much depends on the trait, however. Some traits, like fear of snakes or desire for sex, may have changed little over the last several million years, while others, such as tribal identification and loyalty or the value placed on fatness in potential partners, may have changed significantly even over the past few hundred years.

The Environment of Evolutionary Adaptedness (EEA) (Bowlby 1969) refers to the sum total of environments hominins have occupied since they diverged from the ancestor of chimpanzees and bonobos 6–7 mya. It is within this time period that all hominin traits that were not present in the last common ancestor must have evolved. These are called derived traits; ancestral traits are those that were present in the last common ancestor. The EEA obviously includes a wide range of different environments, and different ones are relevant for different traits. The relevant environment for the evolution of our lungs dates back to the Devonian about 400 mya, for bipedalism to the end of the Miocene 6–7 mya, and for our peculiarly enlarged brain to about 2.5 mya. Lactose tolerance (the ability to digest milk in adults) dates to only about 7,000 years ago, and only in certain populations (Bersaglieri et al. 2004). Given that the relevant period varies with the trait in question, it makes more sense to think in terms of the Adaptively Relevant Environment (ARE) (Irons 1998).

Culture is obviously an important component of the human environment. When we talk about different environments, we are not simply contrasting desert with rain forest, but forager camp with inner-city neighborhood, societies where marriage is arranged by parents with those where people pick their own mates, and societies where food is scarce with societies in which food is guaranteed by a welfare program. Humans have created such varied cultural environments that it is often culture, rather than the physical habitat, that determines which behaviors enhance fitness. Ignoring culture can leave us without a clue (Laland, Odling-Smee, and Feldman 2000). However, there is something unsatisfying about an explanation of one cultural trait by reference to another without any attempt to explain how the first trait came about. For example, people often attribute sexual chastity in some cultures to adherence to religious doctrine. Religion may well be a proximate explanation, but why did a strict religious doctrine evolve in one population and not in another? Here, I attempt to see how much we can understand by reference to the habitat and mode of subsistence. Since among forgers each person must spend much time looking for and processing foods, it is easier to link behavior to the habitat and ecology.

The novel environments we have created can give rise to maladaptive behavior. Maladaptive does not mean bad, only fitness-reducing. This can occur when there has not been sufficient time for selection to produce the appropriate cognitive processing of the new environmental cues. Thus, individuals cannot calibrate the appropriate behavioral response that would maximize inclusive fitness (Richerson and Boyd 2005). It is important to appreciate that decision rules need not be conscious to work, and often it would be inefficient if they were. Imagine a truck coming at you; it is best if you do not have to consciously deliberate and decide whether to jump out of the street. When past selection produced adaptive behavior that is no longer fitness-enhancing in the present, it is called a mismatch. To cite one example, a study found that wealthier men in Montreal did not have more children, though they did have more sexual partners (Perusse 1994). Before contraception, more sexual partners would likely have resulted in more children. Note that what was selected for in the past was desire for sexual partners, not desire for siring offspring. Still, selection never ceases. As long as some people do want to have some children someday (and most people do), reproductive competition continues.

Mismatch is less of an issue among foragers because they are still living in an environment without so many novel cues, and we can expect mostly adaptive behavior from them (Symons 1987, Tooby and Cosmides 1990). There is still much to learn from foragers like the Hadza. Because they live in an area our hominin ancestors inhabited for as long as they existed, where the flora and fauna have not changed much since the Pliocene began 5.3 mya, their ecology is relevant for a long period of human evolution. Mortality risks, energy expenditure, and growth, as we will see in Chapter 6, are probably not so different from what they were 10–20,000 or more years ago. Because the Hadza live outdoors, most of what they do is in full view, which means their behavior can be measured directly. The foods they acquire can be weighed and, with effort, traced to the person who consumes them. We can see what sort of help a parent can give that might impact survivorship or growth. There are few books that report on quantitative behavioral studies carried out in foraging societies (Hewlett 1991, Hill and Hurtado 1996, Howell 1979, Lee 1984). We now have a record of the Hadza going back to the late 1950s, with some continuity back to the 1930s and even a bit earlier. A book-length treatment of Hadza research is long overdue.

CHAPTER 2

Habitat and History

LIVING FOSSILS

In the 1960s, Richard Lee and several other researchers studied many aspects of the Ju/'hoansi (Dobe !Kung or !Kung San) in Botswana (Lee 1984). This research brought renewed interest in hunter-gatherers as a source of information about the human past. After all, our ancestors were all foragers before agriculture first appeared in the eastern Mediterranean about 10–12,000 years ago (ya). The !Kung became the most well publicized hunter-gatherers and were often used to stand in for our Pleistocene ancestors. Lee (1972) described them as pristine foragers "on the threshold of the Neolithic." This sounds like they were frozen in the past because people tend to think about the Neolithic as occurring at a particular time, 10,000 ya. In fact, since the Neolithic refers to the adoption of agriculture and accompanying new tool kits, it did not occur 10,000 years ago everywhere. In most parts of the world, agriculture began much more recently. In northeast Africa, it began 8,000 ya but only spread south of the Sahara 1–2,000 ya, depending on the area. In the New World it began by 7,000 ya, but large areas of North America lacked agriculture when first encountered by Europeans. In Australia, there was no agriculture on the whole continent when British colonization began in 1788 (Scarre 1997).

In one sense, then, the !Kung really were on the threshold of their own Neolithic transition. However, other researchers objected and challenged Lee's portrayal. Citing evidence that cows had been in the area earlier, Wilmsen (1989) proposed that the !Kung were not "pristine" but had possibly once been pastoralists (herders of livestock) who lost their herds and had long been dominated by their Bantu neighbors. They were the dispossessed "rural proletariat" living in a world dominated by the state, a far cry from our Pleistocene ancestors. Lee and Wilmsen hotly contested the historical evidence back and forth in what came to be known as "the Kalahari debate."

The importance of the Kalahari debate for this book on the Hadza is that Wilmsen led many anthropologists and archaeologists to decry the notion of "living fossils." Time was frozen for no one. Of course, no one suggested time was frozen, just that some societies had changed less than others in meaningful ways. While it was important to document all the ways that living hunter-gatherers in the 1960s might differ from those living 11,000 years ago in the Middle East, this new revision was tinged with something more. It was a reaction to the application of evolutionary ecological theory to understanding modern humans. It heralded a postmodern, antiscientific school of anthropology. The interaction of the !Kung with their Bantu neighbors and its possible effects on the patterns of !Kung foraging and social organization is an important question. I suspect that during Lee's early years, the effects were minimal because so much of the behavior of foragers is shaped by the daily necessity of making a living, even for the "original affluent societies," as Marshall Sahlins (1968) called hunter-gatherers like the !Kung who spent less time working than did Americans.

The Kalahari debate turned on how much contact the !Kung had had with their Bantu neighbors, as if this crucially determined how pristine they were. The amount of attention given to this question seems unnecessary from my Hadzacentric perspective. The Hadza have clearly had considerable contact with agricultural tribes for some time, yet it has not changed their daily lives in such a way that undercuts their relevance for thinking about the past. By accusing Lee of falsely portraying the !Kung as "living fossils," Wilmsen led a reaction against those who saw contemporary foragers as useful analogs of our foraging ancestors. It became taboo to suggest they were, as if that would be an insult to those foraging societies. If one does not feel that technologically simple societies deserve condemnation, there is nothing derogatory about describing them as simple. Societies that continue to hunt and gather with bows and arrows resemble the societies our ancestors lived in more than industrialized societies do—that is an inescapable fact. It makes them interesting; it makes them valuable for evolutionary research; it does not make them any less respectable.

THE HABITAT

There are roughly 1,000 Hadza (see Chapter 6). They live in northern Tanzania near Lake Eyasi (which they call Balangida). They occupy an area of about 4,000 km² around Lake Eyasi in northern Tanzania at latitude 03–04°S and longitude 34–36°E (Figure 1.1). This is in the eastern Rift Valley, which runs the length of East Africa. Lake Eyasi is a large body of salt water fed by runoff from the slopes of Mount Oldeani (Sansako to the Hadza), which flanks Ngorongoro Crater at 3,217 meters (Figures 1.1 and 2.1a). Elevation in Hadzaland ranges from 1,000 m to about 1,700 m. Average annual temperature varies little across the year (mean ~ 28°C), but considerably between day and night (avg min = 14°C, avg max = 35°C, August 18, 2008–August 17, 2009, in the Mangola area).

There is a dry season from June through November. During the rainy season, from December through May, the short rains are followed by the long rains. Total rainfall is 300–600 mm, with higher elevations getting more rainfall. There is a stark contrast in the appearance of Hadzaland in the dry and rainy seasons. While the habitat is primarily savanna-woodland, it also includes rocky hills, scrub brush, palm forest, marshland, and some gallery forest around permanent water. With the strong winds that can last all night and into the morning, it is usually cool enough that the Hadza like to stay close to their hearths until 8:00 A.M.

The Hadza distinguish four regions of Hadzaland: Mangola, Sipunga, Tli'ika, and Dunduiya (Figure 1.1). There are about 250 Hadza in each of the four areas. Mangola is in the north of Hadzaland and runs northwest from the Barai River to Endamagha. In the heart of Mangola is an underground spring surrounded by forest with a wide range of plant and animal species (Figure 2.1b). The source of this spring is the runoff from Mount Oldeani. It emerges from the ground in the Mangola area and runs into Lake Eyasi. Because the meandering water creates a marsh, the Hadza were called Watindiga by other tribes (*tindiga* means marsh in Swahili).

Sipunga lies to the southeast of Mangola. This area is hilly, intermittently filled with baobab trees (*Adasonia digitatta*; Figure 2.1c). Along the north end of the Udahaya River is a canopy forest, and flanking the riverbed are steep rocky slopes where the Hadza live sheltered from the fierce winds by rock outcrops and overhangs during much of the year. Further to the east are the Mbulu highlands (a long plateau), where rainfall is much higher (600 mm). These highlands form the southeastern end of Hadza country.

(a)   (b)

(c)   (d)

Figure 2.1. (a) Mount Oldeani from Gola in the Endamagha area; (b) underground springs in Mangola; (c) baobab trees in Sipunga area; (d) hot springs flowing into Lake Eyasi.

Tli'ika is a rocky and wooded range of hills that runs parallel to Lake Eyasi on the southeast side. To the southeast of these hills lies the Yaeda valley, a grassy plain with many gazelles. Tli'ika is the area with the most remote bush camps these days. There are only a few permanent water holes in this large area, but game is plentiful in the hills. To the south is Munguli, where Isanzu agro-pastoralists grow maize and millet and keep herds of goats and cows. Along this border the Hadza had their most extensive contact and intermarriage in the early 20th century, judging from the accounts of early explorers (Bleek 1931, Obst 1912).

In the western part of Hadza country, the eastern Rift wall juts up from the shores of Lake Eyasi. Here among the steep cliffs, a few streams flow into the lake. On top, in the north, live the Masai; further to the southwest live the western Hadza in an area they call Dunduiya. This area is sparsely populated and abuts the Serengeti National Park, Ngorongoro Conservation Area, and Maswa Game Reserve. It is therefore very rich in game. The Hadza from the west (also called Wahi in the past) are somewhat isolated from the rest, but there is enough coming and going to maintain one language and ethnic identity.

One way we might estimate former Hadza occupation is to consider that elevation sets a limit. Today all Hadza live below 1,700 meters. Above that, they complain it is too cold. This was probably true for all people in East Africa long before agriculture and population density grew so high that it forced people up into higher, colder areas. Of course, humans had spread out to occupy much colder habitats in Europe, Asia, and the New World well before agriculture. But this was mainly horizontal expansion. As earlier hominins and humans continued their horizontal expansion into vast unoccupied areas, they adapted by using fire and making warmer clothes. In a world like East Africa before population density was very high, but was growing, hunter-gatherers with minimal clothing would have expanded horizontally before moving up the slopes into colder areas.

THE HADZA, THEIR LANGUAGE, AND THEIR GENETIC RELATEDNESS TO OTHERS

In the literature, the Hadza appear under the ethnonyms Hadzabe, Hadzapi, Hatsa, Tindiga, Watindiga, Kindiga, Kangeju, and Wahi. They call themselves Hadzabe and their language Hadzane. The suffix *ne* is used for the language, and the suffix *be* is used for people, hence the root *Hadza*, which I use because it is the term most commonly used in the literature ever since British social anthropologist James Woodburn began studying them in 1958.

Only the Hadza speak Hadzane; thus, speaking Hadzane is the best criterion for deciding who is or is not a Hadza. Those with one parent who is Hadza usually speak Hadzane, and virtually no one without at least one Hadza parent speaks more than a few words. The only exceptions are the few men who have married Hadza women and taken up life in Hadza camps for many years. They do speak Hadzane fluently. In fact, these men are a special case because they are culturally Hadza and probably ought to count as Hadza.

Hadzane has three types of click consonants—dental, alveopalatal, and lateral—each with a voiceless oral, voiced nasal, or voiceless nasal variant, plus a glottalized variant. These clicks have led several researchers over the years to classify Hadzane together with southern African Khoisan or San languages (Bleek 1929, 1931, Fleming 1986, Ruhlen 1991). Recent evidence suggests that while the click language of the Sandawe, who live a mere 150 km to the south of the Hadza, may be related to San languages, Hadzane is a linguistic isolate (Sands 1995). Hadzane is not at all closely related to any of the languages of the immediate area. This fact illustrates not only that the Hadza have maintained their autonomy as many other groups have moved into the general area, but that the Hadza are likely remnants of a quite different language family that occupied the area, while all others are more recent immigrants.

Like other sub-Saharan Africans, most Hadza speak two or three languages. All but the youngest children and the oldest women know Swahili fluently as a second language. Most research—mine included—has been conducted in Swahili. Hadzane is not in any immediate danger of being lost even though many Swahili words have been borrowed, e.g., words for numbers beyond 4. When Woodburn arrived in 1958, few Hadza knew Swahili, properly called Kiswahili (Woodburn Personal Communication 1998). Instead, many Hadza knew Isanzu, the language of their Bantu neighbors to the south, as a second language. The acquisition of Swahili appears to reflect an increase in its use as a lingua franca by all ethnic groups in Tanzania more than it does an increase in the degree of contact with non-Hadza.

Researchers who did the first genetics work on the Hadza (Stevens et al. 1977) concluded that Hadza, Sandawe, and Khoisan (Khoi + San) populations are quite genetically distinct, but Fleming (1986) concluded that Hadza and Sandawe are not so different linguistically, while Sands (1995) found that they are. A recent study using Y-chromosome and mitochondrial DNA concluded the Hadza and the Ju/'hoansi (!Kung) of Botswana and Namibia are as genetically divergent as any two populations ever tested (Knight et al. 2003). This adds further evidence to the "out of Africa" view that all present-day humans are descended from a population in Africa; if our ancestors have been in Africa longer than anywhere else, then we should expect to find greater genetic diversity there than on any other continent. We would not necessarily expect to find greater diversity between two African populations than between an African and a non-African population unless we were comparing two African populations which split early on. In fact, it appears the !Kung and Hadza have survived as examples of African populations that did split quite early (Knight et al. 2003). Given that the Hadza and !Kung both have clicks, yet are so distantly related genetically and live 2,000 km apart, the authors conclude that the earliest languages must have had clicks which were lost in other languages.

ARCHAEOLOGY

The Hadza have most likely lived in their current area for a very long time. They have no written language, but their oral history contains no stories suggesting they came from some other place. The outer limits of Hadza-land probably have not changed for a long time, since the Hadza have names for landmarks that today form the outer limits of their area, such as Mount Oldeani (Sansako), which forms one side of the rim on Ngorongoro Crater (Figure 1.1), yet they do not have names for landmarks not visible from within the current boundaries of Hadzaland (Blurton Jones Personal Communication 1997). Although many of the best spots within Hadzaland have recently been taken over by outsiders, the Hadza had the whole area pretty much to themselves until the 1950s (Woodburn Personal Communication 1998). The underground spring in Mangola that flows into Lake Eyasi and creates a large marsh with fertile soil has attracted people from various tribes who are now farming onions there. Despite this, the Hadza still have camps around the spring and even continue to hunt the game in the forest that surrounds the water.

In the earliest written descriptions of the Hadza, they lived just where they do now. Hadza ancestry, just like the ancestry of all humans, can of course be traced back to the earliest hominins whose lineage did not go extinct. One difference between the more recent ancestors (past 50–100,000 ya) of most of us and those of the Hadza is where they lived. The ancestors of the Hadza probably lived in East Africa and exploited many of the same resources the Hadza exploit today. Hadza ancestors could have been living in their current area, exploiting many of the same plant and animal foods for almost as long as *Homo sapiens* have existed. This makes the Hadza particularly relevant for exploring the behavioral ecology of earlier hunter-gatherers.

The Hadza live in an area rich in hominin fossils. Olduvai Gorge, with its remains of *Paranthropus boisei*, *Homo habilis*, and *Homo ergaster*, is only 50 km to the northwest (Figure 1.1). Laetoli, the site of 3.6-million-year-old hominin footprints, is a mere 40 km to the north. At the foot of Mumba rock shelter, along the shore of Lake Eyasi near Hadza camps he was staying in, the German explorer Kohl-Larsen found an archaic *Homo sapiens* mandible in 1935 (Kohl-Larsen 1943), which probably dates to at least 130,000 years ago (Mehlman 1987, 1988, 1991). In 2004, a new skullcap was found near the same place, and it has been dated to 130,000 years (Dominguez-Rodrigo et al. 2008). This skullcap has some primitive features that make it appear more like *Homo erectus* (*H. ergaster*) than archaic *sapiens* or modern humans. Surface surveys have yielded a high density of lithic material in Hadzaland, and excavations of rock shelters have revealed continuous occupation back to the Later Stone Age (and possibly the Middle Stone Age) by people who may well be Hadza ancestors (Mabulla 1996).

There are several sites with rock art within Hadzaland. This art has been little studied, although the rock art in the nearby Sandawe area has been (Masao 1982). Most of what I have seen is very faint and depicts animals and humans. The Hadza do not create rock art today. It is therefore not clear whether their ancestors made the rock art, though most Hadza assume it was their ancestors, and some insist that it was (Bala 1998).

If paintings are a mere few hundred years old, it seems less likely that the Hadza would have lost the knowledge that their ancestors used to paint, given their oral tradition. None of the art I have seen includes any depiction of farmers or herders. Thus, there is no evidence the art was done by recent agricultural immigrants who began to arrive around 2,000 years ago. Depiction of bows may put an upper limit on the date (at least if arrows are shown with hafted stone points) (McBrearty and Brooks 2000). Some Hadza say they remember using stone points, and others mention using bone, while all agree that they used simple wooden arrows without any hafted points long ago, which is one type of arrow they still use (see Chapter 4). Thus, the bow could predate the oldest bone and stone arrowheads.

HISTORY AND ETHNIC RELATIONS

Based on the presence of stone tools, rock shelters, and rock art, it appears that before 3,000 years ago, people much like the Hadza lived all over Tanzania. About 2,500 years BP (before present), herding people from Somalia and Ethiopia, who were probably Cushitic speakers, moved into the Rift Valley of Kenya and northern Tanzania (Kaplan 1978). About 1500 years BP, Bantu speakers from West Africa, who were farmers using iron farming implements and weapons, reached Tanzania. Around 200–300 years BP, Nilotic-speaking cattle herders moved south from Sudan into northern Tanzania.

By the 9th and 10th centuries Arabs were sailing along the east coast of Africa, and by the 14th century they had established many trading ports. It was from the interaction of these Arabs with the local Bantu population that the Swahili language and culture evolved; both were largely Bantu, but with heavy Arab influences. During the 1800s, the slave and ivory trades increased. The trade route was only about 300 kilometers south of Hadzaland. We do not know if the Hadza were affected by the slave trade, but they were definitely affected by the ivory trade as neighboring groups came to Hadzaland to kill elephants. The slave trade was not formally abolished until the British blockaded Zanzibar in 1876. Beginning in 1885, the Germans declared part of Tanzania a protectorate (Iliffe 1973). The Germans were in control until the end of World War I, when the British took over and made Tanzania (then called Tanganyika) a territory under their rule. Tanganyika became independent in 1961, and Zanzibar joined to form Tanzania in 1964.

The Hadza population has been increasing slightly since 1900, perhaps partly because it is rebounding from past declines caused by the Masai expansion in the late 1800s and the deaths during the settlement attempts in the 1960s, 1970s, and 1980s (Jones et al. 1992). Table 2.1 shows population estimates over the 20th century. Today the population is about 1,000. A little research has been conducted on the 250–300 Hadza living west of the lake, but most has been conducted with the 700–750 who live to the east of the lake in an area of about 2,500 km^2 (Figure 1.1). Among the latter, about 300–400 still live almost exclusively on hunting and gathering wild foods. The other Hadza mix foraging with various other activities. Some guard the maize fields of their non-Hadza neighbors, receiving maize and the meat of the raiding baboons and vervet monkeys they kill in return. From time to time, a Hadza may work as a game scout or work for the game department; a few have paid government or NGO positions as community development officers. A growing number of Hadza in the Mangola area depend on tourist money, but almost no Hadza has cultivated fields or livestock.

Archaeological evidence shows that farmers and pastoralists have been in the general area around Hadza country for several centuries (Sutton 1989, 1992). Today there are several different ethnic groups that border the Hadza. These include the Iraqw, Datoga, Isanzu, Sukuma, Iramba, and Masai (Figure 1.1). The groups of neighboring people with whom the Hadza interact most nowadays are the Iraqw, Datoga, Isanzu, and Sukuma. These ethnic groups represent three different linguistic phyla (Cushitic, Nilotic, and Bantu), while Hadzane belongs to a fourth, so none are closely related to the Hadza (Ruhlen 1991).

The Iraqw (also called the Mbulu) are Cushitic speakers who migrated south from Ethiopia as early as 3,000 years ago (Ehret and Posnansky 1982, Ochieng 1975, Sutton 1992). They are primarily maize farmers

TABLE 2.1. DESCRIPTIONS OF THE HADZA THROUGH TIME

Year and Source	Population	Camps	Subsistence	Family	Trade and Interaction	General
1890s, explorer (Baumann 1894); officer Werther 1898; geographer Jaeger 1911		Grass huts.	Pegs in baobab trees.		Neighbors had name for Hadza.	Hadza hiding.
1911 (Obst 1912) 8 weeks; German geographer	100	1–3 families 1st camp=55, 25 were "real Hadza"; weeks, months at same place in dry season.	Don't recall herding or farming. Primary diet: tubers, berries, hyrax, baobab, gazelle, antelope, hartebeest, gnu, ostrich, giraffe. Night hunt in dry season. In wet, follow game many days, can go weeks without a big game kill. Watch vultures, scavenge from lion and leopard. 2 kinds of poison.	Levirate. Can't marry mother, sister, can marry niece, granddaughter. Doting mothers, fathers, 5–10 arrows for daughter if she loves man, polygyny often (2 different huts).	Get tobacco, brass neck rings from Isanzu for lion, leopard fur, honey. Sukuma give beads, knives, old hoes. Isanzu captured women and kids during the period of ivory trade.	Circumcision from Isanzu, only 1 man. Wars with Iraqw, Isanzu. No afterlife. Only old buried.

1917–1923 Bagshawe (1924–1925) several trips over 6 years; British colonial district officer	5–600	2–3 men, wives, and children.	No farming, domestic animals or dogs. Meat, honey, fruit, tubers, fish, snakes, lizards, carrion birds, eggs, ants, insects, all but hyena. Kill elephant, scavenge rhino. Had not tasted beef. Seldom lose wounded prey. Kill lions, match by day but eaten by lions when night hunting without fire. Reed fish trap. Running noose snare, no nets.	Bride price 5–15 arrows. Easy divorce. During 1918–1920 famine, some Hadza men married Isanzu women.	Get old spears as scrap iron, beads, tobacco for skins, honey, meat to neighbors on border. Attacked and killed by Datoga who claimed goats were stolen.	No spears or shields, one ax. Often hungry but happy. No religion, burial, magic, medicine, or musical instrument. Cannabis. No "chiefs."
1930 Bleek (1931) 6 weeks; linguist		2–3 families of relations but one may move off by itself; few weeks or months before moving.	No domestic animals or gardens. Roots, fruit, bulbs roasted in ashes, meat cooked on sticks or boiled, liver eaten raw. Seeds	Most own 2 wives in different camps but show children great affection. Girls marry at 16, boys bit later, no ceremony,	Get tobacco, meal from Isanzu, iron scrap from Bantu, paper ear ornaments, clay pots, calabashes, beads, copper rings, stuffs	Remember Masai raids and famines. Dance in circle. Copper arm bands; both sexes wore beads. Medicinal scars. Lukucuko.

(continued)

TABLE 2.1. *(continued)*

Year and Source	Population	Camps	Subsistence	Family	Trade and Interaction	General
			pounded then boiled. Giraffe, ostrich preferred meat. Honey is favorite dish, a treat for kids. Water only beverage. Get some meal from Isanzu. Hammer scrap into arrowhead with iron mallet.	bride price: beads to father. Take to groom's home.	for meat, skins, honey, beeswax (sell at a store).	Burial. No afterlife. No "chiefs."
1931–1938 Kohl-Larsen (1958) Many months; doctor, explorer	450 east, 100 west	From 1 extended family may grow to 60–80 in one camp.	In photos: berries, baobab, tubers, klipspringer, ostrich, killed rhino, hippos. Native ax. Keep dogs.	Monogamy. Men kill adulterer and beat wife. Wife may leave husband if not good hunter, children stay with father.	Get beads, maize, hemp, iron for furs, horns to Isanzu. Brass bracelets, some cloth. For tobacco, women take Isanzu lover.	Girl's fringed apron, tattoos, dancing, epeme items, firedrill. Spear for hippos. "Chiefs."

Source	Population	Settlement	Food	Marriage	Trade/goods	Political
Barlow, S.M. Missionary						"Chiefs."
1945–1947 Cooper (1949) 10 days twice; British colonial game ranger.		5–12 huts, some camps >35, 2–3 men, wives, kids, grandparents. 7–10 days at one spot before deplete baobab.	Baobab main food 5 months. Roots, fruits. Follow honey-guide bird, smoke to stun bees and get honey. Rhino, buffalo, giraffe, wildebeest, hartebeest, zebra, impala, kudu, roan, birds, squirrel, tortoise, some lizards, hyenas when hard-pressed but not snakes, frogs, toads. 2–3 men may drive game.	Marriage after short engagement, bride price few beads; monogamy the rule.	Get iron, millet for meat, skins, but he stopped it. No punishment but ban on rhino hunting to sell horn. Love elephant he shot. Few clay pots.	No spears or shields, few native-made axes. One short camp stay: 2 impala, 2 warthog, 1 porcupine, 1 large bird. No "chiefs."
1950 Fosbrooke (1956) British district officer	Few hundred, <1,000	No fixed abode, small groups move in relation to food.	No herding or cultivation, roots, game, fruits, baobab, smoke native intoxicant plant.		Get cloth, clay pots, gourds. Would not take money, so he gave cloth and beads.	Few make occasional visit to shop in outlying area.

(continued)

TABLE 2.1. (continued)

Year and Source	Population	Camps	Subsistence	Family	Trade and Interaction	General
1958–present Woodburn (1962, 1968a, 1968b, Barnicot et al. 1972). Bennett, Dyson (1977) Many trips; social anthropologist	750 (250 in west, 500 in east; 400 fulltime; foragers 800 (Dyson 1977)	18 (1–100). Large camps at water in dry; small, dispersed in wet. Few weeks in one spot, shorter than food dictates.	By weight: 80% from vegetable matter, 20% from meat and honey (but account for more calories than that). Berries, baobab, tubers. Usually hunt alone, lion, leopard, serval, wild cat, hyena, vulture, zebra, guinea fowl, jackal, impala, eland, giraffe, hyrax (some of which is traded). Don't eat civet, monitor lizard, snake, terrapin	Bilateral descent, Men marry in early 20s. ~60% marriages uxorilocal, few polygynous marriages; divorce rate = 49/1,000 years. Kids live with mother after divorce.	Some intermarriage. Proportions of Hadza ancestry Hadza = 79.8% Isanzu = 17.3% Sukuma = 1.7% Iramba = 1.2% (including grandparents, $n = 437$).	Lukucuko. Musical bow. Attribute disease to violation of epeme meat rules. No territoriality, fluid camp composition. Good health.
1961–1964 Tomita (1966) anthropologist	80 in Mangola	6–11	Hunt alone or in pairs. Berries, tubers, honey, baobab, catch	Eland fat as bride price.	Get corn for baobab. Aluminum pot.	Eland fat used in ceremonies. Small game to family, but

Date/Researcher	Population	Movement	Diet	Social organization	Comments	Summary
1974–1977 Lars Smith anthropologist	Western Hadza = 214+		eels and such fish in Eyasi by hand. Hunt impala, zebra, baboon, warthog, eland, guinea fowl, francolin, but not snakes, lizard, buzzard, and hyena.		larger than impala shared with all.	Arial survey of game (Arusha Region Report 1980)
1980–1981 McDowell (1981a, b) Mangola area, anthropologist	800–1,000 Mangola = 165 (6 camps)	27.7 (22.6–31). Average distance between camps = 3 km; 17.7 moves per year	8 roots, tamarind, baobab, fig, dates, 10 berries. Mostly small game but in calories, large game. Meat eaten 64% of days, honey 21% of days. Daily meat = 0.82 kg./person. Agricultural foods (maize, beans, sweet potato, especially in the late dry season).	All Hadza considered kin. Hadza women marry outsiders in outlying areas, men can't.	Witchcraft fears of neighbors in villages. Only ethnic group in Tanzania to escape tax, shows autonomy.	Good diet and health relative to neighbors. Nonterritorial, egalitarian.

(continued)

TABLE 2.1. *(continued)*

Year and Source	Population	Camps	Subsistence	Family	Trade and Interaction	General
1982–1984 Anne Vincent (1985a, b) archaeologist			Extensive study of Tuber digging in Mangola for 5 tubers for Ph.D.			
1982–2001 Blurton Jones, 1985–1986, 1990 Hawkes, O'Connell anthropologists, archaeologist	1,000 (250 west, 750 east) density = 0.24/km², growth rate = 1.35/year	16.5 (2–48 in 36 bush camps)	Tubers, honey, meat, baobab, berries. Encounter hunt by day, intercept by night. Target large game and took one every 29 hunter-days (4.9 kg/hunter-day). 5 year olds forage at rate capable of meeting half their needs. 5% of calorie intake was agricultural foods.	Divorce rate = 60/1,000 years. TFR = 6.2. Infant mortality = 21%, juvenile = 47%. Life expectancy at birth = 32.5, women at 45 = 21.3.	Some get maize for guarding fields, sweet potatoes for harvesting. Iron, cloth for honey. Cloth, nails, beads from researchers.	Frequent name changes. Epeme dance when no moon, Sun is god. Lobby researchers, negotiate gifts.

1986, 1988, 1997 Henry Bunn, Schoeninger archaeologist, nutrition	Tubers much lower nutritional value than previously estimated by Vincent and O'Connell, Hawkes, and Blurton Jones.	Debate with O'Connell et al. over interpretation of butchering and bone transport.
1992, 1997 Sands (1998) linguist		Hadzane not closely related to San languages.
1992 Mabulla Tanzanian archaeologist (Mabulla 1996)		Lithic surveys, fossils, rock shelter suggest continuous occupation to MSA.
1998 Mountain geneticist (Knight et al. 2003)		Hadza and Ju/'hoansi most divergent populations yet tested.
2001, 2002 Tishkoff and students geneticist		Lactose tolerance in Hadza about equal to surrounding pastoralists.

who live in the highlands, where rainfall is plentiful and temperatures cool. During the 1800s, the Masai expansion caused the Iraqw to take refuge in the Mbulu highlands flanking Hadza country to the east. During the past two decades, the Iraqw population has been growing rapidly (3.5% per year) and is now over 230,000 (Meindertsma Douwe and Kessler 1997). Consequently, many Iraqw have spilled down from the highlands into Hadza country, clearing trees and trying to grow maize in areas that are much better suited for hunting and gathering than for cultivation.

The Datoga (also called Tatog, Barabaig, and Mangati) are Nilotic pastoralists who number 15–20,000 in the vicinity of Hadzaland (Meindertsma Douwe and Kessler 1997). They have been in the wider general area since the 1700s, when the Masai expelled them from Ngorongoro Crater (Sutton 1992). Under German rule, Masai expansion was checked and intertribal warfare and cattle raiding were curtailed, allowing Datoga herds to expand (Klima 1970). In response to Iraqw movement, the Datoga were also pushed out of current Iraqw areas. We know the Datoga have been interacting with the Hadza at least since 1917 (Bagshawe 1924–1925a, 1924–1925b), but it was only in the 1930s and 1940s that they began moving into the heart of Hadza country (McDowell 1981, Tomita 1966). Currently, most bush-dwelling Hadza interact with the Datoga more than with any other group. Datoga herds drink the scarce water in Hadza water holes during the dry season and eat much of the vegetation needed to support wildlife, posing one of the main threats to continued Hadza hunting.

The Isanzu are Bantu agro-pastoralists who live to the south of Hadza country. They may have been in the general area about 500 years (Newman 1995, Nurse 1982, Soper 1982), part of the continuing Bantu expansion into eastern and southern Africa. Hadza access to iron could possibly extend this far back, since the Bantu introduced iron to the Rift Valley area about 500 ya. Isanzu oral tradition tells of colonizing the area near Isanzu and Kirumi just south of Hadzaland around 1850 (Cooper 1949). At least from 1900 until the 1960s, the Hadza interacted more with the Isanzu than with any of their other neighbors. Early European visitors used Isanzu guides and interpreters to communicate with the Hadza (Bagshawe 1924–1925a, 1924–1925b, Bleek 1931, Obst 1912), and there appears to have been much more intermarriage with Isanzu than with Iraqw or Datoga (Woodburn Personal Communication 1998). Perhaps 2% of Hadza today have an Isanzu parent (Blurton Jones Personal Communication 2003).

To the west of Lake Eyasi, the Hadza interact with the Sukuma; the Iramba, who are Bantu; the Masai, who are Nilotic; and now the Taturu, a branch of the Datoga who have been moving into the area in large numbers. The Sukuma have for some time been driving their cattle through Hadzaland on their way to market in Arusha. Long ago, they also made trips in caravans to obtain salt from Lake Eyasi (Senior 1957). There are now a number of western Hadza with a Sukuma parent.

Today in the Mangola area, the Hadza also have contact with a variety of "Swahilis," as the Hadza refer to generic Tanzanians. These Swahilis moved into the area to grow onions beginning in the 1940s, although there were very few until the 1960s and 1970s. In 1962, there were about 900 taxpayers in Mangola, according to the government (Woodburn 1962). Hadza also have contact with the two European families in Mangola, one of which settled there in the 1950s; the first German plantation began there in 1928 (Tomita 1966). A few researchers from Europe, Japan, and the United States have been studying the Hadza on and off since 1958 (Table 2.1).

ETHNOGRAPHIC OBSERVATIONS

The earliest known written accounts of the Hadza are by German explorers in the 1890s (Baumann 1894). These accounts are secondhand descriptions provided by guides, along with direct observations of Hadza huts and wooden pegs inserted in baobab trees, which the Hadza climb to get honey (Jaeger 1911, Werther 1898). The Hadza were presumably hiding from these early European travelers, as they did originally in 1917 from Bagshawe, the British colonial official in the area (Bagshawe 1924–1925a, 1924–1925b). The earliest written accounts of actually seeing Hadza are by Otto Dempwolff (1916–1917) in 1910 and the German geographer Erich Obst (1912). Obst spent 8 weeks with the Hadza in 1911. He described the plentiful game on the Yaeda plain in the middle of Hadzaland; it was then much like Ngorongoro Crater is today, with the world's most diverse and abundant population of large mammals.

At the first camp Obst visited, on the eastern edge of Yaeda valley, Hadza were living with Isanzu (Waisanzu). Obst wrote: "Of the fifteen men, eighteen women and twenty-two children who I met in the camp, barely half—seven men, as many women and eleven children—identified themselves as real Wakindiga *(Hadza)*. The rest were Waisanzu, who were too lazy to farm at home, or who had to escape the reach of the Boma because of some kind of misdemeanor." For this reason, Obst decided to move on to another camp in Mangola where he was told "the inhabitants would be exclusively Wakindiga" and, he hoped, less influenced by Isanzu ways (Obst 1912).

Obst described the Hadza as strictly foragers who kept no animals, not even dogs. Because they had their own words for some domestic animals, Obst speculated that the Hadza might once have been pastoralists. He was told of wars between the Hadza and Masai, and because he assumed that the Masai would only be motivated to fight with other pastoralists, he took this as another indication the Hadza may have been pastoralists who lost their herds. He noted, however, that the Hadza had no memory or stories of having ever been farmers or pastoralists. Obst may have been influenced by those neighbors of the Hadza who, in their condemnation of Hadza backwardness, often say the Hadza are not a real tribe or culture, only an amalgam of the dispossessed "who don't even have a real language" (Woodburn 1997). This view simply reflects ethnocentric bias; Hadzane is clearly not a pidgin language.

The Hadza told Obst they always had to be ready for war with the Isanzu, Iraqw, and Masai. They also told him that the Isanzu sometimes captured women and children. It is possible the Isanzu, who live just to the south of Hadzaland, were capturing Hadza for the slave trade, since the trade route in use until the 1870s was only about 300 kilometers to the south. Obst was told that the danger from the Isanzu subsided once the elephants became rare, so the Isanzu must have been involved in the ivory trade. The Sukuma, he indicated, came from further away and gave old hoes, which the Hadza pounded into arrow points, in exchange for letting the Sukuma hunt elephants. Obst mentioned the Iramba, Masai, Sukuma, Isanzu, and Iraqw, but not the Datoga, suggesting that interaction with them came later.

The next to write about the Hadza was F. J. Bagshawe, a district officer of the British government who made several trips to Hadza country soon after the Germans were defeated in the First World War. According to Bagshawe (1924–1925a,b), a famine in 1918–1920 prompted some Isanzu to take up living and foraging with the Hadza. Although it is usually Hadza women who marry Isanzu men, during the famine, Bagshawe said, some Isanzu women married Hadza men. He said the Hadza kept no domestic animals, not even dogs or fowl. He told a story about their one and only experiment in pastoralism. The Hadza once killed an elephant (which they do not do now, saying their poison will not kill an elephant), and in exchange for the ivory received some goats from a native stranger. The next morning the goats strayed into the bush; no one bothered to follow them because the hunters were feasting on elephant meat. Then the Datoga, declaring the goats had been stolen from them, attacked and killed many Hadza. This shows that, at least since 1917, there has been some hostile interaction with the Datoga, who probably arrived in the area sometime between 1911 and 1917.

In 1945–1947, British colonial game officer B. Cooper (1949) visited the Hadza on two occasions for 10 days each time. He found there were some Hadza around an Isanzu village doing some cultivation. His guide was a Hadza whose father was an Isanzu who had lived in a Hadza camp to escape the hut tax (government taxation). Cooper said that Hadza men sometimes cooperated in pairs or threes to drive game into ambush (which they only very rarely do today) and that men followed the honey-guide birds (*Indicator indicator*) to find honey (as they do today). He described the Hadza as having no tribal authority, but wrote that old men governed their own camp, and that those Hadza on the fringe of Isanzu country paid some allegiance to the Isanzu chief. He indicated that the Hadza were peaceful, settling disputes without bloodshed. Some of the earlier observers talked of headmen or even chiefs; others were explicit about there not being any such leaders (see Table 2.1). Woodburn (1964) argued, and I agree, that this is the result of the inability of the Europeans and their guides to imagine a society without political leaders. Another reason some believed there were Hadza leaders is that the gifts the visitors brought instantly created such demand on the part of the Hadza that anyone who allied himself with the visitor was instantly transformed into something of a leader by virtue of being the conduit for the gifts.

When Woodburn arrived in 1958, he found about 400 eastern Hadza still foraging (1968a). At that time, the Hadza still had much of their area to themselves, but farmers were increasingly moving into the Mangola area, and Datoga into the Yaeda valley. Many other researchers followed (Table 2.1). In the 1970s, Lars Smith began his graduate research and spent much time with the Hadza, getting to know them well. He did not finish his degree but introduced Nicholas Blurton Jones to the Hadza in 1982 and passed on his demographic data. From the time Blurton Jones began in 1982 until he retired in 2001, he conducted censuses roughly every two years. In 1985, he introduced Kristen Hawkes and James O'Connell to the Hadza, and they collected foraging data during a long field season in 1985–1986 and in another, shorter stay in 1990, and many articles have come from this threesome. Blurton Jones also introduced Bonny Sands to the Hadza, and she did linguistic research in the 1990s. I began my fieldwork with Nicholas Blurton Jones in 1995.

Earlier observers had stayed with more assimilated Hadza, who were easier to reach through guides from neighboring tribes. Woodburn and other researchers since have made a point of finding the best bush camps and spending more time in the field. Many of the later descriptions seem to suggest less influence from outsiders, either because such influence actually subsided or because Hadza further from any of their neighbors had always been subjected to less outside influence. However, soon after Woodburn began work, it looked as if Hadza foraging would end as a result of a concerted attempt by the government to settle the Hadza.

SETTLEMENT ATTEMPTS

The first attempt to settle the Hadza and force them to take up farming was made by the British colonial administration in 1927 (Woodburn 1979). The second attempt was also organized by the British colonial government in 1939 (McDowell 1981). It lasted barely a year because the local scout in charge abused his authority and the Hadza left. In 1965, soon after independence from Britain, the Tanzanian government (Mbulu district), with support from an American missionary, attempted to settle the Hadza at Yaeda Chini, where a school and clinic were built. Hadza from even the most remote bush camps were taken to Yaeda in lorries, escorted by armed police. According to McDowell, after some weeks of settlement, "Many Hadza were taken ill and a significant number died, probably of respiratory and diarrheal infections" (1981:7). By early 1966, after only a few months, most Hadza left the settlement to return to foraging.

There was also a settlement established at Endamagha (Mwonyembe to the Hadza) to promote agriculture among the Mangola Hadza from 1971 to 1975. A school, 12 houses, and a dispensary were built; water was piped in and seed provided; and the Hadza were told they could not hunt in the area. The village roll book listed 31 Hadza men in 1973. Then food aid was cut; after a drought and crop failure in 1975, the Hadza left the settlement and returned to foraging. Although many Hadza are still sent to Endamagha to attend boarding school, today Hadza account for only about one-third of the students there.

From time to time, missionaries have provided food and encouraged Hadza settlement. In the southern part of Hadza country, there was a school at Munguli (also built for the Hadza), where many Hadza lived. When a missionary at Yaeda Chini provided food, the Hadza went there and stayed for several months until the food ran out. The Hadza are lured by food not because they are on the verge of starvation, as people often assume, but because, as we should expect of optimal foragers, food that requires no work is irresistible. While the Hadza were off in Yaeda, the school and land in Munguli were occupied by Isanzu (Woodburn Personal Communication 1998). Likewise, at Yaeda, the school and clinic built for the Hadza in the 1960s attracted the neighboring Iraqw and Datoga, who are still there. Another attempt at settlement in Yaeda began in 1979, and the number of Hadza rose from 30 to 300 (Ndagala and Waane 1982), but today only 2 Hadza families with government positions live there. In October 1986, a missionary again tried briefly to get Hadza to settle in Yaeda, which resulted in a measles outbreak and the death of many children, and again the Hadza returned to the bush (Jones, Hawkes, and O'Connell 2005a). Mobile foragers who live outside, at low population densities, have limited exposure and immunity to infectious diseases that become virulent in larger, sedentary, house-dwelling populations.

One Hadza man allied with missionaries even used force in his various attempts to persuade other Hadza to abandon foraging in favor of farming. In 1990, many Hadza were aggressively coerced into settling at Mongo wa Mono, but once local government officials visited and assured them they were free to leave, that is what most did (Jones, Hawkes, and O'Connell 2005a). There is now a fairly permanent settlement at Mongo wa Mono, which was established as an official government-registered Hadza village in 1988. The number of people there varies between 20 and 80, with perhaps 5 to 10 people growing crops at any one time. These efforts have had limited success, and most Hadza there still also forage and simply wait for food deliveries from missionaries or aid workers. The missionaries who try to make converts of the Hadza rarely last more than a few months. Hadza children and teenagers sometimes sing Christian songs, and the Hadza welcome the food provided by missionaries, but there has been little conversion to Christianity. Many observers thought the settlements would mean the end of Hadza foraging, but surprisingly they did not. Although most adult Hadza have lived in a settlement for a few months at some point in time, such experiences have been short-term and have not prevented them from continuing their foraging lifestyle and maintaining their traditional culture.

HADZA CONSERVATISM

Judging from photographs and descriptions, the Hadza visited by Obst in 1911 were remarkably similar to the Hadza I first met 84 years later.

They lived in the same houses in similarly sized camps, used the same tool kit, foraged for the same foods (minus rhino and hippo), traded for the same items, and practiced the same sort of religion. In order to evaluate the degree of interaction with outsiders and the amount of change in Hadza culture, Table 2.1 provides a brief summary of descriptions of the Hadza from the earliest accounts to the present. Table 2.2 lists probable influences from outsiders through time.

TABLE 2.2. INFLUENCES, IN CHRONOLOGICAL ORDER, FROM OTHER ETHNIC GROUPS

Trait or Interaction	The Others	Source
Probably interacted with farmers on border	Engaruka complex at Endamagha (Iraqw) 1700 A.D.	Sutton 1986
Trade for iron, tobacco, beads	Isanzu, Sukuma	Obst 1912
Captured (maybe slave trade), ivory trade	Isanzu 1800s	Obst 1912
Warfare	Masai 1900	Obst 1912
Masai expansion halted	Germans 1890s	Obst 1912
Metal ear ornaments	Isanzu	Obst 1912
Brass neck ring	Isanzu	Obst 1912, Bagshawe 1924–1925, Bleek 1931
Second language is Isanzu	Isanzu	Obst 1912, Bagshawe 1924–1925, Bleek 1931
Killed for "stealing goats"	Datoga	Bagshawe 1924–1925
Intermarriage	Isanzu	Bagshawe 1924–1925
Male circumcision: none today, nor in past say the Hadza	Isanzu	Obst 1912; Bleek 1931 says none
Female clitorectomy	Isanzu or Datoga	Woodburn 1964
Trade for clay pots	Isanzu?	Bleek 1931, Cooper 1949, Fosbrooke 1956
Trade for cloth	Isanzu	Kohl-Larsen 1958
Studied by anthropologists	Europeans	Kohl-Larsen 1958
First settlement attempt	British 1939	McDowell 1981
Loss of range to Mangola village	Mangola European farmers 1950	Woodburn 1962

(continued)

TABLE 2.2. *(continued)*

Trait or Interaction	The Others	Source
Mangola encroachment	Swahili farmers 1960	Woodburn 1962
Yaeda settlement	Tanzania government (Iraqw)	Woodburn 1968a
Second language is Swahili	All neighbors	Woodburn, Pers. Comm.
Aluminum pots	Swahilis in Mangola	Tomita 1966
Sex to remove death pollution	Iraqwi widows seek out Hadza	Matthiessen 1974
Zeze (musical bow) mbira	Isanzu	Woodburn 1970, Marlowe
Guard fields	Iraqw	Jones et al. 1992, Marlowe
Use of father's first name as family name	Isanzu, Datoga, Iraqw, Swahili officials, missionaries	Blurton Jones, Pers. Comm., Marlowe
Get beer	Isanzu, Datoga, Swahilis	Marlowe
Wells dug near waterholes	Datoga	Marlowe
Lion kill celebration	Datoga	Marlowe
Observed, get money	International tourists	Marlowe

Most who read the historical record (Fosbrooke 1956) are impressed with the overwhelming continuity in the descriptions of the Hadza throughout the 20th century. While the overall population has grown slightly, camp size, mobility, diet, and mating system are very consistent (Table 2.1). In 1960, Woodburn (1968b) found average camp population to be 18 (range = 1–100). People camped at one spot for no more than a few weeks. In 1980, McDowell (1981) found the average camp population in the Mangola area to be 28, and camps moved about 18 times per year. Blurton Jones found mean camp population to be 16.5 (Jones, N.G.B. et al 1992). There has very recently been a trend toward slightly larger camps that stay in one place longer in response to encroachment by non-Hadza. However, large camps (e.g., 80–100) during berry season in certain areas also existed long ago (Woodburn Personal Communication 1998).

Just as Bagshawe (1924–1925a,b) and Cooper (1949) reported, the Hadza today have no spears or shields. All observers have found that hunting is done only with bows and arrows, although during Kohl-Larsen's stay a small spear would be used to finish off a wounded hippopotamus in the water after it had been hit with arrows (Kohl-Larsen 1958). As

Obst (1912) and Woodburn (1968a) found earlier, men today usually hunt alone, and many days may pass without any big game being killed. As Obst, Bagshawe, and Woodburn noted, in the dry season, men still tend to hunt in pairs at night, waiting for animals to come to them around the few permanent water holes. As described by Obst and Bagshawe, meat is also obtained by scavenging. And as noted by almost all observers, women and children go foraging for tubers, berries, and baobab.

In 1985–1986, Hawkes and O'Connell found that less than 5% of calorie intake (in one camp) was from agricultural food (Jones, Hawkes, and O'Connell 2002). In 1995–1996 (in 5 camps), I found that 6.6% of all calories entering camps came from non-foraged food. Much of this was maize and millet delivered to one camp by one missionary during one month; the rest was gained through trade with agro-pastoralist neighbors. Across 14 camps up through 2005, 5.7% of food by weight arriving in camp was non-foraged food acquired through trade or begging from non-Hadza, or food deliveries from missionaries or NGOs.

I suspect there was more meat in the diet in the early 1900s. It is clear that with so many people moving in and cutting down trees and their herds eating the grass, the routes of wild animals migrating between the game parks has been affected. The Hadza say that there is less game than in the past. As noted, Obst (1912) reported seeing large herds of big game in the Yaeda valley in 1911, whereas these days it is mostly Datoga cows and some gazelles. Not only were there many elephants (which are fairly rare today), but also rhinos, which are now absent, and many hippos. On the other hand, there are still many impalas, kudus, and giraffes.

As Table 2.1 shows, the Hadza traded with their neighbors throughout the 20th century. Just as they did in 1911 during Obst's visit, Hadza today give meat, skins, and honey in exchange for tobacco, maize, millet, clothes, beads, cooking pots, and scrap iron for making axes and arrowheads. They no longer get clay pots but rather metal pots, mostly from us researchers. Nowadays, the Hadza also receive some beer from their neighbors, sell some crafts to tourists, and receive a variety of goods from researchers, especially nails for arrowheads and clothes (as one can see in the photos in this book).

In contrast to Hadza in the early 1900s, Hadza today are much less shy. Hadza these days will approach a visitor, at least a foreign visitor, rather than hide. Today, the second language for most is Swahili rather than Isanzu. Today, more Hadza attend school. About 20% of Hadza less than 60 years old have had some schooling, and about 40% of those under 30 years have. In the vast majority of cases, this is for 1 or 2 years only.

My impression is that there may be less storytelling nowadays than in the past, since all men can tell stories (see Bala 1998), but only rarely do I observe them doing so now, while I used to see them doing so frequently. There are far more factory-made clothes today, due mainly to us researchers giving them as gifts.

Despite these changes, by and large, I would notice little difference were I to travel back in time to visit a Hadza camp in 1900. The continuity extends all the way to the bows and arrows being exactly the same length, the height of men and women being the same, and the divorce rate and frequency of residence patterns being the same (Jones nd, Jones, Hawkes, and O'Connell 2005b). On balance, one must conclude that, despite the fact that the Hadza have had contact with non-foragers continuously for many decades and perhaps for centuries, they have changed little and conserved much.

Why did the Hadza change so little in the face of contact? Woodburn argued that encapsulation was the result of the immediate-return orientation of Hadza culture, which insulated them from the temptations of agriculture and the entanglements of extensive trade and serfdom (Woodburn 1979, 1988). Woodburn argued that the Hadza are immediate-return, as opposed to delayed-return, foragers. This means that, because they can acquire their food daily throughout the year, they have no need to store food or spend much time and effort investing for some delayed return, the way farmers need to sow and weed for months before harvesting (Woodburn 1980, 1988).

The following are explanations I have offered for Hadza conservatism (Marlowe 2002). First, most areas of Hadzaland are poor for growing crops without irrigation. Where there is plenty of water in Mangola, many non-Hadza have now moved in to farm there. Second, although Hadzaland is a good habitat for pastoralism, before a government eradication program in the 1940s and 1950s, infestations of tsetse flies limited the encroachment of pastoralists. Third, Tanzania has always been relatively undeveloped. Because the country embraced socialism at independence, there was little foreign investment, and development remained minimal until recently. This lack of development and lack of infrastructure (e.g., roads) meant that less change came to the Hadza area than would have occurred otherwise. Fourth, the presence of Ngorongoro Conservation Area, Serengeti National Park, Maswa Game Preserve, and Lake Manyara National Park, all of which surround Hadza country, allowed wildlife to persist. Protected big-game animals migrate through Hadza country, allowing for hunting in addition to gathering. Fifth, the Hadza have long adopted a low-key response to outsiders, hiding from strangers, which may have minimized confrontations that could have resulted in extermination at the hands of enemies. If the Germans had not halted Masai expansion, the Masai might have exterminated or assimilated the Hadza.

We are lucky that the Hadza have conserved so much of their traditional lifestyle. Because about 400 Hadza are still hunting and gathering almost exclusively, the foraging lifestyle can still be studied. At present, my graduate students and I are studying the energetics of foraging and food-sharing, residential mobility, demography, and life history and the psychology of mate choice and cooperation. This book attempts to summarize most of that research along with some of the research done by others.

CHAPTER 3

Social Organization, Beliefs, and Practices

SOCIAL ORGANIZATION

Ecology is an important determinate of social organization. This is true for other species and true for humans, especially hunter-gatherers. For example, living in a desert, a rain forest, or an arctic tundra, each with a very different set of flora and fauna, will determine the sorts of foods available and the technology necessary to acquire them. Ecology therefore determines the pattern of foraging, which in turn strongly influences group size and travel. Social organization may be a response to ecology, but once it exists, it also constrains foraging. For example, whether a species is social or solitary will determine whether cooperative foraging is possible, the extent of scramble or contest competition for foods, and the likelihood of food-sharing. Among human foragers, if women live with their kin, they might have stronger bonds with others in camp than men do, which could influence the nature of their cooperation. For all these reasons, I first describe some basic aspects of Hadza social organization before describing their technology in Chapter 4 and foraging in Chapter 5. Chapter 10 is devoted to the issue of how the foraging niche influences social organization cross-culturally.

The Hadza live in small camps that are mobile. That is to say, the people in these camps move every so often. There is no higher level of organization than the camp, and people move into and out of camps with ease. Hadza do think about those within each of the four main areas of

Hadzaland as sharing some affinity, and they certainly have a Hadza-wide identification, but there is no political structure of any kind, even at the camp level, much less at the tribal or ethno-linguistic level.

People in a camp can organize themselves for a camp move. This does not require a leader; a consensus is usually easy to reach after a little discussion. While men may talk about moving camp, it is usually not until the women are good and ready that a camp actually moves. Moves most often occur when women have exhausted the nearby resource patches and are having to travel too far to get foods. We have not yet analyzed our data to test this, but women often complain they are having to walk too far and want to move.

People can also organize themselves for a daily foray out of camp to forage. Since men usually forage alone, there is little organizing required. Women always forage in groups but seem to have little problem deciding which direction to go and what resources to target. They discuss this a few minutes and come to agreement without any leader.

RESIDENCE PATTERNS

Hadza camps can vary in population from 2 people to over 100. A census of the 53 camps I visited during 1995–2004 revealed a mean camp population of 30.4 (6–139, SD=28.4, median=21). People visit other camps frequently and sometimes move from one camp to another already existing camp. They may also move away from the people in their camp and start a new camp. Although camp residence is fluid, with people moving in and out, there is usually some semblance of a core group. It is common for larger camps to divide periodically into two or three smaller camps. Camps tend to be larger in the dry season. This is because a camp is always located within an acceptable walking distance of a water hole; in the dry season, there are fewer water holes, so there are fewer possible locations for camps (Woodburn 1964). When water is plentiful, the location of camps is less constrained, and people prefer to be in smaller camps.

Our censuses tend to be skewed toward the dry season simply because field seasons are most often during the U.S. summer. They are also skewed toward larger camps since most of our research requires larger samples, and this means we tend to avoid working in the smallest camps even when working during the rainy season. For this reason, dry-season camps are not significantly larger in the whole sample of camps. However, using a more random and representative sample that was obtained simply by traveling from camp to camp in a short period of time to gather GPS and anthropometric data and camp censuses, the difference is significant, with camps being larger in the dry season than in the rainy season ($t=-$2.64, $p=0.012$, $n=42$ camps, unequal variances).

Large camps are noticeably different from small camps. For example, there is more segregation by sex in large camps. Even more striking, as the Hadza themselves note, there is a lot more bickering in large camps. I found that men provide less direct care to their own children in large camps and that there were more single women per reproductive-age man in large camps (Marlowe 1999a). People playing experimental economics games (see Chapter 9) were more generous in larger camps (Marlowe 2004a). In smaller camps, unlike in larger ones, people cannot sneak food into their huts because there is no way to hide anything where there are only 2 or 3 huts near each other and everyone eats together.

RESIDENTIAL MOBILITY

In 2007, I calculated that the Hadza moved 6.5 times per year (4–20). This was based on interviews in which people (23 males, 12 females) were asked to name all places they lived "since this same time last year." Most Hadza moved slightly more often in the past, about 9 times per year in 1995. The Hadza move for a variety of reasons: to be near berries when they come into season, or move away from a location once patches of tubers have been depleted. One important reason for moving camp is that the drinking water is drying up. In the rainy season, drinking water often comes from pools of water on top of big flat rocks (Figure 3.1) and from running streams (Figure 3.2). Hadza camps may also be moved just because someone has died and residents feel that it is bad to stay in that spot.

The main constraint on camp locations is water. Camps are rarely so close to the water hole that animals will not come to drink; the Hadza want the animals to be able to drink so they can be hunted. Yet camps are rarely further than a 10-minute walk to the water hole, usually about 200–1,000 meters away. Camps are often up on a hill where there is a breeze, a view, and good shade. Camps are not located in the middle of very wet areas with many mosquitoes. Around the springs in Mangola, for example, camps are up on the nearby hills, which, even during the rainy season, are much drier and windier and consequently free of mosquitoes. The placement of Hadza camps merits study by paleoanthropologists and archaeologists interested in the most likely places to search for fossil and archaeological remains. If central places were being used, and I suggest they were from very early on (see Chapter 5), they

Figure 3.1. Boys drink from a pool of standing water on top of rocks.

Figure 3.2. A man drinks from a running stream.

should have been located in places like those the Hadza choose for their camps.

The mean distance between camps is 12 km (1.9–27.0 km, $n = 17$ camps, in a synchronic census of three different general areas). This is also the mean distance moved when the people of one camp move to a new location. There is a tendency for the core group to rotate through the same locations in a somewhat seasonal pattern across the year.

TERRITORIALITY

The Hadza are strikingly non-territorial. When people in one camp decide to move to another location, they do not worry about whether they are allowed to move there. They can move wherever they want to, according to Woodburn (1968b), and this agrees with my experience. They know where others are living most of the time and avoid moving to the same water hole. At another time, they will move to that location when no one is there. They would never worry that they are invading an area that belongs to any other group of Hadza. They are clear about the fact that Hadza do not own or control any area of Hadzaland. The freedom to live anywhere has usually extended even to non-Hadza, though the Hadza are beginning to feel that they are losing chunks of Hadzaland and know they will lose more if they cannot exclude outsiders.

The degree of non-territoriality among the Hadza may be somewhat extreme, judging from descriptions of many other foragers. Some of the complex foragers of the Pacific Northwest of North America were extremely territorial and had rights to certain resources, and this was clearly understood by others (Kelly 1995). As many of the complex foragers were sedentary, this is not surprising. Certainly, mobile foragers are more typical of most foragers in the tropics and probably of those of the more distant past. Even if somewhat extreme, the within-tribe ease of movement between camps by the Hadza does not strike me as all that rare in the ethnographic literature: e.g., Agta (Headland and Reid 1989), Mbuti (Turnbull 1983), and Andamanese (Mann 1932); for more on this topic, see Chapter 10.

DOMINANCE, STATUS, AND EGALITARIANISM

It is easy to understand why individuals strive to dominate others and have their way, and it is easy to see how this often results in a dominance hierarchy in social animals. Our closest relatives, chimpanzees, have clear dominance hierarchies. This is especially easy to see among males. Primatologists do not have to observe male chimpanzees for long before they can independently come up with rankings that are in agreement (Walters and Seyfarth 1987). They use a variety of measures: the number of occasions when one individual approaches and another retreats, the times a threat or submissive gesture is given, and the times one attacks and defeats another in an actual fight (Abbott et al. 2003). It is obvious that individuals gain benefits when they are dominant. These benefits usually translate into advantages in passing on their genes (Ellis 1995). Dominance striving in a social species should be taken as a given, and we might expect this to result in a dominance hierarchy because some individuals are larger, stronger, smarter, or just more popular (Krebs and Davies 1993, Sapolsky 2004). Given the logic of dominance hierarchies, one can see why many people are so surprised, even incredulous, when they hear that hunter-gatherers are egalitarian.

The Hadza certainly are egalitarian (Woodburn 1979, 1982a). This does not mean that there are no individuals who would like to dominate others and have their way. It is simply difficult to boss others around. If a Hadza tries to tell others what to do, which does happen now and then, the others simply ignore it; if he or she persists, they just move to another camp. Of course, the bossy person could follow them, but if people move to several different locations, the bossy person cannot control them all at once. Government officials or missionaries, who occasionally show up and try to tell the Hadza what to do, have the same difficulty controlling such a mobile group of people. Woodburn (1979) has described well Hadza egalitarianism and its significance, and I return to this important aspect of the Hadza in Chapter 9.

It is clear why hunter-gatherers without wealth are so much more egalitarian than people in cultivating societies, whether horticulturalists with slash-and-burn cultivation, pastoralists with livestock, intensive agriculturalists with irrigation and plows, or city dwellers. While pastoralists are even more mobile than foragers, they possess wealth in the form of their herds, and a man with many cows can use his wealth to buy favors from others, to buy more wives, and to control children by means of inheritance (Woodburn nd). Sedentary agriculturalists can use land ownership in the same way. The development of hierarchies and stratification in human societies has been extensively investigated and well explained (Boone 1992, Johnson and Earle 1987). The puzzling question is why hunter-gatherers are so egalitarian compared to chimpanzees and other social primates that also do not have wealth. Kristen Hawkes (2000) has suggested that the answer perhaps has to do with the dynamics of hunting and sharing big game among human foragers. Because a hunter who has acquired a large animal has something that everyone wants, he gets positive attention. Because making a kill is so unpredictable, even the best hunter may go a long time without success and often receives meat from a worse hunter. This, she suggests, undercuts the possibility of a stable male hierarchy.

Others have suggested that forager egalitarianism has to do with mobility. The freedom to leave and escape bossy people is surely one important reason hunter-gatherers are so egalitarian (Boone 1992, Lee 1990, Woodburn 1982a). In fact, the availability of viable territories for reproducing appears to be the best predictor of how egalitarian or despotic other species are, especially birds (Emlen 1984, Vehrencamp 1983a). When there are no territories available for reproducing, some birds are forced to stay in a group in which their status is low and their access to mates is restricted. In these despotic societies, dominant individuals have priority of access because they were there first or are older or stronger. Often subordinates serve as alloparents who provision the offspring of the dominant individuals. Subordinates who are close kin of the breeding couple tolerate more exploitation than non-kin since they are at least gaining some indirect fitness (Eberle and Kappeler 2006, Johnstone 2000, Reeve, Emlen, and Keller 1998, Vehrencamp 1983b). When helpers at the nest are not close kin, they will sooner leave and search for a better group if they are exploited too much with no chance to reproduce (although other factors are also implicated) (Covas et al. 2006, Gilchrist and Russell 2007, Nonacs 2007).

The availability of a breeding territory and its effect on the degree of despotism in birds is relevant to the egalitarianism of human foragers because the opportunity to leave rather than put up with being dominated is important in both cases. In the case of most birds, the opportunity has to do with habitat quality and population density. There are only so many spots in a habitat that can serve as a breeding territory (Emlen 1984, 1994). Human foragers are special in having the opportunity to leave and live elsewhere time and time again because, within the ethnic group, coming and going occurs with ease. This is very unlike the movement between groups in most other animals (see Chapter 10).

Among the Hadza, males are dominant over females and adults over sub-adults, but even in these two respects, the difference is slight compared to more complex societies. Some men are clearly much better hunters than others, but this does not result in a dominance hierarchy.

Hunting reputation does seem to come closer than anything else to capturing what little status variation there is. There is also no clear hierarchy among adult females, although older women are afforded a little extra respect, as are older men.

The Hadza have no political specialists. In fact, there is no role specialization of any kind other than the sexual division of labor. Each Hadza knows how to do everything he or she needs to do and does not depend on others. Each man can make his own bow and arrows, his poison, and his ax. Each man knows how to make fire, how to track, and how to make pegs to climb baobab trees and get honey. Each woman knows how to make her own digging stick, how to find tubers and dig them up, how to build a house, and how to make her own clothes, jewelry, and baskets or find gourds to use as containers for carrying water or berries. Even when it comes to medicine, each adult man and woman knows which plants to pick for different ailments. There are no shamans, witch doctors, or religious roles.

Some writers have argued that role specialization (in addition to sex roles) is a human universal and that it results in trade between those with different skills, which facilitates cooperation (Ridley 1996, Sugiyama 2003). Such specialization does seem to occur everywhere once agriculture is practiced as well as in some complex foraging societies. But this is not true of the Hadza. There is simply no routine division of labor except that based on sex. Some trade occurs, but there are no specialists who make certain products for trade either with neighboring tribes or with other Hadza. The only thing that even comes close are the few men who are expert arrow makers, who spend a bit more time at it, and who sometimes give other men arrows in exchange for some other object, but even this is very minor because all men make almost all of their own arrows.

PATTERNS OF MARITAL RESIDENCE

Marital residence is an important issue because it can affect so many other aspects of life. The potential for nepotistic help to have a real impact depends on living near close kin. For example, if resources need to be defended and males are better fighters, it may be better to keep brothers residing in the same place than sisters. Among other species, the sex that stays in its natal group is called the philopatric sex. The other sex usually disperses at maturity. This common pattern of one sex dispersing while the other stays is usually attributed to avoidance of inbreeding. Among most primates and mammals in general, males disperse and often must fight their way into another group. Among chimpanzees and bonobos, however, it is the females who almost always disperse (Pusey and Packer 1987).

The concept of a natal group from which one sex disperses makes little sense when we are dealing with human foragers like the Hadza. A baby (let's say a girl) is born in one camp in one location with one constellation of relatives (and non-kin) and two months later is living in a different location with different relatives (and non-kin), so by the end of the first year, the baby girl has lived in an average of 9 different locations, and the only consistently co-residing relatives may be her parents. Once this girl grows up and marries, it would be impossible to determine whether she left her natal group or natal area or whether her husband did. We can ask which one is residing further from the exact location where he or she was born, but both husband and wife may well be living in the same area where all the different camps they lived in during their first year of life are located. Because of the fluid composition of camp membership and the regular mobility of human foragers in the tropics, the usual terms *philopatry* and *natal group* are irrelevant.

For agricultural societies in which people are sedentary, philopatry is not an irrelevant concept. We can ask which sex moved from its natal village to go live in the natal village of the spouse. In agricultural societies, it is more common for a female to leave her natal area and group to go live in the natal area of her husband and his kin (his natal group) after marriage than for husbands to live with the kin of their wives (Marlowe 2004c). This is largely due to a bias toward male inheritance of land and property, which has a greater benefit on a son's RS than on a daughter's RS (Marlowe 2004c, Trivers and Willard 1973). Because chimpanzees and bonobos are male philopatric and because most human societies, which are mostly agricultural, are male philopatric, some have suggested that this was true of our ancestors as well (Ember 1975, Foley 1988, 1995, Rodseth et al. 1991). However, it makes more sense to consider foragers rather than agricultural societies when extrapolating to earlier hominins. A cross-cultural analysis of foragers shows that they cannot be described as male philopatric (Marlowe 2004c).

Although it makes little sense to ask which sex is philopatric among foragers, we can ask which sex spends more time living with its kin. Virilocality refers to a pattern of marital residence in which a couple lives near the kin of the husband. When a couple lives near the kin of the wife, this pattern is called uxorilocality (van den Berghe 1979). An analysis of hunter-gatherers that takes into account the early years of marriage as well as the later years of marriage reveals that multilocality is the best way to describe the dominant pattern, with virilocality no more common than uxorilocality among tropical hunter-gatherers (Marlowe 2004c).

Geneticists have analyzed the amount of variation in mitochondrial DNA (mtDNA) vs. Y-chromosomes in several populations of humans (Seielstad, Minch, and Cavalli-Sforza 1998). Only males possess Y-chromosomes, which are passed from father to son, while we all inherit our mtDNA from our mothers. If one sex stays in the area where it grew up while the other sex moves, then there should be less within-group and more across-group variation in the sex that is philopatric. Because Y-chromosomes usually show less within-group variation than mtDNA, a number of researchers have drawn the conclusion that virilocality (male philopatry actually) must have been more common than female philopatry throughout human evolution (Foley 1995, Seielstad, Minch, and Cavalli-Sforza 1998). However, one study of 3 virilocal and 3 uxorilocal hill tribes in Thailand found less within-group variation in Y-chromosomes in the virilocal tribes and less within-group variation in mtDNA in the uxorilocal tribes (Oota et al. 2001). These 6 tribes are all closely related (in relation to all humans anyway), and all have taken up agriculture in just the past few hundreds to thousands of years. Given that agriculture alters residence patterns (Marlowe 2004c), we can only conclude that these patterns in Y-chromosome and mtDNA must change rapidly and erase earlier patterns. Otherwise, we would need to posit that these 6 tribes have preserved their different residence patterns for hundreds of thousands of years despite taking up agriculture. Inferences about ancient residence patterns therefore cannot be made from genetic studies of agricultural populations, especially closely related populations (Wilkins and Marlowe 2006).

Hadza marital residence varies considerably. As in so many other aspects of life, there is great flexibility in Hadza residence, though there is a bias toward living with the wife's kin over the husband's kin. Since men are older than their wives by an average of 7 years, some bias is due to the greater likelihood that the husband's parents are already dead, but there are other reasons (Marlowe 2004c). Among couples living in the same camp with the mother of one of the spouses and with both the husband's and the wife's mothers still living, 68% were living in the same camp as the wife's mother (Woodburn 1964, 1968b). Jones et al. (2005b) found that when a mother, a daughter, and a son were all alive, the chance of a mother living with a daughter of age 20 years is 63%, while it is 57% for living with a 20-year-old son. After a woman reaches 40 years of age, the chance is only slightly higher for daughters (about 43% vs. 41%).

Hadza say it is best to live with the wife's mother in the beginning, during the birth of the first few children, and then later to live with the husband's mother. This is a common view among foragers, many of whom expect a new husband to perform bride-service for his wife's parents (Marlowe 2004c). Over the whole span of the marriage, the Hadza are nonetheless more likely to spend more time with the wife's kin than with the husband's kin.

Camps are usually referred to by the name of some senior man usually between 40 and 65 years of age. The core of a camp, however, tends to be a group of sisters, one of whom the man has long been married to. Most people in camp are related to one of these women and her parents or children. In a sample of 8 camps, I found 32% of couples living in a camp where the wife's mother lives, 18% living with husband's mother, 6% living where the mothers of both reside, and 44% living where neither has a mother residing. Although there is a bias toward uxorilocality, couples also live virilocally, bilocally (with the parents on both sides), and neolocally (without the parents on either side). A couple may be living uxorilocally one month, virilocally the next month, and neolocally a few months later. The only appropriate term for such a pattern is *multilocality* (Marlowe 2004c).

KINSHIP

The Hadza have no clans or unilineal kin groups of any kind. Descent is traced bilaterally through both mother and father. Any Hadza can usually decipher some kin connection to any other, given that there are only about 1,000 Hadza and kin ties are so overlapping. In addition, there are broad categories of classificatory kin and frequent use of fictive kin labels. Males refer to each other as *niye* or *hetl'ali* (both meaning brother or cousin), *bawa* (father), or *akaye* (uncle, grandfather), depending on their ages or generations relative to one another. Females refer to each other as *niyeko* (sister or cousin), *aya* (mother), *amama* (grandmother), or *mama* (granddaughter), likewise depending on generation (Woodburn 1964). It often takes some probing to get beyond classificatory and fictive kin to the actual genetic relatedness of two people.

Table 3.1 shows Hadza kin terms. Of the 6 main kinship systems, the Hadza system is closest to that of the Iroquois (Peoples and Bailey 1991, Woodburn 1964). Generation and sex are distinguished (Figure 3.3). For example, sex is distinguished among grandparents, but maternal and paternal grandparents are not distinguished (though a suffix can be added to

TABLE 3.1. HADZA KIN TERMS

Kin	Hadzane
Mother	ayako (aya—Woodburn, aiyako—Sands)
Father	bawa
Sister	niyeko (Niyenakwi, also "cousin," what cowives call each other—Sands)
Brother	niye/mits'i
Daughter	olako
Son	ola
Maternal grandmother	amama
Maternal grandfather	akaye/koku
Paternal grandmother	amama
Paternal grandfather	koko/kuuku?
Mother's older sister	ayadzuwako
Mother's younger sister	ayako kumiko (younger)
Mother's older/younger brother	akaye
Father's older sister	ayadzuwako (ayako?)
Father's younger sister	aya nakwiko (ayako?)
Father's older brother	bawadzua
Father's younger brother	bawa nakwete
Son of maternal aunt	niye/bawa (cannot marry) (nie/murunai—Woodburn)
Daughter of maternal aunt	niye (cannot marry)
Son of maternal uncle	niye/bawa
Daughter of maternal uncle	niye
Son of paternal uncle	!tabe
Daughter of paternal uncle	niye
Daughter of paternal aunt	niye/murunai, also pronounced mnai
Son of paternal aunt	!tale
Mother-in-law	murunai (siteako?)
Father-in-law	bawa/alai (isanzu?) (siteako?)
Sister of your wife	site nakwiko (ame?)
Brother of your wife	ame/nita me
Husband of your sister	ame/nitemekwa
Wife of your brother	nita mekokwa (ame?)
Female ego—sister's husband	ame
Female ego—brother's wife	ame/nitakoko sa or ma
Sister of maternal grandfather	amamako/pakachokowako
Brother of paternal grandmother	koko/akaye
Son of sister	akaye
Daughter of sister	maama/aya (cannot marry)
Husband	edze/ misikana, misika
Wife	misikako/ edzeyako

NOTE: From my work, as well as that of Bonny Sands and of James Woodburn (1964).

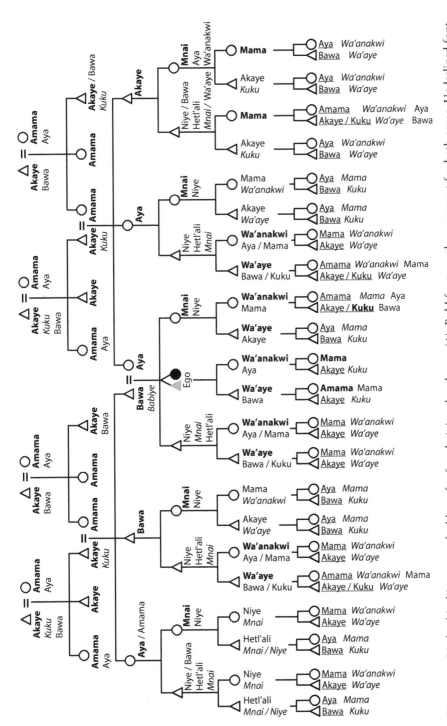

Figure 3.3. Hadza kinship terms of address for female (○) and male ego (△). Bold font equals agreement for both sexes. Underlined font equals male ego. Italics equals female ego. Regular font equals different terms used by Woodburn (m/f) 1964. Underlined followed by italics indicates terms taken from my own field notes. Mnai also pronounced murunai. Diagram made by Geoff Thomas.

distinguish them). Cousins are distinguished by sex, but matrilineal and patrilineal cousins are not distinguished, though some Hadza say one can marry only cross-cousins, not parallel cousins. A parallel cousin is the daughter or son of one's mother's sister or father's brother. A cross-cousin is the daughter or son of mother's brother or father's sister.

A distinction is made between maternal and paternal uncles. Mother's brother is called by a different term (*akaye*) than father, whereas father's brother is called by the same term as father (*bawa*). This could be related to the frequently practiced levirate, in which a man marries his dead brother's widow. Maternal and paternal aunts, on the other hand, are both called by the same term as mother, which differs from standard Iroquois kinship in which different terms are used for opposite-sex siblings in the parental generation on the maternal and paternal sides. Hadza terms reflect the fact that, from a child's perspective, father's sister and mother's sister are both possible substitute mothers. Children often live with a maternal or paternal aunt if the child's mother dies, and sometimes even when she is alive. A child would less frequently live with a maternal uncle, but when a child's father dies, it is common for the child to live with the paternal uncle, who may take the child's mother as a wife.

NAMING

Every Hadza has a name given by his or her parents, which is called the home name. The Hadza usually do not give names right at birth but wait until they feel the baby is "becoming a person" who will survive. This is understandable, given the considerable chances of an infant's dying (see Chapter 6). Often, when the parents do give a name to a child who later dies, they give that same name to the next child of the same sex. Sometimes the husband and the wife argue over the name of the child. In one case, a man was calling his 5-month-old infant by the name of his friend, while his wife was calling the infant Sijui, which means "I don't know" in Kiswahili. She was holding out for another name.

The Hadza do not themselves use family names (surnames), only given names. However, because government officials, missionaries, and researchers have for some time been asking them for surnames, they have adopted the practice of using the father's first name as their second name. Since they often name a boy for the father's father, the father and the son have their two names inverted, and this bounces back and forth each generation. A father may be called Salibogo Ndulumu and his son Ndulumu Salibogo, who then has a son who is called Salibogo Ndulumu. Daughters are often named for their grandmothers or aunts, but because a daughter's second name will be her father's first name, female names are not as confusing.

The Hadza like to change their names frequently. Most Hadza have at least 3 names, and some have had 5 or 6. The individual may use one name this year and the other one next year, then go back to the first one or take on a new one altogether. He or she may use one name with one person and a different one with another person. Many have taken on Bantu or Mzungu (white person in Kiswahili) or Christian names as well. However, they all remember their own home names and usually can remember other people's home names. All the name changing does not make life any easier for the researcher.

There are restrictions on name use or terms of address. For example, a woman is not supposed to say the name of her father-in-law, with whom she has an avoidance relationship. That is, a woman cannot be very familiar or intimate with her father-in-law. Such avoidance relationships are common in traditional or preindustrial societies. When a woman is asked the name of her child whose name is the same as her father-in-law's, she may ask another person to say the child's name. A man has an avoidance relationship with his mother-in-law, but he does not have as much reluctance to say her name as a woman does to say the name of her father-in-law.

SEX AND GENDER

Two genders are recognized, and homosexuality, according to informants and my own observation, is absent, except in the sex play of youngsters. Hadzane has many speech differences depending on whether a female or male is speaking. For example, a woman who wants to say "let's go" says "*Maite.*" A man says "*Maisi.*" Nouns have different suffixes indicating gender. Feminine nouns end in -*ako*, e.g., *nobako* (baobab tree). Masculine nouns lack the -*ako* ending, e.g., *manze* (elephant trunk).

In small camps, there is usually no segregation by sex; everyone sits and talks together. Men still hunt alone, and women go foraging with other women, but in camp all socialize together. A couple will spend much time together as well, especially in the early morning and once it starts to get dark, since they sleep together. In larger camps, couples also spend those hours together, but during the rest of the day, the sexes are often more segregated, not just while foraging but also in camp. Men sit together at the men's place under one tree, working on arrows, while women sit together

Figure 3.4. A woman with cheek scars in the form
of petals.

under another tree, processing food, sewing, or grooming children and
one another.

Both sexes have scars into which ash is rubbed as medicine and small
vertical or horizontal slits on their cheeks they usually get when they are
2 or 3 years of age. These scars are made with a knife by a close relative.
They say these scars serve to mark children as Hadza. Sometimes the scars
are more of an aesthetic statement; for example, the cheek scars of the
woman in Figure 3.4 are shaped like petals or leaves. Both sexes wear their
hair very short; someone else cuts the person's hair with a knife. Women
also use a knife to cut off each other's eyelashes, which they think makes
them prettier.

Women are very hardy. "Hard-working" was the third most often
cited trait that men said is important in a wife (see Chapter 7). Hadza
women speak their minds, and they sometimes have long, loud arguments
with their husbands and, even more often, with other women in camp.
Still, there is very noticeable female-female bonding, especially between
female kin, and it is stronger than male-male bonding between kin. Males
perhaps form stronger male-male bonds with non-kin than females form
with non-kin. Compared to men, women are modest when it comes to
sexual matters.

LIFE STAGES

Though there are no formal age sets, there are terms for the various stages of life. *Ola-pe* (or *olako*) is the term for children from birth to about 4 or 5 years old. *Tsetseya-pe* refers to those from about age 6 to 12 or 13. *Elati-nakwete* refers to boys during their teens and up until they get married at about age 20. *Tlakwenakweko* is the term for girls in their teens until they marry at about age 17. *Elati* is the term for adults of both sexes; *Elati-ka-eh* is the term for someone who has already had 2 or 3 children; *Pa-nekwete* is the term for a person about 45–60 years old; *Pa-nekwete-ka-eh* refers to one in the 70s; and *Balambala* is someone who is really old and frail.

There is no noticeable generation gap. Teenagers look up to adults and get along well with their elders. This is at least partly due to the fact that adults do not try to control them and rarely express strong opinions about whom they should marry. Furthermore, egalitarianism means that each individual has considerable autonomy. The absence of tension between younger and older men is less than in many other cultures, at least partly because polygyny is rare and competition for women is less intense. In addition, since there is no wealth, men do not have the same leverage over their sons that they do in societies where inheritance is important (Woodburn nd).

PUBERTY

Mai-to-ko

At about age 16–17 years, females reach menarche. Around this time, or a little before, they undergo a puberty ritual called *mai-to-ko*, which coincides with the ripening of *undushipi*, the most important species of berry (*Cordia*). Females of the right age assemble in one camp for 2 or 3 days for this ritual. It is important to have more than one female, so this often requires getting girls from more than one camp and sometimes girls of different ages. Girls are normally *tlakwenakweko* and post-menarche when this occurs, though recently I saw 3 girls, 2 of whom were closer to 12 or 13 years old, wearing special attire with beads and feathers, preparing for their *mai-to-ko* because there were so few girls of the right age nearby.

I have witnessed the beginning of a *mai-to-ko* that involved 5 girls around 15 to 17 years of age. Their initiation went on for 3 days. The girls were almost completely naked and covered in animal fat so that they were very shiny, and they were draped in beads. There was much singing and dancing and talking and visiting. Every once in a while, these girls would give chase to older teenage boys and try to hit them with their fertility sticks (*nalichanda*). The boys would run to dodge the sticks the girls wielded but seemed to be having great fun.

On the third day, the females segregated themselves, and the males had to stay away from where the women were. It is at this time that an old woman who is said to be an expert with the knife cuts off the tip of the clitoris (about half) of each young girl (according to male informants).[1] There are now only two old women who know how to do this, making them the only real specialists of any kind among the Hadza. Males are not allowed to observe, but all women in the camp or neighboring camps attend. If men were to watch, it is said they may die. It is not easy to get information about this ritual since women are reluctant to talk about it and men are excluded. Men seem not to know much and give somewhat conflicting answers. When I asked why the clitoris is cut, one man said it is because a baby will not be able to come out without removing this obstruction, while making a gesture with his finger as if the clitoris is large and curved, obstructing the birth canal. Another man said that, if the clitoris is not removed, a woman will enjoy sex too much, which is a problem because she will be moving around and making too much noise during sex (see Chapter 7). After a girl has had her *mai-to-ko*, she is in the marriage market but usually does not marry for another year or two.

The Masai, Datoga, and Iraqw all perform female genital mutilation. This is not surprising, especially in the case of the Masai and Datoga, since it is common among African pastoralists. Since it is rare among foragers, most researchers find it surprising that the Hadza practice clitorectomy. When I ask whether it is a practice the Hadza acquired from their neighbors, they say no, that it is an ancient Hadza practice. Some Hadza men have even told me that occasionally it is the old Hadza woman who performs the operation on the neighboring groups because she knows so well how to do it. Among their Nilotic neighbors, the Masai and the Datoga, there is extensive removal of the labia as well as the clitoris, while only the clitoris is removed among the Iraqw. If the practice was adopted

---

1. In at least one case, much of the labia were also removed, and the girl did not stop bleeding, so she was taken to a clinic by two researchers who are studying the *mai-to-ko* (Power and Mouriki, Personal Communication).

from the Iraqw, who have lived in the area a very long time, it could have been acquired hundreds of years ago, and it is certainly possible the Hadza forgot that it was borrowed.

The Iraqw believe that, after a spouse dies, it is necessary to get rid of the death pollution. They do this by finding a Hadza of the opposite sex, who will shave the widow's or widower's head and take the clothes and belongings of the dead one, after which the surviving spouse has sex with the Hadza, who will carry away the curse and die (Matthiessen and Porter 1974). This is what the Iraqw say, and the Hadza I have asked do not deny it, though they clearly do not believe that it results in their death. It is easy to imagine the Hadza acquiring clitorectomy from the Iraqw in connection with this, or because non-Hadza men from neighboring tribes prefer clitorectomized women (suggested by Ray Hames). Males are not circumcised, and there is no ritual for male puberty, though there is a ceremony (*maito*) that occurs when a young man has killed a large animal and joins the *epeme* men.

ADULTHOOD

Epeme

Epeme refers to the whole complex of manhood and hunting, but also to the new moon and the relationship between the sexes (Woodburn 1964). Fully adult men are referred to as *elati*, or *epeme* men. When a male is in his early 20s and kills a big-game animal, he becomes an *epeme* or fully adult man. Certain parts of all larger game animals can be eaten by the *epeme* men only. Not only can females and sub-adult males not eat the meat, they cannot even see the men eat this meat or, it is said, they could die or get ill or suffer any number of misfortunes. Occasionally, a teenage boy may kill a big animal, in which case he may or may not be deemed ready to join the *epeme* men early. Once a boy of only about 15 killed a greater kudu (*Tragelaphus strepsiceros*), a very large animal, but he was too young to be considered an *epeme* man, though he will likely become *epeme* earlier than most. It is usually not until about 20–25 years of age that males become *epeme* men. I know one man who is close to 30 years old and has not yet killed a large animal and is not *epeme*. This does not mean he cannot marry—he is married and has two children; it just means he does not eat the *epeme* meat, though eventually he will. All men over the age of about 30–35 years are normally considered *epeme* men whether they have killed a big animal or not, and so they join the others when the *epeme* meat is eaten. This is why I am allowed to eat the *epeme* meat.

The *epeme* meat animals are all the largest animals: warthog, impala, greater kudu, eland, giraffe, buffalo, zebra, wildebeest, lion, rhino, hippopotamus, and elephant. The last three are no longer eaten because rhinos have disappeared, there are few hippos, and the Hadza say they cannot kill elephants with their poison. The parts of the animal that are *epeme* meat are the kidney (*!'ukunju*), lung (*hoch'ope*), heart (*nkoloko*), neck (*/uti*) up to and including the tongue (*n/ata*), genitals (*ako*—male, or *akoko*—female), and the upper chest and some of the sides of a warthog.

When the men eat the *epeme* meat, they move just out of camp to a somewhat secluded spot. Once, I attended an *epeme* meat-eating ritual when a young man who had just killed an eland was becoming an *epeme* man. He was in charge of cooking the meat: putting it in the boiling water, stirring it, and taking it out to give to each man. In my experience, the cooking is usually done by the youngest *epeme* man present, though Woodburn (1964) says the oldest man does it. Other than this, very little else is different from ordinary meat consumption, except that no one must see the men eating. Once, in the middle of *epeme* meat eating, some children and women went walking by not too far away. A couple of men yelled at them with urgency and in all seriousness to warn them they were too close and might see us eating the *epeme* meat. The women and children did not look over but continued on their way, apparently not taking the scolding and warning all that seriously, but not looking toward us or slowing down.

Not only is it forbidden for non-*epeme* males and all females to eat the *epeme* meat or see the *epeme* men eating it, it is also forbidden for *epeme* men to eat *epeme* meat alone. They must eat it with other *epeme* men. Once I was with a man I'll call Askania, and we were going to scout out another camp that was about 8 km away from his camp. I wanted to see if I might be able to work there later, even though there was no access by vehicle. As we approached the camp, we noticed lots of meat hanging in the bushes. The man living in the camp, whom I will call Oya, had just killed a greater kudu. Oya was living in this camp with his wife and 2 of his own sons, who were about 7 and 9 years old, along with his half-sister, her two young children, and another half-sister who was pregnant. Thus, he was the only *epeme* man.

My companion, Askania, was happy to discover that after our walk he would be eating meat. The three of us moved a little ways out of camp and ate the *epeme* meat together. When Askania and I were returning to

Askania's camp later in the day, he told me that it was not right for Oya to be living in such a small camp. I asked him why, and he said that there were no other *epeme* men, so Oya could not eat the *epeme* meat by himself. If he did, he could get sick or even die. This is interesting in light of the fact that small camps are not at all rare. When a man kills an *epeme* animal in such a small camp, he is expected to tell *epeme* men in nearby camps to come eat the *epeme* meat with him. Thus, the *epeme* meat ritual and related rules have the effect of guaranteeing middle-aged and older men a certain amount of meat, including some bits high in fat and vitamins. The rules also insure that meat is shared with other men, while also separating the sexes and keeping younger men slightly below the older men in status.

Epeme Dance

The *epeme* dance is considered a sacred ritual. The items that men wear during the dance are also sacred and not to be shared with non-Hadza. The Hadza do not invite strangers to the dance, not even researchers until they have become pretty familiar with them. The dance will usually occur every night when there is no moon in the sky, usually between the hours of full darkness and midnight, at least in camps that are large enough: there need to be at least a few *epeme* men. There can be no moonlight or any other source of light such as a fire; it must be completely dark.

Once it has been dark a while, people begin to assemble in an open area in camp. Little children stay at home asleep, with their older siblings looking after them. Older teenage girls may sit with the women. The females sit together and wait for the men to begin. The men all stay together in a different place, usually behind a rock, an old hut, or a tree or some obstruction, which serves the function of a stage curtain. Only one man dances at a time, while the others sit off stage behind the obstruction. The man dancing puts on a long black cape and a headdress of black or brown ostrich feathers (*kimbakubi*), ties bells (*!ingiri*) to his ankle, and holds a seed-filled maraca gourd (*sengeno*) in his hand.

The man comes out onto the stage and dances, stomping one foot very hard on the ground in a stiff fashion, providing a slow, steady beat with the jangling of the bell and shaking of the maraca. He sings in a call and shout, sometimes whistling to the women the way he does to the honey-guide bird (see Chapter 5), and the women answer him. He only dances a minute or two the first time, then disappears off stage again.

He remerges after a moment and dances again the same way, a bit longer this time. This goes on and on, and each time he dances longer and the women become more animated in their responses to him. At first, the women sing sitting down, but as the dance continues, they get up and dance around the man with more and more feeling. Their movements, unlike the man's, are not stiff, but graceful. Since it is pitch black, no one can see the man but, of course, they can hear him and sort of make out his movements as he sings and dances. While it is difficult for me to say which man is dancing unless I am sitting with the men off stage, it is probably not so difficult for the women who know the men so well.

When the first man finishes, he passes off the *epeme* items to the next man, and the same thing occurs again. Each man has his own style. In fact, most of the observers are probably not fooled long about who is dancing. When I ask men and women who is the best *epeme* dancer, they have no problem giving their opinions, and the women call out each man who is their kin by an affectionate kin term. Woodburn (1964) says that the point of the ceremony is to heal rifts and bring everyone together. The dance can heal those who have violated the *epeme* rules and bring good luck in future hunting.

RELIGION

Most of what we know about Hadza beliefs, ritual, and religion we owe to the work of James Woodburn. Woodburn, who received his Ph.D. from Cambridge and taught at the London School of Economics, began studying the Hadza for his doctoral research in 1958. He early on spent two years with them, learning their language. That was essential in those days because few Hadza knew Kiswahili. He returned many times until his last visit in 1998. His doctoral thesis was on Hadza social organization with special attention to censuses that allowed him to characterize residence patterns (Woodburn 1964). But he also described relations between the sexes, religion, and kinship in detail. My descriptions of these aspects of Hadza culture are to a large extent informed by his descriptions. Almost everything he says resonates for me and other Hadza researchers such as Nicholas Blurton Jones and Lars Smith; we feel he got most everything right. I therefore have more confidence in his descriptions than in my own when it comes to the more difficult to verify realm of norms, beliefs, religion, and rituals, and especially their meaning to the Hadza.

In 1911, when Obst visited the Hadza, he said it was difficult to find out anything about their religion beyond the fact that the sun was God and that prayers were said over dead animals (1912). I have seen many animals killed but have never seen prayers said over them. In the 1920s, Bagshawe (1924–1925a,b) claimed that the Hadza had no religion. In the mid 1940s, when Cooper spent time with the Hadza, he said they had a primitive religion (1949). I can see why these early observers thought the Hadza had either no religion or a very minimal one. When I asked one Hadza man if there was only one god or several, he thought about it a while, then said he was not quite sure. This sums up much about Hadza religion. I think one can say the Hadza do have religion, certainly a cosmology anyway, but it bears little resemblance to what most of us in complex societies (with Christianity, Islam, Hinduism, etc.) think of as religion. There are no churches, preachers, leaders, or religious guardians, no idols or images of gods, no regular organized meetings, no religious morality, no belief in an afterlife—theirs is nothing like the major religions. All the beliefs and rituals associated with the *epeme* dance and *epeme* meat eating are at the heart of Hadza religion.

The sun (Ishoko) is female, while the moon (Seta) is male. The stars are their children. The moon is always chasing after his mate, the sun, but can never catch her. Haine is god, though Ishoko is the sun and is god as well, so it seems to me that Haine may just be a necessary male version, as Ishoko is female. The Hadza have a rich storytelling tradition (Bala 1998), and men are the ones who tell these stories.

The Hadza have a creation myth that explains how people—the Hadza—came to be. Here, I paraphrase Matthiessen and Porter (1974), who himself is paraphrasing Peter Enderlein, a Swede who tried promoting game-cropping in Hadzaland in the late 1960s and related this story: Humans descended to the earth on the neck of a giraffe, sometimes they say humans climbed down from a baobab tree. A giant ancestor, Hohole, and his wife, Tsikaio, lived at Dungiko in a cave beneath the rocks where Haine (god, the sun) could not follow them. Hohole hunted elephants and dispatched them with one blow of his stick, then stuck them in his belt (the way Hadza carry home hyrax they have killed; ironically, the rabbit-sized hyrax are close relatives of elephants). Sometimes Hohole walked hundreds of miles and returned home with 6 elephants under his belt. One day, Hohole was hunting when a cobra bit him on his little toe and he died. Tsikaio found him and fed on his leg for five days until she felt strong enough to carry his body to Masako. There she left him to be eaten by birds. She left to live in a giant baobab tree. After 6 days in the baobab tree, she gave birth to Konzere. The Hadza are the children of Konzere and his mother Tsikaio.

The Hadza also have a story that explains how different tribes came to be. Here, I paraphrase a Hadza man named Gudo Bala from his book of stories and songs (Bala 1998): When god finished making the world, clouds, trees, mountains, sun, moon, and people, he made things for all the peoples of the world. He started with a bow and arrows, then made spears, hoes, rifles, and even medicine. He laid these things out and let each group choose the things they wanted. He started with the Hadzabe. One Hadza chose the bow and arrow and said to god, "I'm done, *nube'eya*" (good). The Hadza left, and a Datoga came forward and chose a spear. Then, an Iraqw person chose a hoe and a spear. Finally, an Mzungu (white person) chose the rifle and several other things; god gave him the medicine and he left. Then, all these different groups went their separate ways to different parts of the world. Note how the stories obviously got revised with mention of the Datoga (in the area less than 100 years), Mzungu (less than 50 years), rifles, and medicine.

There is one story about an old woman called Mambedako, which Woodburn (1964) recounts, and I paraphrase it in condensed form here: Long ago *epeme* meat belonged to the women. The owner of a pot in which *epeme* meat was cooked was an old woman called Mambedako. She dressed like a man, wearing a wildcat skin in front and leaving her buttocks naked. Under the cat skin she had tied a zebra penis. She was married to beautiful wives and had intercourse using the penis. She had a man's bow but hunted zebra only and cut off the penis to replace the one she was wearing when it got old. When men killed animals, they had to carry the *epeme* meat to her hut, and she ate it with the women. One day, mongooses and wildcats who were cooking *epeme* meat inside the hollow of a baobab tree called over a man who had gone hunting. He stopped, and they offered him some of the *epeme* meat, but he refused and told them that men did not eat that meat. They gave him some regular meat and he ate, explaining that *epeme* meat was eaten only by women, with Mambedako as their leader. They told him to kill an eland, and that they would come. After he did kill an eland, Mambedako sent some unmarried women to get water to cook the *epeme* meat. Once the women cooked the meat, big red flies stung the women around their genitalia; then the mongooses and wildcats tied the legs of Mambedako and the other women to the trees, filled their vaginas with sand, beat them with thorny branches, and broke the women's gourds and pots. The mongooses and wildcats gave the *epeme* meat to the men, and from that time on, the *epeme* meat has been the property of the men.

TABOOS, NORMS, AND BELIEFS

The Hadza have very few taboos compared to most ethnic groups in Tanzania. The most serious taboos are against a person who is not an *epeme* man seeing the *epeme* men eating the *epeme* meat, or eating the *epeme* meat, and against an *epeme* man eating it by himself. When the women are performing the clitorectomy, it is taboo for the men to see them. There are more norms than taboos. For example, a man should not work on his poison arrows while his wife is menstruating or even hunt with poison, as his poison will not work (Woodburn 1959, 1982b). One is not supposed to marry a parallel cousin according to some informants.

There are no food taboos. The Hadza do not normally eat fish, but when I have had Hadza men with me on a trip to a nearby town and have opened a can of tuna fish, they have eaten it with gusto. In 1998, when weather conditions created a giant lake complete with giant catfish in the Yaeda valley and Bantu fishermen caught, ate, and sold the fish, some Hadza men took to walking out in the lake and whacking the fish on the head with their bows. They ate the catfish but complained that they did not taste good. They say that fish is bad, "like snake," which they also do not eat. In fact, they eat no reptiles except for tortoises (*k'oloko*; *Geochelone pardalis*). Only women and children eat tortoises and the large land snail (*nlalaka*; *Achatinidae Burtoa nilotica*). When a man is out foraging and finds a tortoise, he is not inclined to think about taking it back to camp, but if I am with him he may ask if I want to take it back. The women and children are glad to get it and promptly cook it and eat it. The men say that if they were to eat the tortoise, it would ruin their arrow poison. Apparently, some men eat tortoises (I have seen one), and younger boys regularly eat them with the women and girls.

WITCHCRAFT

The Hadza do not practice witchcraft but often say they fear the witchcraft of their Isanzu neighbors. More and more these days, a death might be attributed to the witchcraft employed by one of the neighboring groups. Of course, Hadza beliefs about the *epeme* are not too far removed from witchcraft. One Hadza man told me that the Hadza don't know how to perform witchcraft (*uchawi* in Kiswahili) but that the *epeme* is Hadza *uchawi*.

Once we were doing a project that involved getting some Hadza volunteers to let us make imprints of their teeth after controlling their diet for 3 days to analyze microwear patterns. After a woman that I know well and usually see every year volunteered, I discovered that she had lost virtually all of her teeth—teeth she had had the previous time I saw her. I asked her how she lost them. She began to tell me something when a man nearby said that she had eaten *epeme* meat and that is why she lost her teeth. Once he said this, there was nothing else she could say.

Another time 3 Hadza men were in the Land Rover with me. One was the son of an old man who had a mangled hand, all curved and crooked with some fingers missing. The old man's own story was that he wrestled a leopard for some meat and, although he won, almost lost his hand. He has lived many long years and still manages to use a bow with that mangled hand. I was curious about what his son would say. The son began to tell the same story but was interrupted by another man, his senior, who often tries to boss others. This man said it was not a leopard; that the old man's hand was deformed because he had eaten *epeme* meat by himself. Once said, the crippled man's son could not dispute it. It seemed to make him feel sad, embarrassed, and humiliated.

I have never seen anyone contest the accusation of an *epeme* meat rule violation, so it carries some weight and can be used somewhat like witchcraft. But most nice and more humble Hadza do not accuse others of violating the rule; at least, they do not seem to start such a story, even if they will go along with it. Perhaps one difference from witchcraft accusations is that the accused is not said to be a witch who could harm others, only someone who has been harmed for violating the taboo. That is, it is not the case that someone first gets mad at another person and then vengefully accuses that person of violating the *epeme* rule (as is often the case when people believe in witchcraft). Rather, the accusation is merely used to explain a turn of bad luck. It never seems to involve a moral violation such as adultery, theft, or hurting someone either, but simply adherence to rules regarding *epeme* meat eating.

BIRTH

Women may be foraging right up to and even on the day they give birth. When they go into labor, female friends and relatives—a mother, a sister, an aunt, or a mother-in-law—assist them. Men are not present at delivery, though sometimes a husband may be if there are no females to help. The woman squats or sits against a tree in a position to push, or lies down, while midwives massage her.[2] The umbilical cord is cut with a knife. One of the attending women may hold the baby a while as the mother recovers on the ground. The infant nurses soon after, consuming the colostrum with its important antibodies. Women are in remarkably good shape soon after delivery; in most cases, a woman rests only 3 or 4 days before returning to foraging with the newborn on her back.

DEATH

In the recent past, the Hadza tell me, they would simply take the body of a young person who died out of camp and leave it where hyenas would eat it. With an older person, however, they usually left the body in the person's hut, pushed the hut down on top of the person and set it on fire, and moved away from the camp. More and more these days, they bury a body because they know the government does not approve of their leaving the dead out to be eaten. This may also be partly due to the influence of the occasional missionary. According to Woodburn (1982b), however, it was also common in the past to make a shallow grave and to leave the *epeme* ostrich feathers on the grave or to break a decorated gourd used for holding fat over the grave. These days, a young child is usually buried in camp near the parents' hut.

   Deaths and illnesses tend to be explained in one of 5 ways. (1) If someone is really old when she dies, she is said to have died just because she was old. (2) If someone falls to his death, the Hadza say the cause of death is simply the accidental fall. (3) If someone is killed by a lion or a snakebite, this is just part of the dangers of the natural world. Likewise, the Hadza understand that death due to malaria is caused by mosquito bites. (4) When the cause is less obvious, however, and especially when death is sudden, such as from a heart attack or poisoning, and the person had been healthy before, the witchcraft of their non-Hadza neighbors is often said to be the cause of death. Even when a death is clearly caused by a disease, the Hadza may say this was due to witchcraft if the person had quarreled with an Isanzu earlier. The percentage of deaths attributed to such witchcraft is on the rise, and these days even a few Hadza are accused of having learned witchcraft from their neighbors. (5) Finally, there is the supernatural cause related to violating the *epeme*

   2. This information comes from my graduate student, Alyssa Crittenden, who attended one birth.

meat rules. If females or young males eat the *epeme* meat, it is said that they can get ill, get a deformity (like the mangled hand or missing teeth described earlier), or die. In reality, I am pretty sure that only the *epeme* men eat the *epeme* meat, so this attribution of cause of death seems to be an excuse to reinforce the *epeme* meat taboo.

LEISURE, RECREATION, AND THE NONMATERIAL ARTS

Hadza men sometimes gamble for arrows in a game called *lukuchuko*, in which they toss pieces of bark against a tree and determine winners based on how they land. I have mainly seen them doing this, infrequently, in an area where there are vast bushes full of *undushipi* berries (*Cordia gharaf Ehrenb.*) during their ripe season. Hadza come from far and wide to live in the bushes and eat berries every day. This results in very large camps with a regular supply of easy-to-acquire food. It seems that the men gamble there because they have less need to go foraging and plenty of other men are around. Kohl-Larsen (1958) reported on the gambling game when he was there in the 1930s. Perhaps because both Kohl-Larsen and Woodburn had rifles and were shooting animals and feeding the Hadza plenty of meat, Hadza men did not feel they needed to spend as much time hunting. Hadza men tell me that they don't have time to gamble these days. They do spend a lot of time resting, but they are usually working on arrows at the same time. Girls (and, to a lesser extent, boys) sometimes play a game like jacks using small rocks (called *k'ese*). Young girls play with dolls made out of clay or pieces of old cloth. Young boys play together throwing rocks and target-shooting with their bows and arrows for hours every day.

Most of us do not engage in grooming the way our primate relatives do. We probably used to though, back when we had plenty of leisure time each day and lived in small groups out in the open. Hadza grooming is very reminiscent of that of other primates. They pick lice out of others' hair and eat them (Figure 3.5). Women often groom children and other women. Men do not groom or get groomed as much as women and children do, but sometimes a wife grooms her husband and men groom a child. On the other hand, men sit making arrows and talking for hours while in camp. Women sit together talking, sewing, and processing food—for example, pounding baobab seeds.

Stories are a form of entertainment and cultural information. For example, stories like the creation myth (Bala 1998) serve both functions, while daily stories about events provide plenty of laughs.

Figure 3.5. Women groom children and remove head lice.

MUSIC

One form of art the Hadza produce is singing and dancing, which they do often. The main musical instrument is the voice. Occasionally, a teenage boy or young man makes a *zeze*, a stringed instrument made with a gourd, or an *mbira*, a finger piano made from wood and metal, both of which have been adopted from their Bantu neighbors. The only other musical instruments would be the maraca and bells at the *epeme* dance. The bells are also a recent import from their neighbors. The Hadza do not play drums or any other instrument. The voice is the only native Hadza musical instrument (and perhaps the wild gourd used as a maraca).

The Hadza sing often, and everyone can sing very well. When several Hadza get in my Land Rover to go somewhere, they almost invariably begin singing. They use a melody they all know but make up lyrics on the spot. These lyrics may go something like "Here we go riding in Frankie's car, riding here and there in the car. When Frankie comes, we go riding in the car." They take different parts in a three-part harmony, never missing a beat, all seemingly receiving the improvised lyrics telepathically.

They also love to dance and do so in various distinct styles. The *epeme* dance by the men is very different from the dancing of women. And it is also very different from the dancing men do when not at the *epeme*. Sometimes they dance in an up and down motion similar to that of their pastoralist neighbors, but much more sensually. It is hard to believe the same men who dance so stiffly in the *epeme* can move so gracefully and beautifully when engaged in other types of dancing. On rare occasions, there is a dance in which both men and women participate and form a long chain. I saw them do this around the fire at night in one camp. They held onto the person in front and all moved around in a snakelike, sinuous path. They were singing and making noises like animals, and their movements resembled one animal and then another. This dancing is unique and full of soul—the most sensual dancing I've ever seen.

CHAPTER 4

Material Culture

In this chapter, I describe Hadza material culture, which is so integral to foraging and important in situating the Hadza in the context of other cultures in the archaeological record (see also Woodburn 1970 and Kohl-Larsen 1958). Especially in small-scale societies like that of foragers, technology plays a large role in shaping culture. Because the Hadza are so relevant to understanding the past and because paleoanthropologists and archaeologists only have the material culture and fossil remains to work with, it is important to describe how the Hadza use different tools. First, however, I discuss the issue of cultural complexity. Foragers tend to have the least complex societies, but within this category, there is considerable variation.

The Standard Cross-Cultural Sample (SCCS) is a sub-sample of the larger Ethnographic Atlas (EA) of 1,267 mostly traditional societies of all types: foragers, pastoralists, horticulturalists, and intensive agriculturalists. The SCCS consists of 186 societies carefully chosen on the basis of geographic area, language, and cultural cluster to maximize statistical independence. Murdock and Provost (1980) calculated a measure of cultural complexity using the SCCS codes for a range of traits they felt captured complexity. These traits were mode of subsistence, mobility, technological specialization, writing, money, population density, social stratification, and political integration. They summed these to score the complexity of different societies. The scores range from 0 to 40.

TABLE 4.1. CULTURAL COMPLEXITY FOR THE 186 SOCIETIES IN THE STANDARD CROSS-CULTURAL SAMPLE

Societies	Score
Hadza,* Mbuti*	0
Botocudo,* Aweikoma,* Yahgan*	1
!Kung,* Semang,* Tiwi*	2
Aranda*	3
Andamanese,* Kaska,* Paiute,* Klamath,* Siriono*	4
Badjau,* Montagnais,* Chiricahua,* Shavante*	5
Fulani, Vedda,* Copper Eskimo,* Eyak,* Warrau,* Nambicuara, Cayua, Tehuelche*	6
Ainu,* Yukaghir,* Micmac,* Comanche*	7
Nama, Lapps, Samoyed, Chukchee, Slave,* Yurok,* Kutenai,* Gros Ventre,* Yanomamo, Carib, Jivaro, Amahuaca, Lengua	8
Masai, Toda, Lamet, Gilyak,* Ingalik,* Abipon	9
Orokaiva, Saulteaux,* Havasupai, Goajiro, Cubeo (Tucano), Trumai	10
Teda, Aleut,* Yokuts (Lake),* Mundurucu	11
Kimam, Bellacoola,* Twana,* Pomo (Eastern)*	12
Rwala Bedouin, Iban, Pentecost, Haida,* Bribri, Timbira	13
Maori, Hidatsa, Cayapa, Tupinamba	14
Mao, Basseri, Pawnee, Omaha	15
Tuareg, Manus, New Ireland, Trobrianders, Ajie, Callinago, Saramacca	16
Massa, Bogo, Gond, Nicobarese, Tanala, Siuai, Marquesans, Atayal, Papago, Miskito	17
Bemba, Nyakyusa, Otoro Nuba, Somali, Toradja, Kwoma, Tikopia, Western Samoans, Trukese, Huron, Huichol	18
Luguru, Kikuyu, Banen, Tiv, Rhade, Kapauku, Gilbertese, Marshallese, Palauans, Creek, Popoluca	19
Thonga, Lozi, Suku, Nkundo Mongo, Kazak, Alorese	20
Azande, Santal, Garo, Lakher, Tobelorese, Ifugao	21
Mbundu, Mende, Tallensi, Khalka Mongols, Lepcha, Mbau Fijians, Yapese, Natchez	22
Shilluk, Burusho, Cuna (Tule), Mapuche	23
Ibo, Ashanti, Konso, Kenuzi Nubians, Aymara	24
Kaffa (Kafa), Lolo, Zuni, Quiche	25
Songhai, Gheg Albanians, Abkhaz, Manchu, Inca	26
Ganda, Fur (Darfur)	27
Bambara	28
Wolof	29
Fon	30
Amhara, Riffians	32
Hausa, Armenians, Kurd	33
Aztec	34
Punjabi (West), Negri Sembilan, Haitians	35
Hebrews, Khmer	36
Egyptians, Basques, Irish, Vietnamese	37

(continued)

TABLE 4.1. *(continued)*

Societies	Score
Turks, Russians, Burmese, Balinese, Koreans	38
Babylonians, Romans, Javanese	39
Uttar Pradesh, Siamese, Chinese, Japanese	40

NOTE: From Murdock and Provost 1980. Calculated by summing variables 149–158; v149=writing and records, v150=fixity of residence, 151=agriculture, 152=urbanization, 153=technological specialization, 154=land transport, 155=money, 156=density of population, 157=political integration, 158=social stratification; *=foragers.

The Hadza scored 0, along with the Mbuti Pygmies of the Democratic Republic of Congo, as the least complex in the sample, even though there are 35–40 other foraging societies, depending on one's definition of foragers (Table 4.1). The mean (and median) score for foragers was 6 (min=0, max=13).

It does not surprise me that the Hadza ranked at the bottom of the complexity scale; we would be hard-pressed to find a less complex society. While the Tasmanians are often noted as being the least complex of all societies ethnographically described, at least technologically (Flannery 1994, Oswalt 1973), the Hadza certainly would rank below most other hunter-gatherers. With the exception of having the bow and poisoned arrow (and perhaps the ax), Hadza technology is about as simple as that of any society ethnographically described and probably as simple as that of most foragers before agriculture first appeared. Whether nonmaterial culture follows lockstep technological complexity is debatable. Most Australian aboriginal groups had a complicated kinship and spiritual ideology in conjunction with the simplest technology. In general, however, the two surely influence each other. Unlike social insects with genetic castes, a human society is unlikely to have extreme specialization and division of labor (other than one based on sex and age) without somewhat elaborate technology producing wealth, resulting in power differentials and social stratification. Here, I describe Hadza material culture and let the reader decide how simple or complex the nonmaterial culture is.

Table 4.2 shows a list of Hadza possessions and artifacts. Not all of them are made by the Hadza themselves; some are acquired in trade with neighbors and so probably did not exist very long ago, though in many cases, they must have once had an alternative version made of different

TABLE 4.2. HADZA POSSESSIONS AND ARTIFACTS

Possessions and Artifacts	Earliest Possible Date	Earliest Citation	Pre-Neolithic	Post-Neolithic	Frequency of Change in the 20th Century
Hammerstone	> 3 mya		X		–
Anvil for pounding	> 3 mya		X		–
Dig stick	> 3 mya	1911	X		–
Fire drill	> 300,000	1930	X		∨
Hearth	> 300,000	1890s	X		–
House	> 300,000	1890s	X		–
Skin shoes (now tires)[a]			X		∨
Skin belt[a]		1930	X		∨
Leather skirt[a]		1911	X		∨
Leather kaross[a]		1930	X		∨
Leather bags			X		–
Leather sheath		1930	X		–
Sleeping hide			X		–
Gourd container, dipper		1930	X		–
Organic jewelry		1911	X		–
Grass basket			X		∨?
Bow	11–100,000	1911	X		–
Arrow (6 types)	11–100,000	1911	X		–
Two poisons		1911	?		–
Shell (mixing poison)			X		–
Quiver		1931–1938	X		–
Fertility walking stick			X		?

Item					
Medicine horn		1931	X		–
Wood toys		1960	X		?
Wood gambling chips		1930	X		<
Pegs for climbing		1890s	X		–
Stone pipe		1911	X		–
Wooden pipe		1930	X		?
Epeme items: feather or fur headgear, maraca, cape		1931–1938			–
Twine noose snare			X		?
Glass bead jewelry	1300 A.D.	1917		X	>
Epeme items: metal leg bands and bells	1500 A.D.	1931–1938		X	>
Iron arrow point[b]	1500 A.D.	1911		X	–
Metal knife[b]	1500 A.D.	1925		X	>
Metal ax[b]	1500 A.D.	1925		X	>
Metal hammer[b]	1500 A.D.	1930		X	>
Metal chisel[b]	1500 A.D.			X	>
Metal needles[b]	1500 A.D.			X	>
Musical bow with wire	1500 A.D.	1960		X	>
Tobacco[b]	1550 A.D.	1911		X	>
Metal cooking pot	1500 A.D.	1945		X	>
Previously clay pots[b]	1300 A.D.	1930, 1945, 1950		X	<
Factory cloth	1800 A.D.	1911		X	>
Cloth dolls[b]	1800 A.D.			X	>
Plastic beads	1990 A.D.	1990s		X	>

[a]Exist now but often made of different material.
[b]Likely made earlier but of different material.

material. For example, long ago they may have had axes of stone rather than the iron blades used today.

TOOLS

The earliest clear evidence of tool use by hominins are the Oldowan choppers dating to 2.6 million years ago (mya) (Semaw et al. 1997). For a long time, this led many to assume that 2.6 mya was when tools were first used. With the ever-increasing record of chimpanzee and orangutan tool use, including termite and honey fishing sticks (McGrew 1992, Van Schaik, Fox, and Fechtman 2003) and hammerstones (Boesch and Boesch-Achermann 2000), it seems very unlikely early hominins before 2.6 mya went from using no tools to suddenly flaking stones. If their tools were mostly made of wood, the chance of finding them preserved in archaeological sites is next to nil.

The earliest tools used by hominins were probably hammerstones (like those used by chimpanzees to crack nuts) and sticks for a variety of purposes from self-defense, to killing prey, to perhaps termite fishing like chimpanzees (McGrew 1992), and eventually to digging underground storage organs (USOs), such as the tubers Hadza women dig today. Hammerstones and digging sticks are still very important tools for the Hadza. While digging sticks would very rarely be preserved, hammerstones do survive. The problem is distinguishing a hammerstone from naturally occurring stones that have not been used but show wear and abrasion from natural processes of erosion (eoliths). I suspect the reason that no stone tools are recognized before 2.6 mya is probably because it is too difficult to distinguish a hammerstone from an unaltered rock. Hadza hammerstones show varying degrees of wear from usage. Thus, there may already be evidence of hammerstones at the earliest hominin sites that simply cannot be verified.

Wendell Oswalt (1973) introduced a nomenclature and taxonomy for describing and comparing tool kits (Figure 4.1 and Table 4.3). He first classifies tools into those used for subsistence and those used for other purposes. Those used for subsistence he calls subsistants. Subsistants are divided into naturefacts and artifacts. A naturefact is a tool that is not altered before being used, such as a hammerstone. An artifact is altered. A digging stick might be a naturefact if a stick of the right size already sharp enough to use were found; normally, Hadza women cut and sharpen sticks, so they become artifacts. Further, Oswalt divides subsistants into implements and facilities. Traps are facilities that control the movement

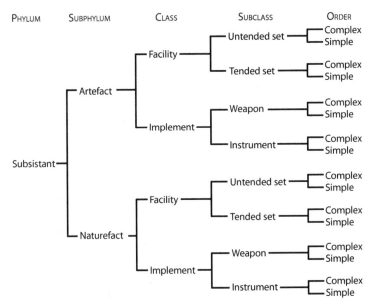

PHYLUM	SUBPHYLUM	CLASS	SUBCLASS	ORDER

Figure 4.1. Wendell Oswalt's tool taxonomy, redrawn from Oswalt 1973, table 2-1, p. 25.

TABLE 4.3. OSWALT'S DEFINITIONS OF TECHNOLOGY

Subsistant	Extrasomatic form that is removed from a natural context or is manufactured and is applied directly to obtain food.
Techno-unit	Integrated, physically distinct, and unique structural configuration that contributes to the form of a finished artefact.
Instrument	Hand-manipulated subsistant that customarily is used to impinge on masses incapable of significant motion and is relatively harmless to the user.
Weapon	Form that is handled when in use and is designed to kill or maim species capable of motion.
Facility	Form that controls the movement of prey or protects it to the user's advantage. *Tended* if physical presence of user is essential for functioning; *untended* if functions in the absence of user.
Naturefact	Natural form, used in place or withdrawn from a habitat, that is used without prior modification.
Artefact	End product resulting from modification of a physical mass to fulfill a useful purpose.
Simple	Retains same physical form before and during use.
Complex	Parts change their relationship with one another when form is used.

NOTE: From Oswalt 1973.

of prey, even when untended, while digging sticks are implements that can function only when being actively manipulated on objects that are not moving; we normally think of implements as tools. A weapon is used to kill prey that can move. Finally, Oswalt introduces the term *techno-unit*, which is structurally and functionally one tool or a component of a tool. For example, a hammerstone or a digging stick has only one techno-unit, while a knife might have two if it has only a blade inserted into a handle with no binding, and three if it also has binding. Some subsistants have many techno-units; one type of Hadza arrow has nine (Table 4.4).

It seems likely that the earliest tools had fewer techno-units, usually one, and were often naturefacts. Artifacts of more techno-units appear later in the archaeological record. It also seems safe to assume that this trend is related to cognitive sophistication and cultural evolution, that is, social learning rather than individual trial-and-error learning by itself, especially since social learning is already present in the tool use of other apes (Lonsdorf 2005). Young chimpanzees learn tool use mainly by watching their mothers, and the same is true of Hadza. Both boys and girls who are nursing sit beside their mother when she is digging tubers or pounding baobab. They watch with great interest and try to imitate her. They also grab and eat the baobab. Because little ones are motivated by the reward of eating some of the food their mothers produce, they are very motivated to watch her and learn. This extra incentive to learn applies to the Hadza just as it does to young chimpanzees (Boesch and Boesch-Achermann 2000).

Carrying devices may not have been invented as early as hammerstones and digging sticks because they might have been more difficult to make. There could be exceptions, as when some naturally occurring material like a bowl-shaped piece of bark is found. In that case, a naturefact makes a decent carrying device for some foods. Some Australians use carrying devices of wood, though they usually carve these from bark (Tonkinson 1978). A naturefact in the form of a gourd can be used to carry water or honey. Both of these examples of carrying devices can provide great benefits because without them the contents must be consumed on the spot rather than taken elsewhere (Tanner and Zihlman 1976). Whole skins of an animal can be used for carrying right after butchering the animal. The Hadza do skin animals with their knives and then use the skins to carry the animals' intestines back to camp. However, butchering and skinning animals requires a sharp tool, and it seems unlikely this occurred during the time of the earliest hominins.

TABLE 4.4. HADZA TOOLS
Their Classifications, Uses, Sex Biases, and Numbers of Techno-Units

Subsistant Category	Tool and Form	Main Use	Artifact or Naturefact	Sex	Number of Techno-Units
Weapon	Arrow (!anako a daniko) wood, iron, feather, poison, ligament, adhesive, ash, fat, leather wrap	Kill prey	A	M	9
Weapon	Arrow (!anako) of wood, feather, ligament, adhesive, iron, ash, fat	Kill prey	A	M	7
Weapon	Arrow (hik'owa) wood and feather, nuchal ligament	Kill prey	A	M	3
Weapon	Arrow (hik'owa) wood, feather, ligament, one barb, twine	Kill prey	A	M	5
Weapon	Arrow (kasama) wood, feather, ligament, iron, adhesive, fat, ash	Kill prey	A	M	7
Weapon	Arrow poison (kalakasy) from plant	Kill prey	A	M	1
Weapon	Arrow poison (panjube) from plant	Kill prey	A	M	1
Weapon	Arrow poison (shanjo) from plant	Kill prey	A	M	1
Weapon	Arrow poison from plant (mixture of panjube and shanjo or kalakasy)	Kill prey	A	M	2.5
Instrument	Ax of wood and iron	Chop tree for honey	A	M	2
Instrument	Bark twine	Tie meat/baobab pods	A	M	1
Facility, tended	Blind of grass, branches, stone, leaves	Conceal hunter	A	M	4
Weapon	Bow (ko'o) wood, nuchal ligament, sinew, fat, skin rings	Kill prey	A	M	5
Instrument	Chisel (shenjoda) iron	Make arrow heads	A	M	1
Facility, tended	Fire drill of wood	To make fire	A	M	2
Instrument	Gourd with handle and rope	Get water in tree	A	M	3

(continued)

TABLE 4.4. (continued)

Subsistant Category	Tool and Form	Main Use	Artifact or Naturefact	Sex	Number of Techno-Units
Instrument	Hammer of wood, iron	Make arrow heads	A	M	2
Instrument	Knife (itl'ako) wood, metal	Cutting meat, bark	A	M	2
Instrument	Leather scabbard, thread	Hold knife	A	M	2
Instrument	Quiver of skin, thread	Carry arrows	A	M	5
Instrument	Stakes of wood	Climb tree for honey	A	M	1
Instrument	Stick (often cut)	Knock off baobab pods	A/N	M	1
Instrument	Stick whittled	Apply poison	A	M	1
Facility, tended	Torch of wood	Smoke and stun bees	A	M	2
Instrument	Baobab pod as cup, bowl, container	Carry honey, drink water	A/N	M/F	1
Instrument	Gourd plus twine handle	Carry water, honey	A	M/F	2
Instrument	Leather pouch, thread, handle	Carry objects	A	M/F	3
Weapon	Stick	Club/flush animal	N	M/F	1
Instrument	Stick (cut)	Pull down bird nests	A	M/F	1
Weapon	Stone	Throw to kill prey	N	M/F	1
Instrument	Stone, usually in place on ground	Anvil to hammer against	A	M/F	1
Instrument	Twig	Extract honey	A	M/F	1
Instrument	Wood pole	To carry meat	A	M/F	1
Instrument	Basket	Carry berries, birds	A	F	3
Instrument	Ceramic, now metal pot	Cooking	A	F	1
Instrument	Digging stick (ts'apale)	Dig tubers	A	F	1
Instrument	Digging stick (ts'apale) iron	Dig tubers	A	F	1
Instrument	Hammerstone (ha!'ako) round stone	Pound baobab/marula nuts	N	F	1
Instrument	Needle (lushinge)	Sewing	A	F	1
Instrument	Porcupine quill, thorn	Extract nut	N	F	1
Instrument	Skin, cloth	Carry nursling, food	A	F	1
Instrument	Thorn	Picking out nut, teeth	N	F	1

Once carrying devices were invented or realized, they must have immediately become very important for carrying infants and foods. Hadza women only carry infants with their hands very briefly. They always use skins or cloths to tie their infants on their backs. They say it would be too difficult to carry an infant in their arms very far. Thus, devices such as skins for carrying infants would likely have been a great leap forward in tool making and used everyday while foraging. In fact, the more one thinks about it, the more difficult it is to imagine how early bipedal hominin females managed without carrying devices.

What follows is a discussion of material objects the Hadza use. I give a brief description of how they use these objects and how they make them.

HAMMERSTONES

Hammerstones (*ha!'ako*) are very round rocks of the right size and weight to be good for pounding (Figure 4.2). Women may pick them up as they need them. When women are going to collect baobab fruit or marula nuts, if they see an ideal stone along the way, they may pick it up and carry it back to camp, where it is used. Occasionally, they do some processing while out on foray, to crack open the marula nut, for example. After this, the nut is picked out with a thorn (another tool, a naturefact if already detached from the tree) and put in a bowl or basket or inside a sling that women wear as they take the food back to camp. Baobab may also be processed out of camp to get the pulp out, but this does not require a hammerstone since the pod can be cracked open by hitting it against a rock or by stomping on it. Pounding of the baobab seeds with the pulp does require the use of a hammerstone because the seeds are very hard (for more about baobab and marula, see Chapter 5). This is done in camp, and so the hammerstone is left in camp right on the big rocks that serve as anvils.

Camps are almost always located where there are big, exposed smooth rocks that women can sit on and use as anvils (Figure 4.2). This is something archaeologists might keep in mind when surveying possible sites. The women do not take the hammerstones with them when they move camp because such stones are plentiful enough that they can always find good ones in the new location. Usually, they use the ones that they, or other women, left there during the previous occupation of that camp location.

Figure 4.2. Women pound marula nuts with hammerstones.

DIGGING STICKS

The digging stick (*ts'apale*) is the main tool for women (Figure 4.3), along with a carrying device. Girls (and, to a lesser extent, boys) begin using them from the time they are 2 years old. After a few years, boys rarely use them, while females continue using them until they die. Anne Vincent studied Hadza women's digging and digging sticks in detail for her Ph.D., so we know a great deal about the tool (Vincent 1985b). Table 4.5 shows the dimensions of my digging sticks combined with those of Anne Vincent. As a woman uses a stick, it gets blunted, and she has to keep sharpening it. Consequently, it keeps getting shorter and shorter until finally she throws it away or gives it to a younger, smaller girl who uses it because it is the ideal size for her—until it gets so short that she throws it away. This accounts for the wide range of lengths of digging sticks.

There are now two or three iron digging sticks being used, and I witnessed the beginning of this. Actually, it seems I contributed to this innovation. During 1997, Nicholas Blurton Jones and I carried out some foraging experiments he thought up to measure skills by age and sex, and that I dubbed "the Forager Olympics." We had females and males of all

Figure 4.3. Women accompanied by young girls dig tubers.

ages digging to see how much they could acquire per hour. In one camp, a missionary had begun to build the foundation of a church. The foundation only got two cinder blocks high before he was made to stop. So the foundation had been sitting abandoned for a few years, and there were 2 or 3 iron rebar sticking up. When I enlisted a group of teenage boys to dig, one 17-year-old boy removed a rebar from the foundation and used it to dig in our experiments. Over the next few days, a few women began to use the iron bar as well. Nowadays, the women have all of the bars from the foundation, sharing them and taking turns using them. They say that a rebar is excellent for digging since it does not need to be sharpened and breaks up the dirt well. However, it is heavier than a digging stick, and for this reason most women still prefer wood.

A digging stick is sharpened with a knife and then hardened by putting the point in a hearth for about a minute and turning it every few seconds. When I began work in 1995, few women owned knives, so a woman usually had to borrow her husband's knife to sharpen her digging stick. Now, since knives are one of the gifts I give, almost every adult owns one.

Digging sticks are very simple one-techno-unit tools, yet they are responsible for acquiring as many kilograms of food as any other tool.

TABLE 4.5. HADZA TOOL DIMENSIONS

Tool	Material Used	Total (cm)[a]	Shaft/Handle (cm)	Point/Blade (cm)	Weight (g)
Bow (Ko'o)	*Dombeya kirkii* (mutateko), *Grewia bicolor* (congolobe) (Woodburn 1970)	154.26 (144–167.5, n=20)			541.5 (342–686, n=20)
Arrow (Hik'owa)	*Dombeya kirkii* (mutateko), *Grewia bicolor* (congolobe) (Woodburn 1970)	96.56 (81–109.5, n=49)			46.00 (34–66, n=49)
Arrow (!Anako) (1, 2 tang) no poison	Tlehako best *Grewia bicolor* (congolobe) (Woodburn 1970)	77.60 (70.2–84.5, n=18)	67.69 (59.1–75.5, n=19)	11.21 (8.6–13.3, n=18)	38.55 (32–44, n=19)
Arrow (!Anako) (1, 2 tang) with poison	Tlehako best *Grewia bicolor* (congolobe) (Woodburn 1970)	79.58 (73.7–88.5, n=14)	69.05 (63.8–84.3, n=14)	10.53 (3.5–13.5, n=14)	41.71 (28–52, n=14)
Arrow (Kasama)	*Dombeya kirkii* (mutateko), *Grewia bicolor* (congolobe) (Woodburn 1970)	79.75 (69.5–89.4, n=13)	69.00 (61.6–78.4, n=13)	11.07 (7.9–13, n=13)	50.62 (38–82, n=13)
Quiver (tl'angase)	Impala skin *Aepyceros melampus* (popoako)	87.17 (87–90.5, n=3)			500.00 (430–630, n=3)

Tool	Material				
Fire drill (miseko)	Tlehako and other types of wood	86.08 (62.25–116, n=3)			30.00 (24–36, n=3)
Knife (itako)	Wood, iron	28.69 (23.5–32.50, n=6)	12.82 (11–17, n=6)	15.88 (11.5–21.00, n=6)	82.40 (70–108, n=5)
Sheath (shapoko)	Skin such as impala or zebra				
Ax (ato)	Wood, iron	53.69 (48–61, n=3)	53.69 (48–61, n=3)	20.63×7.26 (16–26, 7–8, n=3)	949.00 (752–1195, n=3)
Digging stick (ts'apale) (mine and Vincent's)	*Cordia sinensis* (ts'apale), *Cordia* spp. (msakaako), *Dombeya kirkii* (mutateko), *Grewia lilacina* (nguilako) (Vincent 1985b)	112.52 (61.3–164, n=26)			609.25 (330–1030, n=8)
Bird nest stick	Any branch with a fork in it that is long enough	141.25 (116–166.5, n=2)			131.00 (116–146, n=2)

NOTE: These are all adult tools; children's tools are smaller. (Some digging sticks are worn down and passed on from women to girls.)
[a] Total values are mean (minimum–maximum size, number).

Therefore, we cannot assume that more-complex tools are more important. However, the more-complex tools should be capable of producing greater returns per unit time used. Otherwise, it would be difficult
to explain why extra time is invested in making them. Digging sticks
may also be responsible for the successful occupation of more open
habitat by hominins long ago (Laden and Wrangham 2005, Marlowe and
Berbesque 2009, O'Connell, Hawkes, and Jones 1999, Vincent 1985a).
O'Connell has noted how the range of *H. erectus* is roughly coterminous
with that area of the Old World within which tubers are common, suggesting perhaps they were an important component of the hominin diet
and expansion of *Homo*. The digging stick may have been one of the first
tools used by hominins, yet it is still perhaps one of the most important
of tools among tropical foragers today.

KNIVES

Hadza men make knives from larger pieces of metal (Figure 4.4). As with
arrowheads, a man uses a hammer (acquired through trade or from a researcher these days) to pound the metal into a flat surface, and then in-
serts it into a wooden handle with resin glue. He sharpens the blade with
rough stones that function as excellent whetstones. Sometimes, he adds a
covering of impala skin or zebra to the handle. Men often make scabbards
out of impala skin to attach to their belts. These knives are very effective.
Even though I supply the Hadza with very good German-made knives as
gifts, it has not caused men to stop making their own knives.

Given that knives are so important to the Hadza, I assume they were
using knives before iron reached Hadzaland, presumably made of sharpened stones, or else just small flakes like those so common in the archaeological record. The Hadza use their knives to cut and skin meat, to carve
bows and arrows, to cut twine, to cut plants and poke holes in wood, and
as an anvil when making a fire with a fire drill.

BOWS

Every Hadza male from about 5 or 6 years up (and most from 2 or 3
years up) owns a bow (*ko'o*) and arrows. Table 4.5 shows bow measurements and material. We measured bow pulls by having each Hadza male
in our sample grasp a bow scale (Easton Digital) hooked to the string of
his bow and then pull as he normally would. We found that the mean
bow pull for adult men was 69.4 pounds (48.5–94.5, SD = 12.5, $n = 30$).

Figure 4.4. Hadza knives.

Woodburn (1970) said Hadza bow pulls can reach over 100 lbs, and Bartram (1997) said up to 60 kg (132 lbs). Our highest Hadza pull was 95 lbs. According to archery Internet sites, an average adult bow pull is about 40 lbs.

After finding a suitable branch, a man uses his ax to cut it off and shave it down until he can begin to whittle it more finely with his knife so that it is smooth and the ends have a smaller diameter than the middle. The whittling may take two or three days. Once the bow is the right size, the man places the bow in hot ashes to warm it up. Then, he begins to straighten the bow by placing it in the fork of a tree and pulling on it so that the shaft is straight from side to side but also with the right curvature toward the ends. He applies animal fat, which helps keep it from cracking. Then the bow is strung. The string (*acuko*) is made from strips of nuchal ligament of eland, buffalo, or zebra or the sinew of giraffe (Woodburn 1970). These are chewed until soft and then rolled back and forth on the thigh, usually by women. A knot is used to keep the bowstring in place at the bottom of the bow, and the string is wound several times around a piece of chewed ligament at the top of the bow. Since the bow is smaller at the ends than toward the middle, the string does not

slide down. The Hadza often put rings of skin and fur of different animals they kill on the bow which shrink and help keep the bow from cracking. Every man makes his own bow. Adults or older boys make bows for
small boys. Often, it is the mother or father that makes the first bow
for a 2- or 3-year old boy.

ARROWS

The Hadza make several types of arrows (Table 4.4 and Figure 4.5). The
shaft is usually made from the same wood as bows, *congolobe* (*Grewia
bicolor*). All types of arrows have feathers with fletching. One type of
arrow is simply wood with a sharpened point at the end (*hik!owa*). The
feathers are usually from the guinea fowl (*Numida meleagris*) and tied
on tangentially with nuchal ligament (Woodburn 1970). Before iron, the
Hadza may have used only this type of arrow, or they may have also
used stone and bone points. Many Hadza have confirmed that they used
to put poison on these wooden arrows (see also Woodburn 1970). These
arrows are used for all smaller game like birds and hyraxes (*Procavia
johnstoni*), sometimes even dik-dik (*Madoqua kirkii*). There is also a
variant of this wooden arrow that has a wooden barb (*lo'o*) attached
with twine. Some wooden arrows also have several barbs carved right
into the point. If the earliest arrows were like these (and it seems likely
they would have been), archaeologists have little chance of finding any
evidence of them; thus, considering that the bow also consists only of
wood, the antiquity of the bow and arrow could be much greater than
that of the earliest stone arrow points (~ 70 kya, see Chapter 10).

Another type of arrow (*kasama*) consists of a wide, flat, laurel-leaf-
shaped metal point. The Hadza beat the points into the proper shape from
scraps of metal they get from neighbors or from us researchers. Sometimes
they trade meat or honey to acquire a point already forged by an Isanzu
neighbor. This arrow has no poison and is used also on smaller game, especially dik-dik. At close range, a gazelle (*Gazella thomsoni*) may even be
killed with this type of arrow. The wide point insures that a lot of blood
flows out. This is the best type of arrow for stopping a dangerous animal
that is charging, since it has such a large point that the animal feels it instantly and strongly. The metal-tipped arrows usually have vulture feathers,
which are cut in half, and each half is tied on radially, again with nuchal
ligament fletching.

The other arrows have iron-tipped points, with one tang (*!ana* or male)
or two tangs (*!anako* or female). The Hadza make these points by pounding

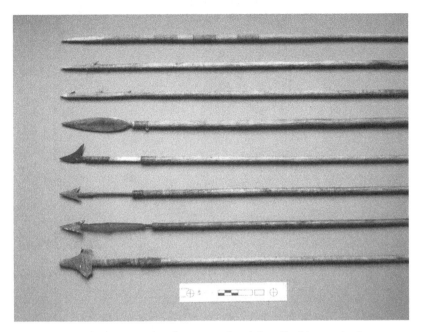

Figure 4.5. Hadza arrows of each type used and described in text in the same order, top to bottom.

large nails with a hammer on a rock anvil (Figure 4.6). These days, we researchers give them the nails. Often a man has some of these with no poison on them, and he will use them for a smaller animal or if he has run out of poisoned arrows. Once a man applies poison, the arrow is called *!anako a !daniko* (literally, a female two-tanged arrow with poison). Poisoned arrows are used on all larger game, those as large or larger than impalas or warthogs.

When making arrows, a man first cuts off a branch of appropriate length, then whittles it with his knife until it is smooth and round. While he is whittling, he often holds the arrow in place with his toes. Periodically, he straightens the arrow by placing it in the hot ashes of a hearth briefly, then bending it with his hands and mouth (Figure 4.7). In fact, men use their teeth so much to straighten arrows that it must contribute to the pattern of wear on their teeth, which are very worn down compared to ours, probably from both the foods and the arrow making (the latter should only show up on men, though women use their teeth when sewing). The use of the teeth as tools may account for some of the wear on fossil teeth as well. The man sights down the shaft after bending it to

Figure 4.6. A man hammers a nail to make it into an arrow point.

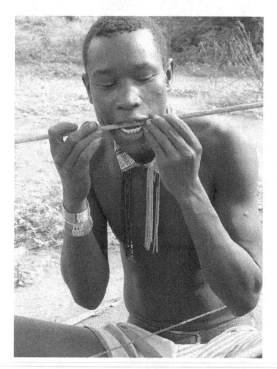

Figure 4.7. A man straightens an arrow using his teeth.

see how straight it is; arrows must be very straight for aerodynamic efficiency. Once a man has finished whittling and straightening the shaft,
the feathering is applied with the nuchal ligament of impala. Finally, on
poisoned arrows, a thin piece of leather is wrapped around the point to
protect the poison from drying out in the sun or getting wet and losing
its strength. It also prevents a person from getting cut and poisoned. Men
often carve finely etched designs of cross-hatched lines along the shafts of
their arrows.

POISON

The Hadza use 3 different kinds of plant poisons (*hach'e'e*) for their arrows: *panjube* (*Adenium obesum*), *shanjo* (*Strophanthus eminii*), and
kalakasy. *Kalakasy* does not grow in Hadzaland but grows just beyond,
and the Hadza do not prepare it but rather obtain it already prepared
through trade with their neighbors. *Panjube* is the most commonly used
poison. It is a succulent that grows only in a few places. Men first either
cut off a branch or pound it into pulp while still attached to the plant.
They can remove the blade in their ax and use the large end of the wooden
handle to pound with, or find a similarly shaped piece of wood. Once the
pulp has been well beaten, the juice is squeezed out and boiled until
the water evaporates, leaving a sticky black substance. When the poison
is ready, it can be carried around in a ball much like clay until a man is
ready to apply it. A small stick (*polok'o*) is used to stir it inside a fresh-
water mussel shell that serves as a small bowl. Then a small amount is
picked up with the stick and applied all around the shaft of the iron ar-
rowhead. *Shanjo*, the other poison, comes from a small tree. Men pound
the seeds and add water, but do not boil it. All three poisons are strong,
and they are sometimes mixed together.

These poisons induce cardiac arrest. Their strength depends on several factors: the particular year and particular plant, its age, and the poisons' exposure to the elements once applied to the arrow. When strong,
they can kill animals the size of a buffalo or a giraffe within an hour and
a smaller animal much sooner. I have seen an impala die within a couple
of minutes of being hit in a good spot, such as the heart or intestines.
When the poison is not strong enough, a man may score a good hit with
his arrow but the animal does not die. I have been on many tracking
expeditions following a blood trail that eventually dries up, and the men
have concluded that the poison was bad and the animal would not die.
There are many animals living in Hadzaland with arrow points in them.

Once I saw an impala killed and butchered, at which time the hunter discovered an old arrow point deep inside a wound that had healed up. Once
one sees how important poison is for the Hadza to kill large animals, it
becomes clear what a major advance poison was in hunting technology,
and consequently how much less efficient big-game hunting must have
been before the use of poison.

AXES

Men make their own axes (Figure 4.8). First, a man must get an already
forged iron blade through trade with a neighboring tribe, usually the
Isanzu. He then finds an appropriate limb, cuts it off, and shapes it until
it is bulbous at one end and tapers down at the other end, where he grips
it. Next he uses his knife to make a small hole in the bulbous end of the
handle. Once he has drilled a small hole, he heats his ax blade until it gets
so hot that it will burn a hole through the handle when he grips the blade
with pieces of wood and skins or cloth and forces it through the small
hole he made. He must do this over and over until he has made the hole
large enough for the blade to fit snugly into the handle. No binding is used.
He can take the blade out easily by tapping the handle against a tree or
rock. After sharpening the blade, he can just as easily reinsert it and tap
it against a tree so that it again fits tightly into the handle.

Men use their axes to shave limbs into bows, as well as to pound
the poison plant *panjube* into pulp. Sometimes they use them to sharpen
women's digging sticks. They use them to crack open giraffe bones to get
at the marrow. The main function of the ax, however, is to open up tree
limbs or tree trunks to get at honey. In smaller trees, bees may have only a
small entrance to the hive—too small for a man's arm to fit in. So the men
must chop around the hole to enlarge it to access the honey. They often
cut the whole branch off and then crack it open on the ground. They also
use the ax to cut small limbs off trees and make stakes to pound into the
trunk of tall baobab trees in order to climb up and reach large beehives to
get honey.

Honey is an important part of the Hadza diet; thus the ax is a very important tool. Since men must get their blades from people who have access to forged iron, they must have used stone axes in the past; it is hard
to imagine they were not getting honey. Twigs are sometimes inserted into
small holes to get honey, which is licked off the twig in the same manner
used by orangutans (Van Schaik, Fox, and Fechtman 2003). But one can
get very little this way. The ax may have been in the tool kit of hominins

Figure 4.8. A couple forages for berries. The man carries his ax on his shoulder.

for almost 2 million years, given that Acheulean hand axes (associated with *Homo erectus* sites) probably were indeed used as axes, possibly to access honey (Allchin 1957, Mitchel 1955). I once watched a Hadza man who had gone on walkabout without his ax; he saw honey in several trees, and he could not resist an attempt to get some. He searched for and found a rock that happened to look very much like an Acheulean hand ax. After 10 minutes or so, he broke into the hive, albeit with much more difficulty than if he had had his ax. Woodburn (1970) mentions men using stones as well. I have also found large flaked stones in Hadzaland that look like they may be old stone axes.

FIRE DRILLS

Men use a fire drill (*miseko*) to make fires. A fire drill is much like an arrow shaft and is sometimes decorated with a feather or tuft of hair. Men carry these long thin sticks with them at all times. Sometimes when a man does not have a fire drill, he uses an arrow as a drill. The drill is placed into a small piece of wood (*pa'ameko*) the man can find on the spot. He uses his knife to whittle a round hole just big enough for the

fire drill to fit in. The bottom piece of wood is then placed on top of a
knife blade or a rock. The man rubs his hands together quickly around the
shaft, repeatedly sliding down the shaft as he does so, for usually about
30 seconds. The friction causes little pieces of wood to become charcoal
and fall onto the knife blade. He picks these up and puts them in a handful of dry grass as tinder and blows to ignite a flame.

Women say they cannot make fire, that it is men's work. I have
not asked them to try, but I suspect they could make a fire if they really
wanted to. Once I did see a woman trying, but after several minutes she
gave up and let her husband do it. Because women often roast some tubers while they are out foraging and these days use matches that I give
them, I have asked them what they did before matches. They say they
used to carry coals in a gourd. In camp, hearths are used 2 or 3 times a
day, so the fire never completely dies out and can easily be rekindled any
time. I have occasionally seen a woman pick a few coals out of a hearth
before she goes foraging.

We collected soil samples of Hadza fires for micro-morphological
analysis (Mallol et al. 2007). We wanted to determine how recognizable
controlled use of fire might be in the archaeological record if human ancestors were making and using fire in a way similar to the Hadza. We used
a full range of Hadza fire types from the most to the least ephemeral and
described all types (Mallol et al. 2007). With the least ephemeral type of
Hadza fires, there may be some hope of detecting high enough temperatures and specific plants used as tinder, but with more ephemeral fires,
such as those used for roasting tubers or a baboon, it may be impossible
for archaeologists to say they reflect anthropogenic fires.

CARRYING DEVICES

Gourds

Carrying devices are much more important than we normally appreciate
(McGrew 1992, Tanner and Zihlman 1976). Without them, only small
amounts of food can be transported, and no water can be taken back to
camp. The Hadza use gourds for carrying water, honey, and coals, and
for storing fat. They poke or cut a hole in one end of the gourd to make
a mouth, and tie some twine or leather on as a handle (Figure 4.9). Today,
they often get the gourds from farming neighbors like the Iraqw who grow
large ones. However, smaller wild variants grow in the area, and sometimes
the Hadza use these, as they must have long ago. Occasionally, a man gets

Figure 4.9. An old ceramic pot, gourds used for carrying water or fat, baskets used to carry berries, and girls' dolls.

some honey but has no container. In this case, he may find a small gourd but more often will find a large baobab pod and cut off about one-third of it so that he can remove the pulp (which he eats) and fill the pod with honey to carry it back to camp.

Baskets

Hadza women weave straw into elaborate and well-made baskets that are usually about the size of the bottom half of a soccer ball (Figure 4.9). These baskets are not decorated but are simply left the color of the straw. They are sturdy and are used mainly to carry berries or processed baobab. It takes a woman 3 or 4 days to make one.

SKINS AND CLOTHES

Animal skins, mostly impala, serve a variety of purposes. They are used as shawls or slings for carrying infants and for carrying food. This requires them to be made supple by tanning. When they are dried to harden, they are used as sleeping mats. They are also used to make quivers, scabbards, knife-handle covers, pouches, and shoes. Skins are what men and women use to make their clothes.

These days, one of the main ways we researchers influence the Hadza is in their clothing. Clothes make good gifts because they are valued and we can give them to everyone. They do not alter people's behavior in any appreciable way, other than letting them spend less time making clothing; even now, they do spend some time sewing to mend the factory-made clothing. We also give them sandals made out of the rubber from old tires. However, they occasionally still make their traditional sandals out of impala skin. Small children usually go naked. They are usually barefoot as well, though sometimes their mother makes shoes for them. Sometimes, little girls wear a pubic apron, usually beaded.

In the past, men wore nothing but skins. When I began work in 1995, there were still some men wearing impala skins like skirts. Many women, especially older women, wore only skirts of skin. Women's skirts are made from the skin of female impalas. They sometimes have a few beads sewed on for decorations. Skins are still used, but much less so for clothes. Men most often wear short pants they get from us, and women wear *kangas*, pieces of cloth with print on them that are popular all over East Africa. These too we give as gifts (compensation) for letting us conduct our research.

ART

The main form of art is body adornment. It seems likely this would have been the first form of art. Both sexes may adorn themselves to attract the attention of others. The Hadza do not have anything that serves as a mirror to look at themselves, except for pools of water (see Figure 3.1). When we are there, people often spend long periods looking at themselves in the side-view mirror of the Land Rover. Women make necklaces and sew beads onto skins for skirts. Most all the jewelry the Hadza make out of glass beads they used to make out of organic materials, and one can still see plenty of this traditional organic jewelry worn. They use bones, often finger and toe bones of baboons, little hollow sticks, pods of various sizes, the quills of porcupines, shells, the scales of pangolins (*Smutsia temminckii*), teeth, and occasionally feathers. Nowadays, women use glass beads to make headbands, which both men and women wear, but as some of the earliest pictures in the 1930s show, they have been doing this for a long time (Bleek 1931, Kohl-Larsen 1958).

Both sexes also wear necklaces and bracelets, also usually made by women. Women often wear earrings and occasionally anklets. Toddlers wear anklets made of bells so that they are easy to keep track of. The bells are either made from scrap metal or obtained pre-made through trade with neighbors. Toddlers are sometimes covered in beads, which might be a case of parents showing off that they have many beads. These various kinds of jewelry are often made from the standard Czechoslovakian glass beads that are so popular with the Masai. It is from the Masai and other neighboring people that Hadza used to get the beads, but today they get them from us researchers. Older women wear many strings of beads under their outer garments. Beads are the closest thing they have to a currency; the beads can always be traded with some non-Hadza neighbors for anything they need. This explains why it is the old women who wear them; older women are best at saving things. They wear more clothes than men, and it would not be safe to leave the beads in their huts with Datoga passing by. Men's artwork consists mostly of carving various items, such as a fertility stick or arrows, and sometimes they carve geometric designs in a gourd used to carry water or honey (Figure 4.9).

HOUSES

In much of the dry season, there is little chance of rain, and the Hadza sleep outside next to their hearth near or inside bushes that serve as a windbreak. The bushes also serve as a shelf on which to place bow and arrows or a piece of cloth. A couple sleeps on a large impala skin.

In certain areas, such as the hills of Sipunga and in Dunduiya to the west of Lake Eyasi, camps are sometimes made in rock shelters. The overhang shields them from rain or wind. In these camps, the best location is right under the shelter, which means that each time the place is occupied, hearths and sleeping areas are virtually in the exact same spot, unlike in more open sites. Thus, they are ideal places for archaeological excavation of sites that have been occupied and reoccupied each year for a long time (Mabulla 1996). Figure 4.10 shows one of these rock shelters, which is occupied every year, mostly in the rainy season.

During the rainy season and even into the early dry season, the most common type of house for the Hadza is a grass hut. Women build these huts. Usually two or three women work together, first getting branches that are flexible. They bend the branches into an inverted U shape and stick both ends into the ground. Once they have crisscrossed several branches to form an upside-down bowl-shaped structure, they begin stuffing dry grass

Figure 4.10. A rock shelter camp.

Figure 4.11. A typical grass hut constructed in the rainy season (with drying impala skin on top).

into the branches until the whole house is finished, which takes about 2 hours (Figure 4.11). In the Sipunga area, the Hadza often live where dry grass is less plentiful and where rain is more plentiful. There, they make huts that are covered with large strips of bark and big leaves of various kinds, rather than grass.

TOOL USE

Table 4.4 lists tools used by the Hadza. Tools for carrying are used by women for more time each day than any other tools, at least by women who have nurslings, since they are always carrying infants on their backs. As women are gone about 4 hours per day and are also carrying their infants on their backs even in camp much of the time, they are probably using a sling or kaross about 7 or 8 hours per day. Women without infants are also wearing a carrying device—skin or cloth—when they are out of camp so they can carry food back to camp. Women are actually digging with digging sticks about 33% of the time they are on forays (6–72%, $n = 24$). In 42% of all forays, women use digging sticks at some point.

Men always have their bows and arrows with them when they go out of camp. They also always have knives and fire drills with them. If honey is available in the area at the time, men also often have their axes, which they carry on their shoulders (Figure 4.8). This means that men have these items with them on average 6.5 hours a day. Hammerstones may be used everyday as well, but they are used mainly by women for processing foods back in camp, perhaps an hour per day at most times of the year.

Females spend more time processing or preparing food than males do (Table 4.6). This sex difference begins at an early age, soon after weaning. Males pound baobab or marula nuts with hammerstones when young, but females do much more of this across all ages, and the time spent pounding climbs with age.

Men spend much of their time in camp working on arrows. By age 15, males are spending considerable time making bows and arrows for themselves, and this continues into old age (Table 4.6). The more complex the tool, the more time is spent making or repairing it. As Table 4.4 shows, arrows have the most techno-units of any tools. This is one reason so much time is spent on arrows, but another reason is that arrows sometimes get lost or broken and so must be replaced or repaired. Each man needs to have 15 or 20 arrows at all times.

Among chimpanzees, females learn how to use tools earlier, use them more often, and get more proficient at using them than males. The tools

TABLE 4.6. PERCENTAGE OF TIME SPENT
PROCESSING FOOD

	% Time All Processing Food	% Time Pounding with Hammerstone	% Time Making Bows and Arrows
Males (all ages)	0.8	0.17	2.1
Females (all ages)	9.3	3.0	0.05
Men (≥18 years)	0.7	0.14	3.5
Women (≥18 years)	11.2	3.8	0.06

NOTE: Food processing includes pounding baobab or marula nuts, and making and repairing bows and arrows.

TABLE 4.7. TECHNO-UNITS OF
TOOLS USED BY MALES
AND FEMALES

Sex Bias	Mean Number of Techno-Units per Tool
Male bias	2.9 (1–9, $SD = 2.3$, $n = 26$)
Both sexes	1.4 (1–3, $SD = 0.8$, $n = 7$)
Female bias	1.3 (1–3, $SD = 0.7$, $n = 8$)

they use more often are used for work that is more complicated, e.g., termite fishing and nut cracking (Lonsdorf, Eberly, and Pusey 2004). In contrast, Hadza men, and probably men in other forager societies judging from Oswalt's (1973) description of tool kits, make more complex tools than women. Assuming that the last common ancestor we share with chimpanzees was somewhat similar to extant chimpanzees, we must assume that male tool use became as important as female tool use at some point in hominin evolution. It must have become important enough that selection favored greater tool complexity and greater time spent using tools. Among the Hadza, the tools used predominately by males have a higher mean number of techno-units than the tools used predominantly by females (Mann-Whitney $U = 52.5$, $p = 0.035$, $n_1 = 26$, $n_2 = 8$). Table 4.7 shows this sex bias in the number of techno-units of tools. The sex differences in tool use among human foragers are related to the sexual division of foraging and processing labor (discussed in Chapter 5).

From the list of tools in Table 4.2, it is clear that the main effect of contact with other cultures is the acquisition of iron. It is also clear that contact affects the technology that men use for acquiring food more than the technology that women use for acquiring food (Table 4.4). Thus, when using the Hadza (or other similar foragers) as guides for reconstructing the past, one of the main caveats to note is that they possess iron. This makes their tools more efficient than they would have been prior to contact with more-complex societies. The tools and foraging activities females engage in are probably more similar to those of much earlier hominins than are the tools and activities males engage in (Marlowe 2005a).

CHAPTER 5

Foraging

OPTIMAL FORAGING THEORY

Optimal foraging theory (OFT) assumes that animals exploit foods in an efficient way within a set of constraints (Krebs and Davies 1993, Stephens and Krebs 1986). One constraint is, of course, the particular diet an animal can utilize. Another constraint is the danger posed by predators. For example, a squirrel may scurry out in the open to pick up a nut and return to a tree to eat it in safety. If there were no threat of predation, it could save the energy used in retreating to a refuge to eat. Models assume that animals are maximizing benefits in terms of a specified currency, such as net energy intake, which should be a good proxy for RS. There are numerous models to capture different foraging decisions. One model captures the decision regarding prey choice (Pulliam 1974). The patch-choice model assesses the time an animal should spend in a resource patch before searching for another patch (Milinski 1985, Price 1983). The diet breadth model analyzes how many foods should be included in the diet (Hames and Vickers 1982). The central-place foraging model addresses the decision to take food back to a central place and how much to take (Orians and Pearson 1979). The processing-transport model asks whether a forager should process certain foods in the field or take them back to a central place whole (Metcalfe and Barlow 1992). Finally, some models address the optimal group size of the foraging party (Smith 1985). Several of these OFT models have been applied to human foragers (Bliege-Bird and Bird 1997, Hill 1987, Hill and Hurtado 1996, Smith 1981, 1983, 1985).

Often, reality does not quite match the model. Some critics seem to think this reflects poorly on OFT (Pierce and Ollason 1987). The reason for the lack of agreement is usually that the model makes some simplifying assumptions that are too simple or just wrong. Of course, this is the only logical way to build a model at first; once the model has been tested, we can let the data guide future models to greater sophistication (Smith 1983, Smith and Winterhalder 1985, Winterhalder 1996b, Winterhalder and Smith 2000). If currently there is a lack of great interest in OFT in human behavioral ecology, it is probably due more to the fact that it is so successful in general and is considered less than groundbreaking. There are also fewer foragers to study, and while the models often lend themselves to analyzing non-forager decisions, field tests are more relevant when people are actually foraging. Few OFT analyses have been conducted with the Hadza (Jones and Marlowe 2002, Hawkes, Jones, and O'Connell 1995, Hawkes, O'Connell, and Jones 1991, Marlowe 2006a, Porter and Marlowe nd-a), but we now have voluminous foraging data and plan on testing OFT models in the future.

One challenge for OFT is to explain why certain foods are not included in the diet. In some cases, the answer is pretty obvious; in others, it is not clear at all. It would be satisfying if we could explain both foods that are taboo and those that are merely ignored, as well as those perhaps in between. In the case of the Hadza, few foods would be considered taboo. The one exception is the *epeme* meat taboo on females and young males. Other foods are simply not eaten. Termites, for example, are not eaten even though they are abundant and are eaten by people in some other cultures. When I ask the Hadza why termites are not eaten, the answer I get is that they will bite you as you are eating them. But this could be avoided by cooking them first. Perhaps, an OFT analysis would reveal that they simply are not worth taking, that the net caloric gain from termites would be lower than the lowest ranked foods that are included in the diet.

Snakes and lizards are also not taken, though they too are abundant. When the Hadza see a snake, they usually promptly kill it and throw it away. It appears that their healthy fear of snakebite (there are several species that are quite dangerous in Hadzaland) may lead them to rule out eating snakes, which would require them to learn how to distinguish the poisonous from the nonpoisonous snakes. When I ask the Hadza if the species we just saw is poisonous, the answer is yes about 90% of the time, which leads me to believe that they consider almost all snakes poisonous. Snakes should not be considered taboo the way the *epeme* meat is. They are simply avoided, which is not surprising, given the danger they pose. As noted, men do not eat tortoises and the land snail; only women and children do. It is tempting to think that women may have introduced and promoted this idea so as to reserve these foods for themselves to compensate for not getting to eat the *epeme* meat.

One interesting and important exception to the success of OFT is the human sexual division of foraging labor. OFT models usually assume the generic adult forager of a given species. In that case, the forager should either include a food item in its diet or pass it up for a more profitable food yielding a higher net return of the relevant currency. When one sex takes certain foods and the other sex takes different foods that are later shared to some extent, it is no longer straightforward whether a forager should harvest or pass up a given food type (Jochim 1988). I return to this at the end of this chapter.

CENTRAL-PLACE PROVISIONING

The Hadza, like most human foragers, are central-place provisioners (CPP), a term I prefer to central-place foragers (CPF) for those who take food back to a central place. Central-place provisioning (CPP) is an important feature of human foragers that distinguishes them from other primates (Isaac 1978, Lovejoy 1981, Washburn and DeVore 1961). There has been considerable discussion of the signals that might reveal when hominins began using central places (Binford 1980, Bird and Bliege-Bird 1997, Bunn, Bartram, and Kroll 1988, O'Connell 1997, Potts 1994, Rose and Marshall 1996). Surprisingly little attention has been paid to why our ancestors began using central places; avoidance of predation is likely the initial reason, but I argue that taking food back to a central place may have been favored by the benefit gained from leaving young weaned children behind with an adult babysitter while foraging. There have been few attempts to compare the ranging and sleeping patterns of humans to other species (Fruth and Hohmann 1994, Potts 1987, 1994).

According to Orians and Pearson (1979), "Many foragers . . . do not consume their prey where they are captured but return with them to some fixed central place where they are eaten, stored, or fed to dependent offspring (Central Place Foraging)." This definition implies that CPF consists of taking food back to a central place, but some have begun to call those who return to a central place to sleep—without taking food back—central-place foragers as well (Chapman, Chapman, and McLaughlin 1989, Whiten 1992). Because it is important to distinguish between those who return to a central place without food and those who return with food, we need two distinct terms for them.

To avoid confusion, I propose recognizing 3 patterns of ranging: (1) In feed-as-you-go (and sleep-where-you-are) foragers, individuals search for food, eat it where encountered, and sleep wherever they end up. Chimpanzees (*Pan troglodytes*) exhibit this pattern (Boesch and Boesch-Achermann 2000, Chapman and Wrangham 1993, Goodall 1986). (2) In central-place foraging (CPF), individuals search for food, eat it where encountered, and then return to a central place to sleep. This pattern is characteristic of hamadryas baboons (*Papio hamadryas*) (Kummer 1995). (3) In central-place provisioning (CPP), individuals search for food, may or may not eat some where encountered, but also take some food back to a central place, usually to share with others, especially the young, or to store it for later consumption. This is the pattern seen in beavers (*Castor Canadensis*), meerkats (*Suricata suricatta*) (Clutton-Brock et al. 2002), and human foragers (Kelly 1995). CPF occurs in several species of primates, but CPP is rare. On the other hand, CPP is common in many birds, carnivores, rodents, and insects. Although most optimal foraging models of CPF deal with taking food back to a central place (Isaac 1978, Marlowe 2006a, Metcalfe and Barlow 1992, Orians and Pearson 1979, Potts 1994, Stephens and Krebs 1986), others address issues such as travel costs and location of the central place in relation to food patches, issues that apply equally to those who do not take food back.

Children who are too big to carry and too young to keep up with adults during foraging pose a problem that can be solved by leaving them behind in a central place where others can look after them. Those who go out foraging must bring food back to feed the people who stay in camp with young children. A crèche is the place and people who look after the young of others, something that is typical of lions as well as the Hadza. The photo on the back cover of this book shows a mother who took her nursling with her foraging and has returned to camp with a basket of *undushipi* berries that are being eaten by her toddler, who was left in camp with others. I have argued this is one reason for CPP, at least among the Hadza, and probably for most human foragers in the tropics, where women do much of the foraging. It may allow women to resume cycling sooner and have shorter inter-birth intervals (IBI) than chimpanzees (Marlowe 2006a). The mean IBI is 3.3 years for human hunter-gatherers (Marlowe 2005a) and 5.46 years for chimpanzees (Robson, van Schaik, and Hawkes 2006). These shorter intervals mean that a woman may have a new nursing infant when her previous child is still toddling. The ability to acquire more food by leaving weanlings in camp, and the availability of weaning foods, enables women to wean earlier than chimpanzees. For human foragers, the mean age at weaning is 2.6 years (Marlowe 2005a); the mean age for chimpanzees is 4.5 years (Robson, van Schaik, and Hawkes 2006).

LEAVING WEANLINGS IN CAMP (THE CRÈCHE)

Hourly scan observations in 6 camps in which 218 people lived were used to see if weanlings were in camp more than others. Weaning occurs between 2 and 3 years of age, with most children completely weaned by 2.6 years (Marlowe 2005b). When age is coded into three categories—(1) infants under 2 years old ($n=21$), (2) weanlings 2–3.9 years old ($n=14$), and (3) older children 4–8 years old ($n=31$)—both infants and older children are gone from camp more than weanlings. Nurslings are out of camp 3.6 hours per day compared to 1.9 hours per day for weanlings ($U=40$, $p<0.0005$, $n_1=21$; $n_2=14$). Children 4–8 years old are gone from camp 3.7 hours per day ($U=71$, $p<0.0005$, $n_1=14$; $n_2=31$). This is because women take their nurslings with them foraging, but leave their weanlings in camp. When weanlings are gone from camp, they are usually in playgroups with older children just beyond the edge of camp.

Leaving weanlings in camp necessitates taking food back for them and for those who are looking after them (their alloparents). Provisioning depends on the ability to acquire surplus food; thus central-place provisioning (CPP) depends on a certain diet like hunted animals, an extractive technology such as digging sticks, or containers to carry large amounts of food such as honey or berries back to camp (Hawkes, O'Connell, and Rogers 1997, Kaplan et al. 2000, McGrew 1992). The sick, the injured, and the very old can also be left in the central place, and they too need to be provisioned. Rest and recovery of the sick and injured should result in lower adult mortality rates and potential selection for increased longevity (Sugiyama 2004).

Human foragers may bring food back to camp with the goal of provisioning the members of their households, but because they live in larger social groups composed of several families, provisioners will likely encounter others who have no food and who may expect or demand shares (Marlowe 2004e). The more people demanding shares, the costlier it is to say no (Jones 1987, Winterhalder 1996a). The fact that people living in

Figure 5.1. Men skin an impala with the help of children.

one camp split into smaller foraging parties and come back together when they return to camp means that surplus food arrives in camp asynchronously, increasing both the opportunities for scrounging and the payoffs to the delayed exchange of the same foods or in-kind reciprocity (Kaplan and Hill 1985, Ofek 2001, Winterhalder 1986). In addition, the sexual division of foraging labor increases the benefits of simultaneous trade (meat or honey for fruit or tubers) (Milton 2000). Whether due to trade, in-kind reciprocity, or scrounging, one important consequence of CPP is the extensive camp-wide food-sharing observed among human foragers (Figure 5.1; see Chapter 9 for a fuller discussion).

One important cause of central-place foraging (CPF) appears to be safety while sleeping (reviewed in Anderson 1998). One important consequence, therefore, is probably reduced mortality. The need to sleep in a safe place could lead individuals to adopt CPF if the central place is a particularly protected site. Protection would be needed to offset the disadvantage of predators knowing where to find those individuals (Reichard 1999). Alternatively, if the sleeping group is large enough to defend against predators, no central place is required unless the group breaks up into smaller parties during foraging. Thus, it is necessary to distinguish between fission-fusion and cohesive grouping. Reuniting each night requires deciding where to reunite; having a central place solves this problem. The need to be near some essential resource like water or shelter on a daily basis could also lead to CPF (Binford 1980).

The need to leave a hut, hearth, and tools behind could favor CPF if such items are important, difficult to carry during foraging, and time-consuming to reproduce. It takes the Hadza 2–3 hours to construct even the simplest rainy-season hut, which would be too costly to build each night in a different place. The more tools that are used, the more difficult it is to carry them while foraging. If the Hadza were feed-as-you-go (and sleep-where-you-are) foragers, they would need to carry a cooking pot, ax, knife, bow, all their arrows, digging stick, hammerstone, fire drill, and carrying device such as a large gourd or basket. They do just this when they move camp, but moving camp happens only once every month or two. The average move is 11 km and can take 6 or 7 hours; longer moves take two days. In such cases, the group can go as slowly as required for the wean-lings who are slow, and can rest as often as necessary along the way. Keep-ing all these possessions may have become feasible only after CPF; thus, when viewed in dynamic (rather than static) terms, the possessions could be considered consequences rather than causes of CPF. When subsistence practices depend on mobility to access resource patches, this should trump other considerations. It should be only when subsistence lends itself to a sufficient diet without moving that sedentism can occur.

Among mammals, it is usually the females who carry infants. This may have paved the way for a foraging division of labor in our ancestors. Once there is a sexual division of labor with regard to foraging, with males spe-cializing in hunting and females in gathering, the two groups cannot forage together because they are targeting different prey. This requires adopting a fission-fusion pattern of splitting up during the day into male hunting parties and female gathering parties. Fissioning into smaller par-ties means there would be no way of reuniting at night without a central place to return to. Some species, such as bonobos, use vocalizations to call each other back together (Barbara Fruth, Personal Communication 2004), but that would be impossible if foragers ranged as widely over a full day as the Hadza do.

One consequence of fissioning into same-sex foraging parties is that most human foragers cannot spend all day within sight of their mates, which makes direct mate-guarding impossible. The resulting weakening of pair-bonds could be offset by household provisioning or trade of male and female foods. If sharing different types of food within a household is one payoff of the hunting versus gathering specialization, then CPP is almost required so couples can reunite each night.

The Hadza are quite typical of central-place provisioners. The central place is moved several times a year in response to resource availability, and the composition of camps is fluid, which allows for access to foods that are patchy in space and time. Such flexibility and individual autonomy is precluded by the sedentary life of agriculturists.

SEASONALITY

Seasonality is very noticeable in Hadzaland; the parched, dry landscape turns very green during the rainy season. Hadza foraging also varies from season to season. For example, during the rainy season when honey becomes plentiful, husbands and wives often go foraging together, with the man looking for honey and the woman digging tubers or collecting baobab. During December to May, the season when the best berries are ripe, large numbers of males and females, children and adults, go foraging together. Toward the end of the dry season, men go to hunt in pairs at water holes all night long. During most of the year, the typical foray for men is to go alone to look for game, while women go in groups to dig, usually accompanied by some older children.

Berries may be available in July and August, but they mostly come into season toward the end of the dry season and continue throughout the first half of the rains; honey then becomes plentiful. Baobab is least plentiful at that time. Tubers are available throughout the year (Vincent 1985a). Tubers appear to be fallback foods (Marlowe and Berbesque 2009). Fallback foods are those which are taken when other, more preferred foods are not available. Tubers are eaten much less often when foods like meat, honey, berries, and baobab are plentiful. By switching to different foods, the Hadza are able to acquire a fairly level intake of daily kilocalories throughout the year (Marlowe and Berbesque 2009, Sherry and Marlowe 2007). Although seasonality is very noticeable, the Hadza do not report one season as more difficult than others. One might think the dry season would be a lean season, but people do not lose weight during the dry season, mainly because at that time men take more meat through ambush hunting at water holes.

DAILY ROUTINE

The Hadza wake at sunup, between 6:30 and 7:00 A.M. year-round (given the proximity to the equator, there are just about 12 hours of sunlight and 12 hours of darkness year-round). It is still cool at dawn, so they usually huddle around the hearth for an hour, becoming active only gradually. They may sit and talk, or eat a bit if there is any food left over from the previous day. On most days, the women are ready to go foraging by 8:00 or 9:00 A.M.

Hadza take 1–2 hour naps around midday until the heat subsides. Even when they are out foraging far from camp, they usually take a long break for a midday rest. Women and children go for firewood and water around 5 P.M. When there is food, dinner is eaten just after dark, around 7:30 P.M.; bedtime is around 9 P.M. On nights of an *epeme* dance, the adults may stay up dancing and singing until about midnight. Below, I describe the most important foods in the Hadza diet and how they are acquired.

TUBERS

A tuber is an enlarged underground stem that serves as a storage organ, sometimes called an underground storage organ (USO), usually with only a vine above ground. The Hadza eat at least 10 species of tubers (Table 5.1). Figure 5.2 shows one species of tuber called *//ekwa* (*Vigna frutescens*), which is the one most commonly taken, along with baobab fruit and three species of berries. Tubers are mostly acquired by women, who use the digging sticks described in Chapter 4. Women's foraging groups usually range from 3 to 10 women, often accompanied by girls 8 or 9 years old who also dig. Sometimes younger boys and girls go. Women also take their nursing infants with them.

The women usually walk for about 10–30 minutes to a spot where they know tubers are available. Then they look for tubers by spotting the lianas growing up and wrapping around a bush or tree. Using the blunt end of their digging sticks, they tap the ground, listening for the sound that suggests a large tuber. Once they are satisfied with a spot, they begin to dig. The women may be close together or spread out, but they always stay within earshot. They may soon give up on one patch and walk on to another patch, which could be another 5–10 minute walk. Sometimes, they visit 6 or 7 different patches—usually not too far from each other—in one foray.

Digging tubers requires learning how to recognize the plant, how to assess the size of the tuber and its orientation in the ground, and how to judge its maturity. Strength and stamina are essential for the 10–20 minutes of vigorous digging needed to expose a big tuber and pull it up. Boulders often hamper the digging because several tuber species tend to

TABLE 5.1. FOODS EATEN BY HADZA

Category	Hadzane Name	English Name	Scientific Name
Tuber	Makalita		*Rhynchosia comosa or Eminia entennulifa*
Tuber	Matukwayako		*Coccinea surantiaca or aurantiaca*
Tuber	Panjuako		*Ipomoea transvaalensis*
Tuber	Shumuwako		*Vatoraea pseudolablab or Vigna sp.*
Tuber	//Ekwa		*Vigna esculenta*
Tuber	//Ekwa hasa		*Vigna frutescens*
Tuber	Do'aiko/Shakeako		*Vigna macrorhyncha*
Tuber	Penzepenze		*Vigna sp. (Papilionoidea Leguminosae)*
Tuber	Sakala		*Vigna vexillata Benth.*
Tuber	!Hibi (Mangola)		
Vegetable	Sasa ndo		*Peponium vogelii*
Berry	Mbilipe		*Grewia flavescens Juss., Grewia platyclada*
Berry	Hlukwayabe		*Grewia villosa Willd.*
Berry	Congolobe		*Grewia bicolor Juss.*
Berry	K'alahaibe		*Opilia campestris Engl.*
Berry	Tafabe		*Salvadora persica L.*
Berry	Tl'atanako		*Grewia pachycalyx K. Schum.*
Berry	Undushipi		*Cordia gharaf Ehrenb.*
Berry	Ngwilabe		*Grewia similis K. Schum.*
Berry	Ts'apaleko		*Cordia sp. (Cordia ovalis)*
Berry	Sememambuga		*Grewia lilacina K. Schum.*
Fruit	Mashalope		*Vangueria acutiloba Robyns or V. apiculata*
Fruit	Ghagha		*Momordica sp.*
Fruit	Hogoyoko	Fig	*Ficus sycomorus L.*
Fruit	Hogoko	Desert date	*Balanites aegyptiaca Del.*
Fruit	N//obabe	Baobab	*Adasonia digitata L.*
Fruit	Mhuibe	Tamarind	*Tamarindus indica L.*
Fruit	Wika		*Maerua edulis/Courbonia glauca*
Fruit/nut	Pawe-be	Marula	*Selenicereus megalanthus*
Fruit/nut	Mnyangube	Doum palm	*Hyphaene coriacea/ventricosa*
Honey	Ba'alako	Honey	*Apis mellifera unicolor/adansonii*
Honey	N!ateko	Honey	*Trigona erythra junodi*
Honey	Kanowa	Honey	*Trigona ruspolii Magrettii*
Honey	Mulangeko	Honey	*Trigona beccarii*
Honey	Tsunako	Honey	*Trigoma (H.) gribodoi Magretti*
Honey	Bambahau	Honey	*Lestrimellitta (Cleptomellitta) cubiceps*
Honey	Lulindi	Honey	*Trigoma denoiti Vachal*

(continued)

TABLE 5.1. *(continued)*

Category	Hadzane Name	English Name	Scientific Name
Insect	Tsunako	Bee larvae	*Apis mellifera unicolor/adansonii*
Mammal	Ne'e'ko	Baboon	*Papio anubis*
Mammal	Nakomako	Buffalo	*Syncerus caffer*
Mammal	Chacha	Bush baby	*Galago senegalensis (lesser)*
Mammal	Ndonoko	Bush baby	*Otolemur crassicaudatus (greater)*
Mammal	Gewedako	Dikdik	*Madoqua kirkii*
Mammal	Komati	Eland	*Taurotragus oryx*
Mammal	Bililiko	Fox	*Otocyon megalotis*
Mammal	Lalako	Grant's gazelle	*Gazella granti*
Mammal	Lalako	Thompson's gazelle	*Gazella thomsoni*
Mammal	Tsokwonako	Giraffe	*Giraffa camelopardalis*
Mammal	Chasho	Tree hyrax	*Dendrohyrax arboreus*
Mammal	Ch'abako	Rock hyrax	*Procavia johnstoni*
Mammal	Popoako	Impala	*Aepyceros melampus*
Mammal	Molola	Jackal	*Canis adustus*
Mammal	!Namako	Klipspringer	*Oreotragus oreotragus*
Mammal	!Naname	Greater kudu	*Tragelaphus strepsiceros*
Mammal	!Nana	Lesser kudu	*Tragelaphus imberbis*
Mammal	/Bisoko	Wildebeest	*onnochaetes taurinus*
Mammal	Lola	Rabbit	*Lepus saxatilis? Or Pedetes capensis?*
Mammal	Doloka	Elephant shrew	*Elephantulus sp.*
Mammal	Setse'eko	Common duiker	*Sylvicapra grimmia*
Mammal	Tsimangana	Bushbuck	*Tragelaphus scriptus*
Mammal	Numbili	Vervet	*Cercopithecus aethiops pygerythrus*
Mammal	Kwahi	Warthog	*Phacochoerus aethiopicus*
Mammal	Tlaha	Bushpig	*Potamochoerus larvatus*
Mammal	Dongoako	Zebra	*Equus burchelli*
Mammal	Goyogoda	Genet	*Genetta genetta*
Mammal	Sindi	Squirrel	*Euxerus erythropus?*
Mammal	Janjai	Leopard	*Pathera pardus*
Mammal	Seseme	Lion	*Panthera leo*
Mammal	Udzameko	Spotted hyena	*Crocuta crocuta*
Mammal	Mbugida	Wild dog	*Lycaon pictus*
Mammal	Ukulukakako	Pangolin	*Smutsia temminckii*
Mammal	!Eleako	Hartebeest	*Alcelaphus buselaphus*
Mammal	Kukula	Topi	*Damaliscus lunatus*
Mammal	Wet sai iako	Hippopotamus	*Hippopotamus amphibius*
Mammal	O sai eh	Aardvark	*Orycteropus afer*

(continued)

TABLE 5.1. *(continued)*

Category	Hadzane Name	English Name	Scientific Name
Mammal	Sipiti	Porcupine	*Hystrix cristata*
Reptile	K'olowako	Leopard tortoise	*Geochelone pardalis*
Snail	N//alaka	Land snail	
Bird	Ch'aako	Guinea fowl	*Numida meleagris*
Bird	Quali	Quail	*Coturnix d. delegorguei*
Bird	Daladala	White stork	*Ciconia ciconia*
Bird	Daladala	Yellow-billed stork	*Mycteria ibis*
Bird	Congozako	Black stork	*Ciconia nigra*
Bird	Nyambulu	Marabou stork	*Leptoptilus crumeniferus*
Bird	Owania	Gray-crowned crane	*Balearica regulorum gibbericeps*
Bird	!Tatamu	Saddle-billed stork	*Ephippiorhynchus senegalensis*
Bird	Gijiko	Sacred ibis	*Threskiornis aethiopicus*
Bird	Gogo gogo	Greater flamingo	*Phoenicopterus roseus*
Bird	Gogo gogo	Lesser flamingo	*Phoeniconaias minor*
Bird	!Ah gwing gwiako	Hamerkop	*Scopus umbretta*
Bird	Bunguako	Black-crowned night-heron	*Nycticorx nycticorax*
Bird	Daladala kulwa	Great white pelican	*Pelecanus onocrotalus*
Bird	Batako	Knob-billed or comb duck	*Sarkidiornis melanotos*
Bird	Gu ih u quali	Rock pratincole	*Glareola nuchalis*
Bird	Qela qeta pe	Collared pratincole	*Glareola pratincole fuellerborni*
Bird	Qela qeta pe	Violet-tipped courser	*Rhinoptilus chalcopterus*
Bird	Ge ge ripi	Two-banded courser	*Rhinoptilus africanus gracilis*

NOTE: Many more birds not shown are eaten.

Figure 5.2. Hadza foods: baobab fruit on left; //ekwa tuber on top; three species of berries on bottom.

grow in rocky spots (Figure 5.3). Removing these boulders often requires the cooperative work of two women; one wedges her digging stick under the rock and levers it up, while the other digs rapidly to free the tuber. Finally, after carving out the length of the tuber, a woman grabs it and pulls. This requires strength because the tubers are held in the ground by many little roots shooting off in all directions. When a woman has pulled most of the tuber up, she uses a knife to cut the tuber free.

Women usually spend about 2–3 hours digging. By then, it is very hot, and they will have a hefty pile of tubers. A woman may get 2 or 3 different species of tubers, or specialize in just 1 type during that day's foray. When they have finished digging, the women usually build a small bonfire. Each woman has her own pile of tubers and puts a few on the roaring flames. Sometimes one woman may put all of her tubers on the fire, to be repaid later with a share of a different woman's haul. The women roast //ekwa for about 5 minutes (Mallol et al. 2007), then peel off the outer covering with a knife and cut the inside, which is virtually all juicy fiber, into pieces. //Ekwa cannot be swallowed, but must be chewed for some time to extract the juice. The remaining mass of fiber is then spit out. After eating their fill and resting for about 30 minutes, the

Figure 5.3. A woman digs tubers in rocky soil.

women pick up the remainder of the tubers and return to camp. More tubers are then roasted for the children and others in camp.

BERRIES

Berries comprise the largest share of the Hadza diet as measured by kilo-calories. However, since they are somewhat concentrated in the late dry and the rainy seasons, they cannot be eaten continually throughout the year as are tubers (Marlowe and Berbesque 2009). Berries are very important because they totally dominate consumption every day they are available. Usually a camp is located in the midst of the berry bushes, especially the favorite berry *undushipi* (*Cordia gharaf Ehrenb*; Figure 5.4) (Berbesque and Marlowe in prep). The Hadza diet includes 10 species of berries that we have identified plus a few yet to be identified (Table 5.1). Berries are high in simple sugars, as one would expect, but unlike the domesticated berries that we are familiar with, these wild berries are very fibrous, with only a little pulp around a large seed. This means the Hadza need to eat huge quantities of them.

During berry season, a much lower percentage of the daily food consumption takes place in camp. Because anyone and everyone can acquire berries, everyone but the youngest nurslings eat them on the spot and

Figure 5.4. A couple forages for *undushipi* berries.

usually until full. When a camp is located in the middle of berry bushes, children who are 3 years old or older wake up, climb above where they were sleeping, and begin picking and eating berries, so they can feed themselves the bulk of their diet during this time. Sometimes, however, women fill baskets and take the berries back to camp after they have eaten their fill, especially when the bushes are far away from the camp. Berry foraging parties are often very large, sometimes consisting of the whole camp—30 or 40 people of all ages and both sexes. Everyone picks berries and eats rapidly in the morning, then rests in the shade of the berry bushes at midday. After a long rest, they pick and eat more, fill baskets, and return to camp.

BAOBAB

Baobab (*Adasonia digitata L.*) is a very important food for the Hadza. In fact, it contributes more kcals to the diet than any other single species. It is high in vitamin C, and the seeds are high in fat. It is also available throughout most of the year because one tree will produce pods at a different time than other trees; thus, there are usually a few trees in any area with ripe pods. All Hadza pick baobab pods up off the ground when they pass them. They stomp on the pods or whack them against a rock to crack them open, then pull the white chalky pulp out and eat it (Figure 5.2). Because there are large, hard seeds inside, one must suck on the pulp and then spit out the seeds. Sometimes women make special trips out of camp to get baobab, collecting numerous pods. They always know the location of the most productive tree at any given time. Their haul is then taken back to camp for processing. Occasionally, a man will climb the tree and go far out on a limb to shake the pods free while women wait below to collect them. Men also use heavy sticks to throw up at the pods to knock them off the tree. When men are heading back to camp empty-handed after hunting or checking beehives, they often stop and load up with many baobab pods so as to take something back to camp.

HONEY

When men are out on walkabout, they always have their bows and arrows, but they often stop at trees to check on beehives. They can tell by watching the bees whether there is much honey ready to harvest. A man often puts his ear to a tree trunk to listen to the bees. After monitoring trees in the area around their camp, they may decide that it is time to raid hives, and then they carry their axes (in addition to their bows). If they should see game worth pursuit, they abandon the search for honey and pursue the animal until they kill it or it gets away. Honey collecting does not pose a substantial tradeoff with hunting; the Hadza (especially men) are very opportunistic foragers, which makes it difficult to code their forays into honey vs. game vs. baobab search time the way optimal foraging models suggest can be done.

Hadza take honey from 7 different species, though 3 species dominate: *baalako*, *nateako*, and *kanoa*. *Baalako* is the best and juiciest and comes in the largest quantities. *Baalako* is made by the fierce stinging bees (*Apis mellifera adansonii*) which prefer to make their hives high up in baobab trees. When a man sees a hive that looks promising, and if he thinks it will have substantial honey, he sets about making a fire and cutting pegs for climbing up the baobab tree. After cutting pegs and using his ax handle to hammer the first peg into the tree bark, a man will carry a torch, climb up and hammer the next peg in, and continue like this until he reaches the hole, whereupon he will use the torch to smoke the bees to stun them (Figure 5.5). It is then easier to reach in and grab the honeycomb because he will less often be stung.

Figure 5.5. A man uses his ax to hammer pegs into a
baobab tree and climbs to reach the beehive above
his torch.

Men often follow the honey-guide bird (*Indicator indicator*). This
bird approaches and makes noise to get a man's attention. The man then
whistles back to the bird and starts following it; it keeps squawking at
him until it has arrived at the tree and the man sees the hive. After the
man opens up the hive and extracts the honey, the bird gets to clean up
the leftovers. The bird leads men to hives of *Apis mellifera* only. There
has been coevolution between the honey-guide bird and humans. This
presumably followed earlier coevolution between the honey-guide bird
and honey badgers, or ratels (*Mellivora capensis*), since they too open up
hives after following honey-guides (Estes 1991).

There are also several different species of stingless bees that make
other kinds of honey, the most common one being *kanoa. Kanoa* is
made by the sweat bees (*Trigona ruspolii Magrettii*) that make their
hives lower down in Commiphora trees (*Commiphora africana*). Even

women take this kind of honey because it requires little climbing and no risk of bee stings. It is fairly rare to see women get much honey east of Lake Eyasi, but in the west, women use their husbands' axes and go on forays that involve considerable time and effort to get *kanoa*. *N!ateko* is also made by stingless bees and is usually located in smaller trees. Another type of honey, *lulindi* (*Trigoma denoiti Vachal*), is located underground and can require elaborate digging to excavate.

HUNTING

Walkabout/Encounter

Men usually forage alone. During the dry season, a man may leave at 5 or 6 A.M., well before the sun rises, to surprise animals that have been drinking at a water hole in the safety of darkness. After shooting at prey and missing, a man rarely follows or tracks that animal because it is too difficult to find when it is aware of him. The man has a better chance just waiting for the next encounter with a different animal. Hadza men rarely run. They may run briefly to get a second shot at a large herd. Occasionally, when they see a small animal like a hyrax, they may run to cut it off before it can reach its home in a rock crevice, or they may run after a burrowing animal before it can reach its burrow.

Women occasionally kill small mammals. Outside of mammals and birds, the only animals eaten are tortoises and large land snails, both of which women usually acquire. Bee larvae are eaten along with honey, and in one area, children eat winged termites and locusts, according to one Hadza who says they roast them first (I have not witnessed this).

Water-Hole Ambush Hunting

Men hunt at night during the late dry season, waiting to ambush animals coming to drink at a water hole. They always do this in pairs because of the danger from lions and leopards using the same strategy. The hunters arrive at the water hole before dusk and build up a small mound behind which they make a fire; as the fire dies, the remaining embers provide warmth all night without giving off light. Then they wait. This needs to be done on moonlit nights so the hunter can see the animals well enough to hit them. The animals may come to drink soon after sundown, but at other times, the wait is long and the hunters take turns snoozing. One can get cold lying outside all night with no covering, but the strategy is effective, and more meat is acquired in the dry season than in the wet.

In the dry season, men also employ ambush hunting during the day. This is usually done alone. A man wakes early to get to his chosen spot before it is very light, since animals tend to come very early for a drink. He hides behind a simple blind that he makes out of branches and leaves. If he misses any animal that comes in the morning, he may get a few more chances throughout the day, but his next best chance will be once the sun is going down. Hence, this strategy requires great patience. The hunter must lie still and be quiet for up to 12 hours straight. But it can also be quite rewarding when the animal is a large buffalo.

SCAVENGING

Hadza men often scavenge meat from carnivores, including lions, leopards, hyenas, wild dogs, foxes, and jackals. They listen for the sounds of predators killing prey at night, the time when most kills are made. From the cries of the dying animal, they can tell the species of prey. They can also tell the species of predator (usually a hyena, leopard, lion, or wild dog) from its vocalizations. From the sounds, they can tell the exact location. The next morning, the men wake at dawn and head directly to the spot; if a large animal was killed, there may be plenty of meat left.

The Hadza are also alert to vultures in the daytime. If they arrive on the site of a lion kill and see the lions have sated themselves, they shoot an arrow near the lions to run them off the kill. If they arrive before the lions are sated, they sit and wait patiently at a safe distance until the lions are sated. The Hadza sometimes find meat stashed in a tree by a leopard. One Hadza man with only one eye claims he lost an eye when he was stealing meat from a leopard (he did get the meat). The Hadza themselves sometimes stash game in trees when they need to leave it and go back to camp. Occasionally, a Hadza man kills a lion or leopard, which the Hadza then eat. Women also scavenge. A group of women armed only with digging sticks can run a leopard off its kill (O'Connell, Hawkes, and Jones 1988). In 1985, James O'Connell found that scavenging accounted for 20% of medium to large carcasses taken, amounting to 14% of all meat by weight (O'Connell, Hawkes, and Jones 1988).

FOOD PROCESSING

Certain foods are always processed, some are never processed, and others are only sometimes processed. For example, baobab is eaten unprocessed when eaten out of camp. When it is taken back, the pulp and seeds are pounded into flour with a hammerstone. When a little water is added, it becomes a paste, which is the main weaning food. When honey or certain berries are available, they are sometimes added to the tart baobab pulp and water to make a delicious sweet and tart drink.

Meat is always roasted or boiled, though marrow is eaten raw. Sometimes a man roasts and eats some of his game before taking the rest back to camp. Game the size of a gazelle or smaller is often carried back whole to camp, while larger game is butchered at the kill site. In the case of very large game (buffalo or giraffe), the hunter will carry as much back to camp as he can and those who are in camp (men, women, and children) will go out to the kill site to cut off and carry back to camp their own pieces. Honey is eaten raw, though it is sometimes mixed with baobab. Berries are usually eaten raw and fresh, but they may be dried toward the end of berry season. Tubers are roasted about five minutes before they are eaten, although Hadza are willing to eat tubers without roasting them. This raises a question: Why do Hadza roast tubers? It may be that roasting is done mainly to make it easier to peel the outside off the tuber, since only the insides of most tubers are eaten. Perhaps roasting enhances the nutritional value or detoxifies the tuber, though so far we have no evidence of this in the few nutritional analyses carried out. One species, *panjuako* (*Ipomoea transvaalensis*), is not usually roasted. It tastes similar to jicama or a juicy raw potato.

FORAGING PARTIES

Most prime-age adults go foraging every day for some period of time, though occasionally they may stay in camp all day. There are usually some camp residents in camp at any given hour of the day, especially in larger camps. Across 8 camps, the percentage of the camp population present in camp ranged from 0% to 100%. The hour when the fewest people were present was 11:00 A.M., when on average 48% (median = 43%) of the total camp population was in camp (Figure 5.6).

Figure 5.7 shows the amount of time people are gone from camp by age and sex. The mean time spent foraging per day is 4.1 hours for women and 6.1 hours for men 18 years and older. Those between ages 2

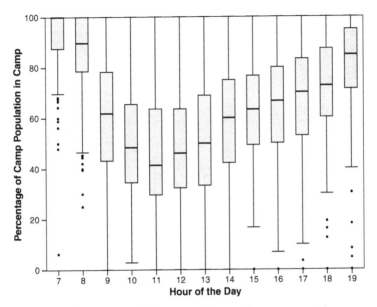

Figure 5.6. Percentage of all camp residents who are present in camp by hour of day across 8 different camps throughout the year (n=number of hourly scans for each hour shown; midlines indicate medians; boxes indicate quartiles; 25th to 75th percentiles; whiskers indicate extremes excluding outliers shown by dots).

and 4 years old were least likely to be gone from camp because, as noted, toddlers are too young to walk very far and too heavy to carry.

Women walk an average of 5.5 km (range=0.25–13.50) per foray (n=110) at an average moving speed of 3.5 km/hour and expend a mean of 698 kcal (n=102). Men walk an average of 8.3 km (range=1.57–27.20) per foray (n=57) at an average moving speed of 3.6 km/hour and expend 716 kcal (n=44). Men travel significantly further than women (t=4.01, p<0.0005, df=74.8, equal variances not assumed). Even in a camp during berry season, when the disparity between men and women is least pronounced, GPS tracks of men's forays are noticeably longer than those of women (Figure 5.8).

A woman carries her nursing infant in a kaross when foraging. She keeps her sleeping infant on her back even while digging tubers, occasionally swinging the infant to the front to nurse. Although weanlings are usually left in camp (Marlowe 2006a), by the time children are 8 years old (especially girls), they often go foraging with the women. By age 10, children can acquire about half their daily caloric needs (Blurton Jones

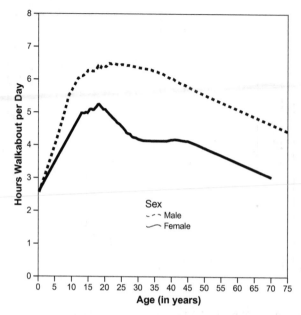

Figure 5.7. Mean number of hours per day males and
females are gone from camp (as a proxy for foraging
time) by age ($n = 110$ females, 108 males). Fit lines are
Loess Epanechnikov.

1993, Hawkes, Jones, and O'Connell 1995). I discuss children's foraging returns in the context of life history theory in Chapter 6.

PARTY SIZE

The mean size of foraging parties for men is 1.7 (SD = 2.09, median = 1,
$n = 199$). For women, mean party size is 5.31 (SD = 3.93, median = 4,
$n = 95$). For mixed-sex adult parties, mean party size is 4.06 (SD = 3.07,
median = 3, $n = 33$). Party size varies considerably with the type of foray.
For women going mainly for tubers, the mean party size is 3.8 adult
women plus infants and some older children (2–12, $n = 55$). During berry
season, there are more mixed-sex parties, and mean party size for
berries is 7.7 (1–24, $n = 40$). When baobab is the main food brought
back to camp, mean party size is 4.6 (1–14, $n = 11$).

Men go foraging for honey with other men in parties of two or three
sometimes, but they most often go alone. There are also some mixed-sex

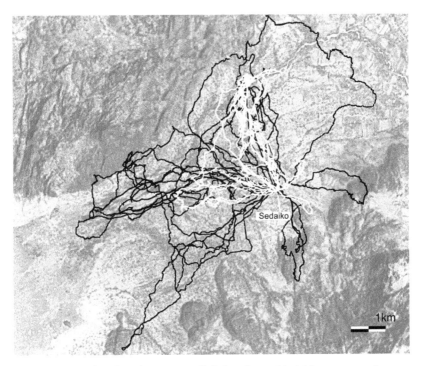

Figure 5.8. Tracks of Hadza women (light) and men (dark) in one camp in January 2004, when *undushipi* berries dominated the diet.

parties when couples go foraging together and men get honey. Average party size for honey is 2.0 (1–8, *n* = 28).

Men in encounter hunting have an average party size of 1.5 (1–16, *n* = 124). Men usually go hunting alone because when using bows and poisoned arrows, one man can kill an animal as large as a giraffe with a good shot (Figure 5.9). The advantages of two hunters looking for game are probably outweighed by the increased likelihood of being detected before getting close enough to get a good shot. Getting close enough for a good shot is the most difficult aspect of hunting, based on my observations during many follows of men hunting. I have to be very careful to be quiet and alert at all times in order not to ruin the hunter's chance of getting a shot.

One drawback to hunting alone is that after a man kills an animal too large to carry back to camp, he must abandon what he cannot carry. He often hides the remainder under branches or up in a tree. This means that hyenas or leopards might well get the rest. If men hunted in pairs,

Figure 5.9. A man on walkabout carrying his bow and arrows and hunting by himself.

one could stay to guard the remainder of the carcass, or two could possibly carry it all back in one trip. The fact that men hunt alone despite this risk is further evidence that net returns are probably higher for lone hunters in most walkabout forays.

Foraging party size has been analyzed for several species (Basabose 2004, Chapman, White, and Wrangham 1994, Newton-Fisher, Reynolds, and Plumptre 2000, Symington 1988) and for a few societies of human foragers (Minnegal 1997, Smith 1985, 1991). While we now have many data on Hadza foraging party size, we have so far only tested whether women's party sizes are predicted by type of food acquired, that is, whether there is an optimal size for each food type and if that is the modal party size (Porter and Marlowe nd-a). Party size made little difference in the amount of foods acquired per hour or per foray. In other words, it does not appear that women forage in optimal sized parties, or else there is no clearly optimal size. This is presumably because women forage in parties that are large enough to provide sufficient safety from predators or from men of other tribes. A boy who is old enough to be sufficiently skilled with a bow to protect the women often goes with them (Figure 5.10).

Figure 5.10. A boy accompanies the women when they go foraging for baby birds (*Quelea quelea*).

There may also be little cost to going in large parties. Perhaps the women would acquire about the same amount per capita even in smaller parties. Since women do only forage in groups, they may all need to go together in one party when they live in smaller camps. In larger camps, there are enough women to form 2 or 3 parties, and often 2 or 3 different groups do go out in different directions. This suggests that parties can be too large, or that women prefer to go with women they like most and so form 2 or 3 different parties. The fact that women can acquire sufficient food in fairly large groups allows humans to live in multi-female, multi-male groups, unlike East African chimpanzees whose females are fairly solitary most of the time, presumably to avoid feeding competition (Wrangham and Peterson 1996).

THE DIET

In the past couple of decades, there has been growing interest in the diet of our ancestors, the paleo-diet, for two main reasons. First, diet is a fundamental component of selection and should explain a great deal about human evolution. Second, those who want to know what diet is healthiest for humans have begun to consider that it might be the diet to which we are adapted. For these reasons, there are numerous recent publications on the hominin diet (Eaton 2006, Eaton, Shostak, and Konner 1988, Somer 2001, Stanford and Bunn 2001, Ungar 2007, Yeakel et al. 2007). The Hadza diet is as relevant in this regard as we could hope to find in any extant society. Because the Hadza are still foraging, we can still measure how much they eat of each species, which can therefore guide collection of those species for nutritional analysis. Not only are the Hadza still eating this wild diet, but they live in East Africa, where the hominin record is continuous over the whole 6 or 7 million years of hominin evolution, and most species they eat were present throughout that time across a range of East African habitats (Bobe, Alemseqed, and Behrensmeyer 2007, Foley 1987).

The Hadza diet consists of more than 880 species (Table 5.1). The vast majority of species are mammals and birds (Table 5.2). In terms of frequency and in terms of kilograms or kilocalories (kcals), the diet is dominated by far fewer species (Table 5.3 and Table 5.4). Table 5.3 shows the percent of foods (in kilograms) brought into camp across 5 food categories. These data come from 5 years of data in 24 camps spanning 11 years.

In Table 5.4 I have sorted the diet across 6 camps in 1995–1996 into 6 food categories and show their importance as measured by daily kcals arriving in camp. Daily kcals refers to the total amount of kcals of one food species a person brought to camp over the course of one camp stay (usually 1.5 months), divided by the number of days that person was observed, and summed for all individuals in the camp. This means we can make fair comparisons across camps and seasons, regardless of camp population. The 6.6% of the diet consisting of "other" includes a variety of foods ranging from figs and other fruits to green leafy vegetables. It also consists of maize and millet given to the Hadza by a missionary or acquired through trade with neighboring agro-pastoralists. Since food like maize would be consumed in camp only, and since about one-third of consumption occurs while foraging, the percentage of domesticated food in the total diet is actually less than shown (perhaps 4%) in the camps we work in.

During berry season, the bulk of the diet is berries, and since they are mostly eaten while foraging, they surely comprise a greater percentage of the diet than Table 5.3 implies. When combining berries with baobab to calculate total fruit, fruit composes the largest fraction of the diet (40% by weight) that is eaten in camp (Table 5.3). The second row of

TABLE 5.2. NUMBERS OF SPECIES BY TYPE OF FOOD IN HADZA DIET

Type of Food	Frequency	Percent
Domestics	7	0.8
Berries	26	3.0
Fruits	8	0.9
Mammals	56	6.4
Tubers	18	2.1
Honeys	7	0.8
Birds	741	84.4
Reptiles	2	0.2
Invertebrates	1	0.1
Berry or fruit	2	0.2
Fruit/nut	3	0.3
Greens	1	0.1
Insects	1	0.1
Vegetables	2	0.2
Eggs	1	0.1
Root?	2	0.2
Total	878	100.0

TABLE 5.3. PERCENTAGE OF FOODS BROUGHT INTO CAMP BY FOOD CATEGORY

Sample	% Baobab	% Tuber	% Honey	% Berry	% Meat
All ages, both sexes, 24 camps	11.5	24.7	8.1	28.5	27.1
One camp (January)	10	8	1	67	14
Women 24 camps	25	30	1	37	7
Men 24 camps	19	1	24	2	54

NOTE: From 5 years of data in 24 camps spanning 11 years. Foods were measured in kilograms. The second row shows how much berries dominate during the *undushipi* season. The third and fourth rows show how different are the foods targeted by women and by men (the only substantial overlap is in baobab).

Table 5.3 represents one camp during January when *undushipi* was available. It shows that berries completely dominate the foods brought back to camp during berry season, and again because the vast majority of berries are eaten while picking them out of camp, the amount consumed is even greater than suggested by Table 5.3 or Table 5.4.

TABLE 5.4. HADZA DIET CONSUMED IN
6 CAMPS DURING 1995–1996

Contribution Group	Berries	Tubers	Honey	Baobab	Meat	Other	Total
Both sexes of all ages	17.2%	23.5%	14.2%	19.2%	19.3%	6.6%	100%
Women (≥18 years old)	24.8%	38.8%	0.7%	25.6%	1.2%	8.9%	100%
Men (≥18 years old)	6.3%	5.0%	30.2%	13.8%	39.6%	5.1%	100%

NOTE: Percentages show the amount that each food type contributed to the diet, as measured by daily kilocalories of food brought into 6 different camps during 1995–1996.

We have yet to finish analyzing total consumption both in and out of camp, but I estimate that, as a fraction of the total food acquired, about 50% of berries, 40% of honey, 25% of tubers, 20% of baobab, and 15% of meat is consumed out of camp. The 5 food categories that provide the most calories, judging from kilocalories in Table 5.4, are, in descending order, (1)berries, (2) meat, (3) baobab, (4) tubers, and (5) honey.

Across all ages, females are responsible for obtaining 60% of all kilocalories that come into camp (Figure 5.11), at least among the eastern Hadza; meat is much more plentiful in the west. For adults 18 and up, the percentage acquired by females is about 57%, while among married couples 50% of kcals are brought in by women (Table 5.5). If the wife is nursing an infant, however, she brings in only 31% (Marlowe 2003a). Even though it is impressive that a woman can dig with an infant sleeping in a kaross on her back, data show that her productivity is reduced when she has an infant (see Chapter 8).

The Hadza diet is surely instructive for those interested in the paleodiet. The Hadza diet is high in fiber. Tubers contain so much fiber that they are nothing like the food we eat, even the food highest in fiber. Rather, Hadza consumption of fiber is more like the amount many other primates, like chimpanzees, get in their diet. They try to avoid fiber, while we are told we need to eat more fiber because we in affluent nations have cultivated a diet that is very low in fiber. The Hadza diet includes very few plants that contain vitamin A, and they rarely eat those few that do. Yet they do not appear to be seriously lacking in vitamin A, probably because

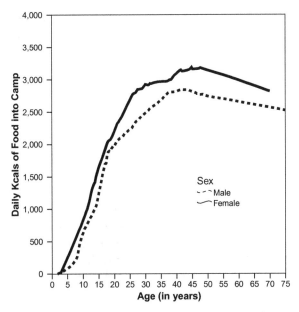

Figure 5.11. Daily kilocalories brought into camp by
age of Hadza females (*n*=94, solid line) and males
(*n*=93, dotted line). Fit lines are Loess Epanechnikov.

TABLE 5.5. HADZA MEAN FORAGING RETURNS
(KCAL/DAY) AND RETURN RATES (KCAL/HOUR)

Sample	Females		Males	
	Kcal/Day	*Kcal/Hour*	*Kcal/Day*	*Kcal/Hour*
All ages (*n*=187)	2,226 (58%) SD=1,866 (*n*=94)	561 SD=463 (*n*=94)	1,633 (42%) SD=1,962 (*n*=93)	343 SD=555 (*n*=93)
Adults (18 and up)	3,076 (57%) SD=1,726 (*n*=59)	795 SD=414 (*n*=59)	2,792 (43%) SD=1,966 (*n*=51)	597 SD=646 (*n*=51)
Married adults	3,016 (50%) SD=1,900 (*n*=41)	764 SD=435 (*n*=41)	2,990 (50%) SD=2,025 (*n*=40)	666 SD=706 (*n*=40)

NOTE: Mean foraging returns are measured by daily kilocalories of food brought into camp, and return rates are measured by kilocalories per hour. Percentages in parentheses next to daily kcal are the proportion of the whole diet (100%) contributed by males and by females within the sample in each row.

they get it from meat (see Chapter 6). The Hadza crave fat because often the game they eat is lean by our standards, and they do not eat meat every day.

SEXUAL DIVISION OF LABOR

Table 5.4 shows a pronounced sexual division of labor with regard to foods brought back to camp. This is one of the more remarkable features of humans in cross-species perspective. While there is a considerable range of variation across foragers in the degree of sexual division of foraging labor, there is a marked division in all human societies compared to all other vertebrates (Marlowe 2007).

Husbands and wives often go foraging together once they get older (Figure 5.4). Even younger couples forage together occasionally during the honey season. The wife takes her infant with her, and sometimes even older children will accompany their parents, though, as noted, toddlers are almost always left in camp. There are large mixed-sex foraging parties during berry season and during the time that the weaver bird, the red-billed quelea (*Quelea quelea*), has its mass reproduction. For about two weeks before the chicks are fledged, the Hadza pull down the nests, using a long branch to reach those higher up, and gather the chicks by the thousands. When they do this, they go in large groups, often comprising the whole camp—men, women, and children. As noted, women in the west acquire considerable honey. Outside these exceptions, there is a marked difference in the amounts of certain foods men and women acquire the vast majority of time. Baobab is the food with the most overlap between the sexes as far as food coming into camp.

In camp, women do most of the food processing and cooking. However, men butcher large animals and then sometimes put the meat on a fire to roast it. Women, on rare occasions, kill some small animals, and they often butcher smaller animals and roast or boil the meat. Women and children fetch water and firewood every day. Women usually tend the hearth. This makes it all the more puzzling that women say they do not know how to make a fire with a fire drill, but rather need to carry embers when no matches are available. Women do the sewing and also build the grass huts.

The sexual division of foraging labor with males and females targeting different foods that are later shared is a very important trait of human hunter-gatherers. (Food-sharing is discussed in Chapter 9.) Nothing like it exists in other mammals. It may well be the most important form of human cooperation. However, the foods men bring into camp, especially large game but also honey, are shared more widely outside the household than the foods women bring home. For this reason, it is less clear that men's foods represent household provisioning (Hawkes, O'Connell, and Jones 2001a). When a child's mother dies, the child is more likely to die, but the child is not more likely to die if its father has died (Jones et al. 2000a). Given that the Hadza practice the levirate, perhaps there is no father-effect on mortality because the father's brother often marries his widow. Of course, it is also possible that the woman's own kin help most. As we will see in Chapters 7–10, the main effect of a husband's help among many warm-climate foragers may be to increase fertility rather than to decrease mortality. Men's foraging goals in relation to household provisioning or reputation building are addressed in Chapter 8.

CHAPTER 6

Life History

LIFE HISTORY AND DEMOGRAPHY

Life history theory deals with the timing of certain important events like weaning, puberty, reproduction, and death (Charnov 1993, Stearns 1992). Life history traits are interrelated. If we know growth rate and age at maturity or first reproduction in females, we can calculate average adult female body size because growth ceases (approximately, anyway) at maturity in mammals. If we know that the extrinsic juvenile mortality rate from predation is high, we can expect maturity to occur early. Individuals that take too long to mature run the risk of getting eaten before they can reproduce, so selection favors genes that promote earlier maturity. Conversely, if extrinsic mortality is low and there are advantages to growing larger, selection favors later maturity (Charnov 1993). With Charnov's equation $dW/dt = A W^{0.75}$, where dW is the increase in weight (W) per unit of time (dt) and AW is a taxonomic constant (A) times weight (W) to the 0.75 power, we can predict the length of the period from weaning to maturity.

Growth rates within taxa tend to adhere to the same power function. However, it is not so clear what determines growth rate for a given species. Growth rate must be related to available energy in the diet, but beyond that there are many unanswered questions. For example, why do animals like grazers such as buffalo that eat mostly low-quality food grow so large in such a short time, while other animals, from insectivores to carnivores, that eat more energy-dense foods grow more slowly to a smaller size? Presumably fast rates of growth can be sustained on lower-quality foods as long as they are abundant and continually available, and of course low-quality foods are more abundant than higher-quality energy-dense foods. But this relationship is opposite to the pattern within a given species: More energy-dense food usually results in faster growth to a larger final size (Walker et al. 2006). This probably occurs only when the high-quality food is continually available, as it is in complex human societies like ours.

We know that with a higher-energy, higher-fat diet, people grow faster. Children grow faster in developed countries than in underdeveloped countries (Bogin 1999). Most hunter-gatherers grow much slower to a smaller adult body size than do people in industrialized societies. The Hadza appear to develop fast in the first couple of years of life when they are nursing on demand, but after weaning, they clearly grow much more slowly than Americans. However, their growth velocity is very similar to that of other foragers, and it is not all that different from that of chimpanzees (Jones 2006). Hadza females reach menarche around 16–17 years, much later than the 12.5 years of American females (Chumlea et al. 2003, Okasha et al. 2001). The increasingly younger age of menarche in affluent industrial societies has been noted for some time and is clearly related to diet (Cole 2000, Okasha et al. 2001, Thomas et al. 2001). Girls in the United States eat whenever they are hungry and eat foods high in fat and calories, so they grow larger faster and reach menarche earlier.

Some have argued that, to account for the body size increase that occurred in *Homo erectus*, the foods they exploited must have been of higher quality compared to the foods of earlier hominins (Aiello and Key 2002), or the foods were enhanced through cooking (Wrangham et al. 1999). If this link is so straightforward, why are many species with the most energy-dense diets (e.g., insectivores) so small? Presumably, they require a high metabolism to find their foods and so have a high basal metabolic rate (BMR), and presumably it is difficult for them to find enough high-quality food. So we cannot necessarily posit a shift to larger hominin bodies with a shift to higher-quality food. More continuously available food is a more likely explanation. One way food could have become more continuously available is if the amount of food-sharing increased at this time. The most likely explanation for what could have caused sharing to increase is that central-place provisioning (CPP) began. Central-place foraging could have long preceded it. With *H. ergaster*, more-efficient tool use could have led to surplus food, which allowed foragers to take the surplus back to camp, and this resulted in nepotistic sharing and camp-wide scrounging.

Life history theory is one important way hunter-gatherer data can help us reconstruct the past. Some foragers exhibit mortality and fertility rates that must be similar to populations in the past. This is because they are probably eating the same foods their ancestors were eating over at least the past 15,000 years, maybe the last 100,000 years in the tropics, and to some extent over the past 2 million years, or as far back as ancestral hominins had body sizes similar to contemporary hunter-gatherers. In Hadzaland, the diet of baboons (*Papio anubis*) overlaps greatly with the Hadza diet. Baboons eat small game, baobab, and the same berries the Hadza eat, as well as the marula fruit, bits of honey when they can get it, and even shallow tubers. It seems likely that early hominins without bows and arrows would have overlapped even more with baboons in their diet than the Hadza do.

We know something about body size, brain size, and eruption of teeth from the fossil record, which, along with data on living primates and hunter-gatherers, can help us make educated guesses about life history evolution. Two important aspects of human life history that stand out in contrast to our ape relatives are our late age at first reproduction (late maturity) and the post-reproductive phase in women (menopause). Hadza data have been used to shed light on both of these (Jones, Hawkes, and O'Connell 2002, Jones and Marlowe 2002, Hawkes et al. 1998, Marlowe 2000b). Given that women start reproducing later than chimpanzees (17 years vs. 12 years) and that both cease reproducing about the same time, the only way to compensate for the later maturity and menopause is through shorter inter-birth intervals, and human foragers do have a shorter IBI. This means humans were probably able to achieve fairly high birth rates even before agriculture. The fact that humans spread around the globe well before agriculture began is evidence of high birth rates and population growth. I discuss these issues only briefly because Nicholas Blurton Jones is writing a book dedicated to Hadza demography and life history.

AGE ESTIMATES

Hadzane has words for numbers up to 4 only (1 = *ichame*, 2 = *piye*, 3 = *samaka*, 4 = *bone*). Beyond that, they say "many" or else borrow from Kiswahili, e.g., 5 = *botano* and is *tano* in Kiswahili, so they have clearly borrowed this word. Even *bone* for 4 appears to be borrowed from Bantu speakers (perhaps Isanzu), while *samaka* for 3 was perhaps recently borrowed from the Datoga (Bonny Sands and Kirk Miller, Personal Communication 2009.). Some younger Hadza now know the Kiswahili words for numbers, but most of them do not count the passing years, unless they have had several years of schooling. Consequently, the Hadza have no idea how old they are. You can ask a man who looks to be 70 years old how old he thinks he is, and he may guess 10 years old. The Hadza do, however, know whether they were born before or after another Hadza, so we can use relative age ranking to make our estimates more accurate. With most of those born since the early 1960s, we have a good record. There are even a few old people who appeared in photos from the 1930s and 1940s, which makes ages of some older people more reliable. In addition, there was a magnitude 6.3 earthquake very near Hadzaland in 1964. Those who were old enough to remember it can tell us whether they were children or adults at the time and whether some child was born before or after the earthquake. With the youngest people, age data are mostly precise, since births and deaths have been recorded at least every two years since 1982. After a while, one gets pretty good at guessing ages. My age estimates are highly correlated with those of Nicholas Blurton Jones ($r = 0.979$, $p < 0.0005$, $n = 482$).

SEX RATIO

Most populations of most species have a roughly equal sex ratio. Sex is determined in mammals and birds by one sex being homogametic: In mammals, it is females with two X-chromosomes and males with one X- and one Y-chromosome; in birds, females are the heterogametic sex. Because the chances of a sperm carrying an X- or a Y-chromosome are about equal, one might assume that equal sex ratios are simply the expected consequence and require no further explanation. However, sex is not always determined this way, and sometimes sex ratios are skewed (Hamilton 1967, Hardy 2002).

It was the geneticist Ronald Fisher (1930) who explained why selection should favor equal sex ratios in general. From a potential parent's perspective, the sex that is rarer is likely to give them a greater number of grandchildren. Given that all offspring have one father and one mother, the contribution to the next generation is the same for females and males. When one sex is rare, say with only half as many as the other sex, the average individual of the rare sex will have twice as many offspring as the common sex, and parents would do better to have the rare sex. Thus, whenever the sex ratio gets out of balance, selection will nudge it back into balance.

There are 916 people in my Hadza census data, though I have not tried to find those who married out or are living somewhere else in a town; those people would probably bring the total very close to 1,000. The best estimate of the number alive in any one year is 976 according to Nicholas Blurton Jones, and he did make an effort to locate and count all those living outside Hadza camps (Jones, Hawkes, and O'Connell 2002). The overall sex ratio, that is, counting people of all ages and dividing the number of males of all ages by the number of females of all ages, is 0.97, which is very close to equal (450 males, 465 females). The operational sex ratio (OSR), defined here as ages 16–49 years for females and 18–60 years for males, which seems to be the ages that males and females are getting married and reproducing, is 1.14 (273 males, 239 females). For those under 5 years of age, the sex ratio is usually male-biased, but males die at a higher rate in the early years. By the later years (greater than 60 years of age), the sex ratio becomes female-biased (0.73). These patterns are common, and not just among foragers but even in the United States to a lesser extent.

HEALTH

The Hadza live wholly outside during the half of the year when it is dry and sleep in minimal grass huts only during the rainy season. Because they live out in the open at low population densities and move frequently, they are less vulnerable to many of the contagious diseases that spread among their farming and herding neighbors. As noted, within a few months of one settlement attempt at Yaeda Chini, many Hadza contracted measles and died. In the previous settlement attempt there, others died with "respiratory and diarrheal infections" (McDowell 1981).

A team of medical researchers accompanied James Woodburn to Hadzaland back in the early 1960s and conducted several brief studies (Barnicot, Bennett, and Woodburn 1972, Barnicot et al. 1972, Barnicot and Woodburn 1975, Bennett et al. 1973, Stevens et al. 1977). This is how Hadza health was described by two of them, Jelliffe and Jelliffe (Work et al. 1973):

> Our survey mainly concerned the nutritional status of the children. Sixty-two children—about 25% of the entire child population—were examined; nutrition was surprisingly good. There was no protein-calorie malnutrition whatsoever. No children appeared to be below standard weight for age,

although it is difficult to be certain that existing international standards of anthropometry could be used. There were, however, some eye signs: Bitot's spots, suggestive of vitamin A deficiency, were noted. As these people did not appear to eat any green vegetables or carotene-rich fruits, it is possible that they were lacking in vitamin A, although other stigmata were not seen . . . no evidence of anemia. . . . The situation was much better than in the nine other tribes that the team had examined in neighboring Uganda. There was only a 27% parasitemia, a mixture of Plasmodium falciparum and P. malariae. . . . Among the 62 children examined, only 7 were found with parasites—3 with Giardia and 3 with tapeworm infestation.

Night blindness is a symptom of vitamin A deficiency. When I asked many Hadza if they have night blindness, none said they did. This agrees with my observations of Hadza who can see at night far better than I can. It suggests that most are not too deficient in vitamin A. It is certainly true that there are few green leafy vegetables in the diet and these few are eaten very rarely. They likely get sufficient vitamin A from the considerable amount of meat they eat. Many do have eye problems, but these are related to the constant smoke from their hearths.

Jelliffe and Jelliffe go on to say, "More recently, one of the original survey teams returned to the area and examined Hadza relocated in a static village as part of government policy. The changes in health status were clear-cut. Kwashiorkor and marasmus were present. Children had parasites, such as hookworm, that had not been found in the original survey, probably because it is difficult to contract a massive infestation when soil contamination is minimal as a result of nomadic camping."

The overall conclusion the medical team drew is that bush-dwelling Hadza have good health, much better than most other rural Africans who are agricultural. The Hadza have a much less monotonous diet than their agricultural neighbors, who eat maize or rice almost every day with only the occasional bit of meat. The Hadza eat a variety of berries; tubers, honey, and baobab fruit; and a wide variety of birds and mammals. There is probably more fluctuation in the quantity of food consumed by the Hadza than there is among their agricultural neighbors, except when the farmers and herders experience famine, which they do occasionally.

Young Hadza children from ages 2 to 6 usually have large bellies. Upon first seeing this, many people think they have kwashiorkor and are malnourished. But the medical team that visited the bush-dwelling Hadza in the 1960s found no evidence of that. The Hadza diet consists of such a large amount of fiber in tubers and berries that the gut must be fairly large, which makes children's bellies look swollen. As Hadza children age, their bodies grow to catch up with the size of the belly, and they no longer appear to have swollen bellies.

While the Hadza are often hungry, they are never starving and cannot recall any Hadza ever starving to death. When a big animal is killed, Hadza will gorge themselves for days. During *undushipi* season, they may eat almost nothing but that one type of berry for two months. When the weaver birds, the red-billed Quelea (*Quelea quelea*), have their mass synchronized reproduction, Hadza eat almost nothing but the little chicks for 2–3 weeks. However, they do desire variety and usually try to get other things, especially meat, during berry season. Meat and other foods are shared widely among all those in an average-sized camp, and this sharing helps minimize the variance in daily consumption (Sherry and Marlowe 2007). When Hadza are analyzed within age-sex groups, there is surprisingly little variation in their physical condition. The percentage of body fat shows the most variation, but even it is quite similar for all women between 30 and 40 years old and for all men between 40 and 50 years old, for example (Sherry and Marlowe 2007). The extensive sharing of food that is taken back to a central place, which is typical of foraging populations, must have had a significant impact on human life history, since it subsidizes the young after weaning much more than occurs in our closest primate relatives. As noted in Chapter 5, however, children begin foraging for themselves quite early (Jones, Hawkes, and O'Connell 1989).

The amount of foraging children do varies considerably across societies. How difficult food is to acquire seems to predict the amount of food children acquire (Jones, Draper, and Hawkes 1994, Jones, Hawkes, and O'Connell 1989). There is a long tradition in anthropology that considers late maturity in humans "delayed or deferred maturity" to provide ample time for children to learn many things that go into adult foraging (Bogin 1999, Kaplan et al. 2000). However, late maturity may simply be a function of constrained growth rates and the length of the reproductive period, with human maturity occurring at the age expected for a primate of our size and longevity (Bliege-Bird, and Bird 2002, Jones and Marlowe 2002), providing we also count the post-reproductive period. I return to this later in this chapter.

MEDICINE, MORBIDITY, AND MORTALITY

The Hadza receive little or no medical treatment. When injuries occur or someone is seriously ill, unless someone like a researcher is around to dispense medicine or take them to the nearest clinic or hospital, they simply endure (though they do have certain of their own medical practices, described below). There is one hospital, which is quite good by Tanzanian standards, only one or two day's walk from part of Hadza country, but since it is still a long walk up steep hills, Hadza rarely walk there for treatment. There are three small clinics with very limited facilities and medicine a bit closer for some Hadza, but unless someone pays for them, Hadza are rarely treated. For the most part, the Hadza continue to exhibit natural mortality and morbidity, only slightly (if at all) influenced by medical attention, and this was especially true until sometime after 2000 (Jones, Hawkes, and O'Connell 2002). Due to their foraging lifestyle, however, they have extremely good eyesight, hearing, teeth, and diet. There is no obesity and apparently little cancer. No cancers have been noted in the Hadza and most other foragers, but with such a small population, it is difficult to assess. Reproductive cancers may be rare in natural fertility populations where women have far fewer menstrual cycles due to more pregnancies and longer nursing (Eaton, Konner, and Shostak 1988, Eaton et al. 1994, Jasienska et al. 2006).

The Hadza have several types of their own medical treatments (for a fuller description, see Woodburn 1959). There is a plant that is boiled and the liquid drunk to relieve the symptoms of malaria. Several plants are used to cause a person to vomit after being bitten by a poisonous snake. With the most poisonous snakes, there is little hope, since they can kill a person in minutes, but these plants can apparently work with less poisonous but still deadly snakes, and several people say they have been saved this way. Bark from a certain tree is boiled and made into a tea to treat syphilis and gonorrhea. One plant is given to someone who falls down with a seizure, presumably epilepsy, which must be rare, given that there are only 1,000 Hadza. There is also a plant that is supposed to help men overcome impotence. Some say there are plants that can induce miscarriage in the early stages of pregnancy, though it seems that they are rarely used or that they are ineffective. The women who told me about such plants went on to complain that they cannot stop having babies.

When one has general pain in the body, a horn is used to create suction to suck "the poison" out. A knife is also used to make cuts and let blood run for general pain. Some Hadza have several scars on their arms and backs as a result. When one is badly cut, a tourniquet is applied after boiled animal fat or honey is applied to the wound. The Hadza do not like to wear bandages and believe it is better to let wounds have fresh air. This is probably true most of the time, but the Hadza also have a problem keeping wounds clean and free of infection, since hygiene is not feasible when one lives outside, sleeps on the ground, and has limited access to clean water.

With the exception of the few older women who know how to perform a clitorectomy, there are no medical specialists or specialists of any kind among the Hadza. Every adult Hadza knows about the various medicinal plants and practices. It is usually men who keep the snake medicine with them. Any adult present may treat someone with an ailment. When anyone is injured and cannot forage for a while, the close kin usually attend to the person and bring food until he or she recovers.

Common illnesses and injuries include scabies, backache, malaria, eye infections due largely to smoke from hearths, broken bones, and wounds from accidents. There are many tsetse flies, but it seems they do not usually carry African trypanosomiasis (sleeping sickness) in Hadzaland. Hadza often scavenge meat from the kills made by lions, leopards, and hyenas, and this sometimes gets them injured by one of these predators. The scavenged (and sometimes very rotten) meat also gives them stomachaches, even after they cook it, but not often enough to keep them from eating it. Causes of death include measles, tuberculosis, malaria when young, viral diarrhea, falling from baobab trees when collecting honey, murder by another Hadza, and snakebite. Out of 75 deaths, Nicholas Blurton Jones found that 16% were attributed to measles; 15% to TB, pneumonia, or some other respiratory illness; 12% to oldness; 7% to childbirth; 7% to poisoning or bewitching; 5% to homicide; 4% when in the hospital or in a jail; 1% to falling from tree; and 33% to "other" (Jones, Hawkes, and O'Connell 2002).

The murder rate among the Hadza is roughly the same as that in the United States. The U.S. murder rate in 1997 was 5.5 for every 100,000 people. During the 30 years between 1967 and 1997, there were 2 murders of Hadza by other Hadza (that I was aware of). Since the population is 1,000, this equals 2/30,000 person-years, which equals 6.6 per 100,000. Men are slow to anger, but when they do become angry, they can quickly kill with a poisoned arrow. All murders of other Hadza that I am aware of, except one (a mentally ill woman who killed her child), were committed by men, and all were apparently disputes over women (jealousy) in some form.

GROWTH

Table 6.1 shows Hadza height, weight, body mass index (BMI), percentage of body fat, and grip strength. These anthropometric measures are almost identical to those of the biomedical survey conducted by Nigel

TABLE 6.1. HADZA ANTHROPOMETRICS

	Adult Male	Adult Female
Height	162.00 (142–179, SD = 6.83, $n = 253$)	150.48 (135–166, SD = 6.49, $n = 238$)
Weight	53.04 (37–73, SD = 6.01, $n = 252$)	46.33 (32–72, SD = 6.9, $n = 238$)
BMI	20.20 (15–26, SD = 1.7, $n = 252$)	20.4 (15–30, SD = 2.3, $n = 237$)
Percentage of Body Fat	10.6 (2–21, SD = 3.4, $n = 250$)	19.6 (3–42, SD = 7.3, $n = 232$)
Grip Strength Right	32.8 (5–51, SD = 8.0, $n = 240$)	20.4 (5–36, SD = 6.4, $n = 218$)
Grip Strength Left	33 (2–50, SD = 7.1, $n = 240$)	21.3 (4–40, SD = 6, $n = 218$)

Barnicot, James Woodburn, and others in 1966–1967 (Hiernaux and Hartono 1980). This is one indication that there has been little change during that time, at least in terms of the number of calories consumed and the energy expended foraging.

Figure 6.1 shows distance curves for stature (height) across all ages of Hadza males ($n = 377$) and females ($n = 377$). Stature peaks at age 24 years for females and 25 years for males. This is later than it peaks in populations in developed countries. In the United States, for example, height peaks at age 20. There is only a very minor adolescent growth spurt among Hadza females or males (Jones 2006). The growth spurt has long been assumed to be universal across humans but not a general primate trait. However, it is possible that this is largely an artifact of agriculture and does not characterize the human life history pattern of foragers. Hadza growth is much more similar to growth among other mammals and, in particular, to our closest relatives, chimpanzees (Jones 2006).

Figure 6.2 shows weight by age for Hadza females ($n = 383$) and males ($n = 380$). There is a little less disparity between the Hadza and

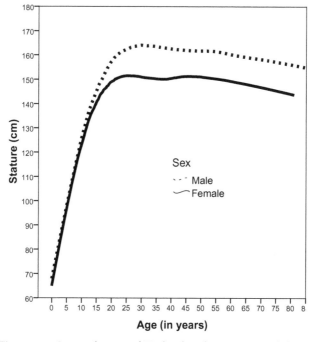

Figure 6.1. Stature by age of Hadza females ($n = 377$, solid line) and males ($n = 377$, dotted line). Fit lines are Loess Epanechnikov.

Americans in curves of weight by age because the growth spurt is not as noticeable in weight as it is in height, even in the United States. However, again the Hadza show more gradual development than Americans. Hadza continue to gain weight at least until age 30. These patterns suggest that under normal subsistence conditions faced by our preagricultural ancestors, there may have been a pattern of growth much more similar to that of other primates, with the main exception being age at maturity. The pattern in developed countries illustrates that we have a norm of reaction that allows us to take advantage of extra food calories or consumption that varies less from day to day. This, however, may have rarely resulted in the rapid catch-up growth of the adolescent growth spurt seen in the United States (Jones 2006).

The degree of height sexual dimorphism among Hadza adults is 1.08 (mean male height = 162.0 cm divided by mean female height = 150.48 cm), while the median for all foragers around the world where data exist is 1.07

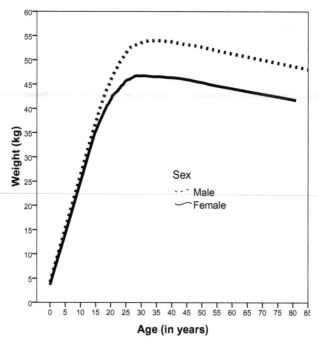

Figure 6.2. Weight by age of Hadza females ($n = 383$, solid
line) and males ($n = 380$, dotted line). Fit lines are Loess
Epanechnikov.

($n = 119$ societies). The degree of Hadza weight sexual dimorphism is 1.14
(mean male weight = 53.04 kg divided by mean female weight = 46.33 kg),
while the median for all foragers is 1.20 ($n = 32$).

The degree of sexual dimorphism across species of mammals has
been related to the degree of polygyny in the mating system (Alexander
et al. 1979, Clutton-Brock 1985, Mitani, Gros-Louis, and Richards 1996).
Where some males gain sexual access to several females and sire several
offspring, and other males fail to gain sexual access and sire no offspring,
sexual selection favors the traits that help males gain sexual access to
females. The males who are reproductively successful pass on their genes,
and the traits that benefited them in gaining sexual access spread throughout the population, but may benefit males only. When larger size is the
trait that helps males gain sexual access to females because they must
fight for access, there will be selection for larger males. But there will be
limits on male size. A larger male needs to eat more and could have difficulty getting enough to eat. The size that is optimal for acquiring suffi-

cient food to sustain oneself may be smaller than the size that is optimal for fighting, though evidence for the benefits of small size is sparse (Blanck-enhorn 2000).

The degree of variation in number of offspring produced is referred to as reproductive skew, and there is a sizable literature on the factors that affect skew (Gilchrist 2006, Kutsukake and Nunn 2006). When reproductive skew among males is greater, male-male competition to gain reproductive access to females should be intense. This often favors larger males and results in males being larger than females. Since females do not need to fight for access to mates, we should expect them to be the optimal size based on diet and energetic tradeoffs (sometimes females are called the ecological sex). One attempt to see if the same relationship between polygyny and sexual dimorphism found across species holds across human populations found that it does not (Alexander et al. 1979). Alexander et al. concluded that if the societies that impose monogamy socially are excluded, those with "ecologically imposed monogamy" are less dimorphic. In a large sample of foragers, I found that there is no relationship between polygyny and height dimorphism, but significantly greater weight dimorphism in more polygynous societies (Marlowe nd-c). Given that body mass rather than height is the measure usually used for other species, this result is consistent with the literature on other species. Height is quite strongly correlated with climatic variables. Foragers in higher latitudes (colder climates) are taller, although at the very highest altitudes arctic foragers are short (Marlowe nd-b). In addition, in populations that are taller and heavier, there is greater dimorphism. It is perhaps not so surprising then that polygyny does not predict height dimorphism. It is perhaps surprising that it does predict weight dimorphism, given that men usually do not gain access to women by fighting.

Body mass index (BMI) is weight (kg) divided by height squared $(m)^2$. BMI is a good indicator of whether an individual is underweight or overweight. Adult Hadza males and females have a mean BMI of about 20, which is close to ideal for athletes, so they are not undernourished. Figure 6.3 shows BMI by age and sex. The mean BMI for 30–39 year-old U.S. women is 26.4, while for 30–39 year-old U.S. men, it is 25.9. Given that we are experiencing an epidemic of obesity, it is more useful to compare the Hadza to what is considered an ideal U.S. BMI: 19–24.

For U.S. women, the normal range of percentage of body fat is 15–25%, and for U.S. men 10–20% (National Center for Health Statistics). Figure 6.4 shows percentage of body fat of the Hadza by age and sex. These data also show that the Hadza are not malnourished but are in quite good

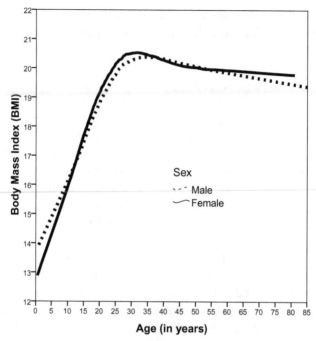

Figure 6.3. Body mass index (BMI) by age (weight in kg/height in m²) of Hadza females (*n* = 373, solid line) and males (*n* = 376, dotted line). Fit lines are Loess Epanechnikov.

shape, with men having plenty of muscle and women plenty of fat. Body fat is 20% for women and 11% for men, just about what we would expect in athletes. Of course, with all the exercise the Hadza get, they are athletes. Percentage of body fat is probably especially important for women's fertility, even though it is the fluctuation in the percentage of fat that is the best predictor of hormonal levels indicative of fecundity (Ellison 2001). Body fat also appears to be the one measure of body condition that varies the most seasonally and across individuals of the same age (Marlowe and Berbesque 2009, Sherry and Marlowe 2007). This suggests that it may be the physiological variable most worth investigating in relation to female fertility and RS.

Figure 6.5 shows Hadza grip strength by age and sex. Strength peaks about age 30 for males and age 25 for females. This is later than we expect among Americans; we consider male athletes in the most physically demanding sports to be old at 38 years of age. One noticeable difference between the Hadza and Americans is handedness. Only 2% of all Hadza

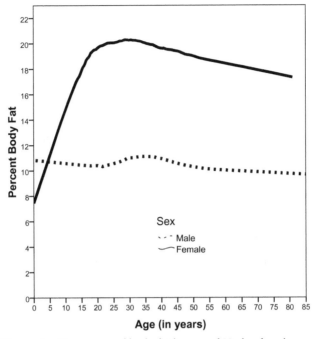

Figure 6.4. Percentage of body fat by age of Hadza females ($n = 356$, solid line) and males ($n = 334$, dotted line). Fit lines are Loess Epanechnikov.

are left-handed, compared to 10–13% of Americans. Although there is a very strong bias for right-handedness among the Hadza, they are nearly equally strong in both hands. In males, there is no significant difference between grip strength between the right and left hands. In females of all ages, the right hand is significantly stronger than the left, though this significance disappears when the sample is limited to adult females. Both men and women use their right and left hands for foraging activities that require strength. But both use their right hand to throw, except for the 2% of left-handers (throwing was the trait used to assess handedness).

Despite being in good health generally, the Hadza have a hard life, and many have had broken bones or serious wounds. This is reflected in their levels of fluctuating asymmetry (FA). FA is a measure of the deviation from perfect symmetry in bilaterally symmetrical traits. For example, our ears, eyes, arms, and legs are bilaterally symmetrical because, in the absence of some environmental insult, our genes build them to be symmetrical, with a population mean equal to zero because some

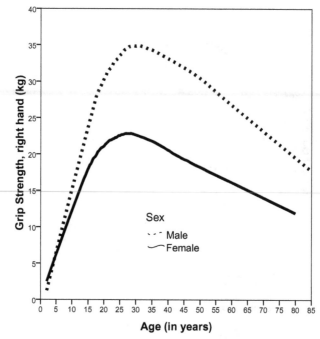

Figure 6.5. Grip strength of right hand by age of Hadza
females (*n* = 329, solid line) and males (*n* = 338, dotted line).
Fit lines are Loess Epanechnikov.

individuals have a larger left and others a larger right. If an organism is
asymmetrical in bilateral structures, it must be due either to a genetic defect or environmental stressors preventing the genes from carrying out
the default program. Though there is considerable debate regarding its
importance, FA is generally assumed to reflect the degree of environmental stress experienced by organisms, as well as their ability to withstand
such stress when the degree of stress is controlled (Moller 2006, Pertoldi
et al. 2006).

After measuring 10 body traits using the same methods used by previous researchers (Gangestad and Thornhill 1999, Manning 1995), we
found that Hadza FA is significantly greater than FA in a U.S. sample
(Gray and Marlowe 2002). The Hadza sleep on the ground on an impala skin with only a thin shawl to keep off the cold. While foraging,
women use digging sticks in hard ground to access tubers, and men use
axes to chop into trees to get honey, and both of these activities are jar-
ring to the body. While FA may serve as a marker of genetic quality, it

appears to increase with environmental stress. Of course, so long as most individuals within one society are exposed to similar environmental conditions, those who can withstand them better should be more symmetrical.

We found that FA increases with age among the Hadza, which is what we would expect since the effects of environmental insults accumulate through time. Older females had significantly higher FA. FA increased with age in males, but not significantly (Gray and Marlowe 2002).

FERTILITY

Total fertility rate (TFR) is the number of children born to women during their lifetime. The Hadza have a mean TFR of 6.2 (Jones et al. 1992). Fertility should depend on age, copulation frequency, ability to conceive, sexually transmitted disease-related infertility, and energetic status (Ellison 2001, Wood 1994). Given a TFR of 6.2, the energetic status of the Hadza appears to be good (the median for all warm-climate foragers is 5.4; see Chapter 10). Sexually transmitted diseases (STDs) and subsequent sterility are not as common in the Hadza as they are in some other foragers such as the Efe Pygmies of the Congo and the !Kung of Botswana, who have more sexual contact with their agricultural neighbors (Pennington 2001, Pennington and Harpending 1988).

Much research has emphasized how pair-bonds may have played a key role in lowering offspring mortality for humans. While this may be true, in a sample of foraging societies where demographic data exist, I found that the amount of male contribution to diet, controlled for habitat productivity, was unrelated to mortality rates. Greater male contribution to diet did, however, predict higher TFR (Marlowe 2001). Of course, the TFR is an absolute number, while mortality rate is a percentage of those born who died. This means that as TFR increases, the mortality rate can increase even though a larger absolute number of children survives. Thus, female reproductive success (measured as number of children who survive to age 15) can increase even as the mortality rate also increases. Rather than lowering the percentage of children who die, a husband's help must primarily raise the number of children born. It thus appears that the main way women benefit from forming pair-bonds is by speeding up their rate of reproduction while holding the mortality rate (the percentage that die) about constant. In the most comprehensive data set on forager demography (see Chapter 10), TFR is the best predictor of female reproductive success (Marlowe 2001).

MORTALITY

Even though the Hadza are sometimes spared epidemics that hit their neighbors, they have appreciable infant and juvenile mortality rates. Infant mortality is the percentage of infants who die in the first year of life. For the Hadza, this is 21%. Juvenile mortality is the percentage of children who die by age 15, which among the Hadza is 46% (Jones, Hawkes, and O'Connell 2002, Jones et al. 1992). While to Americans this sounds very high, Hadza infant and juvenile mortality rates are just equal to the median values for all foragers (see Chapter 10).

We do not really know what kills so many infants in the first year. It appears to be mostly respiratory and diarrheal infections and, at a later age, measles, but we cannot yet be more specific than that. Clearly, malaria takes a toll on the very young. It seems that it would be difficult for parents to do anything that might save an infant from these diseases. The mortality rate in the first few years is not so different from the rate at which chimpanzees die (Hill et al. 2001). However, the mortality rate for the Hadza (and other foragers) drops below that of chimpanzees after age 5, so that human foragers survive at noticeably higher rates (Figure 6.6; see also Chapter 10). Still, by the standards of industrialized nations, the rate remains very high throughout life. Because most Hadza adults have experienced a child dying, they take it rather well by our standards. The mother cries the day she loses a baby and grieves for some time afterward. Fathers may not cry but clearly grieve and console the mother. However, both soon get on with life and usually have another child within a year or two.

Because the main killer of infants may be diseases that are difficult for mobile foragers with no medical care to avoid, it may be that Hadza women, and women in other warm-climate foraging societies, would experience similar rates of infant mortality with or without husbands. We should expect a mother to invest as much effort as it pays her in final lifetime RS to keep the child alive. Therefore, the main effect of husbands helping might be in getting the children who do not die weaned earlier. This should shorten birth intervals and raise fertility. On the other hand, if keeping infants alive is such a burden for mothers that they are in worse condition, it might be that their condition could impact the survivorship prospects for the infant, in which case a father's help could possibly indirectly lower infant mortality rates. So far, however, we have found no clear evidence that father presence or absence affects child mortality among the Hadza (Jones et al. 2000).

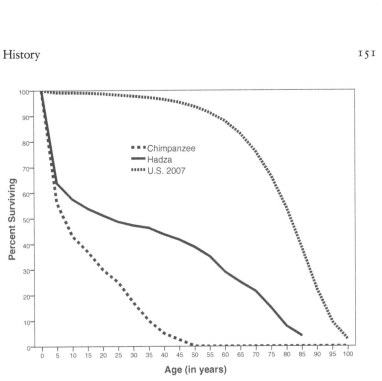

Figure 6.6. Survivorship by age of chimpanzees (dashed line) (from Hill et al. 2001); Hadza (solid line) (from Jones et al. 2002); and United States (dotted line) (from U.S. Census Bureau 2007). Fit lines are Loess Epanechnikov.

REPRODUCTION

The average age of menarche in Hadza girls is about 16.5. This was esti-mated by asking older girls and younger women if they have begun menstruating. Menarche is probably followed by a year or two of sub-fecundity, during which time women are not very likely to conceive even if they are already having regular sex, though there are exceptions, and some can have their first child at 16 years of age.

Median age at first marriage is about 17 years for Hadza females, compared to 25 years in the United States, and median age at first birth is 19 years compared to 24.2 in the United States in 1997 (CDC 2000). American women have a younger age at first reproduction than at first marriage, but this is mainly because those women who are more likely to give birth marry at younger ages. Usually, Hadza women get married before giving birth, but often they marry after giving birth, and there is only a very slight stigma, if any, attached to having a baby without be-ing married. Median age at marriage for males is about 20 years, com-pared to a median of 27 years in the United States (U.S. Census 2004).

In countries like the United States, it is as though we have greatly extended the juvenile period if we define it as ending when marriage occurs. If we define the end of juvenility as when sex first occurs, there is probably much less difference. If we defined maturity as age at reproductive capacity, the juvenile period is shorter in the United States. For the Hadza, reproductive capacity, marriage, and first reproduction are all closely connected—the product of selection on human life history. The U.S. pattern is the product of recent ecological and cultural changes. In India, reproductive capacity, marriage, and first reproduction are still tightly connected, and all occur much earlier than among the Hadza—about 13–14 years of age among less-educated women (Bagga and Kulkarni 2000, Bhadra, Mukhopadhyay, and Bose 2005).

Primary sterility is rare among the Hadza, with only 7 women known to have reached the age of 27 without giving birth (Jones, Hawkes, and O'Connell 2005b). Since this is out of roughly 500 females, 45% of whom (225 women) would be 27 years and older, the rate of sterility is about 3%. For comparison, the rate for the !Kung was 14% (Howell 1979). This suggests that STDs are not so common, or else that the medicine the Hadza use for syphilis and gonorrhea actually works and prevents infertility.

There is no evidence that infanticide is commonly practiced. The Hadza say that a baby might be killed only in the case of severe deformity. Even when twins are born, the Hadza do not kill or neglect one, though the probability that one will die is higher, since it is difficult to rear two at the same time. From a preliminary analysis, the mean interbirth interval of all closed intervals, whether the child lives or dies, is 3.4 years.

Median age at menopause was estimated by one preliminary study among the Hadza to be 43.4 years of age ($n = 68$), but one woman who was 45.9 years old appeared to be pre-menopausal (Phillips et al. 1991). I have estimated the age of some women to be 48 or 49 years when they had their last baby. Menopause is experienced very differently among the Hadza than it is in our society. Most women do not know when they reach menopause because they are nursing a child when it occurs and because they menstruate much less often than women in the United States. When asked if they have reached menopause, they may simply shrug and say, "We have to wait and see," meaning they will know only if they do or do not resume regular menstruation or get pregnant again after weaning the current child. Hadza women may experience fewer side effects of menopause, such as hot flashes, since no such symptoms have been reported. Nursing during this time may counteract the effects of hormonal changes at menopause.

FORAGING SKILLS

Maturity in humans happens quite late, 17–18 years among foragers, compared to 12–13 years in chimpanzees and, coincidentally, in girls in developed countries. Some have argued that maturity is delayed in humans to allow time for juveniles or adolescents to learn and practice their foraging skills as well as to learn many other things ranging from child care to the ways of negotiating adult status and competition (Bogin 1999, Kaplan et al. 2000). Kaplan et al. (2000) developed a comprehensive view that several human life history traits derive from the fact that our ancestors exploited a diet that required extraction and considerable skills, with the payoff being high-quality (nutritious) foods. This, they suggest, is responsible for our longevity, our large brains, and our late age at maturity. The adolescent growth spurt is seen as catch-up growth to hasten maturity after the period of learning is over (Bogin 1999, Walker et al. 2006).

As noted, Nicholas Blurton Jones and I conducted experiments we called "the Forager Olympics" to measure Hadza foraging skills across ages in both sexes. We were interested in seeing what predicts skill level. Figure 6.7 shows how many kilograms of tubers Hadza could dig per hour, once they found a patch to dig in. There is no significant difference between the rates of males and females (Jones and Marlowe 2002). While males learn to dig when they are young and go foraging with their mothers, they do little digging after they are 6 or 7 years old. Still, they are able to dig as effectively as females. Since females have much more experience at this than males, the time spent practicing and learning how to find tubers does not appear to be so crucial that it takes 18 years to master. We also found that lost experience due to time in boarding school for some young Hadza did not lead to a deficit in skills, probably because size and strength are more important (Jones and Marlowe 2002). There was no support in the Hadza data for the hypothesis that maturity is delayed to master these foraging skills. As noted, Hadza growth shows little difference from a general mammalian pattern and that of chimpanzees, except that it continues for longer (Jones 2006). The age at maturity among the Hadza is what is expected for a species with our adult life span, based on Charnov's life history invariants (Charnov 1993). Of course, some of that adult life span is post-reproductive for females, a topic to which I return below.

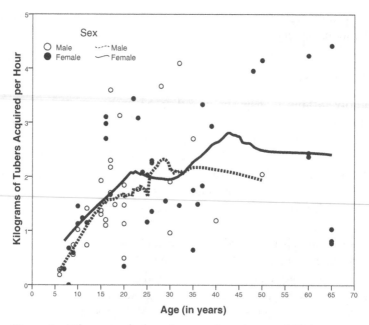

Figure 6.7. Kilograms of tubers dug per minute by age of Hadza females ($n=38$, solid line) and males ($n=30$, dotted line). Fit lines are Loess Epanechnikov.

Figure 6.8 shows the archery scores for men by age. Notice that some men are almost as good in their 20s as others at any age, though there is a slight peak around 35–40 years of age and only slight decreases from then on. Compare how different this looks from the actual amount of meat coming into camp by age of man in Figure 6.9. The difference between archery skill and hunting returns suggests that more than targeting skill alone is involved in successful hunting. Hunting probably takes considerable learning of animal behavior (McDowell 1984) and experience reading spoor, footprints, blood trails, and the wind (to stay downwind), and stealth. Good hunting probably also depends on good eyesight, hearing, strength, stamina, coordination, reaction time, and persistence. The problem with the life history scenario of Kaplan et al. (2000) is that the difficulty of hunting and the importance of male provisioning are used as arguments for delayed maturity even in females. While male foraging and female age at maturity may be linked in some way, Kaplan et al. do not address why the late peak of male foraging success results in a late age at first birth in females.

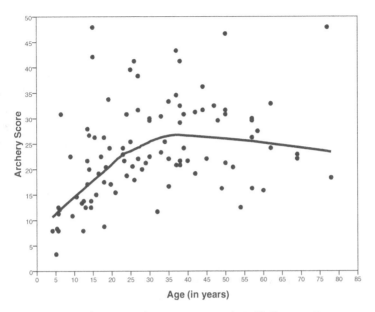

Figure 6.8. Archery score by age ($n = 98$ males). Fit lines are Loess Epanechnikov.

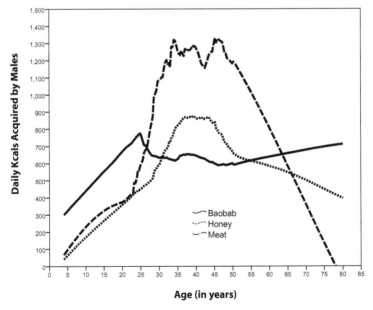

Figure 6.9. Male's food into camp by age for three main foods ($n = 144$). Fit lines are Loess Epanechnikov.

THE LIFE COURSE

Infancy and Weaning

Infants are carried on their mothers' backs in a skin, or these days in a piece of cloth, at almost all times during the first 6 months of life, and they nurse on demand. Occasionally, the mother may put her weanling on the ground to sleep or to play. At about 1 year of age, children begin walking. They are still carried on their mothers' backs much of the time, but more and more they are beginning to play with other, mostly older children.

From scan data on the frequency of nursing, I calculated the median age of weaning to be 2.5 years (1–3 years, $n=33$). A few children nurse till they are 3 years old, but most nurse at low frequency by age 2 (Marlowe 2005b). By the age of 2, most children are occasionally being left in camp when their mothers go foraging. This is a time of great unhappiness for the child, who usually cries in protest as its mother is leaving. Mothers may continue to nurse the children when they return to camp, but finally the nursing tapers off as the child is being more frequently left in camp. A small number of children still protest loudly even at the age of 3 when their mothers refuse to nurse them.

Children are given foods to eat well before they are weaned; some of these foods are chewed by the mother first. Even before a child is 1 year old, it is sometimes given meat, such as a leg of a dik-dik or a rib of a large animal, and the child sucks on the meat even though it cannot yet bite or chew. Children are also given tubers to suck on at this age. However, as noted in Chapter 5 the most important weaning food is baobab paste.

Juveniles and Adolescents

By age 4 or 5 years, children spend most of their time in mixed-sex playgroups in camp or just outside. They are already getting much of their own food. After watching 3–4 year-olds playing a while, one eventually realizes that the children are not just playing but are actually digging small tubers and eating them. They often do this for an hour or two right in camp. Foraging simply emerges gradually from playing and involves very little teaching. It involves a natural interest on the part of the young child watching older people forage and imitating them.

Girls 4–8 years old bring in 361 daily kcals, which is about 25% of their requirements. Boys at the same age bring in only 277 daily kcals.

Figure 6.10. Target practice by boys in camp.

Most of what they acquire they eat while out foraging. Both sexes probably eat more out of camp than they take back to camp. That means they
are probably acquiring at least 600–700 kcals per day, which is about half
of what they need, by the time they are 8 years old, at least during certain
times of the year. During berry season, they might be getting 80–90% of
their own food.

Girls 8 years old and up usually go with their mothers on foraging
forays, while boys usually stop going with their mothers once they are 6
or 7 years old and begin going foraging with other young boys. By age
8–10, both sexes look after their younger siblings, though girls do more
of this (Crittenden and Marlowe 2008). These girls also begin taking
food back to camp to share with others.

Boys get their first bows by about 3 years old and thereafter spend
hours every day in target practice, often shooting at a gourd on the ground
(Figure 6.10). By 5 or 6 years of age, boys are good enough to kill birds
and small rodents. It is through repeated practice and observation of
older boys that they hone their skills. Boys almost never go hunting with
their fathers, at least until they are grown (and even then it is rare). By the
time boys are 8 or 9 years old, they go hunting for small animals, usually
in twos. By 13 or 14 years of age, they usually go hunting by themselves,
killing hyraxes, bush babies, dik-diks, and birds of all kinds. They may be

gone nearly all day, longer than any other age-sex class. For example, males age 10–17 are gone an average of 7.3 hours a day. Most of what they acquire they eat while out foraging.

We tend to think of people being able to feed themselves when they reach adulthood, and it is true that by age 18 years males and females acquire and bring back to camp as many daily kcals as they need to sustain themselves (see Figure 5.11). However, no one ever really stops getting food from others among the Hadza. Parents are still giving food to their children into their 50s, and also receiving food from their children. Older women still go foraging every day and bring in as much food as younger women. These older women even spend slightly more time foraging than younger women with dependent offspring. Still, it is noteworthy that the average kcals acquired at age 18 equals the amount required by an 18-year-old person. This means that food-sharing among adults could be a win-win proposition because the average adult is capable of pulling his or her own weight.

When females in countries like the United States, where menarche occurs much earlier than among foragers, give birth as soon as they are capable (~14 years), they are much less mature psychologically than Hadza women who give birth as soon as they are capable (19 years). However, this is mainly because American girls are not treated as adults until they are 18 years old, even though many could give birth at 13–14 years of age. In countries like India, it is very common for an uneducated girl of 14 to have a baby, and she is much more mature psychologically, partly because it is considered normal to have children that young. In the United States, the period of sub-fecundity after menarche usually lasts till about 18 years of age, and the regularity of ovulation peaks even later (23 years) (Wood 1994). Among the Hadza, sub-fecundity appears to last only until about age 18, since mean age at first birth is 19 years, but it appears that women age 30–45 years may actually have a higher chance of conceiving (Phillips et al. 1991). In the United States, fecundity peaks at 25 years of age and begins to drop by age 30.

Adulthood

Being in a natural fertility population with frequent births, nursing, and strenuous exercise and mere subsistence-level intake of calories, Hadza women do not cycle frequently. They probably have less than one-quarter of the number of menses of American women, perhaps 80–100 in a lifetime compared to 400 for Americans. The much more frequent cycles and much less time spent nursing may have detrimental effects on American women, given the apparent association between frequent hormonal cycles and higher levels of uterine cancer, and the association of lower levels of lactation with more breast cancer (Eaton et al. 1994). A Hadza man, whose wife is so much more often pregnant or lactating and unable to cuckold him at those times, should need to guard his mate less than an American man. However, there is notable variation in the period of lactational anovulation among Hadza women. Most have inter-birth intervals of 3 to 4 years, while some have intervals as short as 1 year.

The much lower amount of time spent cycling among foragers like the Hadza casts doubt on the popular idea of menstrual synchrony as an adaptation in humans (McClintock 1998). If we assume that Hadza women are cycling from age 17 to 45, they must have a reproductive career of about 28 years. The mean age of 19 at first birth and the mean age of 43 at last birth yields 24 years of reproducing on average. During those years, Hadza women manage to give birth 6.2 times on average. They nurse 2.5 years on average with each child that survives that long. They are likely pregnant overall for 56 months. We can subtract 56 months from the 288 months (24 years) of reproductive career, which leaves 232 months. If we assume that lactational amenorrhea lasts about 2 years and occurs 5.5 times (this assumes that 20% of the 6.2 offspring die in the first year), then 11 years or 132 months can be subtracted from the 232 months above, leaving 100 months. This means that women are cycling 34% of the time. Given that the median Hadza camp has 21 people, with 7 adult women per camp, there will be 5.3 women of the right age to be cycling. Multiplying 5.3 women times 0.34 (the percentage of time cycling) yields 1.8 women who might be cycling at any given time. This means that there are usually fewer than 2 women who would even have the chance to synchronize their cycles. Menstrual synchrony would have little opportunity to occur and virtually no chance to serve any adaptive function (Foley 1996, Strassman 1997).

The Hadza have no menstrual huts where women are expected to go when menstruating. I have never seen a woman bleeding, so they are able to conceal the blood with whatever material (nowadays, mostly the pieces of cloth I give them). In the not too distant past, they would have had only animal skins to use. Hadza women say they tend to bleed only for about 3 days rather than the 5 days typical in the United States. In addition, their bleeding is apparently less copious than is typical for American women, according to my female research assistants.

Figure 6.11. A married couple in their 80s relaxes in camp.

The Aged

Hadza life expectancy at birth is 32.5 years (Jones, Hawkes, and O'Connell 2002). People commonly misinterpret this to mean that there are no old people. In fact, it only means that many people die very early. There are plenty of Hadza in their 70s and some in their 80s, such as the couple in Figure 6.11. The low life expectancy at birth is due to high mortality in the first few years of life. A person who survives to adulthood is likely to live a long life. Women who reach age 45 have another 21.3 years of mean life expectancy (Jones, Hawkes, and O'Connell 2002).

Men do not live quite as long as women. Old men are the most likely to fall out of tall baobab trees to their deaths, since they continue to try to collect honey into old age. They usually continue to forage until they die, but get foods that are easier to acquire, such as berries and baobab, and often just enough to feed themselves. Old men are shown extra respect until they reach the age of perhaps 70, when their status begins to drop a bit. They sometimes keep watch over children in camp when they are not out foraging and when other adults and older children are all gone from camp.

Most elderly women are single. This is because their husbands have either died or left them for younger women. Out of 71 women 55 years old and up, 63% were single. These women usually live in the same camp as one or more of their daughters and help tend their grandchildren. They certainly do not feel useless or unneeded. They are an integral part of the camp and family life, but many do express some bitterness over the fact that men leave them once they get too old.

MENOPAUSE AND HUMAN LIFE HISTORY

As noted, Hadza women who make it to age 45 can expect to live to age 66 (Jones, Hawkes, and O'Connell 2002). Many women live well beyond that, at least into their 80s. Most Hadza women, therefore, live 20 or more years beyond their ability to reproduce. A woman gives birth to her last child in her 40s. The median age at menopause was estimated from hormonal analysis (urinary LH) to be 43.4 years (Phillips et al. 1991). This compares to a median age of 49.6 for European women (Brand and Lehert 1978, cited in Phillips et al. 1991). Thus, menopause probably occurs earlier than it does among Europeans. Because menarche is later and menopause is earlier, the total reproductive span is shorter for the Hadza than Americans (26 years vs. 30–35 years). This is likely due to the effect of less energy coming in from food and more energy being expended in acquiring food. Women remain hardy well into their 70s; they bring in more daily calories of food than any other age-sex category. Hardworking Hadza grandmothers have received attention, especially in connection with the evolution of long life spans (Jones, Hawkes, and O'Connell 2002, Hawkes, O'Connell, and Jones 1997).

Menopause is certainly no artifact of modern life (Jones, Hawkes, and O'Connell 2002, Hawkes et al. 1998, Marlowe 2000b). Menopause is rare in animals but has been documented in the short-finned pilot whale (*Globicephala macrorhynchus*) (Marsh and Kasuya 1986) and the killer whale (*Orcinus orca*) (Foote 2008). Menopause is a very special human trait and an evolutionary puzzle. It is not clear how selection would favor any trait that decreases one's chance to reproduce, much less make it impossible. Senescence is partly the result of pleiotropy (genes having more than one effect). Genes that have beneficial effects early on but deleterious effects later on are not selected against if the probability of reproduction drops by the time the deleterious effects occur (Hamilton 1966, Williams 1957).

The first adaptive explanation of menopause offered was that ancestral females gained more reproductive success by turning off reproduction early to avoid dying in childbirth, the better to survive and rear remaining children (Williams 1957). Alternatively, it might have been that selection favored increased longevity so that women simply outlived their supply of oocytes. In that case, there was no selection for turning off reproduction, only for outliving the reproductive career, and this argument has been made for similar reasons: that females were able to increase their RS by helping rear grandchildren, by provisioning them the way elderly Hadza grandmothers do, which is called the grandmother hypothesis (Hawkes et al. 1998). Elderly Hadza women (age 40–70) do bring more daily kcals back to camp than any other age category (see Figure 5.11).

Because a Hadza grandmother is so productive as a forager, and because she tends to reside in the same camp as her daughter, she is a reliable and important source of help for a woman who is raising a young child. With the Hadza as an example, the grandmother hypothesis is not only plausible but compelling. On the other hand, grandmothers cannot always live with all their daughters. The importance of this was not lost on Jones et al. (2005b), who found fewer than expected positive effects on offspring survivorship when maternal grandmother was coresident. This was likely the result of the grandmother going to live with the daughter who most needed help, which makes the most sense from the grandmother's perspective, but her help just brings up the survivorship of that needy daughter's offspring to equal that of the less needy, erasing the difference in offspring survivorship of the two daughters.

In some foraging societies, elderly women are not reported to be such productive foragers as they are among the Hadza (Hill and Hurtado 1996). But if we accept the grandmother hypothesis, we must explain why men live so long as well. Because men can continue to reproduce, male longevity is not the puzzle that female longevity is. It is, therefore, easier to model how greater male longevity could have been selected for. It is interesting that in virtually all human societies, older men have higher status than they would if status were based on physical strength. Longevity could have been selected for in males with the greatest access to mates who garnered the largest share of progeny and who could continue to add to their reproductive success even into old age if their status did not decline in synch with their physical strength (Marlowe 2000b).

Hadza men who have reputations as good hunters are more likely than other men to remarry after one wife reaches menopause. In this way, they can double their reproductive output if they can acquire a young enough wife. To explore alternative ideas about the evolution of menopause, I proposed that selection favored greater longevity in males once status was no longer so closely tied to physical strength and vigor (Marlowe 2000b). If longevity-promoting genes were not on the Y-chromosome, women would inherit these genes and live longer as well. Because women's oocytes are still depleted, extra life span results in menopause as a by-product of selection for greater male longevity. Because oocytes experience a geometric decrease through atresia, it may be difficult for selection to favor an increase in number of oocytes because ovaries would have to be much, much larger just to add a few years to the reproductive span.

Selection for greater longevity must be accompanied by lower mortality rates; selection would not favor slower senescence when the probability of mortality is high across the whole life span. Humans not only outlive chimpanzees, but they also have less chance of dying at each age (with the exception of the first few years). We could also posit several factors that may have reduced mortality rates. Medicine does not appear to be a factor, since the Hadza have limited access to medicine (Jones, Hawkes, and O'Connell 2002). Perhaps it was with greater foraging productivity, due to more efficient tool use, that our ancestors could better afford to provision others, who could then serve as alloparents. Food-sharing on a regular basis would buffer each individual in terms of daily caloric intake and perhaps reduce mortality risk.

There is nothing special about human life history in the earliest years. In juvenile mortality, there does appear to be something special going on. Whether it is related to pair-bonds or just to the generalized food-sharing and lack of predation is less clear. What is clear is that, compared to a population like that of the United States, mortality does strike at all ages among the Hadza. The most significant thing that has happened to humans in rich industrialized societies like the United States is that we have basically eliminated mortality as a factor in natural selection because nearly all mortality occurs well after the age of reproduction (Figure 6.6).

While the overall sex ratio among the Hadza is very close to even (0.97), there are more males during the early years and more females at older ages; consequently, there are more adult females than males. If we count everyone over age 16, there are 322 females and 297 males, a female-biased sex ratio of 0.92, which means there should be slight polygyny since any male should be willing to take on a second wife when there is a surplus of women. If we count only those women who may be fertile (age 16–49) and men in the age range that brackets most male reproduction, the sex ratio is 273 men / 239 women or 1.14. This slightly male-biased

OSR means that monogamy is more likely than it would be if women continued to reproduce until they died. As the number of women falls below the number of men, we can expect male-male competition to increase because each man should be quite eager to get at least one wife, which should result in more monogamy. Menopause, therefore, makes monogamy more likely than it is in other species with similar overall sex ratios.

CHAPTER 7

Mating

SEXUAL SELECTION

Natural selection is the process that determines which genes are passed
on to the next generation, a process that entails survival and reproduction. Sexual selection is the more narrow process that determines access
to mates and reproductive success. Sexual selection consists of intrasexual selection (often called male-male competition) and inter-sexual
selection (often called female choice) (Andersson 1994, Darwin 1871).
Female-female competition and male choice are less common but do
exist, especially in pair-bonded species like humans.

Male-male competition for access to mates is very common in animals. Males in many species have evolved morphological traits such as
antlers for the purpose of fighting, and females in those species often accept a mating with the winner of a contest. As noted in Chapter 6, males
of such species are often larger than females because their larger size
gives them an advantage in fights with other males. Larger males and
better fighters often end up with greater access to mates, so sexual selection favors these traits.

In many species, males are brightly colored and ornamented; peacocks, with their long, colorful tails, are the classic example. Such traits
are not useful in fighting other males but have evolved because they attract the attention of females, which results in greater mating success for
these males. In these species, females themselves are often drab to avoid

detection by predators. Thus, the other form of sexual selection, female choice, explains why males are so often more brightly colored than females. In most monogamous pair-bonded species, however, males and females are often the same size and color, and it is often difficult to tell them apart: e.g., Whooper swans (*Cygnus cygnus*).

A mutation could result in a female preference for a random male trait. Once there is even one female with a preference while other females have none, the males with the preferred trait will have an advantage over other males. This advantage will result in greater RS for those males, and they will pass on the trait to sons and the preference to daughters. Thus, the trait and preference should coevolve until they spread throughout the population via runaway sexual selection (Fisher 1930). Alternatively, a preference may evolve in females for another reason: Selection may favor females who accurately assess male quality in some way. For example, a cock's wattle that is brighter red indicates a lower pathogen load and perhaps a better immune system (Hamilton and Zuk 1982). Hens presumably prefer brighter colors because offspring sired by such cocks will have a better chance of survival (Johnson et al. 1993). Thus, female choice may be based on choosing "good genes" rather than following a random fad. There is a growing consensus that preferences (both male and female) usually fall into this category rather than being whimsical runaway selection (Andersson 1994, Kokko et al. 2002).

MATING OR BREEDING SYSTEMS

Mating (or breeding) systems are a consequence of sexual selection on females and males. Many different mating tactics may occur within one species and one population, so the term *system* does not imply uniformity (Reynolds 1996). Nonetheless, we can easily see the difference between the pair-bonded human mating system and the promiscuity of chimpanzees. Competition for mates influences mating systems, and this competition is influenced by several factors, such as the potential for mate-guarding in relation to ranging and grouping patterns (Emlen and Oring 1977) and the level of parental investment (Trivers 1972).

Competition for mates begins with the differences in gametes. Females are the sex with larger gametes. Eggs are costly to produce and contain energy to nourish the zygote. Males are the sex with smaller gametes. Sperm are small and plentiful because each one is cheap to produce. This means males of most species tend to be eager to mate with any female, while females are more choosy (Bateman 1948). This typical pattern may be overridden when males invest heavily in offspring; in which case they too become more choosy (Trivers 1972).

Even when males invest heavily, however, the number of offspring they can produce is determined mainly by the number of mates they have access to, which is not true of females. We can say males have a higher potential reproductive rate (PRR) (Clutton-Brock and Parker 1992). In mammals, females invest heavily in gestation and lactation, which limits their PRR, and thus it pays them to be more discriminating when choosing a mate.

Other forces affecting competition for mates include the operational sex ratio (OSR). When there are relatively few females, male-male competition should increase. Of course, it is potentially fecund females that count; since mammalian females gestate and then nurse for a considerable period of time, there are almost always fewer potentially fertilizable females than potentially reproductive males. This means the OSR actually almost always favors greater male-male competition than female-female competition, all else being equal (Mitani, Gros-Louis, and Richards 1996).

If females insist on forming pair-bonds before mating, this can affect male-male competition. We must distinguish between the effective mating system and the social mating system. The effective mating system refers to the actual parentage of offspring, which in animals with internal fertilization we can only know by conducting DNA paternity tests. When there is greater variance in male RS than female RS, this equals effective polygyny. This may occur even when males and females are seemingly monogamously paired (the social mating system). In humans, even if we find that men and women are monogamously married and there are few extra-pair conceptions, if men can remarry later in life while women do not, then some men may continue to produce more offspring in a second or third marriage than other men and may thereby cause the variance in RS among men to be greater than among women. Hadza males have greater variance in both births and living children than do females, at least in terms of putative children (Table 7.1). This is mainly through remarriage, not through simultaneous polygynous marriages.

Pair-bonds do not have to be monogamous. A male may have a harem of several mates and therefore be mated polygynously, while the females may be bonded only to him, so those females are mated monandrously. When females need access to resources controlled by males,

TABLE 7.1. ADULT MALE AND FEMALE FERTILITY AND NUMBER OF LIVING CHILDREN

Statistic	Females (n=93)		Males (n=95)	
	Children Born	Children Living	Children Born	Children Living
Mean	4.58	3.05	4.55	3.18
Variance	7.70	4.20	14.31	7.98
SD	2.78	2.05	3.78	2.83
Minimum–maximum	0–12	0–9	0–16	0–12

NOTE: Note the greater variance in both number of children born and living among men.

they may do better to become a second mate of a male with more resources than the only mate of a resource-poor male. The point at which
female fitness is equal between the two options is called the polygyny
threshold (Orians 1969). At that point, the female has access to equal
amounts of resources sharing a richer male with another female or being
the sole mate of the poorer male. In some human societies with wealth,
such as many pastoralist societies in which men have very different numbers of cows or among farmers with different amounts of land, marriage
may often fit the polygyny threshold model (Borgerhoff Mulder 1988b,
Marlowe 2000a). Among foragers like the Hadza without wealth and
property or without much defense of resources, the polygyny threshold
model is surely less applicable, though male provisioning could mean
that it is not completely irrelevant (Marlowe 2003b).

GROWING UP AND COURTING

Hadza girls and boys begin "playing house" literally, building little grass
huts, around the age of 7 or 8. There is some sex play when they enter the
huts. Sometimes sex play among children occurs in full view of everyone;
sometimes it is between two children of the same sex. Once, several Hadza
and I watched two girls about 8 years old hugging and rolling around on
the ground, clearly enjoying themselves in a sexual way. With increasing
age, this sex play disappears; at least, it disappears from view.

When I have asked the Hadza if homosexuality exists among them,
I have always been met with a puzzled look and invariably the answer
"no." They say that with the exception of little children experimenting,

like the two girls I just described, no one is homosexual. Still, perhaps homosexuality exists without others knowing about it. Even if the percentage of exclusive homosexuals were the same as in the United States (2–3%) (Michael et al. 1994), there might be little chance for one homosexual Hadza to find another. Perhaps a Hadza would experience ridicule if he or she was discovered to be a homosexual, but I have no reason to think so. In fact, given how much individual freedom each Hadza has, it seems that the lack of adult homosexuals cannot be due to social disapproval. In this regard, it is interesting that no man over 45 years of age is without at least one child born, which means that no men are completely excluded from access to wives.

Around the time females reach menarche or a little before, they undergo the puberty ritual *mai-to-ko*. Soon after, they get a lot of attention from males. One may see teenage boys or young men taunting girls 16–18 years old, and these taunts can turn into wrestling bouts which bespeak sexual interest just the way they do on our playgrounds in elementary or junior high school, albeit at a younger age in the United States, where physical maturity occurs earlier. The young women seem to enjoy the attention and often end up courting two or three young men at once. The men may get so jealous that they threaten to kill their rivals, and sometimes do. Everyone in camp is concerned and impacted because they are related to the woman or the men. Twice I have witnessed this concern lead to meetings among all adults to tell the young woman that she needed to choose between her suitors before someone got killed. Once I was in a camp when a man did try to kill a rival competing for an 18-year-old single woman. It caused the camp to split into two different camps, mainly based on kinship with one of the two men.

After girls reach menarche and when boys are 17 or 18 years old, they begin to have sex. A go-between often facilitates this. For example, the boy's sister may tell her friend that her brother likes her, or perhaps the girl sends a message to the boy. Either way, when the word comes back that their interest is reciprocated, the young lovers sneak off at night. The boy may sneak over to the girls' hut, where the young single girls sleep together, or the couple sneaks just out of camp to begin their affair. Although the premarital sex is discreet, it may not be such a well-kept secret. Perhaps most people know what is going on from the gossip, but there is no public acknowledgement that they are together until the woman builds a house and the couple begins to live together. The Hadza are pretty good at keeping secrets when it comes to premarital affairs and even better when it comes to extramarital affairs.

FEMALE CHOICE AND MARRIAGE

In 1911, Obst observed: "What I could find out about the Wakindiga's [Hadza's] family life suggests that they treat each other more cordially than the surrounding Bantu families do. No father would sell his daughter to somebody if the girl does not love the man or had not made arrangements with him" (Obst 1912:24). This is still true today. Female choice appears to be the main factor influencing Hadza marriage.

While marriage is not arranged, parental approval is valued about the same as it is among Americans, and the new couple usually goes together to tell the parents and listen to what they have to say. Since the parents really have little control, the couple can get married regardless, but they do feel that it is better when parents of both spouses approve, and they usually do approve. Only in rare cases do parents of one of the spouses protest vigorously and try to convince their son or daughter not to marry. This happened in one case when a man who lived in a village and was deemed to be a drunk by the parents was coming to live in the camp where the daughter lived with her parents. In another case, the parents tried to prevent a marriage when the young woman was deemed by the man's mother to be too promiscuous. In both cases, the parental objections were ultimately ignored by the couples. In both cases, however, the couples did not stay together very long. The parents, it turns out, had valid objections. When women get married a second or third time, they are a little older, and there is even less than the minimal influence from parents that may occur in a first marriage.

Occasionally parents try to influence things in the opposite direction. Once, a well-respected old man expressed strong sentiment to his daughter and her husband that they should stay together and not divorce. This was after his son-in-law had been pursuing another woman and had tried to kill a rival male competing for the same unmarried young woman. Very firmly, he told his son-in-law to be a good, faithful husband to his daughter. The pressure worked for a while, but eventually the couple divorced.

There is no exchange of gifts between couples upon marrying, even when it is the woman's first marriage, though in the past it may have been a bit more common for a man to give a few arrows to his father-in-law (Woodburn 1964). A man is expected to provide meat to his mother-in-law if he wants to keep her happy, and it is important for a man to keep his mother-in-law happy. If she thinks he is not bringing in enough meat, she may advise her daughter to look for someone else. This suggests that Hadza women think that male provisioning is important. There is an oral tradition of Hadza men telling stories, and the pressure men feel from their mothers-in-law shows up in the stories they tell. For example, the stories sometimes feature a mother-in-law who transforms into a monstrous beast, chases her son-in-law, and bites off hunks of his flesh as he flees.

Premarital affairs may not last long, but if the couple continues to be together for perhaps a week or a few weeks, they may begin living together and are then considered married. Marriage involves no ceremony but is defined by cohabitation. For some cultural anthropologists (and social conservatives) focused on symbolism, there can be no marriage without a ceremony. However, once a woman has built a new house and the couple begins sleeping together in that house, everyone treats them as married. There is no confusion about their status; they are referred to as *edze a edzeyako*, the only translation of which is husband and wife. When speaking in Kiswahili, the Hadza use the term *kuoa* or *kuolewa* (to marry) and *bwana na bibi* (husband and wife). The daily behavior of Hadza couples does not seem to differ in any notable way from that of couples in many other societies where there is a ceremony.

Median age at first marriage is 21 years for men and 17 years for women, with mean age at first reproduction for women being 19 years (Jones et al. 1992). Hadza say there is a postpartum taboo and that couples should wait until a child is weaned before resuming sex, but in fact some women are still nursing a child of about 1 or 2 years old when they are already noticeably pregnant again, so occasionally a birth interval may be only 1–1.5 years, even though the average is 3.4 years.

The Hadza often practice the levirate: When a man dies, one of his brothers may take his widow as a wife and take on the role of father to her children. This is most likely to be a brother who has no wife at the time, but sometimes it results in polygyny with the brother taking the widow as a second wife. When I say the Hadza "practice the levirate," I do not mean that it is a strong rule that cannot be violated. The widow does not always marry her brother-in-law; the likelihood probably varies with the woman's age and number of close kin, as well as the number and the personalities of the dead man's brothers. However, it is quite common, and Hadza talk as if doing it is a good and normal thing. The sororate, in which a woman marries her dead sister's husband, is not practiced. It might occur sometimes, but it is not common and is not spoken of as expected.

The mating system is serially monogamous. There is no overt polyandry (women with 2 or more mates), other than the cases of young single women who sometimes have 2 or 3 suitors at the same time. Obst (1912) refers to some Hadza men as having 2 wives. Cooper (1949) said that monogamy was the rule, with a few beads as bride price. During Woodburn's early work, there was only slight polygyny as well, so it seems that the mating system has not changed much over the past century. Since I have been working with the Hadza, about 4% of men have 2 wives at any given time, but never more than two wives, and these polygynous marriages are not very stable. I usually find that the 2 or 3 men who had 2 wives in the previous year have all lost 1 wife and are back to being monogamous when I return the following year, while 2 or 3 other men now have 2 wives.

Considering that the Hadza are surrounded by more numerous and powerful neighbors, a surprisingly small percentage (4%) of Hadza women marry non-Hadza men (Jones, Hawkes, and O'Connell 1996). Hypergyny, or women marrying men of higher social status than their own, is a common trait in stratified societies. Among foragers without wealth, the same factor explains why it is common for forager women to marry men from an outside group of non-foragers who do have some wealth. Among Efe foragers in the Congo, for example, 13% are married to non-Efe men, and among the !Kung of Botswana, 10% are married to Bantu men (cited in Jones, Hawkes, and O'Connell 1996). Kohl-Larsen (1958) says that, in the 1930s, Isanzu men frequently stole Hadza wives. Even in 1995, I found that women who were out foraging would scream or hide in fear upon seeing a Datoga pastoralist man. They told me they might be captured and taken away (or perhaps raped). They would yell for a Hadza man, if one were within earshot, to come and protect them. They would also tell me to take my bow and arrows so that I cold protect them. I am not sure how much they were joking or if they really believed I could protect them. This makes one wonder why women don't learn to use a bow and carry one with them while foraging.

Occasionally, a Hadza woman marries a non-Hadza, moves away, and has a child with him. Very often, however, the woman eventually leaves her husband and returns to raise the child in a Hadza camp. This seems to be because Hadza women are too independent to put up with the sort of treatment they get from non-Hadza men. Hadza women have a good deal of independence and often speak their minds. But with non-Hadza men, they are looked down on, given orders, and more often beaten, so they want to leave and return to a Hadza camp. When Hadza women return to a Hadza camp, they do not experience any notable stigma, nor does a child with a non-Hadza father; if there is any stigma, at least it is slight. Such children are considered Hadza, as they are if they have a Hadza father and a non-Hadza mother, which is much less common. Occasionally, non-Hadza men take up life in a Hadza camp with their Hadza wives, and these marriages are more enduring because the men treat their wives better; in fact, they begin to behave just like Hadza men.

Obst (1912) said that a man could marry anyone other than his mother or sister and that one man even married his granddaughter. The Hadza, like people in most societies, say that it is not acceptable to marry anyone who is a parent, child, sibling, grandparent, grandchild, uncle, aunt, nephew, or niece—anyone who shares on average at least 25% of their genes. They usually say it is not good to marry first cousins, thus anyone who shares even 12.5% of their genes. However, as with the few other rules one can elicit from the Hadza, there is little or no enforcement. I know one man who married his niece. One man even married his sister. While other Hadza shake their heads and say it is not right, no one feels compelled to do anything about it. So even though these norms are well understood and recognized by all Hadza, there is simply no strong sentiment that others should enforce them. To a remarkable extent, individuals are free to do what they want.

HUSBAND-WIFE RELATIONSHIP

Husbands and wives sleep together on a skin on the ground close to a hearth with their young children. Once a child is about 9–12, he or she begins sleeping with other similar-age same-sex children. Husbands and wives show no outward signs of affection such as hugging or kissing, but when they sit together, they often talk at length (Figure 7.1). They say they feel love for each other before and after getting married. Contrary to the view that romantic love was invented during the days of medieval chivalry (Bloch 1991, Lewis 1936), the truth may be that it was greatly thwarted once agriculture led to stratified societies and marriages were arranged as calculated economic contracts. Among many hunter-gatherers, though by no means all, girls and boys are free to pursue romances during their teenage years with little interference from adults (Murdock 1964). Some of these romances lead to long-term pair-bonds. That is certainly true of the Hadza.

Most of the time, men and women appear to be coequals. A man may hit his wife occasionally. Usually, others disapprove, and the wife's kin

Figure 7.1. A married couple rests inside berry bushes during midday. The man whittles an arrow and wears a heart rate monitor to measure his caloric expenditure.

may intervene. The fertility stick that a man carves for his wife to insure she conceives is sometimes used to beat her as well, according to some Hadza, though wife beating appears to be fairly rare. Hadza women speak their minds, especially at home. They are quite independent and capable of feeding themselves and their children, especially because they usually live with their kin, who also help feed and care for the children.

Women never go out of camp alone, except to relieve themselves. They are either with other women or with a brother, father, or husband. This is not because there is any great danger of being raped by a Hadza man, but because there is danger of being raped or even captured and taken off by a non-Hadza man. It may also be partly because, without bows and arrows, women are more vulnerable to large carnivores. At least when they are in a group and have their digging sticks, they can cooperate to defend themselves.

Sex usually occurs at night in the hut or around the hearth while others are sleeping. One never hears people having sex, so couples are careful to be discreet and quiet. If they have children, they must have sex while their children are sleeping next to them. There is little opportunity for sex to occur out of camp because men usually forage alone and women forage in groups. Married couples who forage together occasionally may have sex out of camp. A sexual tryst while on a foray would require the complicity of the other women in the foraging group to keep it quiet. Kohl-Larsen (1958) said that women would sometimes conspire and choose one of them to initiate a relationship with an Isanzu man so that she could receive a lot of tobacco from him. She would give much of the tobacco to the elder women so that if her adultery was discovered, the elder women would speak on her behalf.

SEXUALITY

Women are modest and do not talk openly about sex, though some will answer questions about sex in private. Men are less private but still do not talk about sex much in public. The Hadza understand conception; they know it requires semen and that if a woman misses her period, she is pregnant (Marlowe 2004b). A Hadza woman will wash on the last day of her period, and then the couple has sex. Sex is generally avoided during menstruation.

Infertile women feel sad about not having any children, and others feel sorry for them. On the occasions when a man admits to having left his wife (he usually says he was left by her), the reason is most often that she bore no children. Although women sometimes say they wish they could stop having babies, men seem to think more is better.

The main source of conflict that can escalate into violence is competition for mates. Almost all murders of Hadza by other Hadza are related to male jealousy. This may be when a man discovers that his wife has had an affair, in which case he may kill the other man and beat his wife, or kill both of them. More often, however, it is when two men are competing for the same single woman. Since marital infidelity is dangerous for women, and since women never leave camp alone, extramarital affairs are tricky. Men, according to Hadza opinion, are more likely than women to philander. But married women say one must keep an eye on the single women because they will try to steal one's husband.

SEX RATIO

The overall sex ratio, the number of males divided by the number of females, is slightly female biased (450 males/465 females = 0.97). However, the OSR, the ratio of reproductive-age males to females is male biased (1.14). While the overall sex ratio varies from 0.89 to 1.13 across camps ($n=26$ camps), the OSR in one sample of camps varied from 0.25 to 2.33. Because camp composition is constantly in flux, however, a camp that had more reproductive females than males in one week could have fewer females than males 2 or 3 weeks later.

Given that there are more reproductive-age men than women, we should not expect there to be many reproductive-age women who are single—at least, not because they cannot find a man willing to marry them. Nonetheless, in a sample of 26 camps ($n=228$ women), 20% of women within the ages of 16 to 49 were single. Some women are not interested in marrying any of the available bachelors. Many others are simply between marriages. But the largest fraction is made up of those who have not married yet. These are women from 16 to 19 years old who seem to be shopping before deciding on a husband.

The OSR should determine the intensity of male-male competition and affect the degree of polygyny. In reality, it appears that marriage alters this dynamic. There is much more competition for single women than for married women because competing for a woman who is already married is so much more dangerous. The husband will surely feel that he should punish someone for an extramarital affair, while he may not always feel entitled to punish a rival competing for the same single woman (though murders do occur even then). Marriage entails possession that is largely respected by others and at least partially takes those women out of the mate pool so long as they are married. Most single females are single because they are choosy, and those who are already married do not feel like sharing their husbands with other women, all of which suggests that female choice is not constrained and is the main factor driving the mating system.

Male-male competition should also be related to the chance of conception (Mitani, Gros-Louis, and Richards 1996). Therefore, it is not just a woman's age but also her reproductive state that matters. There is only about a 3- or 4-day window during each menstrual cycle when men have a chance of siring offspring (1 day of ovulation plus 3 or 4 days that sperm remain viable). When females are pregnant, they cannot conceive, and when they are nursing at high frequencies, they are much less likely to conceive. Once these factors are taken into account, there should be very few women in a typical hunter-gatherer camp who can conceive on any given day. However, because women have concealed ovulation, men need to compete even when copulation cannot result in conception, unlike the males of species in which females advertise ovulation. Once pair-bonds exist, if they afford some ownership rights even in the absence of active mate-guarding, males may be forced to compete for females even before they can conceive so as not to be left without mates. For all these reasons, using the per-day probability of conception to calculate the OSR is less necessary in humans (and probably other pair-bonded species).

Concealed ovulation has received considerable theoretical attention. Many species of primates, such as chimpanzees and several species of macaques and baboons, have exaggerated sexual swellings that signal when ovulation occurs, so ovulation is advertised rather than concealed. Even in species without swellings, there is usually behavioral estrus when females solicit copulations from males, and this occurs mostly around ovulation. Clearly, women have no swellings, and neither do they exhibit behavioral estrus. Studies of coital frequency among couples show that copulation is equally likely to occur at any point in the menstrual cycle, with a significant hiatus only during menses (Brewis and Meyer 2005, Ford and Beach 1951, James 1971). Menstruation is, therefore, the only clear signal in women, and it signals non-ovulation. Other evidence implies ovulation is concealed from women themselves (Sievert and Dubois 2005), as well as from men (Brewis and Meyer 2005). However, several researchers have suggested that ovulation is not completely concealed in humans. Some argue that libido increases mid-cycle (peri-ovulatory) (Dennerstein et al. 1994, Wilcox et al. 2004); others that women who are near ovulation wear more jewelry or revealing clothing (Haselton et al. 2007). Still others have found that men prefer the smell of women at mid-cycle (Singh and Bronstad 2001). Some have suggested that ovulation may be even more detectable in less hygienic societies similar to those of our hunter-gatherer ancestors (Pawlowski 1999, Small 1996).

The Hadza certainly qualify as a less hygienic culture. Hadza men and women know very well that conception is caused by copulation and semen. Most Hadza believe that women conceive right after their menses (Marlowe 2004b). Given that there is a cross-cultural hiatus in copulation during menstruation (Ford and Beach 1951), selection has clearly favored men and women who avoid copulating during menses, when there is no chance of conceiving. If Hadza men could detect ovulation and concentrate copulations at ovulation, we should expect them to be more likely to say that conceptions result from copulation at mid-cycle. This suggests that ovulation is just as effectively concealed among the Hadza as it is in hygienic cultures like the United States.

DIVORCE

Divorce is common among the Hadza (Jones et al. 2000); thus serial monogamy is the only way to describe the mating system. When a couple ceases to live together, the partners are considered divorced. The probability of divorce is higher for first and second marriages and higher in the early years of a marriage, and thus higher for younger people. However, once a woman passes menopause, the couple also very often divorces. Excluding couples with postmenopausal women, with each passing year of a marriage, the probability of divorce, per year, decreases. For example, in the first 4 years of marriage, the chance of divorce is 0.393 / year, but it drops to only 0.242 / year for couples that have been married for over 13 years (Jones et al. 2000). The Hadza divorce rate is 49 / 1,000 years of marriage (Woodburn 1968b), which is considerably higher than that of the United States, which in 2000 had a rate of 4.2 / 1,000 years of marriage (U.S. Census Bureau 2002). Several foraging societies also have high divorce rates. The Hadza divorce rate is lower than that of the Ache, but higher than that of the Hiwi, and close to the same as that of the !Kung (Jones et al. 2000).

The mean number of wives men have had is 2.46 (0–7, SD=1.62, n=100). The mean number of husbands women have had is 1.63 (1–3, SD=0.74, n=111). For those over 45 years of age, men have had an average of 3.29 wives (1–7, SD=1.81, n=24), while women have had an average of 1.57 husbands (1–3, SD=0.73, n=23). Women appear to be undercounting. Since we have been keeping records for several years and have recorded spouses, we know that a woman sometimes omits the name of one of her previous husbands, perhaps because there is some slight stigma attached to women who have had many husbands. Men may overcount slightly. They may sometimes count a woman they were with for a brief period like a week or two, while the woman might not count that as a marriage. On the other hand, men who have had many wives tend to forget to name some, just as they forget some of their children when they have had many. Overall, it seems likely that men are counting more accurately than women.

Even though divorce is common, perhaps 20% of Hadza stay married to the same person their whole life. Some of these long-lasting marriages result in a large number of surviving children as well. The record number of children living for a woman in my data is 9. Three women have achieved this, all of them with just one husband. This raises the question of whether staying married might improve the chances of children surviving. However, there are plenty of women who have almost that many living children with more than one husband.

Male extramarital affairs are a common cause of divorce. If a man is gone from camp too many days, his wife may suspect that he is seeing another woman in another camp and decide the marriage is over. When the husband returns, he may find that she has a new husband, but he may still consider her his wife. Female extramarital affairs appear to be mostly cases like these, where the woman considers she is no longer married while her husband still claims she is his wife.

I asked Hadza men and women about the reasons for divorce. The reason most often cited for fighting and divorcing was men's affairs (other reasons cited are listed in Table 7.2). When I asked what happens if someone finds out that his or her spouse is having an affair, 38% of men and women said the man would try to kill the other man, 26% said a woman would fight with the other woman, 20% said a man would leave his wife, and 13% said the woman would leave her husband ($n = 55$).

No man said it was all right for women to have 2 husbands, but 19% of women said it was all right. Significantly more men (65%) than women (38%) said it was all right for a man to have 2 wives (Marlowe 2004d). It is interesting that such a high percentage of men and women said polygyny is all right, given that there are usually only about 4% of men with 2 wives. Even though 38% of women said it is all right for a man to have 2 wives, when a married man pursues a second woman and his wife finds out, she usually gets angry. I have seen women yell and throw things at their husbands, accusing them of chasing another woman. When a man does have 2 wives, the women usually live in different camps, and polygynous marriages are less enduring.

Many a Hadza man has told me the reason for his divorce is that his wife left him. When I ask why his wife left, the man usually says it is puzzling and he does not know why. When I ask if he began a relationship with his current wife before his previous wife left him, "yes" is usually the answer. Yet he is actually puzzled about why she left. Men usually have no intention of leaving their wives; they merely want a second woman. Perhaps we should not fault them for not understanding why their wives left them, given that 38% of women say it is all right for a man to have 2 wives. On some level, divorce is something we should expect only women to want. If a man has a reproductive-age wife, there is no reason he should want to lose her; it is clear why he might desire to add a second, third, or fourth wife, especially if he does not need wealth

TABLE 7.2. PERCENTAGE OF HADZA MALES AND FEMALES CITING VARIOUS REASONS FOR FIGHTING AND/OR DIVORCING AMONG COUPLES IN GENERAL

Sex	Extramarital Affairs	Male Extramarital Affairs	Female Extramarital Affairs	Female Work Effort Low	Male Work Effort Low	Strong Words/ Nagging	No Intelligence	Wife Doesn't Want Sex	Disputes over Children	Having No Children
Male n=42	60	45	29	36	26	19	7	5	0	5
Female n=44	70	64	16	9	7	9	7	2	5	0
Total n=86	65	55	22	22	16	14	7	3	2	2

to acquire wives. Divorce in such a situation should be the product of a woman's disinterest in being a co-wife.

In a study of 4 hunter-gatherer societies, divorce rates were best predicted by the fertility units per male (Jones et al. 2000). This is a measure of the potential payoffs to mating effort by males, calculated by multiplying the OSR by the total fertility rate (TFR). Where there are more reproductive-age females per male and where they produce more children throughout their lives, there are more fertility units for males to compete for; when this number is high, divorce rates are high because males stand to gain from pursuing extra mates. This suggests that pair-bond stability is greater where male-male competition is more intense (OSR is higher, controlling for TFR) because there are fewer potential children to be sired by leaving a current wife in search of other women. There is a lower chance of philandering when there is a lower chance that it will result in a fitness gain. In Hadza terms, there is more pair-bond stability because there is less male philandering that causes their wives to leave their husbands.

EFFECTIVE POLYGYNY AND REPRODUCTIVE SKEW

Variance in fertility and RS, measured by the number of living offspring, is greater for adult males (variance $= 7.98$, mean $= 3.18$, $0-12$, SD $= 2.83$, $n = 95$) than for adult females (variance $= 4.20$, mean $= 3.05$, $0-9$, SD $= 2.47$, $n = 93$) (age ≥ 18 years) (Figure 7.2, Figure 7.3, Table 7.1). To the extent that putative paternity reflects the effective mating system, there is slight polygyny. Using those older than 45 years of age, mean male fertility equals 7.87 ($n = 31$), and mean female fertility equals 6.13 ($n = 31$). Mean number of living children equals 5.35 ($n = 31$) for men and 3.87 ($n = 31$) for women. With a larger sample, the mean number of children should be equal for males and females, and to the extent that it is not, the female mean should be slightly higher than the male mean since women are more likely to have children with non-Hadza than men are. However, in a small sample of older men and women, men have more children, probably because some of those older men are married to their second or third wives who are younger and still having children.

SEEKING MATES

People frequently visit other camps and know a great deal about who is living where, which is probably important when seeking mates. In a larger camp, a person may find a suitable mate within the camp, but in smaller

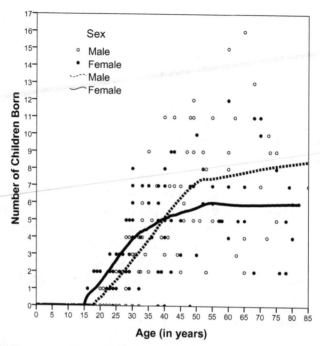

Figure 7.2. The total number of children ever born by age of Hadza females (*n* = 181, solid line and closed circles) and males (*n* = 171, dotted line and open circles). Fit lines are Loess Epanechnikov.

camps, one may have to look elsewhere. Men, especially those without wives, travel further than women, and some of the time they are out foraging is spent visiting other camps, some quite far away, so they usually know where potential mates are. Often, men visit a camp where an unmarried female lives and end up staying there if she reciprocates his interest.

Most Hadza know everyone in their mate pool very well, something that must have been true throughout much of human evolution, but is quite different from people in our own society. Humans should be good at evaluating potential mates and prefer traits that are most likely to enhance our reproductive success. Many studies have found considerable overlap in the preferences of men and women, as well as significant differences (Buss 1989, Ellis 1992, Perrett et al. 1999, Townsend and Wasserman 1998). However, most of these studies have been conducted on college students, who represent a thin slice of cultural variation in an evolutionarily novel environment. In our complex societies, people tend to marry

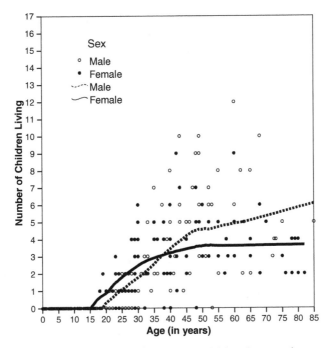

Figure 7.3. The number of still living children by age of
Hadza females (*n* = 181, solid line and closed circles) and
males (*n* = 171, dotted line and open circles). Fit lines
are Loess Epanechnikov.

those of the same race, ethnicity, language, religion, and political affiliation. There is also assortative mating on the basis of height, weight, and
overall attractiveness as measured by the ratings of subjects within the society (Price and Vandenberg 1980, Todd et al. 2007).

One big difference between the Hadza and societies like the United
States is that there is so much less variation for Hadza to choose from.
All potential mates are of the same ethnicity and somewhat similar in
color. They speak the same language, have no political affiliation or specialized knowledge, have the same lack of wealth and education, and
have the same religious concepts and lifestyles. This narrow range of
variation is the context in which more ancient mate preferences evolved.
Still, some people are taller, some are heavier, some have smoother skin,
some have larger breasts, some have more symmetrical faces, some are
smarter, and some are nicer. Of course, age varies in small-scale societies
and complex societies to a similar degree, and age is a very important

factor. Among the Hadza, the husband is older than the wife in almost all couples. In about 1% this is reversed. On average, husbands are 7 years older than wives (median = 6 years).

MATE PREFERENCES

I asked 85 Hadza, "If you were looking for a husband/wife, what kind of man/woman would you want; what is important to you?" Because the open-ended question yielded a wide range of specific traits, I later classified answers into 7 salient categories I treat as the following variables: (1) foraging, (2) looks, (3) character, (4) fertility, (6) intelligence, and (7) youth/age (Marlowe 2004d).

When a woman said she wanted a man who is a good hunter or one who can feed her children, and when a man said he wanted a woman who can get a lot of food, I coded these answers as foraging. All traits that were clearly attributes of the body or the face were classified as looks. The category character includes not only answers like "good character," but also other, more specific traits, such as "nice."

Figure 7.4 shows how frequently the 7 traits were nominated as important in a potential spouse. A higher percentage of men than women placed importance on fertility in a potential spouse. Many men said with great emphasis that it was important that a woman be able to bear many children. When I asked, "How can you tell whether a woman can bear many children?" they would often say you can tell just by looking, though they could not be more specific than that. Hadza men often say they will look for another wife after several years of a childless marriage.

Given that female fecundity ceases at menopause and begins to decline after age 25–30 (Wood 1994) in many populations, though perhaps less so in the Hadza (Phillips et al. 1991), it is not surprising that some men also mentioned youth, while no woman did. My impression is that Hadza men, like men in many societies (Kenrick and Keefe 1992, Perusse 1994), prefer women younger than the age of maximum fecundity, which is usually about age 25. When pair-bonds exist and sometimes last until death, it should pay men to acquire wives who still have most of their reproductive years ahead of them. Reproductive value (RV) is the expected number of future offspring. RV reaches a peak just before reproduction begins because the chance of dying before reproducing (which must be subtracted from expected future offspring) is minimal then, while all reproduction is still in the future. When long-term pair-bonds exist, males should place greater emphasis on RV than on peak

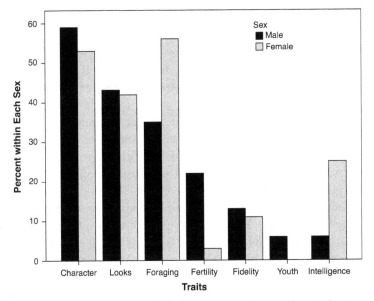

Figure 7.4. The percentage of Hadza women and men who cited various traits as important in a potential spouse (*n* = 36 females, *n* = 46 males). The only significant differences between the sexes are on the traits fertility and intelligence.

fecundity. Because female fecundity is so constrained by age, a man who marries a younger woman stands to gain more offspring than one who marries a middle-aged woman.

When I asked men if they found female breasts attractive, 94% said they did, while 6% said they didn't care about them. Most men liked breasts big and round and firm, "like those of young women," they would often say (Marlowe 2004d). Despite cultural variation in the preferred size, breasts appear to be erotic stimuli, possibly because they reveal a woman's RV, potential fecundity, or both (Jasienska et al. 2004, Marlowe 1998).

In contrast to U.S. men (Singh 1993), Hadza men preferred heavy women over normal and thin women. Also in contrast to U.S. men, they preferred a high over a low female waist-to-hip ratio in frontal views (Marlowe and Wetsman 2001). Waist-to-hip ratio (WHR) might be a clue to a woman's mate value. Women have relatively smaller waists and larger hips (lower WHR) than men, and younger women tend to have lower WHRs than older women. Women with lower WHRs may have greater fecundability (Zaadstra et al. 1993). For this reason, it has often been taken for granted that men universally prefer a low WHR. In frontal views, Hadza

men and men in a few other small-scale societies do not show this preference (Marlowe, Apicella, and Reed 2005). On the other hand, in profile
views Hadza men preferred a lower waist-to-hip ratio (more protruding
buttocks) than U.S. men (Marlowe, Apicella, and Reed 2005). Hadza
men probably preferred fatter women because it is important to store
energy for pregnancy and lactation and no foraging woman, certainly
no Hadza woman, is ever overweight or has too much fat (Marlowe and
Wetsman 2001). When we use both frontal and profile views of WHR to
get a preference more relevant to actual women, on whom WHR is measured with a tape pulled around the waist and around the buttocks, as
well as the hips, Hadza men prefer a 0.78 WHR. This is very close to the
mean actual WHR (0.79) of 18-year-old Hadza women (Marlowe, Apicella, and Reed 2005). Eighteen-year-old U.S. women have a lower mean
WHR (0.72), close to the preferred WHR of U.S. men (0.68), which is
exactly the mean WHR of *Playboy* centerfolds (Katzmarzyk and Davis
2001).

Unlike women in complex societies (Buss 1989, Sprecher, Sullivan, and
Hatfield 1994), Hadza women did not value looks significantly less than
men did. Hadza women clearly do attend to men's looks. Women everywhere probably notice looks, but in some societies they must discount looks
when their welfare greatly depends on access to men's resources—societies
where women are not allowed to work outside the house, for example.
Since Hadza women can forage and take care of themselves quite well, they
do not have to trade off looks for wealth as much as, say, Indian women,
and so we should expect them to care more about men's looks. However,
when fertility and youth (possibly related to looks) were added to looks and
age was controlled in a multiple linear regression, Hadza men did value
appearance more than women did ($\beta=-0.290$, $p=0.011$, $df=79$).

More Hadza women than men placed importance on intelligence. Several studies in complex societies have found that women place greater
value on a potential long-term mate's education than men do (Buss 1989,
Sprecher, Sullivan, and Hatfield 1994). Surprisingly few studies have reported on the value placed on intelligence (Prokosch et al. 2009). In one
study (Buunk et al. 2002), women cared about intelligence more than
men did, while in another they did not (Li et al. 2002). Hadza women
may value intelligence more than men do because it plays a more important role in male-male competition or in male foraging than in female
foraging. Hadza women who themselves had actually divorced often said
that the reason they left their husband was that he had no intelligence
(*akili* in Kiswahili), which also translates as he had no [common] sense.

Hadza men placed considerably more value on a wife's being hard-working (a good forager) than U.S. college men do. Men who placed importance on "hard working" were also more likely to value fidelity. Married women who have affairs run the risk of being hit or killed by their husbands, so clearly Hadza men value fidelity. Unlike women in many societies, Hadza women did not place less value on fidelity than men. This suggests that it costs a woman to share a husband or to lose a husband to another woman. As already noted, Hadza divorce often occurs when angry wives leave their philandering husbands. But it is less clear why there should be costs. Is it because they get less help with direct care of children, less help provisioning children, or less provisioning from other households with no husband to reciprocate and share food with those other households? Could the cost be loss of protection from other men? Rape of a Hadza woman by a Hadza man is extremely rare since the woman's family would not sit idly by; however, Woodburn (1979) describes one unusual case. Any sexual coercion that exists is probably more likely to come from an angry husband. The cost of divorce is therefore unlikely to be loss of a husband's protection, at least once pair-bonds have evolved.

Women placed more value on men being good foragers than on any other trait. This may seem unsurprising to most readers who assume this explains why women in many societies place so much value on male occupation and wealth (Buss 1989, 1999). However, the benefit of having a rich husband in agricultural and industrial societies, where resources can go directly to the household, is straightforward. It is less clear what material benefit the wife of a good hunter receives when meat is widely shared with all in camp, as it is among the Hadza and most other foragers (Kaplan et al. 1984, Kitanishi 1998, Peterson 1993, Woodburn 1998). Hadza women's mate preferences suggest they do benefit from having a husband who is a good hunter (see more on this in Chapter 8). But this might be from his household provisioning or simply because better hunters have a superior phenotype (and presumably genotype). In other words, bringing in lots of food might be a costly way for a man to signal his underlying quality as a mate, even if the household gets no more food (Smith and Bliege-Bird 2000).

FACE PREFERENCES

Figure 7.5 shows Hadza male and female composite faces created by blending 5 different faces (a, c) and 20 different faces (b, d). The degree

(a)

(b)

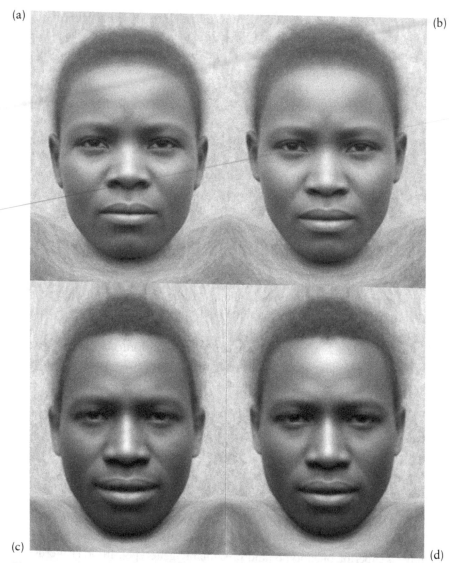

(c)

(d)

Figure 7.5. (a) Blend of 5 Hadza women; (b) blend of 20 Hadza women; (c) blend of 5 Hadza men; (d) blend of 20 Hadza men.

of fluctuating asymmetry was controlled by making all composites equally symmetrical. My graduate student Coren Apicella asked Hadza males and females to choose the most attractive of the two choices of the opposite sex. Both males and females chose the 20-face composite signifi-cantly more often than the 5-face composite (Apicella, Little, and Marlowe 2007). UK males and females also chose the same 20-composite Hadza faces over the 5-composite ones. The best explanation for why composite faces are considered more attractive, as they usually are (Rhodes 2006), is that they inevitably come closer to capturing the mean values of traits (averageness) in a population—mean-size nose, ears, eyes, and color. A preference for the mean value of a trait is called koinophilia (Koeslag and Koeslag 1994). The mean size is the result of past selection. After all, if the mean shows no secular trend, then stabilizing selection must be reinforcing the mean each generation. Great deviations from the mean are more likely to be the result of mutation, and most mutations have undesirable effects (Koeslag 1990, Koeslag and Koeslag 1994).

When presented with composites of British faces, however, the Hadza did not find the 20-face picture more attractive than the 5-face one. This could well be because the Hadza have less familiarity with British faces and therefore do not have any cognitive record of variation or template in the British population with which to compare the photos and assess which picture comes closer to the mean in the UK population. To assess whether a face is closer to the mean, one must have a history of tracking individuals to compute mean values. This cognitive tracking and calculation of sample means is not done consciously; it is presumably an automatic, ongoing process. UK subjects are also not familiar with the Hadza but are familiar with diversity around the world and the variation across different parts of Africa. This variation alone may cause them to pick something closer to the mean for a geographic area, as the British subjects did (Apicella, Little, and Marlowe 2007).

MATING EFFORT

Mating effort is an important determinant of one's reproductive success, yet it is poorly understood and difficult to measure. Reproductive success depends on survival and reproduction, and, to these ends, individuals can allocate their limited time and energy to somatic effort, including such things as resting, feeding, growth, cell repair, and fat storage, or to reproductive effort. Reproductive effort can be further divided into parenting effort and mating effort. Rarely do we specify exactly what should count as mating effort. Mate-guarding is an unambiguous form of mating effort, but if mate retention counts, we may need to count all sorts of behaviors as mating effort: a man fixing his wife's car or carrying out the trash, for example.

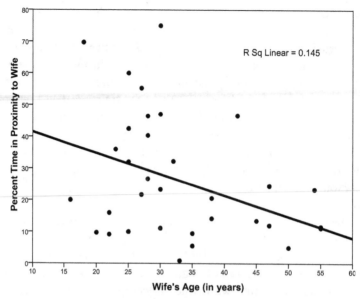

Figure 7.6. A man spends more time interacting with his wife the younger she is ($r = -0.463$, $p = 0.010$, $n = 35$). Fit line is linear.

Mating effort by a man should be related to the mate value of the woman his effort is targeted at, or more precisely to a woman's mate value in relation to his own ability to acquire mates. Women who are capable of conceiving children should have higher mate value than women who are pre-pubertal or postmenopausal. Without pair-bonds, a female's mate value should peak at the age of peak fecundity, but when long-term bonds exist, her value depends on how many years of reproduction she has left (her RV). This means that, even among women in their reproductive years, younger women should have higher mate value than older women. Therefore, if we assume that time around wife is a proxy for time spent mate-guarding or mate-helping, either of which should count as mating effort, we can predict that the younger their wives are, the more time men will spend near them.

In a sample of 5 camps, controlling for man's age, Hadza men spent more time near younger wives (Figure 7.6; $\beta = -0.803$, $p = 0.012$, $df = 32$) (Marlowe nd-d). In general, older men spent slightly less time near their wives, but not if they had wives much younger than they themselves were, which was more likely for older men. Controlling for man's age, the age gap between a man and his wife was also a significant predictor of the time men spent near their wives (Figure 7.7, $\beta=0.470$, $p=0.012$, $df=32$).

Males should vary their mate-guarding in response to the reproductive status of their mates. When a woman is noticeably pregnant, is nursing at high rates, or is postmenopausal, she is not ovulating and cannot conceive a child. Since a husband cannot be cuckolded at this time, he has less reason to guard his wife. Other men may still be interested in her, but probably less so. We might therefore predict that when women are postmenopausal, pregnant, or lactating at high frequency, their husbands will spend less time guarding them.

The reproductive status of a man's wife (cycling or not) was not a significant predictor of the amount of time men spent near their wives. However, if reproductive status is divided into premenopausal and postmenopausal, men did spend less time with postmenopausal wives ($t=-2.9$, $p=0.009$, $df=33$, unequal variances), though this is a less strong predictor than wife's age. Excluding postmenopausal women, there was not a significant difference between the amount of time men spent near their cycling and noncycling wives. Men spend the most time near wives who are around the age of peak fecundity, about 25 years old (Figure 7.7). This may be explained by the fact that the wives need their help most at that age, given that a 25-year-old woman usually has at least one toddler and one nursling already, while an 18-year-old women does not. A man may spend much time with his wife when she needs help most, when pregnant or nursing a young infant, just at the time she cannot cuckold him (Marlowe 2003a). Because she might leave him otherwise, it may behoove a man to help his wife, which would mean even his direct care of children might reflect mating rather than parenting effort (Smuts and Gubernick 1992).

When long-term bonds exist, mate-guarding may not vary as much in response to female reproductive state. This may be especially true when ovulation is subtle and effectively concealed from males, as it is in humans. If males cannot tell exactly when females are ovulating, they cannot increase their guarding at that time. Still, once a woman is clearly pregnant or nursing a very young infant, her husband does know she is not menstruating. Because most women who are premenopausal but not cycling have young infants, their husbands may be spending more time foraging or more time providing direct care. Thus, a man's time near his wife could be increased (greater time in direct care) or decreased (greater time out foraging) in ways that do not reflect mate-guarding, but rather parenting effort.

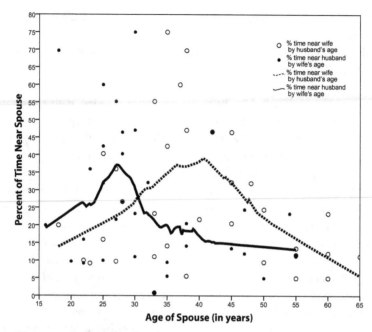

Figure 7.7. Percentage of time a man is near his wife (< 10 m) by his age (*n* = 35, dotted line) and percentage of time a woman is near her husband < 10 m) by her age (*n* = 35, solid line). Fit lines are Loess Epanechnikov.

Because of long-term bonds, concealed ovulation, and language, human mate-guarding is quite different from that of most other species. This is not to say it is unimportant; male jealousy accounts for virtually all murders among the Hadza. But mate-guarding among hunter-gatherers is certainly nothing like the mate-guarding of gorillas or hamadryas baboons, where males try to keep their mates within eyesight at all times. In fact, the very concept of hunting and gathering entails a sexual division of labor that means that men and women target different foods and therefore must be apart most of the time they are foraging (Marlowe 2007). Human mate-guarding involves friends and close kin keeping an eye out for a man and passing on information. Gossip and kin ties mean that humans can guard their mates in absentia.

HUNTING REPUTATION AND MATE VALUE

In interviews, men and women were asked to nominate 3 men as the best hunters. Men's hunting reputation was then measured according to the number of times they were nominated divided by the number of interviewees. Men who have better hunting reputations have wives who are younger in relation to themselves than men with poorer hunting reputations (Marlowe 2000b). If men prefer younger wives with greater RV, then the fact that better hunters have younger wives suggests that better hunters have higher mate value and consequently a greater choice of mates, which is what we can conclude from Hadza women's expressed mate preferences as well. Why better hunters might have higher mate value is the subject of debate (Hawkes, O'Connell, and Jones 2001a, Marlowe 2004d, Smith 2004, Wood 2006). The long-held view that women should prefer to marry better hunters because they and their children would thereby receive more provisioning has been challenged on the grounds that men's big-game meat is shared widely across households in camp (Hawkes, O'Connell, and Jones 2001b), which means that a woman married to a poor hunter may get as much as a woman married to a good hunter. An alternative explanation argues that women might prefer to marry better hunters because hunting success could be a reliable sign of a man's overall phenotypic quality, for example, his health, vigor, coordination, or intelligence (Hawkes and Bliege-Bird 2002).

Not only do men with better hunting reputations have relatively younger wives; as we will see in the next chapter, they also have greater RS relative to poor hunters. They do not have more wives over their lifetimes (nor more often have 2 wives at once), but they are more likely to start a second family after the previous wife has reached menopause (Marlowe 2000b). Divorcing and remarrying a woman of similar age to the previous wife will not necessarily enhance a man's reproductive success, and might even lower it if his children are treated poorly by his ex-wife or a new stepfather. However, when a man leaves a wife approaching menopause and marries a much younger woman than his first wife, he can potentially double his reproductive output. In the next two chapters, we will see that this is how better hunters achieve higher RS. We will also see that Hadza men behave in ways that should benefit their households and their own genetic offspring. In other words, good hunters may indeed be better household provisioners.

CHAPTER 8

Parenting

PARENTING EFFORT

Reproductive effort is composed of mating effort and parenting effort (at least in species with post-zygotic parental investment). When parental investment would increase the odds of offspring survival, selection may favor it, but this depends on just how much it increases survivorship and how costly it is to provide. If a parent gains even more RS from investing in something else, like mating effort, selection may favor little or no parental investment (Trivers 1972). An important factor is whether one or both parents invest. If the difference between no parental investment and one parent investing is a huge increase in survivorship, we should expect some parental investment. When the help of a second parent increases offspring survivorship only a bit more, we can expect there to be a conflict between the parents over how much each invests. It may pay one parent to desert and leave the other parent to do all the investing (Maynard Smith 1977). Of course, this will depend on the chance of gaining access to other mates, which will depend greatly on what others are doing. This is why a game theory perspective is important.

Mammalian females have evolved mammary glands, which makes them the more essential parent, and this makes it much more likely that males will be the sex to desert. In a few species, however, male investment in infants rivals or surpasses that of females (Garber 1997). There may be no tradeoff between mating and parenting effort if a male provides care to his offspring and guards his mate at the same time, but if he pursues extra pair mates, there is a tradeoff.

One illustration of this tradeoff is the accidental discovery that zebra finches (*Taeniopygia guttata*) behaved differently when males were marked with different color leg bands. When Nancy Burley (1988) was banding her birds with red, yellow, green, and blue leg bands, she found that males who had been feeding their chicks before began to feed them less when they had red or yellow bands on. She discovered that females found males wearing red and yellow bands more attractive. Consequently, these males were getting more opportunities to mate. They responded by curtailing their provisioning. They stood to gain much more from extra mating effort than from parenting effort when females found them attractive. When Burley put green or blue bands on those same males, they became less attractive and went back to provisioning. Burley (1988) called her explanation the differential allocation hypothesis.

Parental investment can be divided into direct care, such as holding or nursing, and indirect care, such as territory defense or resource acquisition and provisioning (Kleiman and Malcolm 1981). In mammals, nursing is the most important type of parental investment in the beginning. Because females are so well-equipped for direct care, often provisioning or protection from predators or infanticidal males is the most important form of investment by male mammals, especially primates (Doran and McNeilage 1998, Harcourt and Greenberg 2001, Palombit 1999), though males in some primate species also do considerable direct care (Garber 1997, Rotundo, Fernandez-Duque, and Dixson 2005, Whitten 1987).

PARENTING STYLE

Obst, a German, described the Hadza as doting parents (compared to neighboring Bantu), saying "I never saw in this region such concerned mothers or such active family fathers as among the Wakindiga and even if a subsidiary wife joins the first wife, which is quite often the case, the harmonic family life is not affected" (Obst 1912:25). Another German observer, Kohl-Larsen (1958), said children were not punished. Nicholas Blurton Jones (an Englishman) has described Hadza as harsh, at least compared to the !Kung (Ju/'hoansi) foragers in Botswana (Jones, Hawkes, and O'Connell 1996). It seems that Hadza parenting might therefore be described as affectionate and lenient but apparently not as indulgent and attentive as the Ju/'hoansi (Konner 2005).

Figure 8.1. A 2-year-old smokes while his father and others watch.

Hadza children are allowed to do as they like most of the time (Figure 8.1). By American standards, Hadza adults do very little disciplining or training of children. When a 2-year-old defecates too close to a hearth, for example, adults may make disapproving sounds, take the child's hand, and lead him or her further away. When children are 1 to 3 years of age, they often throw tantrums, during which they may pick up a branch and repeatedly whack people over the head. The parents and other adults merely fend off the blows by covering their heads, laughing all the time. They do not even take the stick away. When the child hits another child who is a little older, however, that child often grabs the stick and hits the little one back. This is the way young children learn they cannot get their way; older children train them. Thus, it is not necessary for adults to discipline them.

Children are rarely spanked (Marlowe 1999a, 2005b). During one year of 30-minute focal individual observations of men who had young children ($n = 32$ men, 53 children), consisting of 139,520 person-minutes, and 5,280 minutes of those children, I saw only one spanking. This was by the one and only stepfather who had a stepchild younger than his own child, since his wife had conceived a child with a non-Hadza man during a period of separation. I have seen women whip 3–5 year old children with a switch during a camp move which was a 6-hour walk.

These children grew very tired and began crying, refusing to walk any-more. They were carried by various adults from time to time but eventu-ally were forced by these women to keep walking to make it to the new camp location.

Children up until they are about 3 years old often cry for long periods when they do not get what they want. The crying can continue literally for hours. Occasionally, a parent may grunt disapproval. Rarely do other adults intervene, although they may complain to us researchers about the crying. When there is a very legitimate reason for a child to cry, for ex-ample, when a scorpion stings it, the mother does rush to pick the child up and inspect it.

Hadza parenting emphasizes self-reliance and independence. In gen-eral, parents and other adults are much less attentive by our standards. For example, an infant may grab a sharp knife, put it in its mouth, and suck on it without adults showing the least bit of concern until they need the knife again. I have not seen infants injure themselves in this way, but they must occasionally. I have seen several children who have burned themselves by falling into a hearth, though the burns are usually not very serious. Children will learn on their own what is dangerous and what they can and cannot get away with.

Children go from being extremely spoiled during their "terrible 2s" and 3s to being perfectly well behaved and respectful of adults—even obe-dient little servants—by the time they are 4 or 5 years old. Five-year-olds fetch anything adults want. Sometimes they fetch things they see the adult will need before they are even asked. For example, when seeing a man get-ting out his pipe and tobacco, a child may grab an ember from the fire and take it to the man to light the pipe. They never complain. In fact, they seem to enjoy being helpful.

Whenever a baby cries or fusses, mothers usually offer their breast right away. Weaning occurs when the child is becoming too big for the mother to carry on her back when she goes foraging. At this time, she begins to leave the child in camp with someone else. The child is usually not at all happy about mother leaving and will cry and follow the mother. Sometimes she relents, picks the child up, and takes it with her, but eventually she will refuse and make the child stay behind. The amount of time children nurse varies from about 20% of daylight hours soon after birth to 5% by age 2, and virtually all are completely weaned by 2.5 years of age (Figure 8.2).

Adults express no sex preference and welcome a male or a female baby equally. Both sexes are reared with equally little discipline. Boys

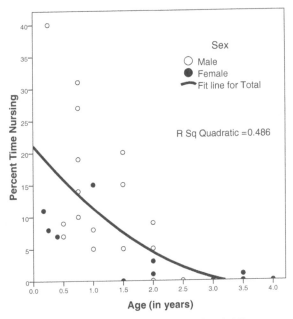

Figure 8.2. Percentage of time nursing by child's age
($n = 11$ females, $n = 30$ males). Fit line is quadratic.

usually go naked until the age of 4 or 5, but girls are given a pubic apron
or skirt around 3 years of age. They may also be taught modesty, for example, to cross their legs so others cannot see beneath their skirt. Otherwise, there is not much difference in the way adults treat boys and girls.
Differences in their behavior begin to emerge nonetheless. For example,
while 3 or 4 years old, boys and girls often play together; by age 6 or 7,
they more often play in same-sex groups. By age 8–10, boys go foraging or
play with other boys, while girls begin to go foraging with their mothers.
Young girls do more work, such as food processing and tending younger
siblings (Crittenden and Marlowe 2008).

DIRECT CARE

Hadza children require considerable direct care only during their first
2 or 3 years of life. By age 3 or 4, they are usually in playgroups with other
children in or near camp, a pattern comparable to that of several other foraging societies, such as the Baka Pygmies of Cameroon and !Kung of
Botswana (Hirasawa 2005, Kamei 2005, Konner 2005). Hadza children

over 3 or 4 years of age are looked after by the older children they are playing with, though it is still necessary that some adult be in camp within earshot; otherwise, lions, leopards, and hyenas would eventually lose their fear of camps during the day, and these children would become easy prey. Toddlers are almost never left in camp without an adult or teenager there, but this can be almost anyone. More than once, all adults slipped out of camp to forage and left me to babysit.

Although Hadza mothers are very nurturing, they are quite willing to hand their children off to anyone willing to take them. The child is not always so willing, however, and if he or she starts crying, the mother will usually retrieve the child. Despite a willingness to leave children with others, Hadza mothers provide the bulk of direct care. Men are affectionate with children and play with them more than women do (Marlowe 1999b).

Humans might be considered cooperative breeders if by this we mean simply that individuals other than parents provide care (Hrdy 2005). Among the Hadza, there is considerable allomaternal direct care, especially in the form of babysitting (Crittenden and Marlowe 2008). Even without allomaternal direct care, the food-sharing among most foraging societies might qualify them as cooperative breeders.

MOTHERING

After nursing, holding is probably the most important form of direct care of nurslings. Hadza women spend an average of 14% of the day (about 3 hours) holding their children of all ages while in camp. In addition, they take their infants with them when they go foraging. The percentage of time that children are held is about 85% soon after birth and drops to near 0% by age 4. Close to 100% of the time that newborns are being held, it is the mother doing the holding. When children of all ages are being held, about 69% of the holding is done by the mother (Table 8.1). Since mothers leave the children they are weaning in camp, someone must stay in camp to watch these toddlers. It is often older children who provide much of the care of their younger siblings (Crittenden and Marlowe 2008).

The percentage of time that children are in close proximity to adults (less than 3 meters) is close to 100% after birth and falls to about 15% by 8 years of age. Children under 9 years old interact most frequently with mother, then father, sisters, brothers, and maternal grandmother, in that order. When limiting the sample to only those children

TABLE 8.1. PERCENTAGE OF TOTAL TIME THAT
CHILDREN UNDER 4 YEARS OF AGE WERE
BEING HELD BY ALL CAREGIVERS

Holder's Relatedness to Child Being Held	Number of Individuals in Each Category	Mean % Time Held	Mean % Time Held Controlled for Camp Residency
Mother	46	68.7	68.9
Father	34	7.1	9.4
Older sister	56	1.2	2.8
Maternal grandmother	16	3.7	9.5
Paternal grandmother	8	1.2	6.1
Maternal aunt	33	1.9	3.5
Other kin	*	3.6	*
Unrelated	77	12.4	*
Total		100	100

NOTE: From Crittenden and Marlowe 2008. Total time is 100%. For children under four years of age, N=68. "Other kin" represents various categories of holders. Because individuals may fall into more than one category, the total number is not known. Residence could not be controlled for the "other kin" and "unrelated" categories because they overlap.

3 years old and older, however, less time is spent interacting with mother and father than with all others combined. This is because children over 3 spend most of their time playing with other children (Table 8.2) (Marlowe 2005b).

ALLOMOTHERING

An allomother is anyone other than the mother who cares for her young. Those who do the most holding of Hadza children tend to fall into the categories in Table 8.3. Since divorce and remarriage are common (Jones et al. 2000), about one-third of all children under 10 years of age are living with stepfathers (Marlowe 1999b). Children almost always live with their mothers after divorce, at least while they are young. In a sample of 41 couples, I found only 1 child living with its stepmother, but 22 stepchildren (≤8 years old) living with 11 stepfathers. There was one man whose wife had left him and had taken their nursling with her, but left him to care for 3 children under 10 years of age.

In a sample of 42 children 4 years old or younger, 27 had a genetic father present in the household, 5 had a stepfather present, and 10 had no father present in the household (though 1 of these had a genetic father

TABLE 8.2. PERCENTAGE OF TIME CHILDREN UNDER 8 YEARS OLD SPENT IN SPECIFIC ACTIVITIES AND INTERACTIONS

Age Category (n)	Percentage of Time in Camp (scans) (n)	Percentage of Time Held (scans) (n)	Percentage of Time Nursing (follows) (n)	Percentage of Time Interacting (in follows) with:					
				Mother	Father	Older Sister	Older Brother	Maternal Grandmother	Others
<1 yr (11)	62.82 (11)	52.84 (11)	16.64 (11)	78.43 (11)	17.78 (9)	18.33 (2)	7.78 (5)	9.44 (6)	29.07 (11)
1–1.9 (11)	71.47 (11)	25.19 (11)	8.30 (10)	43.76 (10)	21.81 (8)	0.00 (0)	30.00 (2)	3.89 (2)	39.79 (10)
2–2.9 (8)	83.64 (8)	15.69 (11)	2.25 (8)	30.06 (7)	21.11 (5)	18.19 (4)	3.89 (4)	9.44 (3)	39.52 (8)
3–4 (12)	73.12 (12)	0.93 (12)	0.08 (12)	7.59 (9)	5.78 (5)	9.63 (3)	7.22 (8)	21.11 (4)	49.70 (11)

Total ≤4 (42)	72.00 (42)	23.69 (42)	7.68 (41)	42.68 (37)	17.37 (27)	17.2 (7)	8.62 (19)	9.74 (15)	40.68 (40)
4.1–5 (4)	79.94 (4)	0.00 (4)	0.00 (4)	21.67 (2)	0.00 (1)	1.11 (1)	0.00 (0)	0.00 (1)	49.70 (4)
5.1–6 (4)	71.40 (4)	0.00 (4)	0.00 (4)	14.44 (1)	13.33 (2)	18.89 (1)	30.00 (1)	0.00 (0)	80.00 (2)
6.1–7 (7)	65.54 (7)	0.00 (7)	0.00 (7)	3.33 (2)	1.11 (2)	0.00 (1)	0.00 (0)	10.00 (1)	59.44 (6)
7.1–8 (11)	55.30 (11)	0.00 (11)	0.00 (5)	6.39 (4)	6.67 (1)	14.07 (3)	8.056 (4)	0.00 (0)	83.33 (5)
Total ≤8 (68)	69.06 (68)	14.65 (68)	4.86 (59)	36.29 (46)	15.52 (33)	13.37 (15)	9.77 (24)	9.18 (17)	52.74 (57)

TABLE 8.3. CATEGORIES OF DIRECT
CARE PROVIDERS

Maternal Kin	Paternal Kin	Other Kin	In-laws	Others
Mother	Father	Sister	Aunt-in-law	Female
Maternal aunt	Paternal grandfather	Female kin	Step-grandfather	Male
Maternal grandfather	Paternal grandmother	Male kin		Female visitor
Maternal grandmother	Paternal uncle			Male visitor
Maternal uncle	Female cousin			Mother's co-wife
Female cousin				Stepfather
				Other child

in the same camp). Among all 42 children, mothers accounted for a far larger share of holding than anyone else (72% of all holding). After the mother, most holding was done by the maternal grandmother (6.7%), followed by the father (6.1%). Females who were not close kin held the children 7.5% of the time. Excluding the mother and the father, maternal kin held children much more (83%) than paternal kin (17%), which is mainly because they are more likely to be residing in the same camp (Jones, Hawkes, and O'Connell 2005b).

In contrast to the figure for all 42 children under 4 years old, the 27 children who had genetic fathers present were held more by fathers (26%) than by maternal grandmothers. Among the 15 children (4 years old or younger) with no genetic fathers present in the household, maternal grandmothers increased their holding and accounted for 70% of all holding, excluding the time held by the mother. The involvement of maternal grandmothers increased even more when a stepfather was present in the household (83% of all holding excluding the mother); they did significantly more holding than they did when a genetic father was present ($\beta = -0.421$, $p = 0.014$, $df = 28$) (Marlowe 2005b).

Hadza grandmothers, especially maternal grandmothers, provide considerable direct care (Figure 8.3) and considerable provisioning (Hawkes, O'Connell, and Jones 1989, 1997, Hawkes et al. 1998). Sometimes a woman who has no husband leaves her children with her parents and lives in another camp, which might make it easier for her to attract a new husband. When there was a genetic father in the household, holding by the genetic father and the maternal grandmother was inversely

Figure 8.3. A grandmother carries her grandchild.

related, controlling for age and sex of child and the amount of time the mother held. The more the maternal grandmother held, the less the father held ($\beta=-0.483$, $p=0.050$, $df=22$). Because maternal grandmothers compensate, there is no difference in the total amount a child is held with a father present or absent.

Mothers do much more holding when no father is present. The maternal grandmother provides the bulk of allomaternal direct care. This is partly because single women are more likely to live with their mothers than are married women (Jones, Hawkes, and O'Connell 2005b). Once a child is being weaned, fathers, grandmothers, and older sisters begin to do an appreciable amount of direct care, especially babysitting (Figure 8.4). Both genetic fathers and maternal grandmothers are important in

Figure 8.4. Two girls babysit and carry their young siblings. Photo by Alyssa Crittenden.

terms of direct care, and it appears that they are alternative sources of help for a woman who depends more on one when the other is not living with her. Thus, a genetic father appears to relieve both the mother and her mother from some holding time either directly or via the assistance of his kin.

FATHERING

Men often babysit toddlers who are left in camp while women are foraging. Sometimes in the dry season, after men have been night hunting, they nap throughout the morning, but if a child screams, they will wake up to investigate. Even if babysitting normally entails little cost to a man and little benefit to a child, all it would take is the occasional potentially deadly accident for babysitting to pay greatly. Babysitting by men allows women to forage unencumbered by toddlers. Men spend 6 daylight hours in camp on average, during which time they could be babysitting.

All caretakers appear to be equally sensitive to fussing and crying, but the mother is far more effective at soothing the child. However, it is usually the father who holds a crying infant in the middle of the night

TABLE 8.4. HOLDING OF INFANTS
The Hadza Compared with Other Foraging Societies

Population	Age of Infants (months)	Father Holding (% of time)	Source
Aka Pygmies	1–4	22.0	(Hewlett 1991)
Efe Pygmies	1–4	2.6	(Winn, Morelli, and Tronick 1990)
Gidgingali	0–6	3.4	(Hamilton 1981)
!Kung San	0–6	1.9	(West and Konner 1976)
Hadza ($n=8$) (scans)	0–9	2.5	(Marlowe 1999b)
Hadza ($n=8$) (% present)	0–9	5.4	(Marlowe 1999b)
Hadza ($n=8$) (follows) day and evening	0–9	5.6	(Marlowe 1999b)

NOTE: Data on Hadza are for genetic fathers only. Data on other societies from Hewlett 1992, presumably also for genetic fathers only.

and sings to get the infant to go back to sleep. Both girls and boys appear to be closer to their mother and spend more time with her, though once boys are about 6 or 7 years old, the time they spend with their father increases.

In one sample, fathers held their genetic infants (9 months and under) for an average of 19.5 minutes per day (2.5% of the daytime) and 30.2 minutes per day plus early evening (5.6% of the time they were in camp during the day and early evening). Table 8.4 shows how the Hadza compare with other foragers.

If direct care were provided only as a form of mating effort to keep the child's mother happy, we should expect no difference between care received by a genetic child and care received by a stepchild. When I tested this and controlled for child's age, men spent more time near their genetic children ($n=30$) than near their stepchildren ($n=11$) ($U=96$, $p=0.017$, $n=41$). They also played more with their genetic children ($U=42$, $p=0.027$, $n=31$). I also calculated a variable I called nurturing, which included holding, feeding, grooming, carrying, and pacifying. Controlling for age and number of all children at home, men nurtured their genetic children more than their stepchildren (Figure 8.5, $\beta=0.295$, $p=0.043$, $df=27$) (Marlowe 1999b). One often sees Hadza men holding their own children affectionately (Figure 8.6).

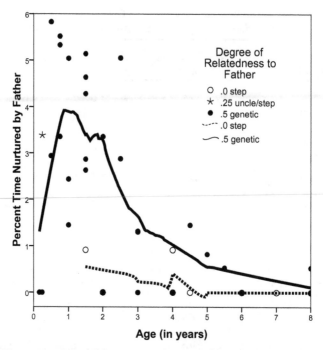

Figure 8.5. Stepchildren receive less nurturing from their stepfathers than genetic children receive from their fathers. One stepfather was also the uncle of the child. Fit lines are Loess Epanechnikov.

Whether fathers, stepfathers, grandfathers, or some other type of household head, men showed a sex bias in their nurturing. In a multiple linear regression controlling for age of the child and its degree of putative genetic relatedness to the man, a male head of household provided significantly less nurturing to girls than to boys ($\beta=-0.331$, $p=0.002$, $df=49$, $n=53$ children 8 years old or younger with a male head of household present). Although men spend more time with boys, women spend slightly (but not significantly) more time with girls, so that overall there is not a significant difference in how much care young boys and girls get (Marlowe 2005b).

Degree of relatedness (r) predicted the amount of nurturing children received from any type of male head of household (e.g., father, uncle, grandfather), controlled for the child's age and sex and the number of all children (≤ 6 years old) at home ($\beta=0.308$, $p=0.013$, $df=48$). One

Figure 8.6. A man holds his child.

stepchild was actually a nephew, since the man had taken on his dead brother's wife. This child's degree of relatedness was 0.25, and he received more care than any other stepchild (Figure 8.5).

Almost all Hadza said that stepfathers feel the same about their stepchildren as they do about genetic children and that they should care for them equally. Upon further questioning, however, only 54% continued to maintain there was absolutely no difference ($n = 70$). Despite the stated norm, the data showed that men do discriminate and provide more direct care to their own children. Still, it is of interest that they say otherwise. As Cronk (1999, 2004) has argued, we can learn something important by eliciting people's comments in addition to measuring their behavior. In this case, a woman and her kin have an interest in promoting good stepfathering, while a man who is interested in marrying a woman has an interest in signaling that he will not be harmful to stepchildren if the woman will have him.

PATERNAL INVESTMENT AND MATING EFFORT

If care enhances offspring fitness, a male with no potential mates should invest in parenting up to the point of no marginal benefit. As the number of potential mates increases, he may gain fitness by allocating more and more time and energy to mating effort, and consequently less to parenting effort. The best measure of mating opportunities is the number of reproductive-age females to males (the OSR). The more females to males there are, the more mating opportunities males have (Jones et al. 2000, Clutton-Brock and Parker 1992, Hurtado and Hill 1992, Kvarnemo and Ahnesjo 1996, Mitani, Gros-Louis, and Richards 1996). Because men should invest more in mating effort and less in parenting effort as mating opportunities increase, we can predict that men will provide less direct care to their own children in camps with more reproductive-age women per man.

In a sample of 21 men who had only genetic children at home, I found that when men had more mating opportunities, they provided less direct care to their children (controlled for child's age and number of genetic children at home). By using a measure of direct care that took into account the age of children and the number of children, I was able to compute something like a per unit investment in direct care. The more reproductive-age women there were per man in camp, the less men played with their children ($\beta=-0.537$, $p=0.014$, $df=18$) and the less physical contact they had ($\beta=-0.591$, $p=0.006$, $df=18$). OSR with only cycling women (that is, excluding those pregnant and lactating more than 5% of the time) was a significant predictor of nurturing. With more mating opportunities, men invested less in nurturing of their own children ($\beta=-0.442$, $p=0.048$, $df=18$). Even if men were not actually trading off parenting for mating effort when they had more mating opportunities (i.e., cashing in on these opportunities), it is possible that when the OSR is more favorable for men, their wives can demand less help with child care from them.

One measure of men's mating effort might be their number of lifetime mates. This is fairly straightforward if we are counting the number of lifetime sex partners, both wives and clandestine mates, or if we are dealing with polygynous societies where a man with 2 or 3 wives invests

more in mating effort than a man with only 1 wife. When we are dealing with a serially monogamous society and have no genetic data on paternity or extramarital affairs, things are less straightforward. A man with
only one wife in a lifetime might invest as much in her over a 30-year period as a man with 2 lifetime wives, one during the first 15-year period,
followed by another in the second 15-year period. However, if we assume
that a man invests less in mating effort aimed at his wife after he has a
stable relationship and after he has children than when he is seeking a
mate or guarding a wife in a new relationship, or at least trying to keep
her happy, it follows that a man who has had only 1 wife probably has
invested less in mating effort than a man who has had multiple wives.
Since Hadza children nearly always live with their mothers, a man with
only one wife may have all of his children at home and invest more heavily
in parenting effort than a man with children spread over different wives.
The latter might be considered more of a "cad" and the former more of a
"dad" (Draper and Harpending 1982).

Hunting reputation, controlled for age, is not significantly correlated
with the total number of wives men have had in life ($r=-0.016$, $p=0.910$,
$df=49$). This says nothing about the number of affairs, of course, of which
I have no measure, but there is no evidence in my data that better hunters
are more likely to be cads. Good hunters had more genetic children, and
their genetic children received more direct care. Stepfathers, on the other
hand, were less successful hunters than genetic fathers (or less motivated), had lower hunting reputations ($t=-2.78$, $p=0.012$, $df=19.4$,
unequal variances), and yet they had had more wives ($t=2.18$, $p=0.040$,
$df=22$, equal variances) even though they were no older. The number of
lifetime wives may be measuring the degree to which men pursue a cad-
like strategy.

There are 3 possible explanations for why stepfathers bring in less
meat. (1) Stepfathers are less motivated to bring back food because
some of it goes to stepchildren. (2) Stepfathers are poor hunters. Because of this, they are of lower mate value to women. Because they are
less preferred, they acquire women only after better hunters have had
their pick. The women available to them may already have young children. This would make poor hunters more likely than good hunters to
become stepfathers. (3) Stepfathers tend to be men who pursue a more
cad-like strategy. They do not provision much (or provide much direct
care). Because they don't invest much, they do not mind marrying women
who have young children. This means cads are more likely to become
stepfathers. If stepfathers are cads, they should have had a higher number

of wives over time, since that is practically the definition of a cad, and they did.

Given a tradeoff between parenting and mating effort, if we assume men who have had more wives are men who have invested more in mating effort, they should also be men who tend to invest less in parenting effort. Thus, we can predict that men who have had more wives will provide less direct care to their own children (controlling for the man's age). Men who had more wives (controlled for the man's age) did provide less nurturing (per unit investment) to their own children ($\beta=-0.556$, $p=0.013$, $df=18$). This suggests that men who have had many wives are just the type to generally invest more in mating effort and less in parenting effort.

It appears that the offspring of men who invest more in mating effort may suffer slightly higher mortality. Controlled for the man's age, men who have had more wives had significantly more children born ($\beta=0.213$, $p=0.031$, $df=48$, $R^2=0.541$). If the mortality rates of their children were no higher than those of men with fewer wives, these men should also have significantly more children living, controlled for age, but they did not ($\beta=0.153$, $p=0.299$, $df=48$, $R^2=0.233$). This suggests that they end up with RS that is not significantly greater because, while they sire more children, those children do not survive at an equal rate. This is in contrast to men with better hunting reputations who did not have more lifetime wives but did have higher RS (more surviving genetic offspring controlled for man's age).

When a man knows a child is a stepchild because he married the child's mother after the child was 2 or 3 years old, the direct care he provides to his stepchild must be counted as mating effort. Some of the direct care men provide to their own children may be mating effort as well, the price of keeping their wives from leaving. We might consider the amount of direct care men provide to stepchildren to be the amount required for mate retention and everything above that to be parenting effort. Since stepchildren receive little direct care, Hadza men invest very little mating effort in the form of direct care.

PROVISIONING

Human pair-bonding has long been considered an adaptation to the demands placed on mothers by needy offspring, and the benefits of provisioning by a mate (Darwin 1871, Lancaster and Lancaster 1983, Lovejoy 1981, Westermarck 1929). More recently, this paternal investment theory of human pair-bonding has been challenged (Hawkes 1991, Hawkes, O'Connell, and Jones 2001a). Among tropical hunter-gatherers, men frequently acquire less food than women (Marlowe 2005a). Hawkes, O'Connell, and Jones (2001a) note that large game is acquired so sporadically that a woman may go long periods without receiving any meat from her husband. They also note that large game is shared so evenly across households that the wife of a good hunter may receive no more meat than the wife of a poor hunter or a single woman (Hawkes, O'Connell, and Jones 2001a, b). Good hunters give out much more meat than they ever get back, so all their giving does not appear to favor their households to any great extent (Hawkes, O'Connell, and Jones 2001b, Woodburn 1998). Nevertheless, as we saw in the last chapter, the trait most frequently cited by Hadza women as important in a potential husband is good forager (Marlowe 2004d). This forces us to ask what benefits forager women gain from being married.

One might think provisioning is more important than direct care, and if the two were inversely related, perhaps men who provided less direct care were actually helping children more via provisioning. Using children as the unit of analysis and controlling for age of child, there were no negative correlations between any measure of direct care received and any measure of father's food acquisition. On the contrary, because there were some positive correlations, men who provided more direct care tended to bring back more food (Marlowe 1999b). So it seems some men just invest more than others in their children overall, and more in genetic children than in stepchildren.

However, in a few extreme cases, men do compensate for lack of provisioning. Two men who were disabled and did not forage, and so were excluded from previous analyses (and who had only genetic children), provided higher levels of direct care than any other men in the sample. If they had been included in the analysis, their effect would have been to strengthen the influence of paternity on level of direct care provided by men.

Table 8.5 shows how many daily kcals of foods of all types married men and women brought into camp. Married women brought into camp 50% of the total kcals among couples. Among couples with offspring under 3 years old, men brought in 58% of the daily kcals of food, and among those with offspring under 1 year old, men brought in 69% of daily kcals (Marlowe 2003a).

I analyzed the food returns of couples by subtracting from each woman's own food returns those of her husband. The more negative the

TABLE 8.5. HADZA MEAN FORAGING RETURNS
(KCAL/DAY) AND RETURN RATES (KCAL/HOUR)

Sample	Females		Males	
	Kcal/Day	*Kcal/Hour*	*Kcal/Day*	*Kcal/Hour*
Married adults	3,016 (50%) SD = 1900 (*n* = 41)	764 SD = 435 (*n* = 41)	2,990 (50%) SD = 2025 (*n* = 40)	666 SD = 706 (*n* = 40)
Married adults with offspring <8 years old	2,697 (47%) SD = 2056 (*n* = 19)	768 SD = 550 (*n* = 19)	3,049 (53%) SD = 2369 (*n* = 18)	642 SD = 855 (*n* = 18)
Married adults with offspring <3 years old	2,346 (42%) SD = 1650 (*n* = 17)	693 SD = 476 (*n* = 17)	3,227 (58%) SD = 2316 (*n* = 17)	678 SD = 867 (*n* = 17)
Married adults with offspring <1 year old	1,713 (31%) SD = 1409 (*n* = 6)	451 SD = 332 (*n* = 6)	3,851 (69%) SD = 1283 (*n* = 6)	690 SD = 137 (*n* = 6)

NOTE: Mean foraging returns are measured by daily kilocalories of food brought into camp, and return rates are measured by kilocalories per hour. Percentages in parentheses next to daily kcal are the
proportion of the whole diet (100%) contributed by males and females within the sample in each row.
Note that while women's returns decline with younger children, men's returns increase.

number, the more a husband compensates for his wife's provisioning.
Even though women beyond their early 50s are not caring for their own
young children, some men do have very young children at 65, so I used
women with husband's aged 18–65 years and controlled for age in the following analyses.

Among married women with a child under 1 year old who was the
offspring of her husband, women brought in an average of 2,138 daily
kcals less than their husbands. Having a child under 1 year old was a significant predictor of the gap between a man's returns and those of his
wife ($\beta = -0.387$, $p = 0.030$, $df = 30$, controlled for woman's age).

Husbands appear to compensate for their wives' food returns until
about the time of weaning. Women who had children less than 3 years of
age who were the offspring of their husbands brought in less food than
their husbands, whereas those who did not brought in more food than their
husbands. Having a child under 3 years old was also a significant predictor of the gap between a couple's daily kcal contribution ($\beta = -0.366$,
$p = 0.048$, $df = 30$, controlled for woman's age).

This disparity between a couple's food returns is not due merely to
the lower returns of women with young children. Men who had a child

≤8 years old at home, young enough to still require substantial provisioning, brought in more daily kcals than men who did not ($\beta=0.358$, $p=0.029$, $df=36$, controlled for man's age).

Some men had both their own offspring and stepchildren at home, and the presence of a stepchild was associated with lower food returns for men. The presence of a genetic offspring ≤8 years old predicted higher food returns for men ($\beta=379$, $p=0.022$, $df=35$, controlled for man's age). Without controlling for the presence of a stepchild, this relationship was obscured.

The difference between the returns of men who did and did not have offspring ≤8 years old at home was greater when meat was excluded from the analysis. Men who had offspring ≤8 years old at home had higher non-meat returns ($\beta=0.464$, $p=0.004$, $df=36$, controlled for man's age). This was due largely to those men getting more honey ($\beta=0.387$, $p=0.018$, $df=36$, controlled for man's age). There was no difference between men who did and those who did not have young offspring in terms of daily kcals of meat.

HUNTING SUCCESS, REPUTATION, AND REPRODUCTIVE SUCCESS

Hadza men with better hunting reputations, controlled for age, had higher overall food returns ($r=0.319$, $p=0.014$, $df=56$) and higher hourly return rates ($r=0.310$, $p=0.018$, $df=56$). Controlling for age, men with better hunting reputations had more children born ($\beta=0.317$, $p=0.043$, $df=39$) and more children surviving ($\beta=0.357$, $p=0.022$, $df=39$) (Marlowe 1999b). Eric Smith (2004) reports higher RS for better hunters among other foragers. He argues that the link between successful hunting and reproductive success may be due to costly signaling (Smith 2004). Because hunting is difficult, a woman might prefer to mate with a good hunter even if she gets no extra food, so long as hunting success is a reliable signal of male quality, e.g., general vigor (Hawkes and Bliege-Bird 2002, Smith and Bliege-Bird 2000).

Hawkes, O'Connell, and Jones (2001a) argue that Hadza men are not trying to provision their children when they target game. They found that Hadza men who were better hunters had wives and children with better nutrition and growth rates, but argue that this is only because better hunters are married to better gatherers, since children's weight gains correlated with mothers' foraging returns, but not fathers' foraging returns. However, they did not distinguish stepfathers from fathers. This makes a difference in my data, with one-third of all Hadza children ≤ 8 years old being stepchildren (Marlowe 1999b). I too found no correlation when stepfathers without genetic children at home were included. But using only those men who had at least 1 genetic child at home, the more genetic children they had at home, the higher their hourly meat return rate ($r=0.488$, $p=0.025$, $n=21$). Men who have more genetic children at home may be more motivated to bring back more food, and they had better hunting reputations ($r=0.439$, $p=0.036$, $df=21$).

Men who had the best hunting reputations, controlling for age of man and number of genetic children at home, did not provide less nurturing to their genetic children ($r=0.050$, $p=0.838$, $df=17$). This is interesting because the hunting as costly signaling hypothesis would lead us to expect that better hunters are more attractive to females, and if better hunters are more attractive, they should do less provisioning and direct care of offspring just like Nancy Burley's zebra finches did, as predicted by the differential allocation hypothesis (Burley 1988).

Men's returns of all foods were more highly correlated with non-meat ($r=0.862$, $p=0.000$, $n=51$) than meat returns ($r=0.486$, $p=0.000$, $n=51$), and all foods were more highly correlated with hunting reputation ($r=0.375$, $p=0.007$, $n=51$). Men with reputations as good hunters, therefore, are not just good at getting big game, but also are good at acquiring all types of food. Focusing only on meat, which is much less predictably acquired than other foods, obscures the benefits of a husband's provisioning, just as does ignoring the presence of a stepchild.

It is possible that male household provisioning is important, even though preliminary data show little effect of a father's presence on offspring mortality (Jones et al. 2000). One way good hunters could gain their reproductive advantage without having more wives (and even without a higher percentage of offspring surviving) is by providing for a wife and children sufficiently to increase fertility and shorten inter-birth intervals (Marlowe 2001).

MEN'S AND WOMEN'S FORAGING GOALS

Hawkes, O'Connell, and Jones (2001a) have argued that Hadza men are targeting large game almost exclusively. However, my data from 1995–2005 show that, although adult men take more large game than Hadza boys, they still take a great deal of small and medium-size game

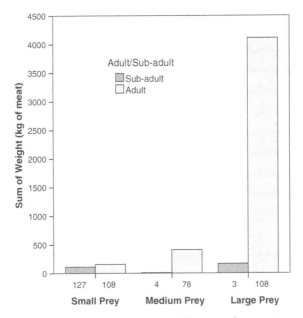

Figure 8.7. Sum of meat weight (kilograms) by prey size acquired by males ($n = 428$ carcasses).

(Figure 8.7). There is certainly no reason to think that teenage boys do not want to kill large game. Yet boys under 18 years old killed only 3 large game animals. This is because they are not capable of killing them. One reason for this seems to be they do not have the necessary strength to sink an arrow deep enough in a large animal to kill it, which we can see in both grip strength tests (Figure 6.5) and archery scores (Figure 6.8).

Based on experiments with snaring, Hawkes, O'Connell, and Jones (1991) have also suggested that Hadza men could acquire a higher daily return by targeting small game. While their experiments show that snaring would yield a more reliable daily take, the Hadza do not snare. A few have done it occasionally after learning how to from their neighbors, the Isanzu, who do set snares. Hadza men have told me emphatically that snaring simply is not a Hadza custom. This may be explained by the fact that anyone who finds the animal can take it and eat it without the one who set the snare eating any or even getting credit for it. Furthermore, it appears that large game yields a much higher total amount of meat in kilograms than small and medium game (Figure 8.7), even if slightly fewer carcasses are taken (108 large vs. 186 small and medium). Actually it would be far fewer carcasses if each and every individual bird were counted during the bonanza of *tso ma* (weaver birds, *Quelea quelea*) when thousands of chicks are taken by men, women, and children. However, those individuals would be nearly impossible to count, as they are in giant heaps in a basket, and here each basket is counted as one when weighed.

I have found Hadza men willing to shoot at almost any mammal or bird they felt they could hit (Figure 8.7; number of prey: small game = 108; medium = 78; large = 108). Hadza men express a preference for larger game because, as they say, "there is more meat." Even though big game is shared more widely in camp than small game, in each encounter with a prey animal, the hunter gets more absolute kilograms of meat (and so do others) when he kills a big animal than when he kills a small animal. For example, 1/20 of a 200-kg zebra shared by 20 people (10 kg) is greater than half of a 3-kg rock hyrax shared by two people (1.5 kg), so Hadza men are happier when they encounter a zebra than when they encounter a rock hyrax.

It may be easier to hit a large target in the open like a zebra than a small one like a hyrax that is seeking refuge in crevices between rocks. This would be true for young boys as well, but because they lack the strength to kill a large animal, they preferentially target small game. Of course, large game are fewer in number than small game, so if men were passing up small game in search of large game, it probably would be true that they could acquire more kcals of meat each day by targeting small game. Since they are not passing up small game, however, the opportunity cost of taking large game is minimal. Furthermore, the processing and transport costs are not usually large enough to offset the extra kcals of meat in a large animal. For one thing, men often get other men to help them track, butcher, and carry meat back to camp. Even though small game is also often shared outside the household, it is the more widespread sharing of large game that poses the main question. But as long as a man's household ends up with a considerably larger amount of meat from a large animal than from a small one, taking big game when possible may not a bad strategy for household provisioning.

My graduate student Brian Wood conducted an experiment to test whether men preferred to be in a camp where there was more meat coming in, or if they would rather signal their own hunting ability. He showed both women and men a picture of two camps: camp A in which there were

3 women and 3 men, and all 3 men were good hunters, and camp B in which the 3 men were not good hunters. He asked which camp each person would rather live in. All women preferred to live in the camp with good hunters with lots of meat coming into camp. Seventy-six percent of men chose to live in the camp with better hunters where there would be more meat for all to eat, even though each man would be less likely to be the only good hunter and have an advantage in signaling his quality to the women. There was no difference between men with dependent children and those without, and the 4 men who were single all chose to live in the camp with better hunters (Wood 2006). These results imply that Hadza men are less interested in showing off than in eating meat.

MOTHER'S PROVISIONING

Women in general, as we saw in Chapter 5, bring back to camp more daily kcals than men, although fathers bring back more than mothers when the sample is limited to couples where the father is the genetic father of the children and there is a child under 3 years of age. Nonetheless, in about half of all married couples, the wife brings back to camp more kcals than the husband. Furthermore, women are targeting more reliable foods: baobab, berries, and tubers. Women almost never return to camp without some food. The foods women target are also shared less extensively outside the household than are men's foods. Because women daily acquire more reliable foods that are shared less outside the household, it is clear their foraging strategy is aimed at provisioning their households. This pattern is true not only of the Hadza but of virtually all tropical foragers (Marlowe 2007).

Even though a woman can dig tubers with an infant on her back, it does lower her foraging returns (Marlowe 2003a). It is clear that women with nursing children could benefit from help with provisioning. Married women who were nursing brought in fewer daily kcals than married women who were not, and the more frequently a woman nursed, the lower were her returns (Marlowe 2003a). In addition, among women with a child under 3 years old, the younger a woman's youngest child was, the lower her hourly return rate (Figure 8.8). This means someone else must compensate for her lower productivity. Postmenopausal women bring many kcals back to camp and are clearly one important source of provisioning for nursing mothers and their families (Hawkes, O'Connell, and Jones 1989). My data show that fathers are another source.

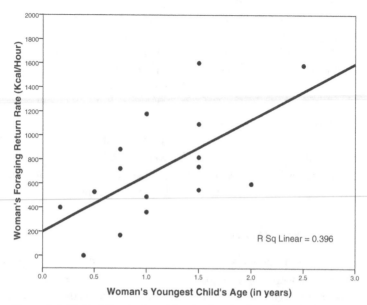

Figure 8.8. Daily kilocalories of food taken back to camp by women per hour of foraging by the age of each woman's youngest offspring ($r = 0.629$, $p = 0.009$, $n = 16$). A newborn lowers a woman's foraging efficiency. Fit line is linear.

FATHER'S PROVISIONING AND HOUSEHOLD SHARE

Hawkes, O'Connell, and Jones (2001a) have suggested that pair-bonds may not be related to male provisioning. They have also suggested that the correlation between men's hunting reputations and RS may result from better hunters marrying better gatherers. This might mean that women marry better hunters because hunting success signals superior qualities that are important, but not greater household provisioning (Hawkes and Bliege-Bird 2002). My data show that once stepfathers are excluded, fathers' returns are correlated with the number of young children in the household. My data also showed that men who have wives who are nursing their own children bring more food back to camp (Marlowe 2003a).

The link between my data on how much food men bring back to camp and my data on how much food their households get was missing. Now, however, we have data on how much of a man's food stays in his household. Data on primary distribution of men's foods collected by my graduate student Brian Wood show that the food acquirer does keep a

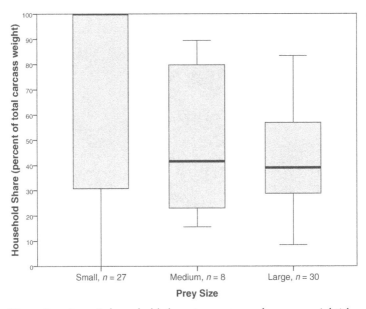

Figure 8.9. A man's household share (percentage of carcass weight) by prey size ($n = 65$ carcasses; midlines indicate medians; boxes indicate quartile 25th to 75th percentiles; whiskers indicate extremes).

larger share of his food than others get (Marlowe and Wood 2007). Data on final distribution is still being analyzed, but preliminary analysis reveals that a greater share of the food a man brings back to camp is eaten by his children than is eaten by children in other households (Wood and Marlowe in prep).

Married men keep a larger fraction of small game than of medium or large game in their households in the primary distribution (Figure 8.9). This does not mean they keep all of even a very small animal because often even something as small as a hyrax is shared outside the household, sometimes with several people. However, sometimes a hyrax may be eaten only by a man's children. That is never true of a giraffe or even an impala. Despite the fact that married men keep a smaller fraction of large game, they still end up with a much greater amount of meat in their households after a primary distribution from large game than from small and medium-size game (Figure 8.10).

A cross-species analysis of birds and mammals revealed that species in which parental care interferes with a mother's foraging were more likely to form pair-bonds (Ember and Ember 1979). This same factor

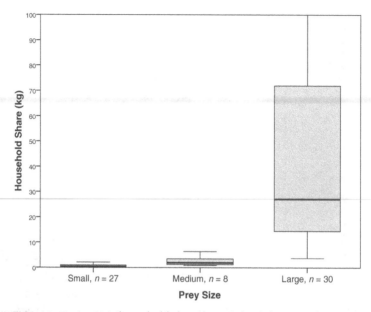

Figure 8.10. A man's household share by weight (kilograms) by prey size (*n* = 65 carcasses; midlines indicate medians; boxes indicate quartile 25th to 75th percentiles; whiskers indicate extremes).

could be important in maintaining pair-bonds in humans. Even if a woman subsidizes her husband most of the time, she might still benefit if he subsidizes her when she is nursing and has reduced foraging efficiency. Hadza women with infants have lower foraging returns than other women (Figure 8.8). Their husbands have higher returns and bring in more food than other men, so long as the children at home are their own offspring and not their stepchildren. Therefore, despite the problem of the unpredictability of big-game hunting which Hawkes and colleagues have pointed out, Hadza women may prefer good hunters because they receive direct benefits from a husband's overall provisioning. Men with good hunting reputations also have reputations as good honey collectors (Figure 8.11; $r=0.557$, $p<0.0005$, $n=109$). Therefore, it appears that some men are just better foragers all around.

Foraging men may specialize in meat and honey because these foods have the highest trade value with women. A Hadza woman is probably more pleased if her husband comes home with meat or honey than with extra piles of tubers and berries, which she can get herself. It is because women acquire foods that can be counted on every day that men are free

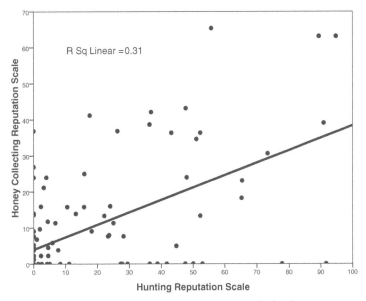

Figure 8.11. A man's honey-collecting reputation by his hunting reputation (n = 109; calculated by percentage of times nominated in interviews). Fit line is linear.

to pursue less predictable, but potentially much larger and certainly more preferred, foods (Marlowe 2007, Marlowe and Berbesque 2009). Still, when men fail to kill game or find honey, I often see them stop on the way home to get baobab to take back. Men also feed themselves to a large extent on more predictable foods while they are out on a foray (Marlowe 2006b).

Women's foraging strategies surely reflect parenting effort more than men's do (Bird 1999, Hawkes, O'Connell, and Jones 2001a, Marlowe 1999b), yet male provisioning could still be an important factor in pair-bonding. Men's foraging might be motivated by gains from increased mate access and retention, rather than increased offspring survivorship (Marlowe 2001, Marlowe 2007). Pair-bonds could be a mate-guarding strategy for males, but a way to get help with rearing children for females. Still, the presence of a stepchild does make a difference. This means either that men are less motivated to provision unrelated children or that better foragers are less likely to be living with a stepchild. If the latter, that would presumably be because good foragers have higher mate value, which affords them greater choice of mates, and they more often choose to marry women who do not already have other men's young children. Even if mate acquisition and retention are what motivates a man's foraging, he gets more fitness benefit if his food goes to feed his own offspring rather than stepchildren.

The paternal investment theory of pair-bonding tends to put the cart before the horse by suggesting that men provision because offspring are needy. Surely, ancestral females did not begin to bear offspring so needy that they could not rear them on their own before others began to acquire more food than they consumed. It was surplus food acquisition that made provisioning possible. Life history traits then coevolved with provisioning. Women in many societies like the Hadza can rear offspring without husbands. But they may take longer to conceive the next child, especially if they do not have a mother around to help. Women should be able to rear more offspring in less time when they also have a husband providing food (Marlowe 2001). Women stand to benefit most from provisioning when lactation places the greatest demands on them. At that time, they are less likely to be ovulating and should be less sexually attractive. Without pair-bonds, then, this is just when they should be least likely to get food from males. Offering men increased paternity confidence through pair-bonding may be the best strategy for women to gain provisioning for themselves and their children during this critical period.

In conclusion, there are several reasons to suspect that Hadza women gain some economic benefit from a husband. They cite good hunter as the single most important trait in a potential husband (Marlowe 2004d). They get angry when they catch their husbands pursuing other women; if they did not risk losing some benefit, it is difficult to see why they should get jealous. Men say they feel pressure from their mothers-in-law to be productive foragers. Men with reputations as good hunters (who are good foragers in general) have higher reproductive success. Good hunters do not have more wives over their lifetimes, but they do have a better chance of marrying reproductive-age women after their previous wives reach menopause (Marlowe 2000b). The most parsimonious explanation to account for all of these observations is that a wife can receive direct benefits from her husband's provisioning. He does not even need to bring home more food than she does, just more than he consumes of his food and hers. However, even a productive husband may go a long stretch without killing a large animal, so without all the camp-wide food-sharing, hunting would make a very poor source of provisioning. As we will see in Chapter 9, there is no shortage of food sharing among the Hadza.

Cooperation and Food-Sharing

COOPERATION

Game theory provides the tools for understanding the evolution of cooperation (Maynard Smith 1982, Nash 1950, Schelling 1960, von Neumann and Morgenstern 1944). The prisoner's dilemma (PD) is the game most often used to explore cooperation (Table 9.1). The PD takes its name from the situation of 2 partners in crime from whom the police are trying to get information. The 2 prisoners are put in different rooms so they cannot communicate, and the police offer each a shorter sentence if they will give evidence against the other one. If one gives evidence (defects) and the other does not (cooperates), the defector gets the best possible outcome (lightest sentence, a score of 5), and the cooperator gets the worst (longest sentence, a score of 0). If both keep quiet (cooperate), they both get short sentences (score of 3), and if both tell on the other (defect), they both get longer sentences (score of 1). In a one-shot game, player 1 should realize that there is no reason for player 2 to cooperate when he could defect and gain 5 points. Realizing this, player 1 should defect. Thus, the only equilibrium strategy in a one-shot game is to defect, with both players getting the punishment payoff (1). Even though they both could get 3 by cooperating, they cannot trust each other and are doomed to get 1 instead. This illustrates the problem of cooperation (Axelrod 1984).

When the PD game is not one-shot but iterated (has several rounds of unknown number), the possibilities for cooperation are greater because

TABLE 9.1. PAYOFF MATRIX FOR
PRISONER'S DILEMMA GAME

	Cooperate	Defect
Cooperate	R = 3, R = 3 Reward for mutual cooperation	S = 0, T = 5 Sucker's payoff, temptation to defect
Defect	T = 5, S = 0 Temptation to defect, sucker's payoff	P = 1, P = 1 Punishment for mutual defection

NOTE: The payoffs to the row player are listed first.

one's decision can be contingent on the previous outcome of an interaction with someone else. If 2 players can trust one another, they can get the reward payoff of 3 each time. The problem is that the partner may be tempted to defect and take the higher payoff of 5.

In an iterated PD game, the simple strategy of tit for tat (TFT), which cooperates on the first move, continues to cooperate if the other player cooperates, but defects if the other player defects, is a good strategy for promoting cooperation (Axelrod 1984). It is still somewhat difficult to get off the ground when the population is full of defectors, but as long as there are some cooperators TFT can increase. Once cooperation exists, however, other strategies do even better in terms of maintaining cooperation. For example, tit for 2 tats is better at avoiding endless feuds (Axelrod 1984). The best strategy of all, Pavlov, cooperates when forced to, but defects when it can get away with it (Nowak and Sigmund 1993). If Pavlov receives either of the 2 higher payoffs (3, 5), it repeats the previous move. If it is playing with TFT, it will continue to cooperate because only then will TFT cooperate. On the other hand, against a dovish strategy which always cooperates, Pavlov will find that it gets 5 each time it defects, and so it continues to take advantage of doves. This is what maintains cooperation in the population because TFT allows doves to increase, and once doves increase, hawks (which always defect) can do very well. Unlike TFT, Pavlov keeps doves from increasing, which keeps hawks from increasing, yet Pavlov will cooperate when forced to, so it is best at maintaining cooperation.

TFT is the strategy we tend to associate with reciprocity. If food-sharing is explained mainly by reciprocity, foragers should behave like TFT and cooperate on the first move. The evolution of reciprocity is facilitated when individuals live in small groups, regularly interact, keep track of others' interactions, and have a high probability of future interactions (Axelrod 1984, Trivers 1971), all features of human foragers. These are conditions that allow givers to monitor others so as to make future giving contingent on receivers reciprocating with sufficient frequency or in sufficient amounts. Without the ability to spot cheaters, free riding will likely erode reciprocity. Since it is more difficult to monitor everyone in larger groups, without special controls, free riding should increase as group size increases (Boyd and Richerson 1988).

COOPERATIVE FORAGING

Much of Hadza food acquisition is individualistic, even among women who always go foraging in groups. Each individual can usually acquire food without the help of others. That does not mean that cooperative foraging is absent. Women often cooperate when digging tubers. Once they settle on a patch, each begins to dig in her own spot. Frequently, however, one woman may stop digging her own tuber to help a companion who is digging a big tuber that is very deep. The two may work together to pull it up after it is exposed.

When men forage alone (which is almost always the case), there is no opportunity to cooperate, unless we consider coordination with other men on the direction each will take upon leaving camp to be cooperation. Men often talk about where they are going before leaving camp, and other men tend not to travel the same path, but the coordination is minimal, and men cross each other's paths frequently. Men do cooperate when tracking game (Figure 9.1). After a man has hit an animal that he knows will not die for an hour or more, he usually returns to camp and gets other men to help him follow the blood trail and footprints to track the prey. Once they find the animal, they take turns butchering or cooperate, with one holding a leg out while the other cuts the skin off (Figure 9.2). Men go to water holes in the late dry season, where they wait all night to ambush animals coming to drink, and they do this in pairs, taking turns dozing and keeping watch. It is not uncommon for men to go for honey in groups of 2 or 3, and one will hand the torch up to the other who then climbs up to raid a beehive and drops the honeycomb down to the other man.

During berry season, men often go foraging with their wives (Figure 4.8 and Figure 5.4). Sometimes, they use their axes to chop off branches so that the women can pick the berries without having to climb into the bush. When the red-billed Quelea (*Quelea quelea*) mass reproduce, everyone in camp may go foraging together over the course of two weeks. Sometimes, one person concentrates on pulling down nests and handing them to another

Figure 9.1. Three men track a wounded animal that one of them has hit with an arrow.

Figure 9.2. Four young males butcher an impala that one of them shot.

person, who takes the chicks from the nests and deposits them in a basket or a sling he or she is wearing. This cooperative foraging is often between a husband and wife and their children. Thus, there are plenty of occasions where Hadza do cooperate, but it is rare for such cooperation to be essential for success in acquiring food. It is usually a matter of making food acquisition a tad bit more efficient, or safer, or more pleasurable.

FOOD-SHARING

Among mammals, when food-sharing occurs at all, it is usually limited to the provisioning of offspring. More widespread sharing does occur among cooperative breeders, such as wild dogs (Solomon and French 1997). Lions may share a carcass, but not without a lot of snarling (Packer and Pusey 1997). When a chimpanzee kills a colobus monkey, others often get some if they steal it or beg with outstretched hand (McGrew and Feistner 1992, Mitani and Watts 2000). In contrast, humans regularly share food outside the household without begging or arguing (Gurven et al. 2000, Kaplan and Hill 1985, Kitanishi 1998, Peterson 1993, Woodburn 1998). When lions are eating on one carcass, we might say they are sharing, though there is no transfer of food from one to another; the term *food transfer* is often used to specify the giving of food to others (Winterhalder 1996b). Here are the relevant hypotheses:

1. Nepotism (food for kin)
2. Mate provisioning (food for mating access or bond maintenance)
3. Not-in-kind exchange (food A for food B)
4. In-kind delayed-reciprocity (food A now for food A later)
5. Costly signaling (food to advertise ability and receive benefits)
6. Tolerated scrounging (food for peace)

Hypotheses

Often, when food is shared in other species like lions or hyenas, the sharing follows cooperative group hunting. The best explanation for the cooperation in the hunt appears to be mutualism (Packer and Pusey 1997). Mutualism occurs when two or more individuals engage in coordinated action which enhances the outcome for both, but entails no temptation for one to defect because defecting would result in the prey escaping. The sharing of the carcass after such mutualistic hunting might simply result from the fact that the best one can do is find a spot on the carcass and eat fast. The following are the most relevant hypotheses to explain the sharing among human foragers when there is a transfer of food from one to another or several others.

Nepotism   Individuals should be willing to give food to kin when the cost (C) to the giver is less than the benefit (B) to the recipient, multiplied by the coefficient of relatedness (r) between giver and recipient ($C < B*r$) (Hamilton 1964). Selection can favor a gene that promotes such behavior, so sharing food with close kin presents no evolutionary puzzle. Female mammals have evolved specialized organs (mammary glands) to do just this. While nepotism surely explains much of the food-sharing among foragers like the Hadza, there are also many food transfers to non-kin that it does not explain.

Mate provisioning   In some species, such as scorpion flies (*Panorpa japonica*), males offer females food in exchange for mating (Thornhill 1984), and in other species, such as the Celebes hornbill (*Penelopides exarhatus*), males feed their mates, who are cloistered with their chicks inside tree holes. It is rare that females offer food to their mates, though it occurs in owl monkeys (*Aotus spp.*), at least in captivity (Wolovich, Evans, and French 2008). Hadza women certainly feed their mates, and so do women among most human foragers. When true monogamy exists and persists until death, offering food to a mate benefits the giver because the giver's own reproductive success is completely tied to that of the mate.

Not-in-kind exchange (trade)   This entails the exchange (often simultaneous) of one type of resource for another, such as meat for berries. This must account for some of the sharing between husbands and wives who bring different kinds of foods back to camp and then eat each others' foods (Winterhalder 1986). Not-in-kind exchange may also include food for nonfood goods (or perhaps services), and may account for cases where a woman gives food to someone who stays in camp to watch her child while she goes foraging.

In-kind delayed-reciprocity   When there is considerable daily variance in foragers' food returns and little correlation in daily returns across foragers, giving food to others will pay, so long as it is reciprocated, since this minimizes the risk of going a day without food (Winterhalder 1986).

One problem with reciprocity is that some individuals may be more productive foragers than others, either because they are more skilled or because they try harder, and end up giving out much more food than they receive (Hawkes, O'Connell, and Jones 1991, 2001b). This makes delayed reciprocity riskier and potentially less balanced than immediate not-in-kind exchange. If lower production is due to laziness, an imbalance might not be tolerated, whereas it might be if it is due to lower skill (since more-skilled foragers expend less effort to equal the production of less-skilled foragers and can therefore afford some imbalance).

Costly signaling An individual may share food that is difficult to acquire because doing so signals information about his or her phenotypic quality. These qualities could include good eyesight, coordination, strength, knowledge, endurance, or bravery. A woman may benefit from mating with a man who possesses such qualities. Her children may inherit those qualities, or the qualities may be associated with general vigor and greater survivorship odds. She may also receive better treatment from others who receive food from, and defer to, her husband and his household. One who can afford to give more than he or she receives demonstrates his or her foraging ability and may gain benefits from conveying that information—for example, a good hunter may gain extra mating opportunities (Gintis, Smith, and Bowles 2001, Hawkes and Bliege-Bird 2002, Zahavi 1995). Hunting may be a good way to signal phenotypic quality because it is difficult and because giving out meat attracts a large audience (Smith and Bliege-Bird 2000).

Tolerated scrounging Glynn Isaac (1978) suggested that sharing among early hominins may have begun with scrounging not unlike that seen among chimpanzees. Richard Wrangham (1975) had described chimpanzees "sharing under pressure," which Isaac called "tolerated scrounging." If individuals realize others will get mad if they do not share their food and may eventually take the food by force, we can imagine how this could have been the reason for early food-sharing. Once language evolved, the fear of being called stingy could motivate human sharing, as it does even nowadays. With large packages of food, the owner will experience diminishing marginal utility with each additional unit he eats after getting full, so those additional units will be worth more to those who have not yet eaten and are hungry, and they should therefore be more willing to contest those units. Because the cost is greater than the benefit of defending additional units, it pays the acquirer to hand them over.

Nicholas Jones (1987) modeled this idea and called it "tolerated theft." Unfortunately, *tolerated theft* is often misinterpreted as outright theft, though that is not what Blurton Jones intended. This is why I use the term *tolerated scrounging* (Blurton Jones used the term *tolerated theft* only because he thought Isaac had used it, Personal Communication 2002).

Once scrounging occurs, producing food can become a game of chicken (Hawkes 1992). Those who receive food without paying the cost of acquiring it gain more than those who acquire food. We can then expect people to wait for others to go get food. This situation can lead to a mixed strategy of producers and scroungers (Vickery et al. 1991), or everyone producing sometimes and scrounging at other times. This will result in depressed production. Costly signaling might be the antidote that spurs production. Even when scrounging is rampant, so long as those who produce more food are judged to be of higher quality and benefit from this reputation, they should be motivated to produce. Foods acquired with considerable daily variance will often be the ones that signal ability. Foods acquired with considerable daily variance, especially in large packages, are also more vulnerable to scrounging (Winterhalder 1996a). And they are the foods most likely to be exchanged in delayed reciprocity, making it difficult to choose between these hypotheses (Bliege-Bird and Bird 1997, Kaplan and Hill 1985). However, tolerated scrounging should apply more to large packages, while package size is not as relevant for reciprocity. We might, therefore, predict that large game is subject to scrounging more than honey is.

TYPES OF FOOD-SHARING

Just as in our complex society, much Hadza food-sharing occurs within households. Within our houses, we have privacy, so most outside-household sharing occurs on special occasions when friends and relatives are invited to dinner. Among the Hadza, without such privacy, there is considerable sharing outside the household on a daily basis, often with everyone in camp. Thus, while nepotism is an important reason for the within-household sharing, it is clearly insufficient to explain all food transfers, especially in the largest camps, where many other households of unrelated people receive shares.

The following scenarios are common occurrences among the Hadza. Each is quite different in terms of possible explanations. (1) Two or three

Figure 9.3. Three men out of camp share honey that one of them acquired.

men share honey when they go foraging together (Figure 9.3). (2) Five women who dig tubers together roast and eat some of the tubers once they stop digging. They may all eat from their own piles, or they may take all of the tubers from one woman's pile, and she eats some of the other women's tubers once they return to camp. (3) Once they return to camp, these women roast and eat more tubers, this time sharing with all the children present. (4) One of these women sends some tubers over to her husband and the other men sitting in the men's place. (5) A man returns to camp with a rock hyrax that he cooks for his children only. If others come and sit at his hearth, they will likely get some of the hyrax, so even small game does not always stay in the acquirer's household. (6) One hunter returns to camp with an impala, which is shared widely across households. Big game is not only shared with other households in camp, but due to the frequent visiting between camps, it is also shared with people from other camps. For example, in a sample of 6 camps, 27.2% of all meat that arrived in camp was killed by men residing in another camp.

Men also eat some small game on the spot, a small bird or squirrel or a leg of a dik-dik, but medium-size game like a gazelle is carried back to

Figure 9.4. Males carry the butchered carcass of an impala back to camp.

camp. If a man has hit an impala and has enlisted other men to help him track it, they may butcher and eat some of the meat before carrying the rest back to camp (Figure 9.4). When men kill very large game, like a buffalo or giraffe, they sometimes take as much as they can carry back to camp, and then others go to the kill site and butcher and carry back their own portions. Sharing of very large game in such cases consists of merely telling others where the carcass is.

Honey is shared widely when many people see it, but its distribution can be targeted to particular individuals more easily than meat because it is easier to hide and does not have to be cooked. I have seen a man sneak honey into his house, where he shared it with his wife and child plus two young single women he discreetly signaled. Still, it can be difficult to hide. Once a man slipped into camp and put his honey under my Land Rover to wait for an opportune time to fetch it and give it to his children. But when he finally retrieved it, others saw it, and he had to share it with everyone present.

Unless men find a lot of honey, they may eat all they find and take no honey back to camp. Men's foods, such as meat and honey, that make it back to camp do so with greater variance and tend to be shared more widely outside the household than women's foods. When picking berries, women will eat many, but they also fill up baskets and take them back to camp, whereas men and children tend to eat all they pick. We can therefore infer that women share berries more than men or children, and that not all of this sharing is within the household. Hadza children forage for themselves from a very early age, but they take back to camp a lower percentage of what they acquire than adults do.

FACTORS INFLUENCING FOOD-SHARING

Food Processing

Several factors influence food-sharing. For example, if foods can be eaten on the spot, there may be less reason to take them back to camp, and they may thus be transferred less often. The need to process foods can increase the likelihood of transfers (Wrangham et al. 1999). Some foods are always processed, some are never processed, and others are sometimes processed and sometimes not. For example, baobab is eaten directly when out of camp, but when it is taken back to camp, the pulp and seeds are pounded into flour with a hammerstone. Meat is always roasted or boiled, though marrow is eaten raw. Berries are usually eaten fresh, but toward the end of berry season, they are dried to preserve them for several days. All species of tuber (save one) are usually roasted for about 5 minutes before being eaten, though all are occasionally eaten without roasting.

Central-Place Provisioning

Different foods are taken back to camp in different proportions. About 50% of berries, 80% of baobab, 75% of tubers, 60% of honey, and 85% of meat are consumed in camp. Most food-sharing among the Hadza occurs in camp. Of course, much of the diet about two-thirds) is eaten in camp, so we would expect there to be more opportunity to share there. It appears that species that routinely share food are more likely to be central-place provisioners (Marlowe nd-a), so one of the main reasons human foragers share food so much more than other primate species is related to taking food back to a central place (CPP) (Marlowe 2006a).

   Table 9.2 shows the frequency of sharing by type of food in two different camps, one in the dry season and one in the wet season. For all 5 main categories of foods, there was more sharing in camp than out of camp per hour of observation. The bias toward in-camp sharing was strongest for

TABLE 9.2. TESTS OF FREQUENCIES OF FOOD TRANSFERS
By Food Category in Camp and Out of Camp for Two Different Camps

Location of Food Transfers	Tubers	Berries	Baobab	Meat	Honey
In camp 131.6 hrs observed (0.41 of total)					
Expected n	77.5	43.5	24.6	30.3	25.0
Observed n	127.0	62.0	51.0	70.0	50.0
	obs. > exp.	obs. > exp.	obs. > exp.	obs. > exp.	obs. > exp.
Out of camp 187.7 hrs observed (0.59 of total)					
Expected n	111.5	62.5	35.4	43.7	36.0
Observed n	62.0	44.0	9.0	4.0	11.0
Total transfers 319.3 hrs observed	189	106	60	74	61
In camp vs. out of camp test	$\chi^2=53.615$ $p<0.003$	$\chi^2=13.405$ $p<0.003$	$\chi^2=48.020$ $p<0.003$	$\chi^2=87.869$ $p<0.003$	$\chi^2=42.322$ $p<0.003$

NOTE: Expected frequencies are derived by assuming the total number of food transfers for each food category would be divided into transfers in camp vs. transfers out of camp in proportion to the number of hours of observation in camp and out of camp. Chi-square tests are Bonferroni corrected for 5 tests of 5 food categories. Total amounts of food transferred are not shown here. Nonetheless, the null assumption would be that the probability per hour of observation of a food transfer in camp and out of camp would be equal if there were nothing special about using central places. For central place foragers, it is likely more transfers would occur out of camp while foraging and eating, as they take no food back to camp. Central place provisioners, on the other hand, can share food out of camp while foraging and back in camp when they take food back. The tests here show that in the case of the Hadza, the probability of a transfer is much higher in camp than while out foraging.

meat, which is not surprising given that men usually hunt alone and have few opportunities to share out of camp. When large game arrives in camp, it is usually shared widely across households (Hawkes, O'Connell, and Jones 2001b, Marlowe and Wood in prep). Berries are the foods with the lowest percentage of in-camp sharing. This too is to be expected because they are so often eaten on the spot. In fact, during berry season, there are days when the Hadza do not take food back to camp but instead live in the berry bushes and are basically feed-as-you-go foragers.

Leaving some members in camp necessitates taking food back, at least for those weanlings and their alloparents. Provisioning depends on the ability to acquire surplus food; thus CPP depends on a certain diet like sizable game, or an extractive technology such as the digging sticks women use to acquire large amounts of underground tubers or the hammerstones used to pound baobab seed and pulp (Hawkes, O'Connell, and Jones 1997, Kaplan et al. 2000).

Hadza may bring food back to camp with the goal of provisioning the members of their households and alloparents, but because they live in groups composed of several families, they end up sharing with others (Marlowe 2004e). Due to the fissioning into smaller foraging parties, surplus food arrives in camp asynchronously. This means that some people have food while others do not, which increases the opportunity for scrounging. The Hadza expect others to give them food, so food-sharing is common. Surely, this is partly due to egalitarianism, but it is also partly responsible for creating egalitarianism.

Being Present or Absent

With all the food-sharing that goes on among the Hadza, one might think that a husband would surely save food for his wife or a wife for her husband, or at least parents for their offspring. In fact, food is almost never saved for anyone not present unless there is so much food around that it does not get eaten up. In other words, people keep food in their huts or hanging up in a tree near their hearths, but this can be for those same people who have already eaten when they get hungry again. If someone like a child or a spouse returns to camp while the food is still there, then of course that person will get some. Otherwise, he or she is just out of luck.

Once I was out with several women and a few children who were digging not too far out of camp. Suddenly, one of the women looked up and yelled to the rest of us. She had found a klipspringer (*Oreotragus oreotragus*), an animal about the size of a mountain goat, hanging in a tree. It was obvious what had happened. The animal had been standing on a big rock stretching its neck to reach some leaves on the tree when it slipped; its neck lodged in the fork of a branch and it hanged itself. It was like manna from heaven, and the women were very excited. They quickly pulled the animal down, butchered it, carried it back to camp, and roasted it. They and the children managed to eat it all up before the men returned. Not a bit was saved for the men. The men would likely do the same if the women were all gone from camp.

A common misconception is that meat is shared because it will spoil and be worth nothing to the hunter. But the Hadza often eat very rotten week-old meat they scavenge from carnivores. The Hadza (and many other foragers) know how to preserve meat by drying it, but they rarely do so because it gets eaten so quickly. Even very large animals usually do not last a week because word spreads (often despite efforts to keep it a secret) and people come from other camps to get some.

Camp Size

Large camps are noticeably different from small camps, with more segregation by sex and more bickering. This bickering may be related to scrounging. The Hadza fight about a number of things, and how much food they are given is one of them. I have seen one couple move out of a camp because the man and woman felt they were given too little when a large bag of maize bought with tourist money was divided up. This is more likely to happen with food that is not acquired by foraging but rather earned by all, or that comes as a windfall, presumably because it is then explicitly communal property.

If we assume that people who bring back to camp less than 1,000 daily kcals are more often receiving food from others, the absolute number of adult scroungers increases with camp population (Marlowe 2004e). In small camps, where there may be only 3 or 4 households, all eat together, and all types of food are shared with everyone present. In the smallest camps, there is absolutely no privacy and no chance of sneaking food in. In a large camp, there may be 20 households. At times, everyone may be sitting on one side of the camp, which means that someone can more easily sneak food into a hut on the other side of camp. In large camps, people will occasionally wait until dark to return and then discreetly signal me to come weigh their food after sneaking it into their huts. This shows that they would prefer not to share with possible free riders. Yet with more scroungers demanding more, it may become more risky not to share for fear of being called stingy.

Mates, Children, and Other Kin

When Hadza men sneak food into their huts, they tell me they are doing so because they want to feed their families. Men do indeed lose much of their food (Hawkes, O'Connell, and Jones 1991, 2001a, 2001b), but this should not count as evidence that they are uninterested in provisioning their households. That would be true only if men were passing up foods that are less likely to be scrounged yet are still highly valued by their wives, which is something I do not see. I see men take small, medium, and large game when they have the chance to hit the animal (see Figure 8.7). Controlling for age, people who had a biological child ≤ 8 years old at home and/or were married took back to camp significantly more daily kcals of food than single people without young biological children at home did.

Some young single males and females without children do bring in many daily kcals, perhaps because having a reputation as a good forager helps one acquire a better mate. "Good forager" is frequently cited by males and females as important in a potential mate (Marlowe 2004d). Males, especially when young and trying to establish reputations, may acquire the foods most subject to scrounging (meat and honey) because they are more preferred (Berbesque and Marlowe nd) and so have the highest trade value. Once they have children, Hadza men often appear to want to direct food to their households but simply lose much of it to scrounging.

PRIMARY DISTRIBUTION

Data on food-sharing is very difficult to collect. When one can grab a handful of meat, honey, berries, etc., the grabbing happens quickly by several people at once, and the eating is just as fast. Sometimes those who got handfuls move off in different directions. If one is conducting a focal individual observation, following someone continuously, there is a better chance of recording each instance of food transferred to or from the focal individual, and we have now collected many such data in and out of camp (though only a small sample has been analyzed). When one cannot weigh the food, getting reliable estimates is challenging. We do not stop people as they are eating to weigh the food, but rather estimate

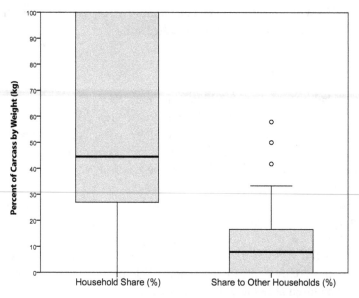

Figure 9.5. A man's household share compared to the mean share of other households by weight (kilograms) of carcasses ($n = 62$; midlines indicate medians; boxes indicate quartile 25th to 75th percentiles; whiskers indicate extremes excluding outliers, which are shown by open circles).

the amount transferred, e.g., one golf-ball of honey. It is a little easier to record where all divisions of an animal go right after it is butchered, what we call the primary distribution. Often, large chunks of meat are sitting on top of a hut or at each family's hearth. Before this portion is all gone, it might be shared in a multitude of ways within and outside the household. That is what we call the final distribution.

Brian Wood managed to estimate final distributions of many foods men brought back to camp. Here, I show only his data on primary distribution. Figure 9.5 shows that, despite the widespread food-sharing, the producer kept a significantly greater fraction of the food he acquired than he gave to other receivers ($Z=-5.7$, $p<0.0005$, $n=62$). One reason is that when he returns and few people are in camp, he puts the food at his hearth and begins eating with those present, which may include some of his family members. By the time everyone else returns, it may all be gone.

Men keep a smaller fraction of large game than of small game (Figure 8.9). Even so, the acquirer still keeps a significantly larger share of large game than the average share received by others (Figure 9.6; $Z=-3.75$,

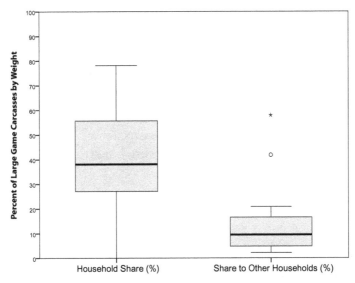

Figure 9.6. A man's household share compared to the mean share of other households by weight (kilograms) of large prey carcasses only ($n = 22$; midlines indicate medians; boxes indicate quartile 25th to 75th percentiles; whiskers indicate extremes excluding outliers shown by open circle and star).

$p < 0.0005$, $n=22$). This is true even though others receive more shares of meat than of honey or baobab, and a man keeps a smaller fraction of his meat than of his honey or baobab. In the end, men do keep a larger fraction of their meat than other households get across game of all sizes (Figure 9.5).

In order to draw conclusions regarding household benefits from a man's or woman's food arriving in camp, we need to know if the primary distribution gives us a reliable indication of the amount eaten in the household when the food is all gone (the final distribution). In preliminary analysis, primary and final distributions are correlated (Marlowe and Wood in prep). Although the correlation is not extremely high ($r=0.443$, $p=0.027$, $n=25$), it does imply that the results for final distribution will show that the forager had an advantage and that his household ate more than other households (Wood and Marlowe 2007 in prep).

Not-in-kind exchange of food (trade) occurs among the Hadza, especially between husband and wife, with men specializing in hunting and women in gathering, and then exchanging their foods. Occasionally, one man has brought meat to camp where several other men have been sitting with honey they got, and each man has eaten some honey and some meat. Even if trade is involved in special cases, it does not explain why good hunters so often supply everyone in camp with meat. Because trade (or mate provisioning) can explain husbands and wives sharing different kinds of food and nepotism can explain sharing with children, grandchildren, and siblings, it is the food transfers to everyone present, child and adult, close kin and non-kin, that is most puzzling. The 3 most relevant hypotheses to explain such widespread transfers are delayed in-kind reciprocity, costly signaling, and tolerated scrounging.

MOTIVE VERSUS PATTERN OF
FOOD TRANSFERS: INSIGHTS FROM GAMES

Most studies of food-sharing focus on the pattern of food transfers and then infer something about the motives and goals of those who give food (Gurven 2004). It is important to distinguish between one's desire to give away food (one's motive), which may or may not be conscious, and the observed pattern of food transfers. Sometimes motives and patterns of sharing coincide; sometimes not. If one's motive for taking food back to camp is to feed one's children (which may be a conscious goal) in order to enhance inclusive fitness (not a conscious goal), and food is given only to one's children, the motive explains the pattern of food transfer and vice versa. But after arriving in camp, if others request and receive shares, then although the motive for taking food back was nepotism, the food transfer might be explained by scrounging. The motive for the transfer to non-kin is then to avoid the costs of defending the food or getting a reputation as stingy.

Five of the 6 food-sharing explanations in Table 9.3 imply that the food giver wants to give out food. Tolerated scrounging explains only why others get shares regardless of the wishes of the giver. Costly signaling is mostly an explanation of motive, not of the pattern of food transfers. The giver may have no preference about who gets food, only that recipients get the information conveyed by the signal (hence, the ? in the third column of Table 9.3). Tolerated scrounging might explain why everyone gets some of the hunter's meat, while costly signaling is invoked only to explain why the hunter bothers to hunt.

The food-sharing hypotheses are more distinct with regard to motives than to pattern of food transfers predicted, yet there has been little in-

TABLE 9.3. MOTIVATION, PATTERN OF TRANSFERS,
AND GAME PREDICTIONS FROM HYPOTHESES

Food-Sharing Hypothesis	Giver's Motive	Food Recipients	Game Predictions
Nepotism	Raise inclusive fitness	Close kin[b]	
Mate provisioning	Maintain bond	Mate[b]	Males give more
Reciprocity			
Not-in-kind exchange (trade)	Optimize diet breadth	One with different foods[b]	
In-kind delayed reciprocity	Reduce daily variance in food consumption	Sharing partners, especially successful foragers[b]	1) High UG/DG offers (50%)[d] 2) High rejection of low UG offers[c]
Costly signaling	Gain mates, allies	Fertile females and worthy allies[b]?	3) High UG/DG offers (≥50%)[d] 4) Male UG/DG offers > female[d]
Tolerated scrounging	Avoid contest[a]	All present, or at least all with leverage	5) Low UG offers[c] (DG=0%)[d] 6) High rejection of low UG offers[c]

[a] = Food-giver has no desire to give
[b] = Recipients are intended recipients
[c] = Hypothesis is supported
[d] = Hypothesis not supported

vestigation of the motivation and decision making involved. Measuring only the pattern of food transfers is akin to noting only the mates people have, not those they would like to have. Without data on mate preferences, we might erroneously assume that people are with their preferred mates. Likewise, without data on sharing preferences (unconstrained by external pressures), we might erroneously conclude that the giver gives the way he or she wants to.

I have used experimental games to investigate Hadza sharing preferences. The advantage of using games is that each person is free to decide how much to keep and how much to give away without others knowing, since the players are anonymous in these games. We can therefore find out what people would like to do when free of constraints, such as coercion, punishment, or fear of damaging their reputations.

Two games that measure sharing propensity are the ultimatum game (UG) and the dictator game (DG). In the UG, the first player, P1 or proposer, must decide how to divide a given amount (the stake) with the second player, P2 or responder. If the responder accepts the proposer's offer, he or she receives that amount, and the proposer gets the remainder, e.g., if the stakes are $100, the proposer offers $10, and the responder accepts, the responder gets $10 and the proposer gets $90. On the other hand, if the responder rejects the proposer's offer, both receive nothing. The responder can, thus, punish the proposer for making a low offer, but at a cost to himself or herself. The dictator game (DG) is played exactly like the UG except that the second player cannot reject an offer. The proposer therefore dictates the division.

Standard economic theory suggests that the UG responder should accept any offer above zero, since something beats nothing. A proposer should figure this out and offer only one unit above zero (10%) in the UG to maximize his or her own earnings. Zero is the expected allocation in the DG. Experiments in complex societies, such as the United States, have shown that proposers offer much more. In fact, the modal UG offer is 50%, and the modal DG offer is between 30% and 50% (Camerer and Thaler 1995). UG offers in complex societies seem irrationally high unless responders often reject lower offers, and they do. Offers under 20% have about a 50% chance of being rejected (Henrich 2000).

I played these games with the Hadza as part of a cross-cultural project that included 20 other small-scale societies (Ensminger and Henrich in prep, Henrich et al. 2005, Henrich et al. 2004, Henrich et al. 2006). Here, I discuss the results from round 1 in 1998 and round 2 in 2002. In round 2, we used the strategy method: Players had to say whether they would accept or reject all possible offers before hearing what they were actually offered.

THE ULTIMATUM GAME

In contrast to the modal offer of 50% that is typical of industrialized societies, the Hadza modal offer was 20% (mean = 33%, SD = 17, $n = 55$) in round 1 in 1998 and 10% (mean = 26%, SD = 17, $n = 31$) in round 2 in 2002 (Table 9.4). Even in round 1, Hadza offers were significantly lower than offers among Los Angeles graduate students (Henrich 2000) ($U = 174$, $p < 0.0005$, $n_1 = 55$, $n_2 = 15$).

The Hadza, unlike several other small-scale societies in our project, were quite willing to reject low offers; 24% of offers were rejected in round 1, and 65% in round 2. The maximum possible overall earnings

TABLE 9.4. RESULTS IN THE 2002 ROUND
COMPARED TO THOSE IN 1998

	DG	UG	TPPG
1998			
Mode	10	20	
Mean ± SD	20 ± 16.2	33 ± 17	
n	43	55	
2002			
Mode	0	10	0
Mean ± SD	26 ± 25.26	26 ± 16.6	26 ± 19.4
n	31	31	27

TABLE 9.5. 1998 ULTIMATUM AND DICTATOR
GAME MULTIPLE REGRESSION RESULTS

Variables[a]	Ultimatum (money as stakes)		Dictator (beads as stakes)	
	β	P	β	p
Age[b]	−0.097	0.562	−0.017	0.926
Sex[c]	−0.174	0.199	−0.203	0.153
Comprehension	0.277	0.067		
Number of siblings	0.010	0.943	−0.196	0.162
Number of children	−0.077	0.634	0.040	0.824
Camp population size	0.475	<0.0005	0.544	<0.0005

[a]Relationship to proposer's offers; 27 male and 28 female proposers.
[b]Age Mean = 37 (17–70).
[c]Sex: male = 1; female = 2 (*n* = 55 males, 55 females).

equal 50% per person when there are no rejections and group benefit is maximized, but because Hadza offers were low and rejections high, their overall earnings were low (mean = 38.1%, SD = 27.5, *n* = 110 in round 1; mean = 32.3%, SD = 24.3, *n* = 62 in round 2). In fact, it appears that their overall earnings were lower than in any other society tested.

The only significant predictor of how much player 1 offered player 2 in round 1 was camp population (Figure 9.7). Offers were higher in larger camps (β = 0.475, p < 0.0005, df = 48), controlling for age, sex, number of children, number of siblings, and a measure of comprehension (Table 9.5). None of these control variables were significant predictors.

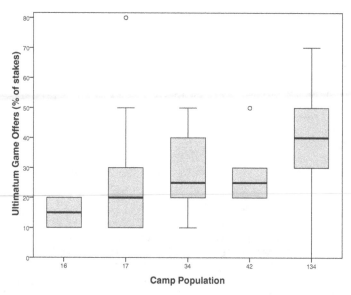

Figure 9.7. Hadza ultimatum game offers by camp population size ($n = 48$ proposers; midlines indicate medians; boxes indicate quartile 25th to 75th percentiles; whiskers indicate extremes, excluding outliers, which are shown by open circles).

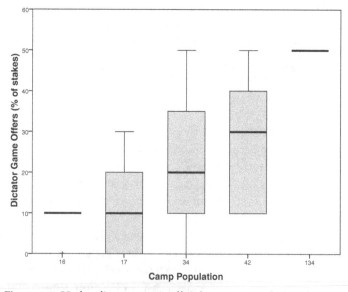

Figure 9.8. Hadza dictator game offers by camp population size ($n = 34$ proposers; midlines indicate medians; boxes indicate quartile 25th to 75th percentiles; whiskers indicate extremes).

THE DICTATOR GAME

In contrast to complex societies, where the modal offer in the DG is 30–50% (Camerer and Thaler 1995), the Hadza modal offer in the DG was 10% (mean = 20%, SD = 16.2%, $n = 43$) in round 1 and 0% in round 2 (mean = 26%, SD = 25, $n = 31$). Again, the only significant predictor of offers was camp population (Figure 9.8). People gave higher amounts in larger camps, controlling for age, sex, number of children, and number of siblings (Table 9.4; $\beta = 0.544$, $p < 0.0005$, $df = 34$).

When the 2002 results are combined with those of 1998 and camp populations are divided into small (16–20), medium (24–42), and large camps (76–134), offers are significantly higher in larger camps in both the DG ($r = 0.335$, $p = 0.004$, $n = 74$) and the UG ($r = 0.321$, $p = 0.003$, $n = 86$). There is more bickering in large camps, which seems to be related to more persistent demands to share food, while the number of free riders increases (Marlowe 2004e). It could be that, even if it is more tempting to hide and hoard food in larger camps, it is also more costly to do so where there are more people to claim shares. Even though the games are anonymous, perhaps players in larger camps still felt compelled to give more than players in small camps.

In round 2, we played one more game, a third-party-punishment game (TPPG). This is a dictator game in which P1 can give P2 whatever allocation he or she wants. However, in this game, there is a third player (P3), endowed with a sum equal to half the total stakes, who can decide whether to punish P1. If P3 decides to punish P1 for giving P2 a low amount, he or she can return one-fifth of the endowment to me and take away three-tenths from the earnings of P1. If P3 does not want to punish P1, he or she can keep all the endowment. In the TPPG, the modal offer from P1 to P2 was 0 (Table 9.4; mean = 26%, SD = 19, $n = 27$), and the mean minimum acceptable offer (MAO) that P1 could give P2 without P3 deciding to punish was 5.65% (Marlowe 2009). This low mean MAO indicates that the Hadza were very reluctant to engage in third-party punishment. Yet they were likely to engage in second-party punishment, because when they themselves are given low offers, they are quite likely to reject them. In fact, the Hadza may exhibit the lowest third-party punishment and the highest second-party punishment of all societies tested (Marlowe 2009, Marlowe et al. 2008).

IMPLICATIONS OF GAME RESULTS

The Hadza share food every day, yet they gave low offers in all 3 games. They were willing to reject low offers given to them, but not inclined to punish anyone who gave a third party a low offer. Because they gave low offers but rejected low offers in the UG, they had very low mean earnings. If all would give generous offers or all would accept low offers, they would get a lot more money from me and maximize group benefit, even if that was at the expense of certain individuals. Any rejection means I keep the money I would have given to one or both of the players. This is emblematic of the difficulty the Hadza have solving collective-action problems. This difficulty is one of the drawbacks to egalitarianism.

Without hierarchical organization and leaders to give and enforce orders, collective efforts such as crop planting and tending, building and maintaining irrigation ditches, or territorial defense would be difficult to accomplish. The Hadza occasionally have meetings where they reach a collective decision—for example, the one mentioned in Chapter 7 when they told the girl to choose one of her 3 suitors. Maybe she will heed their advice, but if she does not, there is little that others can do, and one of the suitors may still kill his rival. Another common problem is defending their area. In discussions, the Hadza may agree on the need to exclude non-Hadza from their land and tell outsiders (mostly pastoralists) they cannot build a house in the hills where Hadza camps are. As soon as the meeting breaks up, one Hadza may go directly to the house of the offending pastoralist and beg for food or make a trade. No one can force others in the group to forego their own interests for the sake of forming a solid defense against outsiders. Hierarchy with a big man on top can accomplish this (Boone 1992). With even the simplest horticulture, sedentism increases, population density rises, and big-men societies become the norm (Johnson and Earle 1987). Hadza egalitarianism and individualism are too strong for them to adhere to group rules that big men, chiefs, kings, or presidents can impose.

Third-party punishment helps enforce cooperation. If people will cooperate with cooperators, defect on defectors, and punish those who defect on others, it is difficult for cheaters to benefit. The Hadza were reluctant to punish third parties. When I ask Hadza what they do if someone in camp is being a slacker or being stingy, the most common answer is "we move away from them," rather than "we make them leave." They are averse to confrontations and solve most conflicts with others by moving. This is what they do when someone in camp is trying to boss them around as well.

When I tell people about these games, they almost always guess that the Hadza, or any foragers who regularly share food extensively, would make more generous UG and DG offers than people in complex societies make. This is because they assume generosity and reciprocity explain food-sharing. One would be hard-pressed to find a society with more extensive food-sharing than the Hadza, yet they made low offers in all 3 games. If tit for tat, which cooperates on the first move, captured Hadza norms in any situation where one has to decide whether to give to another, we might expect them to cooperate in the role of player 1. We should expect Hadza P1s to give 50% in these games. Instead, they gave much lower amounts, close to the lowest of all societies tested. TFT reciprocity, therefore, seems a poor explanation for the ubiquitous food-sharing we observe among the Hadza. Of course, money is not food, and these games are not food-sharing, but it is precisely because money is not food that we gain insight. Money does not have to be shared because it can be hidden, while food usually cannot be. When certain foods can be hidden, the Hadza will often do just that, until they can sneak them into their household.

Just as we say it is bad form to keep close tabs on the balance of favors, so too do the Hadza. In fact, it seems to be the overriding ethic. In a camp of 30–40 people, there are probably many more days when even the best hunter has no food and someone else has food than when the best hunter has food. If there are 10 men and each man averages a kill once every 2 weeks, the average man will not have food 13 out of 14 days. but on 10 of those 14 days someone will have made a kill. Even the best hunter might only score a kill once per week, so he would have no food on 6 of 7 days. Therefore, it will often be in his interest to request or demand shares from others. The same cannot be said of women, who target more predictable foods. Their food returns depend more on effort and strength or stamina than on luck or skill (Jones and Marlowe 2002), and women who are more hard-working tend to bring more food back day after day.

From costly signaling theory, we would expect Hadza men to give hyper-fair offers, but they gave the lowest offers of all societies. True, there is no audience to whom to advertise one's generosity in these anonymous games, but neither is there any reason to give generous offers in the DG the way so many Americans do. Americans presumably do so in order to feel good about themselves; this may be because we are so often reciprocating or signaling generosity, and it might be common, even useful, to behave the same way whether others are looking or not.

Tolerated scrounging is the hypothesis best supported by the game results (Table 9.3). Offers were low by comparison to complex societies, but there was a high rejection rate of low UG offers. It is presumably the rejection of low offers that motivates much of the outside-household sharing. The Hadza expect a fair share of what others have, and in real life, this expectation is not irrational. Instead of a one-shot decision, they can keep pressure on until someone hands over a fair share. Between Hadza, no begging or threatening is required for sharing to occur; the mere sight of someone's food usually suffices. There is no need to say "please." Nor after receiving a share, is there any need to say "thank you." I suspect that a survey of all languages would reveal that those languages which lack words for "please" and "thank you" are mostly those of egalitarian hunter-gatherers. No one need put up with bossy people. They can easily make quick alliances when their interests overlap, as when someone has a lot of meat and everybody else wants some of it.

Once I had 2 Hadza men with me traveling from camp to camp. As we headed toward the next camp, they spotted vultures and told me to stop. We found an impala carcass freshly killed by wild dogs (*Lycaon pictus*). They set about butchering the carcass and hid the meat on the floor of the car. These two men were married, but they were hoping to have an affair with women in the camp we were going to next. When I asked if they could increase their chances of an affair by giving meat to a woman, they said they were sure going to try. They failed, however, because as soon as we arrived, a crowd gathered around the car and everyone present ended up getting some of the meat. It must be rare that a man can exchange meat for sex directly; it is just too difficult to hide meat. The inability to make direct exchanges is precisely why a man might need to signal his quality via widespread food-sharing.

Except for their rejection of low offers, the Hadza come pretty close to the expectations of rational choice theory, very unlike more complex, market-oriented societies in the cross-cultural project. For example, the modal offer of player one in all 3 games in round 2 was the income-maximizing offer (IMO): 0% in the DG and TPPG, and 10% in the UG. It is the rejection of low offers that seems irrational. But surely we can understand UG player two being disappointed with low offers and wanting more. In real life, a person who is given only a small portion of food may object and ask for more. The person very likely will get more. These games do not allow for bargaining since they involve one-shot decisions.

It is the high rate of rejection of low offers that helps explain Hadza food-sharing in real life, which is not a one-shot anonymous game.

Food is shared by the Hadza in different contexts, and it seems likely that all 6 food-sharing explanations are relevant. Nepotism clearly explains household provisioning by women and sometimes by men. Mate provisioning must be at work when men feel compelled to bring enough food back to camp to keep their mothers-in-law happy. Trade occurs when men give women meat and women give men tubers. Reciprocity may account for some sharing; my anecdotal observations suggest that the best hunters tend to give other good hunters portions of their kills first. But tolerated scrounging seems most apt to explain the widespread sharing of meat and honey when they cannot be hidden. Costly signaling is likely involved to some extent, especially when teenage boys give away their meat to all and they do not even have wives or children yet.

Costly signaling could well be important, as those who give away more shares do gain reputations as good hunters, at least in a small sample of men so far analyzed ($r=0.665$, $p<0.0005$, $n=27$). In interviews, I asked men and women to name their 3 best friends, as well as the 3 best tuber diggers, honey collectors, and hunters. Preliminary analysis indicates that women with reputations as the best tuber diggers may be preferred as camp coresidents. I found that men who are named as best hunters are more often named as friends ($r=0.362$, $p<0.0005$, $n=109$). Men named as the best honey collectors were even more often named as best friends ($r=0.440$, $p<0.0005$, $n=109$), even though honey can be acquired more predictably than large game. The question is whether this helps men or only makes them more vulnerable to having an entourage following them from camp to camp to scrounge more. For a man to gain by having a reputation as a better forager, he needs to be deferred to in competition or gain an extra mate or a higher-quality mate. If he gains a higher-quality mate, which we saw men do in Chapters 7 and 8, we do not necessarily need to invoke costly signaling so long as the higher-quality woman is choosing him on the basis of his provisioning potential.

In evolutionary perspective, the way the Hadza played these games makes sense; they wanted to keep a larger share for themselves, yet they wanted others to give them an equal share. The Hadza do not steal anything from other people, only from other species (I have avoided the term *tolerated theft* for this reason). When it comes to food, one does not need to steal because it simply must be shared with anyone who sees it. It appears that Hadza take food to camp to feed their households, but once there, others often get some because scrounging is tolerated. The Hadza share their food on a daily basis with many others, while we in complex societies do not. Only after one experiences such constant demands to share can one fully appreciate how strong the desire can be to escape it. Tolerated scrounging is certainly partly responsible for Hadza egalitarianism.

PRIMITIVE COMMUNISM: PROPERTY AND EGALITARIANISM REVISITED

After studies of the Ju/'hoansi (!Kung foragers of Botswana) began to document the amount of time people spent working to gain their food, some anthropologists began to argue that hunting and gathering was not a harsh life of continual struggle to get enough food to avoid starvation (Lee 1968). Thus, the view promoted by Thomas Hobbes's (1651) description of humanity in its primeval state as a life of "continual fear and danger of violent death . . . and the life of man being solitary, poor, nasty, brutish, and short" was replaced by its antithesis, "the original affluent society" of hunter-gatherers who spend less time working than we in the developed world do (Sahlins 1972). Sahlins also drew attention to the boundless sharing of hunter-gatherers and described this as generalized reciprocity among kin and balanced reciprocity among non-kin.

Richard Lee used the term *primitive communism* to describe the sort of political and economic life of the !Kung (Lee 1988) and other foragers (see also Testart 1985, 1987). This is usually interpreted to mean that the equal sharing (especially of food) that occurs is part of a voluntary communism based on generosity and commitment to the egalitarian ethic. The inability to dominate others and resist sharing is a more apt explanation. Sahlins argued that hunter-gatherers were affluent because they had little desire for material goods. This portrayal could not be further from the truth in the case of the Hadza. The Hadza want and request anything and everything they see. It is their persistent demands for gifts that cause most outsiders to make a hasty retreat. On the other hand, the Hadza can do without material possessions. While they want gifts of all kinds, they do not develop attachments to possessions. When they lose something, they take it in stride. In fact, few material goods survive long when one lives outside in the elements, and when something gets ruined by the rain, the Hadza do not fret over it. Furthermore, they like to move frequently, which severely limits the amount of permanent possessions they can keep.

Among the Hadza, there is minimal private property. Each woman has her jewelry, clothes, and digging stick, and sometimes a cooking pot; these are her private property that she may lend to others, but no one would steal them. A man has his bow and arrows, clothes, and jewelry, and a few tools. Other than these, there is no property. The land and resources on it are there for anyone, and there is no defense of areas. Trees with good beehives do not quite qualify as defended resources. Men keep an eye on the trees and hives near their camp, and when they check a hive, they often place a rock in the hole to keep other animals out of it. They can often tell who put the rock in a tree hole when they see one. The rock acts a little like a claim to the tree and the hive. However, when I ask if that means that they should not take the honey from a tree that another man has placed a rock in, the answer is invariably no, and I see them take it all the time. It is as if they try to privatize the honey, but the effort simply fails. They would not really be able to keep others from taking it, and they are too interested in taking that which others have marked to abide by any rules that respect ownership of food resources. On the other hand, there is something a little special about honey. Once a man has collected a lot of it, he may give a little to other Hadza and then say he is saving the rest to trade with a non-Hadza. Others seem to respect his wishes to save it, but not always. Sometimes the pressure is just too strong, and he ends up sharing it before he has the chance to trade it.

The Hadza do not value saving the way people in societies that must delay gratification do. These days, if they get money, it never lasts longer than it takes to get somewhere they can spend it. This explains why the Hadza never make alcohol, even though they will drink it when someone from another tribe makes some. The Hadza know how their neighbors, the Datoga, turn honey into mead (alcohol), but despite how much they like alcohol, they always eat the honey in short order, except for those few times a man saves some for a day or two to trade with a Datoga for meat, tobacco, or iron. They simply would never delay eating the honey long enough for it to ferment. The Hadza also know how to dry meat to make it last longer, but they rarely get the chance to do so because it gets eaten so quickly.

Woodburn (1980) described the Hadza as an immediate-return society. Delayed-return societies are those where considerable effort is expended in preparation for harvesting foods in the fairly distant future. This includes all agriculturalists but some foragers as well. For example, foragers in the Pacific Northwest of North America constructed labor-intensive weirs and dams across rivers and built large permanent smoke houses for drying the fish they caught. Some of these fish would be eaten months later, long after the fish runs were over. This sort of planning for the distant future is something the Hadza do not do. They do not need to because foods are available year-round. Most foods vary between the rainy and the dry seasons, but one kind of food or another can be acquired and eaten the same day, day in and day out, year-round. There is simply no need to store food.

The Hadza do take advantage of bonanza resources such as the weaver birds (*Quelea quelea*) described in Chapter 5. But this does not lead to long-term storage or require any preparation other than finding an appropriate stick for yanking down the nests. They eat the chicks in short order, and a few days after the birds are all fledged, there are no more supplies to eat, even when they lay some out to dry. The same goes for the *undushipi* berries. In both cases, the portion that was dried is eaten every day and gone within a week or less.

Presumably, most tropical hunter-gatherers are, like the Hadza, immediate-return societies. Small-scale societies in the cross-cultural experimental economics project engaged in less third-party punishment. They probably less often enforce norms of cooperation required to solve collective action problems because they less often face such problems (Marlowe et al. 2008). In the next chapter, we will see that there is nothing so peculiar about the Hadza when it comes to tropical hunter-gatherers. In fact, we will see that they appear to be about as typical or representative as one could find.

CHAPTER 10

The Median Foragers

Humans in Cross-Species Perspective

THE HADZA AND OTHER HUNTER-GATHERERS

Now that I have described the Hadza, in this chapter, I place them in the context of all other hunter-gatherers. One way the Hadza stand out is the length of time they have survived as hunter-gatherers without taking up agriculture or disappearing altogether. Consequently, we can study them using new technology like GPS devices, heart-rate monitors, and bio-impedence measurements of body fat, as well as using more rigorous methods for collecting behavioral data. Data on most other foragers are limited to mostly qualitative ethnographic descriptions. Many of the quantitative data on other foragers in this chapter are actually coded from more qualitative data or are quantitative estimates in the original ethnographies. My goal here is not only to see how the Hadza compare to other foragers but to see how humans compare to other species.

To know which of our traits are derived and therefore require a separate explanation from ancestral traits we share with *Pan* (chimpanzees and bonobos), we must first characterize the three extant species. When we compare traits like diet, group size, home range, mating system, or mortality rates in humans with other species, it is best to measure the traits in foragers if we want to understand the relevant selective forces that shaped modern *Homo sapiens*. In this chapter, I examine some basic relationships between habitat, technology, and social organization.

Social organization is a cultural trait. When I argue that habitat variation predicts social organization, it may seem that I am making a functionalist argument at the level of culture, not individuals, or a group selection argument. In many if not most cases, however, the behavior that is most advantageous for the individual is adopted by most individuals. If using a bow is more efficient than using a spear, one individual will benefit by using a bow, and we should not be surprised to see the whole group eventually adopting the bow. Likewise, if residing in a camp with the wife's kin for a while and then later in a different camp with the husband's kin is beneficial, we may find it typical of the whole group. In other words, the habitat leads to certain behaviors that individual selection favors, and these usually become widespread, whether they are technology or social arrangements. This in no way eliminates all the ways in which the behaviors of individuals are in direct conflict within the group. One individual may benefit from hoarding food or cuckolding his neighbor, and most individuals might have such an inclination, but neither of these enhances group welfare.

THE FORAGER DATA SET

I have previously analyzed the complete forager data set (Marlowe 2005a), but here I focus on the foragers most relevant for earlier time periods, those living at lower latitudes in warmer climates. I use all the data on foragers I have been able to find (Figure 10.1). I borrow heavily from several other anthropologists (Binford 2001, Kelly 1995, Murdock 1967), the World Cultures CD (World Cultures 2005), and the *Ethnologue* (Grimes 2000), as well as other sources cited in Marlowe (2005). In the complete data set, there are 478 foraging societies, with almost all deriving less than 10% of their diet from domesticated foods. In reality, many of these societies no longer exist, but for convenience I use the "ethnographic present" and write as if they did.

The median value of a variable is the midpoint of the distribution; half of the sample lies above it, half below. While the mean is influenced by extremes, the median is not. It is usually the best measure of how average or typical a particular case is. With each variable I report on, I am comparing the Hadza mean value to the median value of all foragers, but note that the median of all foragers is calculated from each society's mean value. In many traits, the Hadza lie near the median value for my sample of foragers. When building models of evolution with parameter estimates taken from ethnographic data, it is important to know just

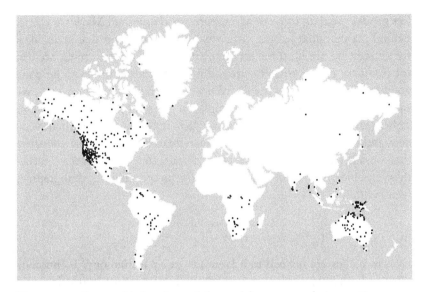

Figure 10.1. Geographic locations of the total forager sample ($n = 478$).

how typical or atypical a society is in general and with respect to foragers in a certain geographic area or type of habitat (Marlowe 2005a).
It makes little sense, for example, to use the diet and foraging techniques
of arctic foragers as a proxy for human ancestors living in the tropics.

By analyzing how climate, flora, and fauna influence ethnographic
foragers, we can infer how Pleistocene foragers might have differed from
Holocene foragers, given differences in the ecological conditions that
prevailed then and now. The Holocene is our current epoch, and it began
13,000 ya (years ago) when the last major glaciation ended. Because foragers in warm, wet habitats tend to occupy smaller home ranges than
those in cold, dry habitats, we can assume that during the late Pleistocene,
when much of the earth was colder and drier, most foragers had larger
home ranges. However, tropical areas were less changed than temperate
zones during the Pleistocene.

One might argue for using foragers in richer habitats as analogs of
earlier foragers if one thinks ethnographic foragers occupy more marginal habitats than they would have before more powerful agriculturalists existed (Alexander 1979, Bigelow 1972, Dickson 1990, Lee and
DeVore 1968). The assumption that foragers occupy more marginal
habitats, however, is not supported by the only test of that assumption.
When the cold-climate foragers are excluded, forager habitats are no

less productive than those of agriculturalists (Porter and Marlowe 2007). Behind the marginal habitat criticism is the assumption that areas ideal for agriculture are ideal for foraging and areas bad for farming are bad for foraging. However, some areas unsuitable for planting can be quite good for foraging. From the distribution of foragers in Figure 10.1, we can see that the main bias in the sample is a geographic one due to history rather than ecology. The absence of foragers in the circum-Mediterranean area and most of Eurasia is not because there is richer arable soil there than on other continents, but because complex state societies arose earlier there and incorporated or eliminated all the foragers before ethnographies were written.

ECOLOGY AND TECHNOLOGY

Human niches are defined to a large extent by technology. Technology allowed human foragers to occupy the full spectrum of terrestrial habitats, resulting in a wide range of variation. While our ancestors must have varied considerably, it appears that the first modern humans arose from a particular population living in Africa 160,000–200,000 years ago (Goldstein et al. 1995, White et al. 2003). It also appears there was a bottleneck when the breeding population was as small as 10,000 (Harpending et al. 1998). This means there would have been a limited range of variation in that population at that time. As modern humans spread to diverse habitats and developed diverse technologies, sociocultural variation increased. Because we can assume there was less efficiency in extracting resources as we go further back in time, we need to subtract the effects of increased productivity associated with the more complex technology of ethnographic foragers when we extrapolate to much earlier times.

To illustrate how ecology and technology shape social organization, consider the North American foragers who became specialists hunting bison from horseback during the 1700s, after the Spaniards introduced the horse (Shimkin 1983). The horse increased hunting success rates and lowered travel costs, which allowed the Plains Indians to specialize on the high-yielding bison and follow them over vast distances in large groups (Boone 1992, Shimkin 1983). Consequently, these equestrian foragers have much larger home ranges and significantly larger local (residential) group or camp populations than nonequestrian foragers.

If we are interested in periods before horse domestication, we can exclude the equestrian foragers. If we are interested in the period before 30,000 ya, we can exclude the arctic foragers, since it was only during the last 30,000 years that such cold areas were occupied by modern *sapiens* (Vaughan 1994). Because I am concerned with extrapolation to the more distant past (at least back to the origin of modern humans in East Africa), I use a warm-climate subset of all foragers. This sample includes those where effective temperature (ET) is $\geq 13\,°C$. ET is a measure of temperature that reflects the growing season by using a formula that relates the temperature of the warmest and coldest months. $ET = (18 * W - 10 * C) / (W - C + 8)$, where W = mean temperature (°C) of the warmest month, and C = mean temperature (°C) of the coldest month (Kelly 1995). This sample excludes foragers with the horse. There are a total of 237 societies in the warm-climate nonequestrian sample, and it is these to which I refer below.

HABITAT VARIATION AND SOCIAL ORGANIZATION

One measure of habitat productivity is net primary productivity (NPP). NPP is calculated here with an equation that uses data from satellite images (for a full explanation, see Porter and Marlowe 2007). The program takes a reading that can estimate leaf cover and then calculates net new plant growth per year. Net new production is the best way to assess habitat quality because humans and the animals they eat tend to eat reproductive parts of plants (new growth) such as seeds, fruit, and leafy parts. The benefit of this measure is that it can be calculated for any spot on the earth within an area of 1 square kilometer. One limitation of NPP is that it does not count animal biomass. However, animal biomass is greatly influenced by plant production and tends to go along with NPP in terrestrial habitats.

Table 10.1 shows how the Hadza compare to other foragers on several environmental variables. The Hadza have an ET of 17°C, which is close to the median for the warm-climate sample (16.3°C). The Hadza have an NPP of 607 g/m²/year, slightly higher than the median for the warm-climate sample (515 g/m²/year, $n = 186$). Figure 10.2 shows how NPP varies across latitudes.

DIET

Mainly as a consequence of temperature effects on primary plant production, gathering falls off in colder temperatures at higher absolute latitudes, whereas hunting and fishing increase (Binford 2001, Kelly 1995, Lee 1968) (Figure 10.3). Males in the total forager sample (cold

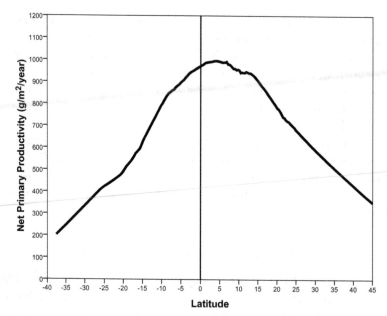

Figure 10.2. Net primary productivity (NPP) of the warm-climate sample by latitude ($n = 178$). The Southern Hemisphere is plotted with negative latitudes. Fit lines are Loess Epanechnikov.

and warm climate), therefore, contribute more to the diet at higher absolute latitudes, that is, further north and south of the equator ($r = 0.480$, $p < 0.0005$, $n = 158$). Male contribution to diet is also higher where fishing is more important ($r = 0.510$, $p < 0.0005$, $n = 155$). In the warm-climate sample, males contribute more to the diet where there is more fishing ($r = 0.317$, $p = 0.011$, $n = 63$), and although they contribute more to the diet at higher absolute latitudes, this is not significant in the warm-climate sample.

In the warm-climate sample, the median percent of the diet coming from gathering is 53%, from hunting 26%, and from fishing 21% (Table 10.1). The Hadza diet consists of 75% gathered food and 25% hunted food. This is one way the Hadza differ considerably from the median of all warm-climate foragers. However, the median values for the African foragers are 67% gathering, 32% hunting, and 1% fishing ($n = 20$). African foragers, for some reason, avoid taking fish. It is interesting that chimpanzees, bonobos, and gorillas also do not take fish, even when fish are present in the habitat. Thus, if we are interested in earlier African foragers, the Hadza are close to the median value.

TABLE 10.1. THE MEDIAN FORAGERS
The Hadza Compared to All Warm-Climate
Nonequestrian Foragers

Trait	Warm-Climate, Nonequestrian Foragers (median)	Hadza (mean)
Mean temperature C	20.5 (9.7–29, $n=187$)	19.6°C/28°C day
Effective temperature C	16.3 (13–25, $n=190$)	17°C
Mean yearly rainfall (mm)	794 (41–3,912, $n=188$)	300–600 mm
Rainfall wettest month (mm)	150 (6.4–754, $n=187$)	150 mm
Rainfall driest month (mm)	5.3 (0–212, $n=187$)	2.6 mm
NPP (modis) g/m²/year	515 (77–1,738, $n=186$)	607 g/m²/year
Gather, hunt, fish	53%, 26%, 21% ($n=179$)	75%, 25%, 0%
♀/♂ diet cont.	48%/52% ($n=57$)	50%/50%
Number moves/year	7 (0–58, $n=174$)	6.5, 9
Ethnic population	565 (23–11,800, $n=175$)	1,000
Total area (km²)	3,905 (46–230,000, $n=174$)	4,000 km²
Population density (per km²)	0.18 (.004–3.09, $n=174$)	0.24/km²
Camp population	26 (13–250, $n=133$)	30.4 (med: 21, 6–139, $n=53$ camps)
Local group area (km²) (minimum home range est.)	175 km² (22–4,500, $n=125$)	122 km²
Total fertility rate	5.5 (0.81–8.5, $n=28$)	6.2
Age at weaning (yrs)	3 (1.25–4.5, $n=18$)	2.5 years
Inter-birth interval (yrs)	3.08 (1.75–4.0, $n=9$)	3.25 years
Infant/juvenile mortality	21% (10–46, $n=12$)/ 46% (20–61, $n=14$)	21%/46%
♀/♂ age marriage (yrs)	13.5 (8–21, $n=100$)/ 20 (12–35, $n=87$)	17/20 yrs
Polygynous men	8% (0–70, $n=113$)	4.3%
Women with co-wives	10% (0–90, $n=31$)	8.6%

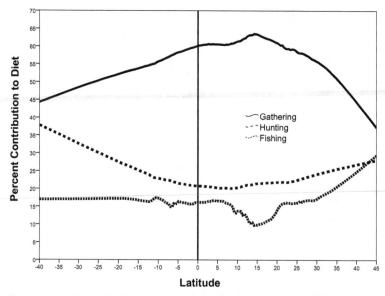

Figure 10.3. Contribution to diet from gathering, hunting, and fishing by latitude ($n = 179$). The Southern Hemisphere is plotted with negative latitudes. Fit lines are Loess Epanechnikov.

POPULATION DENSITY

The median population density in the warm-climate sample is 0.18/km². Hadza population density is 0.24/km². As expected from basic ecological theory, population density increases with greater habitat productivity (higher NPP; $r=0.195$, $p=0.008$, $n=185$), but it peaks at an NPP of about 750 g/m² and then drops again (Figure 10.4). In the total sample, there are high-density foragers at NPP ranging from 400–1,000 g/m². These are mostly the foragers of the northwest coast of North America. Their rich supplies of salmon, which they preserve and consume year-round, allow them to live in small territories in sedentary, socially stratified groups, often with frequent warfare and even with slavery (Ames 2003). It is not habitat richness per se that explains the special qualities of the complex foragers, but the seasonally abundant anadromous fish. Anadromous fish are those, like salmon, that return from the ocean to spawn in the rivers where they were born. The seasonally abundant salmon promote storage and investment in time-consuming technologies, such as weirs and smokehouses. As noted, these are delayed-return foragers (Woodburn 1980). For modeling earlier periods, we

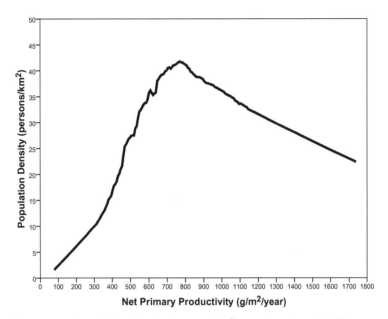

Figure 10.4. Population density (persons/km²) as a function of habitat NPP (*n* = 174). Fit line is Loess Epanechnikov.

can exclude them, and most are absent from the warm-climate sample used here.

GROUP SIZE, AREA, AND MOBILITY

Foragers typically have three salient types of groups: the ethno-linguistic group (tribe), the residential or local group (camp or band), and the daily foraging group (party). Most foragers have several types of fission-fusion. For example, every day the local group (camp) splits up into smaller foraging parties; some remain in camp while others go foraging and then return to camp to sleep. Foraging parties may also fission or fuse. Camps also show fission-fusion when one camp splits into two, then later rejoins others. Individuals also move back and forth between camps. There is residential mobility of a different sort when the whole local group moves the camp to access new resource patches. The vast majority of foragers are, like the Hadza, quite mobile. The median number of moves per year is 8.5 in the warm-climate sample, while the Hadza average 6.5–9 moves per year.

The median size of the local group (camp) population among the warm-climate foragers is 26. Mean camp population is 30 for the Hadza,

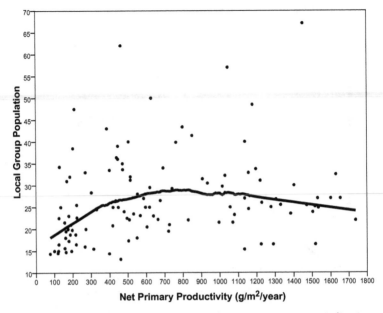

Figure 10.5. Local group population by habitat NPP ($n = 126$). Fit line is Loess Epanechnikov.

but the median Hadza population is 21. We might think that local groups would be larger in richer habitats because a larger number of people could be supported on the amount of food contained within each square kilometer. It is therefore interesting that there is no correlation between local group size and NPP. There is a higher population density in richer habitats, which means that smaller areas are occupied in order to minimize travel energy expenditure, but across the full range of NPP, local groups tend strongly toward something under 30 individuals (Figure 10.5). This suggests that warfare isn't as important as the energetics of acquiring food. If warfare were very prevalent, we should expect foragers to prefer, when at all possible, to live in larger local groups to defend themselves more effectively. Larger groups would be more sustainable in richer habitats, so the fact that local groups are not larger in richer habitats suggests that warfare is not that influential.

As we saw, Hadza camps are at their smallest during the rainy season and at their largest at the end of the dry season because there are only so many permanent water holes, which limits the number of possible camp locations and forces more people into each of the fewer camps. When rain removes this constraint, the default is to disperse into smaller groups, where the Hadza say there is less bickering. This suggests that the explanation for the remarkable consistency in local group population across forager habitats may be that free-rider problems set an upper limit on optimal or equilibrium group size (Boone 1992, Boyd and Richerson 1988). Beyond 30, conflicts between families may cause fissioning, and it is only when there are external constraints, like the prevalent warfare of some equestrian and complex foragers, that there are larger local groups. Median local group population for the anadromous fishers (complex foragers of the Pacific northwestern coast) is 75 ($n=22$) and for the equestrian foragers is 92 ($n=33$). By making bison so easy to kill, the horse removed the constraint that food availability would have otherwise placed on group size.

Because few home range data exist, I calculated a minimum estimate of home range that I call "local group area," which is the total area of the ethno-linguistic group divided by the number of local groups (which itself was calculated by dividing the total population by the mean local group population). The median local group area (home range) is 175 km² for the warm sample, while it is 122 km² for the Hadza (Table 10.1 and Table 10.2). This estimate is probably low because it assumes no overlap with other local groups, when in reality there usually is considerable overlap, and in the case of the Hadza very high overlap.

The more hunting contributes to the diet, the larger the local group area is ($r=0.219$, $p=0.004$, $n=172$) and the more frequently camps are moved ($r=0.310$, $p<0.0005$, $n=174$), while there is less mobility where fishing accounts for more of the diet ($r=-0.279$, $p<0.0005$, $n=174$). Local group area is also smaller where fishing contributes more to the diet ($r=-0.299$, $p<0.0005$, $n=172$). Local group area (home range) decreases as NPP increases, since resources are more concentrated. But once NPP reaches about 500 kg/m², local group area does not continue to decrease (Figure 10.6). This implies that most warm-climate late Pleistocene foragers, even in rich habitats, probably had very large home ranges of about 175 km² (Table 10.2), too large an area to defend as an exclusive territory (Mitani and Rodman 1979), given the population density (median=0.18 km²). Residents might still have repulsed outsiders upon encounter, as they do among some carnivores with large home ranges and some human foragers in the ethnographic record (Brown and Orians 1970, Cashdan 1983, Dyson-Hudson and Smith 1978). Much trespassing, however, would go unnoticed.

TABLE 10.2. TRAITS FOR THE WARM-CLIMATE NONEQUESTRIAN SAMPLE BY HEMISPHERE

Region	Statistic	Primary Biomass (kg/m²)	% Diet Gathering	% Diet Hunting	% Diet Fishing	% Male Contrib. to Diet	Ethno-linguistic Pop.	Ethno-linguistic Area (km²)	Pop. Density (persons per km²)	Local Group Pop.	Local Group Area (km²)	Number of Moves per Year
Old World	Mean	15.59	54.78[a]	24.23	20.78	46.83	991	18,476	0.24	30.52	473.13	8.86
	N	96	98	98	98	29	97	96	96	77	73	96
	SD	16.54	20.12	13.23	24.69	15.73	1526	34,364	0.24	31.30	838.55	9.40
	Min	0.12	0.00	0.00	0.00	25.00	35	46	0.00	13.10	21.76	0.00
	Max	59.27	90.30	55.00	90.00	80.00	11,800	230,000	1.23	250.00	4,500.00	45.00
	Median	*10.14*	*55.00*	*25.00*	*7.50*	*45.00*	*528*	*5,500*	*0.17*	*24.85*	*152.50*	*8.00*
New World	Mean	13.28	49.01	26.84	23.78	59.90[a]	1,451	7,185	0.40[a]	47.53[a]	419.82	8.75
	N	79	81	81	81	32	78	78	78	53	52	78
	SD	14.04	14.19	13.31	19.97	13.98	1,571	8,968	0.49	45.04	414.74	12.78
	Min	0.02	10.00	5.00	0.00	33.33	23	310	0.01	14.50	46.72	0.00
	Max	46.25	76.00	62.00	70.00	88.89	6,500	40,500	3.09	250.00	1,830.00	58.00
	Median	*5.65*	*50.00*	*25.00*	*20.00*	*57.50*	*875*	*3,185*	*0.23*	*32.00*	*278.76*	*5.50*
Total	Mean	14.55	52.17[b]	25.41[c]	22.14[c]	53.68[c]	1,196[c]	13,414[c]	0.31[b]	37.46[c]	450.96[c]	8.81
	N	175	179	179	179	61	175	174	174	130	125	174
	SD	15.46	17.87	13.29	22.66	16.12	1,558	26,758	0.38	38.28	692.63	11.01
	Min	0.02	0.00	0.00	0.00	25.00	23	46	0.00	13.10	21.76	0.00
	Max	59.27	90.30	62.00	90.00	88.89	11,800	230,000	3.09	250.00	4,500.00	58.00
	Median	*9.86*	*55.00*	*25.00*	*15.00*	*52.50*	*565*	*3905*	*0.18*	*25.58*	*174.90*	*7.00*

[a]Significantly higher mean values in one hemisphere.
[b]Significantly higher values for the warm-climate sample totals.
[c]Significantly lower mean values for the warm-climate sample than the cold-climate sample.

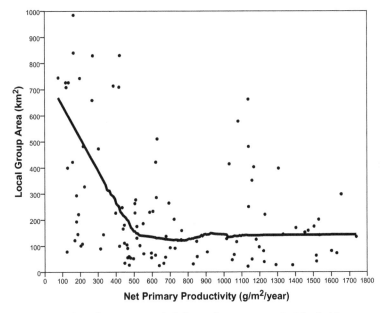

Figure 10.6. Local group area (minimum home range size) by habitat NPP for warm-climate, nonequestrian foragers ($n = 122$). Fit line is Loess Epanechnikov.

TERRITORIALITY

The Hadza are notably non-territorial. But how typical is this of other hunter-gatherers? Among the Australians, even those in the central desert where population density was low and ethnic divisions less clear, inheritance of areas from one's father (usually) was something of great importance, especially inheritance of certain sacred places (Tonkinson 1978). Greetings were ritualized so that approaches by outsiders could be made without violence (Hiatt 1996, Peterson 1976). Among the !Kung, there were *n!ories*, areas of land the rights to which were controlled and inherited (Cashdan 1983, Lee 1979, Marshall 1976), although it seems that others were usually given access if they asked (Cashdan 1983, Marshall 1976, Silberbauer 1981). Yellen (1976), however, found there was no !Kung word for *territory* nor any defense of areas which were often occupied by two different groups at once. The Andamanese are noted for their perpetual warfare (Kelly 2000). They were often considered as one group, but they saw themselves as 10 distinct tribes, and the warfare over territory was between tribes rather than within the tribe.

The Hadza have occasionally had wars with their pastoralist neighbors. These were usually provoked by the pastoralists. Sometimes the pastoralists killed Hadza to punish them for hunting their livestock. It is extremely rare for one group of Hadza to ever attack another group of Hadza. What is clear is that territorial exclusion within an ethnic group of foragers was much less strict than that between ethnic groups. This is one way humans differ from almost all other species.

HUNTING AND THE SEXUAL DIVISION OF FORAGING LABOR

Many people seem to take it for granted that hunting is usually done cooperatively by a group of several males. This is much less common than is solitary hunting among the Hadza, and that appears to be true for many foragers in the ethnographic record (Porter and Marlowe nd-b). There are notable exceptions, such as net hunters who coordinate in driving animals into a net (Hewlett 1988). Much has been written about the importance of cooperative hunting in the evolution of human cooperation (Hill 2002, Stanford 2001). It is possible that cooperative hunting was more prevalent for earlier hominins before the bow and arrow and spear thrower were invented.

When human foragers like the Hadza are compared to other species, the most remarkable form of cooperative foraging is not what the term usually implies—namely, working together to get one food item; rather, it is the sexual division of labor. When one forager can count on another to return to camp and share meat or honey in exchange for tubers or berries, we can only view such foraging and sharing as cooperation based on specialization by sex. The main form of cooperative foraging among humans, then, is this sexual division of foraging labor (Marlowe 2007).

Among chimpanzees, 71–90% of hunting is done by males (Stanford 2001), so perhaps early hominin males did more hunting than females. One might assume that the amount of hunting by early hominins just continued to climb from an original starting point similar to that of chimps. But early bipeds with limited technology in more open habitat were probably much slower and less efficient hunters than chimpanzees are in the trees, where most of their hunting occurs (Mitani and Watts 2000). The amount of hunting may therefore have decreased in the earliest hominins. The specialization in hunting by males and gathering by females that we see in contemporary human foragers may have begun much later and entailed scavenging first, perhaps as early as 2.5 million years ago (de Heinzelin et al. 1999).

The common view that males only hunt and females only gather is not true. Australian females do considerable hunting of small animals (Tonkinson 1978), while males in many foraging societies like the Hadza collect honey and gather fruit (Marlowe 2007). Hadza men know how to get the foods females get and often feed themselves on baobab and berries (tubers very rarely) while they are out hunting. Our experiments revealed that males' return rates were equal to the return rates of females when the men were asked to find and dig tubers (Jones and Marlowe 2002). Nevertheless, the human sexual division of foraging labor stands in real contrast to our ape cousins and other mammals. Even though Hadza women will kill game (usually small animals) when they have the chance and men will gather fruit, Table 5.4 shows that there is a marked division of foraging labor. Relative to all other foragers in the Standard Cross Cultural Sample, the Hadza rank near the middle on a scale that scores the division of foraging labor (Hadza = 125, median = 145, range = 60–200). They rank 14 out of 36, though the top 10 are all tied at 200 (Marlowe 2007). Among the 17 warm-climate foragers, the median is 120, so again the Hadza are almost the perfect median foragers.

LANGUAGE, ETHNICITY, AND MULTILEVEL SOCIAL STRUCTURE

As NPP increases, the total area of the ethno-linguistic group in the warm-climate sample shrinks, but the total population remains fairly stable (median = 565, mean = 1,196, 23–11,800, $n = 175$), compared to 1,000 Hadza. Presumably, there are only so many foragers who can remain tied together in terms of language (Birdsell 1968). Foragers tend to have friendly, coequal relations with other local groups of the same ethnic group but not with other ethno-linguistic groups, at least when the other groups are agriculturalists. To understand what it may have been like before agriculture existed, we can look at the Australians, since at the time of European contact, all were foragers. While there were ethno-linguistic boundaries, they were not very sharp, and there was some intermarriage between adjacent groups (Peterson 1976, Tindale 1953), especially in the central desert with its low population density (Spencer and Gillen 1899, 1904, Tonkinson 1978), but there was also some warfare

(Hiatt 1996). Along with the evolution of language came both the means to tie together several local groups and the basis for dividing one cluster of local groups from others. Since the ethno-linguistic group is largely defined by language, there is no good analog of ethnicity in other mammals, and the continuous movement of individuals back and forth between local groups within the ethno-linguistic group may be unique to humans.

KINSHIP

Bilateral descent is more prevalent among foragers (75%) than among agriculturalists (25%) (Marlowe 2004c). The Hadza trace kinship bilaterally and have no clans. Agriculturalists are most often patrilineal (Marlowe 2004c). One advantage of such unilineal descent is that it is easier to assemble a large group of reliable allies in times of warfare or disputes, since people know which unilineal clan they belong to and where their loyalties lie. This is one reason unilineal descent dominates among agriculturalists (van den Berghe 1979).

The advantage of bilateral descent among foragers is that it maximizes the number of kin ties across camps, facilitating visiting, mate seeking, and moving to access seasonal resources (Murdock 1949). This is the reason that most mobile foragers have a multilocal pattern of residence (Marlowe 2004c). Since one traces one's kin through both mother and father with bilateral descent, if having kin in a camp makes it more likely one will be welcomed there, then the person can probably double the number of camps he or she can move to. Bilateral descent is possible only if one knows one's father as well as one's mother, and since it is highly unlikely one will know who one's father is without pair-bonds, multilocal residence likely evolved after pair-bonds evolved.

MATING SYSTEMS

There is a common assumption that the decrease in sexual dimorphism seen in *Homo ergaster* and *H. erectus* about 2 mya (million years ago) relative to the earlier australopithecines reflects the origin of pair-bonds. However, there can be pronounced dimorphism with bonds (polygynous gorillas) or no bonds (orangutans), and slight dimorphism can exist with bonds (humans and monogamous gibbons) or no bonds (chimpanzees and bonobos). Therefore, we cannot conclude anything about bonds from the degree of sexual dimorphism by itself in the fossil record.

There is considerable variation in the mating system of foragers, ranging from the Andaman Islands, where polygyny is said not to exist at all (Radcliffe-Brown 1964), to Australia, where 70% of married men among the Tiwi are polygynous (Goodale 1971) (Table 10.1 and Table 10.3). Polygyny in Australia is related to gerontocracy; old men have much higher status (and more wives) than young men. The percentage of married women with co-wives better captures the degree of reproductive skew, since a polygynous man may have 2 wives or 10, which will affect the number of bachelors and thus male-male competition. In the warm-climate sample, the median percentage of women with co-wives is 10% (0-90%, $n = 31$), and among the Hadza, it is about 9%. Even where there is considerable polygyny, most marriages are still monogamous (Marlowe 2003b), and except for Australian societies, 2 wives is often the maximum.

Where male contribution to diet is higher, there is less polygyny (Marlowe 2003b). Hence, the variation across human foraging societies fits a pattern seen across mammalian species in general; males are most likely to invest in offspring in socially monogamous species, while in the vast majority of species, males invest little or nothing, and effective polygyny prevails (Clutton-Brock 1989, Kleiman and Malcolm 1981). Recall, however, that among the Hadza, men's foods (especially larger game) are shared widely outside the household, and this pattern appears to be true of most foragers (Hawkes and Bliege-Bird 2002, Kaplan and Hill 1985, Kelly 1995). This camp-wide sharing of men's foods makes it less clear that human pair-bonds are related to male provisioning. As we saw, however, among the Hadza, a man's household did keep a larger fraction of his foods than other households got (Marlowe and Wood in prep).

In the warm-climate sample, median age at weaning is 3 years (1.25-4.5 years). Mean age at weaning is 2.5 years for the Hadza, which is considerably younger than the 4.5 years for chimpanzees (Robson, van Schaik, and Hawkes 2006) (see Tables 10.1 and 10.3). Median infant mortality across the warm-climate sample is 20.6% (10-46%), the same as the mean for the Hadza (21%), and juvenile mortality is 45.5% (20-61%), again almost exactly the same as the Hadza (46%). Median total fertility rate (TFR) is 5.5 (0.81-8.5). It is 6.2 for the Hadza. A higher mean male contribution to diet across foraging societies predicts a younger age at weaning, a higher total fertility rate, and greater female RS (measured as mean number of children surviving to age 15), but not lower infant or juvenile mortality rates. Female RS is correlated only with TFR and not with mortality rates (Marlowe 2001). This implies that women use food from men mainly to speed up their rate of reproduction.

TABLE 10.3. DEMOGRAPHIC TRAITS FOR THE WARM-CLIMATE NONEQUESTRIAN SAMPLE BY HEMISPHERE

Region	Statistic	% Infant Mortality	% Juvenile Mortality	Total Fertility Rate	Female Age at First Reproduct. (years)	Age at Weaning (years)	Inter-birth Interval (years)	% Married Males Polygynous	% Married Females with Co-wives
Old World	Mean	24.35	40.48	4.87	18.15	3.13	3.08	19.07	21.56
	N	11	11	23	5	12	7	68	22
	SD	10.23	11.95	1.54	1.79	0.71	0.81	19.22	29.47
	Minimum	10.30	20.00	0.81	15.90	2.00	1.75	0.00	0.00
	Maximum	46.00	56.40	7.00	19.96	4.50	4.00	70.00	90.00
	Median	*21.00*	*45.00*	*5.25*	*18.00*	*3.00*	*3.40*	*11.00*	*6.50*
New World	Mean	11.6000	48.33	6.38	19.50	2.40	3.04	10.22	29.89
	N	1	3	5	1	6	2	45	9
	SD	.	13.01	2.29	.	0.81	0.06	8.91	20.01
	Minimum	11.60	35.00	2.80	19.50	1.25	3.00	0.00	4.00
	Maximum	11.60	61.00	8.50	19.50	3.50	3.08	33.00	55.00
	Median	*11.6000*	*49.00*	*6.80*	*19.50*	*2.29*	*3.04*	*5.00*	*37.00*
Total	Mean	23.2917	42.16	5.14	18.38	2.88	3.07	15.55	23.98
	N	12	14	28	6	18	9	113	31
	SD	10.42832	12.13	1.75	1.69	0.80	0.70	16.46	27.01
	Minimum	10.30	20.00	0.81	15.90	1.25	1.75	0.00	0.00
	Maximum	46.00	61.00	8.50	19.96	4.50	4.00	70.00	90.00
	Median	*20.6000*	*45.50*	*5.50*	*18.75*	*3.00*	*3.08*	*8.00*	*10.00*

CENTRAL-PLACE PROVISIONING

Central-place provisioning (CPP) is typical not only of the Hadza but of most human foragers as well as of many birds and social carnivores (Table 10.4). One reason for taking food back to a central place is to feed the young who are left in a safe place (Marlowe 2006a). Hadza mothers leave their weanlings in camp, so someone needs to stay there to look out for them, and that means food must be taken back. Camps across warm-climate foragers may tend toward populations of 26 when adults have young children, because if there were fewer than this, there would be too few allomothers to stay in camp and look after the weanlings.

Central-place provisioning increases food-sharing because taking food back to camp creates more opportunities for scrounging (Jones 1984, Isaac 1978, Marlowe 2006a). In addition, because a group of individuals among human foragers can and do bring down any would-be dominant individual, human foragers tend to be egalitarian (Boehm 1999). This could also contribute to the prevalent food-sharing among foragers. Food-sharing would have lowered variation in daily food consumption (Winterhalder 2001), which should have lowered mortality rates and altered life history patterns (Kaplan et al. 2000). Because central-place provisioning makes food-sharing and egalitarianism more likely, if central places can be detected archaeologically, their earliest appearance might set an upper limit on the antiquity of human egalitarianism. If central places were detected archaeologically, it would likely indicate CPP rather than central-place foraging (CPF) because a central place would be detected only via refuse, tools, and bone assemblages, something much more likely to show up once food is taken back to camp.

THE CROSS-SPECIES PERSPECTIVE

Human societies are so diverse that they are in many ways more like different species than like different populations of one species. Still, some features are common to almost all human foraging societies. In some of these near-universal features, humans resemble social carnivores more than our closest primate relatives. Like wild dogs, foragers have long day ranges, large home ranges, central places, offspring provisioning, food-sharing, and bisexual dispersal (Table 10.4). In humans, many of these traits are due to technology that allows us to acquire large food surpluses that can be transported, and food is consequently more likely to be

TABLE 10.4. COMPARISON OF BEHAVIORAL-ECOLOGICAL CHARACTERISTICS OF HUMAN FORAGERS, AFRICAN APES, AND SOCIAL CARNIVORES

Trait	Foragers Homo sapiens	Chimp Pan troglodytes	Bonobo Pan paniscus	Gorilla Gorilla gorilla	Wild Dog Lycaon pictus	Lion Panthera leo	Hyena Crocuta crocuta
Dietary Niche	Omnivore	Frugivore/folivore	Frugivore/herbivore/folivore	Folivore/herbivore/frugivore	Carnivore	Carnivore	Carnivore
Dispersal	Bisexual, multilocal (Marlowe 2004c)	Female (Pusey and Packer 1987)	Female (Furuichi et al. 1998)	Bisexual (Pusey and Packer 1987)	Female (Kingdon 1997), bisexual (Moehlman and Hofer 1997, Waser 1996)	Male, bisexual (Waser 1996)	Male (Waser 1996)
Group (local)	26	40	34	11, 6mt, 9 lowland	10	13 (Estes 1991)	55
Population Min–max	13–250	15–120 community = 50 (Wrangham and Wilson nd)	30–60 (Cheney 1987)	2–20 (Estes 1991)	20/60 (Estes 1991)		3/80 (Estes 1991)
Population Density (individuals per km²)	0.18 0.00–3.09	0.09–5 (Cheney 1987)	2–3 (Cheney 1987)	0.5–10 (Whitfield 2003)	<0.05 (Estes 1991)	0.12–0.38 (Estes 1991)	1.77 (Estes 1991) Ngorongoro
Group Composition	Multimale, multifemale camps	Multimale, multifemale community, parties	Multimale, multifemale groups, parties	Unimale, multifemale groups	Multimale, multifemale packs	Multimale, multifemale prides	Multimale, multifemale clans
Mating System	Pair bond, monogamy, polygyny	Promiscuity	Promiscuity	Pair bond, harem polygyny	Monogamy, cooperative breeding	Promiscuous but estrus pairs	Promiscuous
Sexual	None	Exaggerated	Exaggerated	Slight	None	None	None

Division of Foraging Labor	Yes	No	No	No	Male provisions pregnant female (Moehlman and Hofer 1997)	No (Estes 1991)	No (Estes 1991)
Provisioning beyond Weaning	Yes	A bit (McGrew and Feistner 1992)	A bit	No	Yes	Yes	No
Food Sharing among Adults	Yes, lots	A bit (McGrew and Feistner 1992)	A bit (Nishida and Hiraiwa-Hasegawa 1987)	No (Estes 1991)	A lot (Estes 1991)	Yes, grudgingly (Estes 1991)	Yes, grudgingly (Estes 1991)
Foraging Pattern	Central-place provisioning	Feed as you go	Feed as you go	Feed as you go	From den only when infants	From lair only when infants	From burrow or den only when infants
Grouping Pattern	Fission-fusion, ♂'s often alone	Fission-fusion, ♀'s often alone	Fission-fusion, ♀'s more social than chimp	Cohesive ♂ harem group, bachelors out	Fission-fusion, group hunt	Fission-fusion	Fission-fusion hunt alone, pairs
Day Range (km) ♀/♂	9.5/14.1 n=8/n=6	3/5 (Wrangham and Wilson nd)	2.4/2.4 (Wrangham and Wilson nd)	1.1/1.1 (0.5–2.1) (Doran and McNeilage 1998)	10 (Estes 1991)	4.5/8 (1.9–14.4) (Schaller 1983)	10 (Estes 1991)
Home Range Min–max (km²)	175 (median) 22–4,500	12.5 .5–50 (Estes 1991)	45 30–60 (Cheney 1987)	24.4 8.2–40 (Doran and McNeilage 1998)	1,700 1,500–2,000 (Kingdon 1997)	200 20–400 (Estes 1991)	500 30–2,000 (Estes 1991)

NOTE: Numbers are means or medians, followed by ranges.

shared. While technology has intensified greatly in just the past 100,000 years, if the hominin divergence from *Pan* entailed a shift to difficult to acquire but high-quality foods, as well as continuously available fallback foods, dispersed in a more open habitat with increased threat of predation, some increase in technology may have been selected for from the very beginning (Bartholomew and Birdsell 1953, Oswalt 1973).

TRAVELING BACK IN TIME AND SUBTRACTING TECHNOLOGY

Human behavioral evolution must be reconstructed trait by trait because the adaptively relevant environment and timing are different for different traits (Foley 1995, Irons 1998). The ethnographic foragers are relevant for only the past few thousand years with regard to certain traits, like iron tools, but for other traits, like digging sticks, they are probably relevant analogs of hominins millions of years ago. Table 10.5 shows some of the important technologies and their probable effects.

Many foragers acquire iron through trade and use it to make arrowheads. Iron first appeared about 2000–1500 B.C. in western Asia (Waldbaum 1978), and by 600 B.C., it had spread far and wide in the Old World, though not to Australia. Iron's superiority for durable, effective tools and weapons explains why it is so highly valued and spread so rapidly. Most contemporary foragers use iron rather than stone or bone points, which means they spend less time on tool manufacture per tool than did Pleistocene foragers. Traps, snares, and nets are examples of other fairly recent hunting technologies (Table 10.5). Some of them greatly affect many aspects of behavior; for example, net hunting can alter the sexual division of labor when males and females hunt together (Hewlett 1991). The possession of iron tools, cooking pots, and factory-made buckets and cloth make contemporary foragers different from Pleistocene foragers, but most of these items do not eliminate the value of using foragers to test many hypotheses that pertain to past selection.

HUNTING VERSUS SCAVENGING

The signs of cut marks on bones that imply meat-eating at least as early as about 2.5 million years ago have led to a debate over whether hominins were hunting or were only scavenging after other predators such as hyenas had killed large game (Blumenschine 1995, Bunn, Bartram, and Kroll 1988, Dominguez-Rodrigo 1997, 2002, O'Connell, Hawkes,

Trait	Earliest Evidence	Where	Probable Effect
Iron	3,500 ya (Waldbaum 1978)	Southwest Asia	Time-saving in arrow making, axes, more trade
Poison	11,000 ya, cited in Clark 1970	Zambia	Fast killing of large game by lone hunter, more meat
Bow (see arrow points)	11,000 ya (Cattelain 1997)	Germany	Effective killing at a distance
Spear thrower	17,000 ya (Knecht 1997)	France	Uni-male hunting, killing at a distance, more meat
Nets	22–29,000 ya (Soffer et al. 2000)	Czech Republic	Bisexual hunting, effective fishing
Microliths (arrow points), bows implied	65–70,000 ya (Barham 2002, Elston and Kuhn 2002, McBrearty and Brooks 2000)	Tanzania South Africa	Effective killing at a distance, uni-male hunting, more meat
Fishing harpoons	75,000 ya (McBrearty and Brooks 2000) 80,000 ya (Henshilwood et al. 2001)	Congo	Greater male contribution to diet, lower mobility
Shellfish	125,000 ya (Deacon and Shuurman 1992)	South Africa	Coastal niche
Spears	400,000 ya (Thieme 1997)	Germany	Hunting of larger game, before this mostly scavenging, more meat, and better defense
Fire	790,000 ya (Goren-Inbar et al. 2004) 1.6 mya (Bellomo 1994)	Israel, Africa	Protection from predators, lower mortality, warmth, cooking
Acheulean handax, cleaver	1.7 mya (Asfaw et al. 1992)	East Africa	Butchering, more meat, or opening beehives to get more honey
Oldowan chopper, hammerstone, scraper	2.6 mya (Semaw et al. 1997)	East Africa	Food processing, scavenging, tool manufacture

(continued)

TABLE 10.5. *(continued)*

Trait	Earliest Evidence	Where	Probable Effect
Carrying devices	?	Africa	Infant carrying, leather, straw or wooden devices to carry food to a central place
Wooden digging stick?	?	Africa	Digging tubers, thus adaptation to more open habitat, larger home range
Pounding/ throwing rocks, hitting and jabbing sticks?	6 mya?	Africa	Protection from predators, food processing, pre-adaptation for more open habitat

NOTE: ya = years ago.

and Jones 1988). When one has watched how difficult it is for Hadza men with effective bows and poisoned arrows to make a kill, it inevitably tilts one toward the scavenging proponents in the debate about early hominins.

The Hadza often hit animals that do not die because the quality of their arrow poison can vary. Hadza men usually hunt alone because the challenge is getting close enough to prey to get a shot before being detected. Once the bow was invented, it may have caused a switch from group hunting to more individual hunting, or at least hunting in smaller groups. Although game may have been more plentiful in the Pleistocene, early hominins did not have nets or the bow and arrows, iron points, and poison, so it is difficult to imagine that they could have matched the hunting success of the Hadza. If group hunting with spears had been so effective, individual hunting with bows likely would not have replaced it. The archaeological inference that some very early populations had diets dominated by large game that was hunted seems unlikely; it is much more likely that bones from large game animals simply dominate remains because they are so much more likely to survive. When the Hadza abandon a camp, all that remains after a short period are the large bones of large game. Yet we know that meat of all kinds, from very small game up, composes only about 25% of the calories in the diet.

Foragers without the bow are probably the most useful analogs for humans living before 100,000 ya, at least the male half. With very few exceptions, it is in Australia that spear hunters continued to exist long enough to be described ethnographically. Even they had the spear thrower (or atlatl), which greatly enhances efficiency. Wooden spears without stone points have been found in Germany, associated with horse bones dating to 400,000 ya (Thieme 1997). Without a spear thrower, a lone hunter would have great difficulty killing large game, especially if spears were used to thrust rather than throw, since that requires getting very close to game. Thus, spear hunters, before the spear thrower, most likely hunted in groups. The successful big-game spear hunters, like the pastoralist neighbors of the Hadza, the Masai and Datoga, throw their spears and kill lions and buffalos. But their spears are very heavy with huge iron points. It seems unlikely that spears with stone points would have been anywhere near as deadly. If large-game hunting occurred, it probably required cooperative groups. Before effective projectiles, hunters may have run down and clubbed small game or extracted animals from burrows (Hill and Hawkes 1983). The slow speed of bipeds would not have prevented them from eating large game acquired by scavenging, however. Recall that Hadza women, armed with only their digging sticks, occasionally scare off a leopard and take its kill (O'Connell, Hawkes, and Jones 1988).

MALE CONTRIBUTION TO DIET

Before effective hunting, males could have focused more on honey and plant foods, so their daily hauls of food did not have to add up to fewer kcals, but the food species must have been different. Male contribution to diet is significantly lower in Australia, where there was no bow, than in the rest of the warm-climate sample (38% vs. 57%), even after controlling for NPP, though this might reflect faunal differences rather than technological differences.

Even in the warm-climate sample, male contribution to diet is significantly higher where fishing accounts for more of the diet. When it is ≥ 20% of the diet, males contribute significantly more than when it is < 20% (58% vs. 49%). Since there are several other traits associated with fishing, such as lower mobility and smaller home ranges, dating the origin of fishing is important (Table 10.5). In the ethnographic record, fishing is done with spears, bows, weirs, nets, baskets, and poison, and since many of these do not appear prior to modern *H. sapiens*, we should probably exclude those who do much fishing for extrapolating to earlier periods. Hadza male contribution to diet is 50% among married couples (Table 5.5 and Table 8.5). The median male contribution to diet for all warm-climate foragers is 53% (mean = 54%, 25–89%, $n = 61$).

While some tool use may have existed throughout hominin evolution, there has been a rapid increase in technological sophistication in our species. Given the somewhat recent evolution of complex projectiles, male foraging long ago had to be quite different, but female foraging did not. Female foraging and related behavior are therefore more instructive for earlier periods. Hadza females forage in groups of about 5 women, with some infants and older children. They collect baobab fruit that falls to the ground, gather berries, and dig up a variety of tubers with digging sticks. They also use their digging sticks to defend themselves if need be. Hadza women, and women in other warm-climate foraging societies with simple technology, could be reasonable guides to hominin foraging patterns over a very long period. Females may have pioneered the earliest and still important technologies: digging sticks (O'Connell, Hawkes, and Jones 1999), rocks for pounding nuts and seeds (McGrew 1981, 1992), and devices for carrying infants and foods (Tanner and Zihlman 1976) (Table 10.5). Among the Hadza, the digging stick is responsible for acquisition of the food type (tubers) that makes up the third largest portion of the diet by kilograms and is the food most regularly arriving in camp.

IMPLICATIONS

The forager data allow us to explore relationships between habitat and social organization and compare humans to other species. Such relationships, in conjunction with the fossil and archaeological record, can help model the behavior of our ancestors at different times in the past. The main obstacle is technology. All foragers in the ethnographic record possess complex technology compared to all hominins before modern *sapiens*. However, even lower Paleolithic technology may have afforded some surplus production, which in several ways made hominins more like social carnivores than other apes.

In so many traits, from the NPP of their habitat, to their camp population, to the number of times they move camp each year, to their infant mortality rate, the Hadza mean value is very close to the median value across all the warm-climate foragers. The Hadza appear to be the median foragers. This means that when we use data values on the Hadza (and similar foragers) as parameter estimates for plugging into various models of human evolution (Aiello and Key 2002, Hawkes and O'Connell 2005,

Leonard and Robertson 1997), we can at least be confident that they are not so atypical of tropical foragers, especially in Africa. If we are modeling the evolution of modern human life history and the timing of certain traits, such as age at weaning or first reproduction that was typical of most early modern humans, the Hadza mean value might be a good estimate.

The median human foragers have a much larger home range (area used throughout the year) than chimpanzees. This is mainly because their more open habitat requires greater movement to access available foods. Bipedalism is an efficient mode of locomotion for long-distance travel. Of course, it could not have been so efficient in the very beginning. Given that all foragers depend on technology for extracting parts of their diet, and given that chimpanzees use tools, it seems likely that our last common ancestor used tools. Increased dependence on tools (that unfortunately do not preserve or cannot be confidently identified) may have been the main response to the increasingly open habitat where hominins evolved. This response could be what favored bipedalism, resulting in the *Homo-Pan* split.

The traits that are derived in hominins are shown in Table 10.6. The median foragers are compared to our closest relatives, the African *Pan* apes (chimpanzees and bonobos) and gorillas. Derived traits are those which are typical of humans but not any of the African apes: e.g., the white sclera on either side of the dark-colored iris, which allows us to tell where someone is looking, a trait possibly related to our ability to read other's minds or intentions so well, something referred to as theory of mind (TOM). Traits that we do not share with *Pan* but do share with the less closely related gorilla, such as pair-bonds and absence of sexual swellings, are considered possible ancestral traits, with *Pan* having derived them after the *Pan-Homo* split. Similarly, traits that appear to be common to gorillas and early hominins (australopithecines), but not to *Pan* or modern humans, such as extreme sexual dimorphism, are considered possible ancestral traits unless gorillas and early hominins evolved this trait independently (homoplasy). We resemble bonobos more than chimpanzees in some traits, such as our egalitarianism, because of the lack of a very clear hierarchy in bonobos (White and Wood 2007). In other traits, such as our considerable tool use, we resemble chimpanzees more.

While the Hadza are not analogs of early hominins, the foraging activities of Hadza females could be similar in many ways to those of our female ancestors 3 mya. The use of hammerstones and digging sticks could have begun with the earliest hominins. The mean Hadza camp population

TABLE 10.6. IMPORTANT DERIVED TRAITS, POSSIBLE SELECTIVE FORCES, AND EFFECTS IN HUMANS

Human	Pan (C=chimp, B=bonobo)	Gorilla
Bipedalism (tools, carrying objects)	Knuckle-walking	Knuckle-walking
Small canine (< biting in fights, hunts)	Large canine	Large canine
Vertical face	Prognathic face	Prognathic face
White sclera (follow eye gaze T.O.M)	Iris fills eye	Iris fills eye
Hair loss, variable color skin	White skin under hair, else black	White skin under hair, else black
Very large brain (1,350 cc)	400 cc	400 cc
Low sexual dimorphism	Low sexual dimorphism	Extreme sexual dimorphism
Concealed ovulation	Sexual swellings	No swelling but behavioral estrus
Permanently swollen breasts	Breasts swell only when lactating	Breasts swell only when lactating
Pair bonds in multi-male groups	Multi-male/female promiscuity	Pair bonds in unimale groups
Extensive tool technology	C—termite twig, hammer nuts, log weapon	Few
Surplus production	No	No
Sexual division, more hunting	C—> insects ♀, > hunt ♂, B—small animals	Small animals but rarely
Food-sharing	C—meat-sharing, C, B—mother-offspring	Almost no food sharing
Egalitarianism	Dominance hierarchy, C—m, B—m, f	Dominance hierarchy
Controlled use of fire (cook, safety)	No	No
Shorter IBI (3.5 yrs)	C—6 yrs, B—5–6 yrs	3 yrs
Late maturity (19 yrs)	13 yrs	10 yrs
Max. lifespan (85 yrs), menopause	C—53 yrs, B—50 yrs, no menopause	54 yrs, no menopause
CPP, allomothering in camp	Feed-as-you-go C—fis-fusion, B—cohesive	Feed-as-you-go, cohesive
Language	No, though can learn	No, though can learn
Multilocality, ethnoling. group	C—defend community, B—cohesive	Silverback defends harem
Clothes, art, music, culture traits	No, except tools, behaviors	No, few cultural traits

could well be representative of human ancestors millions of years ago. Without such efficient weapons and before controlled fire, however, our hominin ancestors should have been much more vulnerable to predation than the Hadza are. Still, in cooperative groups with sticks and stones, they may have been able to run predators off their kills, adding more meat to the diet. Skins from animals could have been used to carry all sorts of foods back to a central place. CPP may have begun with early *Homo* 2–2.5 mya, leading to extensive food-sharing, lower mortality, and shorter inter-birth intervals, the formula for the success and spread of *Homo* throughout Africa and beyond to Eurasia.

Afterword

The Hadza Present and Future

LIVING FOSSILS?

Over the past 20–30 years, some anthropologists have dismissed—even condemned—the notion that contemporary foragers can serve as windows into the past (Barnard 1999, Schrire 1980, 1984, Wilmsen 1989). This is partly for good reasons, like the fact that some "foragers" have been greatly dominated and influenced by their agricultural neighbors, have acquired new technology such as guns, and get much of their food from government handouts or from a store. Mostly, however, the criticism is a backlash against evolutionary approaches to explaining human behavior.

The Hadza are not living fossils. They have not been frozen in time; we have a written record of them going back to 1911, so we can see changes that have occurred, whether it be Kiswahili replacing Kiisanzu as the main second language, or metal pots replacing ceramic ones, or the disappearance of hippos and the small hippo spear. That said, the amazing thing is how little they have changed.

The Hadza, and a few other foraging societies, have preserved much of the technology of the past, and along with it many other attributes. The Hadza (at least some of them, the ones we spend the most time with) still exhibit many of the same patterns of behavior they did in early descriptions. They live in small groups and move every month or two, use the same tools to acquire and eat most of the same foods, marry and raise children in the same way, and seem to have similar fertility and mortality rates. These attributes make them very different from almost all other populations in the world today.

To most people, *primitive* is a derogatory adjective. But why? The Hadza are viewed by many Tanzanians as primitive and inferior. A few Hadza men who once went to Dar es Salaam told me how people there asked them "Where are your tails?" Once in a government office, the district commissioner (D.C.) told a Hadza man who was with me that "The Hadza should come on down out of the trees and do something productive with the land they occupy." This same D.C. was later quoted in a local newspaper as saying she needed to "look out for the Hadza and protect their dignity." It is because people equate *primitive* with *subhuman* that the term is an insult. Just because subsistence practices and technology vary, there is no reason to think that some people are any less human than others. An informed evolutionary perspective is the best antidote to such thinking. We all belong to one species. The constellation of traits that make us human evolved in societies that must have resembled the Hadza in many ways. Human variation is fascinating. It can be studied. It need not be viewed as dangerous in its implications. Being conservative and preserving traits over the past hundred years, and several thousand years in some cases, does not make the Hadza inferior. Nor does possessing a simple technology.

The Hadza clearly have changed less than most other societies. It is this that makes the Hadza so likable. The foraging lifestyle is not as Hobbes imagined: nasty, brutish, and short (Hobbes 1651). Rather, it is to a great extent peaceful, healthy, and fulfilling. That is not to say it is the idyllic existence conjured up by Rousseau's (1762) noble savage (even though Rousseau himself did not paint as rosy a picture as his interpreters did). The views of Hobbes and Rousseau are both too extreme.

THE PRESENT

While the Hadza have changed remarkably little since they were first written about, today many influences are changing them. There is the ever-increasing number of non-Hadza in their area. The populations of many neighboring groups are increasing rapidly, and this pressure pushes more and more farmers into Hadzaland. The farmers cut down and burn trees to clear areas for planting maize. This continues to threaten the wildlife populations and the future of hunting by the Hadza. The neighboring pastoralists are growing in number. This also puts pressure on the wildlife population because the cows and goats leave less for wild animals to eat. Neighboring tribes enter Hadzaland to hunt the game. They usually come with homemade guns or snares. In the east, the pastoralists have virtually eliminated lions, and agro-pastoralists have all but killed off the buffalo. In the west, a private hunting company leases the land from the government and charges foreign hunters to hunt, while occasionally arresting Hadza for poaching on the land they have long occupied. There has been a recent attempt to take over virtually the rest of Hadzaland by someone who wants to use it as his personal safari vacationland. We shall see how that turns out.

One threat to the foraging lifestyle today comes from the tourists who come to see the Hadza precisely because they are foragers. During 1995, there was about one car full of tourists per week visiting Hadza camps only in the Mangola area and only during the 3–4 month tourist season. Now there must be 10–20 times that number. Tourism would not be so troubling if the Hadza received food rather than money. Once the tourists leave, neighboring tribes waste no time bringing the Hadza alcohol and leaving with all the tourist money. Most Hadza simply cannot have a few drinks; once they begin, they drink until completely passed out. I have seen a few Hadza in Mangola die from drinking every day over a few years. Drinking leads to arguments and fights and injuries and murder. A few recent alcohol-related murders have caused the murder rate to soar.

Tour guides in Mangola usually cut a deal with one man and pay him well, by Tanzanian standards, to bring tourists to see the members of a camp sing, dance, and shoot their bows and arrows. It is up to this "headman" to convince the others to go along and accept how much he wants to give each person. Of course, the reader now knows there are no headmen among the Hadza. The tour guides are creating them by virtue of giving them money to distribute. This arrangement works well for the tour guides because it is much easier to negotiate with one person who has a lot at stake, and let him haggle with others to get them to agree, than it is to deal with the whole camp. It is also much cheaper for the tour guides. Sadly, they are not even aware that they are creating headmen by their actions.

It may be that Hadza culture, which has remained little changed despite long contact with more powerful neighbors, will finally succumb to outside influences, largely because the tourists are a source of money. The irony is, of course, that the tourists come because they want to see foragers; once they have completely eliminated real foraging, they will no longer come, leaving the Hadza with no source of income but with an insatiable appetite for alcohol. When I began work, most people in bush camps, especially women, much preferred gifts to money, since they did not ever go to a village and had no way to spend money.

There are some positive effects of tourism, however. The visibility of the Hadza is enhanced, which gives them a modicum of clout with local officials. Tourism can be conducted responsibly and can actually be a good influence. There are some tour operators who do consider their impact on the Hadza and take care not to cause harm.

THE INFLUENCE OF RESEARCHERS

We researchers, too, have an impact on the Hadza. We spend so much time observing them, weighing their foods, measuring their heights, and asking questions that it would be wrong not to compensate them. What to give is a problem, because whatever we give has some impact that we would rather not have. Food would be a good thing to give, but since we are studying their foraging, this is one thing we cannot give. We want to give things they value, so we give tobacco, matches, knives, beads, short pants, cloth, blankets, and sandals made from old tires (many of the items you see in the photos in this book). Although we researchers benefit from continued Hadza foraging, I try to do nothing that would hasten or prevent change. I only hope our publications do not result in greatly increased tourism.

THE FUTURE

For decades, missionaries have tried to convert the Hadza in exchange for handouts of food. The government still wrestles with the ambiguous status of Hadza rights to hunt and use their area as they see fit. NGOs are now involved, some wanting to educate or develop the Hadza, some wanting them to gain rights and resist changes that don't benefit them. Government officials, missionaries, and some NGOs have tried to get the Hadza to take up farming, with very little success. Attempts to get them to practice pastoralism have not fared any better. Once, beehives were given to Hadza at the settlement of Mongo wa Mono. This seemed like a good idea, given that the Hadza are bee and honey experts. The hives eventually got destroyed by honey badgers, and that was the end of that experiment. The immediate-return orientation of the Hadza is difficult to change; tending hives that will produce much later is something alien to them, whereas checking on wild hives when they are on a walk-about is not.

There are no simple answers. Some Hadza want to change; others do not. As long as those who are hunting and gathering can continue to do so, they really are probably much better off than they will be under most plans that are likely to be forthcoming any time soon. To most Tanzanians, especially officials, the life of the Hadza appears awful. They think the Hadza are miserable and starving, impoverished and ignorant without going to school. I hope no one has gotten the wrong impression from my description of Hadza food-sharing that Hadza life is harsh. While it would be difficult for most of us to endure others daily expecting to eat our food, the Hadza take it well because each person is receiving as well as giving. They know so much about their environment that they can always get some food. They have plenty of leisure time. To me, their life is in many ways much better than the average Tanzanian's life.

As of this writing, the Hadza are still foraging. We continue to collect data and are able to find enough camps where virtually the whole diet comes from foraging. This can be said of very few other societies today. I have tried my best to portray the Hadza accurately. I hope one day this book will be of value to their descendents.

References

Abbott, D. H., E. B. Keverne, F. B. Bercovitch, C. A. Shively, S. P. Medoza, W. Saltzman, C. T. Snowdon, T. E. Ziegler, M. Banjevic, T. Garland, and R. M. Sapolsky. 2003. Are subordinates always stressed? A comparative analysis of rank differences in cortisol levels among primates. *Hormones and Behavior* 43:67–82.

Aiello, L. C., and C. Key. 2002. Energetic consequences of being a *Homo erectus* female. *American Journal of Human Biology* 14:551–565.

Alexander, R. D. 1979. *Darwinism and human affairs*. Seattle: University of Washington Press.

Alexander, R. D., J. L. Hoogland, R. D. Howard, K. M. Noonan, and P. W. Sherman. 1979. Sexual dimorphism and breeding systems in pinnipeds, ungulates, primates, and humans. In *Evolutionary biology and human social behavior: An anthropological perspective*, ed. N. Chagnon and W. Irons, 402–435. North Scituate, MA: Duxbury Press.

Allchin, B. 1957. Australian stone industries, past and present. *Journal of the Royal Anthropological Institute of Great Britain and Ireland* 87:115–136.

Ames, K. M. 2003. The northwest coast. *Evolutionary Anthropology* 12:19–33.

Anderson, J. R. 1998. Sleep, sleeping sites, and sleep-related activities: Awakening to their significance. *American Journal of Primatology* 46:63–75.

Andersson, M. 1994. *Sexual selection*. Princeton, NJ: Princeton University Press.

Apicella, C. L., A. C. Little, and F. W. Marlowe. 2007. Facial averageness and attractiveness in an isolated population of hunter-gatherers. *Perception* 36:1813–1820.

Asfaw, B., Y. Beyene, S. Semaw, G. Suwa, and T. White. 1992. The earliest Acheulean from Konso-Gardula. *Nature* 360:732–735.

Axelrod, R. 1984. *The evolution of cooperation*. New York: Basic Books.

Bagga, A., and S. Kulkarni. 2000. Age at menarche and secular trend in Maharashtrian (Indian) girls. *Acta Biologica Szegediensis* 44:53–57.

Bagshawe, F. J. 1924–1925a. The peoples of the Happy Valley (East Africa): Part I. *Journal of the Royal African Society* 24:25–33.

———. 1924–1925b. The peoples of the Happy Valley (East Africa): Part II. *Journal of the Royal African Society* 24:117–130.

Bala, G. G. 1998. *Hadza stories and songs*. Los Angeles: Friends of the Hadzabe.

Barham, L. 2002. Backed tools in Middle Pleistocene central Africa and their evolutionary significance. *Journal of Human Evolution* 43:585–603.

Barnard, A. 1999. Images of hunters and gatherers in European social thought. In *The Cambridge encyclopedia of hunters and gatherers*, ed. R. B. Lee and R. Daly, 375–383. Cambridge: Cambridge University Press.

Barnicot, N. A., F. J. Bennett, and J. C. Woodburn. 1972. Blood pressure and serum cholesterol in the Hadza of Tanzania. *Human Biology* 44:87–116.

Barnicot, N. A., D. P. Mukherjee, J. C. Woodburn, and F. J. Bennett. 1972. Dermatoglyphics of the Hadza of Tanzania. *Human Biology* 44:621–648.

Barnicot, N. A., and J. C. Woodburn. 1975. Colour-blindness and sensitivity to PTC in Hadza. *Annals of Human Biology* 2:61–68.

Bartholomew, G. A., and J. B. Birdsell. 1953. Ecology and the protohominids. *American Anthropologist* 55:481–498.

Bartram, L. E., Jr. 1997. A comparison of Kua (Botswana) and Hadza (Tanzania) bow and arrow hunting. In *Projectile technology*, ed. H. Knecht, 321–343. New York: Plenum.

Basabose, A. K. 2004. Fruit availability and chimpanzee party size at Kahuzi montane forest, Democratic Republic of Congo. *Primates* 45:211–219.

Bateman, A. J. 1948. Intrasexual selection in Drosophila. *Heredity* 2:349–68.

Baumann, O. 1894. *Durch Massailand zur Nilquelle*. Berlin: D. Reimer.

Bellomo, R. V. 1994. Methods of determining early hominid behavioral activities associated with the controlled use of fire at FxJj 20 Main, Koobi Fora, Kenya. *Journal of Human Evolution* 27:173–195.

Bennett, F. J., N. A. Barnicot, J. C. Woodburn, M. S. Pereira, and B. E. Henderson. 1973. Studies of viral, bacterial, rickettsial and treponemal diseases in the Hadza of Tanzania and a note on injuries. *Human Biology* 45:243–272.

Berbesque, J. C., and F. W. Marlowe. In review. Sex differences in food preferences of Hadza hunter-gatherers.

Bersaglieri, T., P. C. Sabeti, N. Patterson, T. Vanderploeg, S. F. Schaffner, J. A. Drake, M. Rhodes, D. E. Reich, and J. N. Hirschhorn. 2004. Genetic signatures of strong recent positive selection at the lactase gene. *American Journal of Human Genetics* 74:1111–1120.

Bhadra, M., A. Mukhopadhyay, and K. Bose. 2005. Differences in body composition between pre-menarcheal and menarcheal Bengalee Hindu girls of Madhyamgram, West Bengal, India. *Anthropological Science* 113:141–145.

Bigelow, R. 1972. The evolution of cooperation, aggression and self-control. In *Nebraska symposium on motivation*, vol. 20, ed. J. K. Cole and D. D. Jensen, 1–57. Lincoln: University of Nebraska Press.

Binford, L. R. 1980. Willow smoke and dogs' tails: Hunter-gatherer settlement systems and archaeological site formation. *American Antiquity* 45:4–20.

———. 2001. *Constructing frames of reference.* Berkeley: University of California Press.

Bird, D. W., and R. Bliege-Bird. 1997. Contemporary shellfish gathering strategies among the Meriam of the Torres Strait Islands, Australia: Testing predictions of a central place foraging model. *Journal of Archaeological Science* 24:39–63.

Bird, R. 1999. Cooperation and conflict: The behavioral ecology of the sexual division of labor. *Evolutionary Anthropology* 8:65–75.

Birdsell, J. B. 1968. Some predictions for the Pleistocene based on equilibrium systems among recent hunter-gatherers. In *Man the hunter*, ed. R. B. Lee and I. DeVore, 229–240. Chicago: Aldine.

Blanckenhorn, W. U. 2000. The evolution of body size: What keeps organisms small? *Quarterly Review of Biology* 75:385–407.

Bleek, D. F. 1929. *Comparative vocabularies of Bushmen languages.* Cambridge: Cambridge University Press.

———. 1931. The Hadzapi or Watindega of Tanganyika territory. *Africa* 4:273–285.

Bliege-Bird, R., and D. Bird. 1997. Delayed reciprocity and tolerated theft: The behavioral ecology of food-sharing strategies. *Current Anthropology* 38:49–78.

———. 2002. Constraints of knowing or constraints of growing? Fishing and collecting by the children of Mer. *Human Nature* 13:239–267.

Bloch, R. H. 1991. *Medieval misogyny and the invention of Western romantic love.* Chicago: University of Chicago Press.

Blumenschine, R. J. 1995. Percussion marks, tooth marks, and experimental determinations of the timing of hominid and carnivore access to long bones at FLK Zinjanthropus, Olduvai Gorge, Tanzania. *Journal of Human Evolution* 29:21–51.

Bobe, R., Z. Alemseged, and A. K. Behrensmeyer, eds. 2007. *Hominin environments in the East African Pliocene: An assessment of the faunal evidence, vertebrate paleobiology and paleoanthropology.* Dordrecht, The Netherlands: Springer.

Boehm, C. 1999. *Hierarchy in the forest: The evolution of egalitarian behavior.* Cambridge, MA: Harvard University Press.

Boesch, C., and H. Boesch-Achermann. 2000. *The chimpanzees of the Tai Forest: Behavioural ecology and evolution.* Oxford: Oxford University Press.

Bogin, B. 1999. *Patterns of human growth.* Cambridge: Cambridge University Press.

Boone, J. L. 1992. Competition, conflict, and the development of social hierarchies. In *Evolutionary ecology and human behavior*, ed. E. A. Smith and B. Winterhalder, 301–337. New York: Aldine de Gruyter.

Borgerhoff Mulder, M. 1988a. Behavioural ecology in traditional societies. *Trends in Ecology and Evolution* 3:260–264.

———. 1988b. Is the polygyny threshold model relevant to humans? Kipsigis evidence. In *Mating patterns*, ed. C. G. N. Mascie-Taylor and A. J. Boyce, 209–230. Cambridge: Cambridge University Press.

Bowlby, J. 1969. *Attachment and loss*. New York: Basic Books.

Boyd, R., and P. J. Richerson. 1988. The evolution of reciprocity in sizeable groups. *Journal of Theoretical Biology* 132:337–356.

Brand, P. C., and P. H. Lehert. 1978. New way of looking at evironmental variables that may affect age at menopause. *Maturitas* 1:121–132.

Brewis, A., and M. Meyer. 2005. Demographic evidence that human ovulation is undetectable (at least in pair bonds). *Current Anthropology* 46:465–471.

Brown, J. L., and G. H. Orians. 1970. Spacing patterns in mobile animals. *Annual Review of Ecology and Systematics* 1:239–262.

Bunn, H. T., L. Bartram, and E. M. Kroll. 1988. Variability in bone assemblage formation from Hadza hunting, scavenging, and carcass processing. *Journal of Anthropological Archaeology* 7:412–457.

Burley, N. 1988. The differential allocation hypothesis: An experimental test. *American Naturalist* 132:611–628.

Buss, D. M. 1989. Sex differences in human mate preferences: Evolutionary hypotheses tested in 37 cultures. *Behavioral and Brain Sciences* 12:1–49.

———. 1999. *Evolutionary psychology: The new science of mind*. Boston: Allyn and Bacon.

Buunk, B. P., P. Dijkstra, D. Fetchenhauer, and D. T. Kenrick. 2002. Age and gender differences in mate selection criteria for various involvement levels. *Personal Relationships* 9:271–278.

Camerer, C. F., and R. Thaler. 1995. Anomalies: Dictators, ultimatums, and manners. *Journal of Economic Perspectives* 9:209–219.

Cashdan, E. 1983. Territoriality among human foragers: Ecological models and an application to four Bushmen groups. *Cultural Anthropology* 24:47–66.

Cattelain, P. 1997. Hunting during the upper paleolithic: Bow, spearthrower, or both? In *Projectile Technology*, ed. H. Knecht, 213–240. New York: Plenum.

CDC. 2000. Birth statistics, ed. N. C. f. H. Statistics.

Chapman, C. A., L. J. Chapman, and R. L. McLaughlin. 1989. Multiple central place foraging by spider monkeys: Travel consequences of using many sleeping sites. *Oecologia* 79:506–511.

Chapman, C. A., F. J. White, and R. W. Wrangham. 1994. Party size in chimpanzees and bonobos: A reevaluation of theory based on two similarly forested sites. In *Chimpanzee cultures*, ed. R. W. Wrangham, W. C. McGrew, F. B. M. DeWaal, and P. G. Heltne, 41–57. Cambridge, MA: Harvard University Press.

Chapman, C. A., and R. W. Wrangham. 1993. Range use of the forest chimpanzees of Kibale: Implications for the understanding of chimpanzee social organization. *American Journal of Primatology* 31:263–273.

Charnov, E. L. 1993. *Life history invariants: Some explorations of symmetry in evolutionary ecology*. Oxford: Oxford University Press.

Cheney, D. L. 1987. Interactions and relationships between groups. In *Primate Societies*, ed. B. Smuts, D. L. Cheney, R. M. Seyfarth, R. W. Wrangham, and T. T. Struhsaker, 267–281. Chicago: University of Chicago Press.

Chumlea, W. C., C. M. Schubert, A. F. Roche, H. E. Kulin, P. A. Lee, J. H. Himes, and S. S. Sun. 2003. Age at menarche and racial comparisons in US girls. *Pediatrics* 111:110–113.

Clark, J. D. 1970. *The prehistory of Africa*. New York: Praeger.

Clutton-Brock, T. H. 1985. Size, sexual dimorphism and polygamy in primates. In *Size and scaling in primate biology*, ed. W. L. Jungers, 211–237. New York: Plenum.

———. 1989. Mammalian mating systems. *Proceedings of the Royal Society of London* 236:339–372.

Clutton-Brock, T. H., and G. A. Parker. 1992. Potential reproductive rates and the operation of sexual selection. *Quarterly Review of Biology* 67:437–456.

Clutton-Brock, T. H., A. F. Russell, L. L. Sharpe, A. J. Young, Z. Balmforth, and G. M. McIlrath. 2002. Evolution and development of sex differences in cooperative behavior in meerkats. *Science* 297:253–256.

Cole, T. J. 2000. Secular trends in growth. *Proceedings of the Nutrition Society* 59:317–324.

Cooper, B. 1949. The Kindiga. *Tanganyika Notes and Records* 27:8–15.

Covas, R., A. Dalecky, A. Caizergues, and C. Doutrelant. 2006. Kin associations and direct vs indirect fitness benefits in colonial cooperatively breeding sociable weavers *Philetairus socius*. *Behavioral Ecology and Sociobiology* 60:323–331.

Creel, S. 1991. How to measure inclusive fitness. *Proceedings of the Royal Society of London, Series B* 241:229–231.

Crittenden, A. N., and F. W. Marlowe. 2008. Allomaternal care among the Hadza of Tanzania. *Human Nature—An Interdisciplinary Biosocial Perspective* 19:249–262.

Cronk, L. 1999. *That complex while: Culture and the evolution of human behavior*. Boulder, CO: Westview.

———. 2004. *From Mukogodo to Maasai: Ethnicity and cultural change in Kenya*. Cambridge, MA: Westview Press.

Darwin, C. 1859. *The origin of species*, 2003 edition. London: Penguin.

———. 1871. *Descent of man and selection in relation to sex*. Princeton, NJ: Princeton University Press.

Dawkins, R. 1976. *The selfish gene*. Oxford: Oxford University Press.

Deacon, H. J., and R. Shuurman. 1992. The origins of modern people: The evidence from Klasies River. In *continuity or replacement: Controversies in homo sapiens evolution*, ed. G. Brauer and F. H. Smith, 121–129. Rotterdam: A. A. Balkema.

de Heinzelin, J., J. D. Clark, T. White, W. Hart, P. Renne, G. WoldeGabriel, Y. Beyene, and E. Vrba. 1999. Environment and behavior of 2.5 million-year-old Bouri hominids. *Science* 284:625–629.

Dempwolff, O. 1916–1917. Beiträge zur Kenntnis der Sprachen in Deutsch-Ostafrika. Teil 12: Wörter der Hatzasprache. *Zeitschrift für Kolonialsprachen* 7:319–325.

Dennerstein, L., G. Gotts, J. B. Brown, C. A. Morse, T. M. M. Farley, and A. Pinol. 1994. The relationship between the menstrual-cycle and female sexual interest in women with PMS complaints and volunteers. *Psychoneuroendocrinology* 19:293–304.

Dickson, D. B. 1990. *The dawn of belief*. Tucson: University of Arizona Press.

Dominguez-Rodrigo, M. 1997. Meat-eating by early hominids at the FLK 22. Zinjanthropus site, Olduvai Gorge (Tanzania): An experimental approach using cut-mark data. *Journal of Human Evolution* 33:669–690.

———. 2002. Hunting and scavenging by early humans: The state of the debate. *Journal of World History* 16:1–54.

Dominguez-Rodrigo, M., A. Mabulla, L. Luque, J. W. Thompson, J. Rink, P. Bushozi, F. Diez-Martin, and L. Alcala. 2008. A new archaic *Homo sapiens* fossil from Lake Eyasi, Tanzania. *Journal of Human Evolution* 54:899–903.

Doran, D. M., and A. McNeilage. 1998. Gorilla ecology and behavior. *Evolutionary Anthropology* 6:120–131.

Draper, P., and H. Harpending. 1982. Father absence and reproductive strategy: An evolutionary perspective. *Journal of Anthropological Research* 38:255–273.

Dyson, T., ed. 1977. *The demography of the Hadza in historical perspective. African historical demography.* Edinburgh, Scotland: University of Edinburgh.

Dyson-Hudson, R., and E. A. Smith. 1978. Human territoriality: An ecological reassessment. *American Anthropologist.* 80:21–41.

Eaton, S. B. 2006. The ancestral human diet: What was it and should it be a paradigm for contemporary nutrition? *Proceedings of the Nutrition Society* 65:1–6.

Eaton, S. B., M. Konner, and M. Shostak. 1988. Stone agers in the fast lane: Chronic degenerative diseases in evolutionary perspective. *American Journal of Medicine* 84:739–749.

Eaton, S. B., M. C. Pike, R. V. Short, N. C. Lee, J. Trussell, R. A. Hatcher, J. W. Wood, C. M. Worthman, N. G. Blurton Jones, M. J. Konner, K. R. Hill, R. Bailey, and A. M. Hurtado. 1994. Women's reproductive cancers in evolutionary context. *Quarterly Review of Biology* 69:353–367.

Eaton, S. B., M. Shostak, and M. Konner. 1988. *The Paleolithic prescription: A program of diet and exercise and a design for living.* New York: Harper and Row.

Eberle, M., and P. M. Kappeler. 2006. Family insurance: Kin selection and cooperative breeding in a solitary primate (*Microcebus murinus*). *Behavioral Ecology and Sociobiology* 60:582–588.

Ehret, C., and M. Posnansky. 1982. *The archaeological and linguistic reconstruction of African history.* Berkeley: University of California Press.

Ellis, B. 1992. The evolution of sexual attraction: Evaluative mechanisms in women. In *The adapted mind*, ed. J. Barkow, L. Cosmides, and J. Tooby, 267–288. New York: Oxford University Press.

Ellis, L. 1995. Dominance and reproductive success among nonhuman animals: A cross-species comparison. *Ethology and Sociobiology* 16:257–333.

Ellison, P. T. 2001. *On fertile ground.* Cambridge, MA: Harvard University Press.

Elston, R. G., and S. L. Kuhn. 2002. *Thinking small: Global perspectives on microlithization*, vol. 12. *Arceological Papers of the American Anthropological Association.* Arlington, VA: American Anthropological Association.

Ember, C. R. 1975. Residential variation among hunter-gatherers. *Behavior Science Research* 10:199–227.

Ember, M., and C. R. Ember. 1979. Male-female bonding: A cross-species study of mammals and birds. *Behavior Science Research* 14:37–56.

Emlen, S. T. 1984. Cooperative breeding in birds and mammals. In *Behavioural ecology: An evolutionary approach*, ed. D. L. Krebs and N. B. Davies, 305–339. Oxford: Blackwell.

———. 1994. Family-structure influences mate choice in white-fronted bee eaters. *Behavioral Ecology and Sociobiology* 35:185–191.

Emlen, S. T., and W. Oring. 1977. Ecology, sexual selection, and the evolution of mating systems. *Science* 197:215–223.

Ensminger, J., and J. Henrich, eds. In prep. *Fairness and punishment in cross-cultural perspective.*

Estes, R. D. 1991. *The behavior guide to African mammals.* Los Angeles: University of California Press.

Fisher, R. A. 1930. *The genetical theory of natural selection.* Oxford: Clarendon Press.

Flannery, T. 1994. *The future eaters.* New York: Grove Press.

Fleming, H. C. 1986. Hadza and Sandawe genetic relations. *Sprache und Geschichte in Afrika* 7:157–187.

Foley, R. 1987. *Another unique species: Patterns in human evolutionary ecology.* New York: John Wiley and Sons.

———. 1988. Hominids, humans and hunter-gatherers: An evolutionary perspective. In *Hunters and gatherers: History, evolution and social change*, ed. T. Ingold, D. Riches, and J. Woodburn, 207–221. New York: St. Martin's Press.

———. 1995. The adaptive legacy of human evolution: A search for the environment of evolutionary adaptedness. *Evolutionary Anthropology* 4:194–203.

Foley, R. A. 1996. Is reproductive synchrony an evolutionary stable strategy for hunter-gatherers? *Current Anthropology* 37:539–545.

Foote, A. D. 2008. Mortality rate acceleration and post-reproductive lifespan in matrilineal whale species. *Biology Letters* 4:189–191.

Ford, C. S., and F. A. Beach. 1951. *Patterns of sexual behavior.* New York: Harper and Row.

Fosbrooke, H. A. 1956. A stone age tribe in Tanganyika. *The South African Archeological Bulletin* 11:3–8.

Fruth, B., and G. Hohmann. 1994. Nests: Living artefacts of recent apes? *Current Anthropology* 35:310–311.

Furuichi, T., G. Idani, H. Ihobe, S. Kuroda, K. Kitamura, A. Mori, T. Enomoto, N. Okayasu, C. Hashimoto, and T. Kano. 1998. Population dynamics of wild bonobos (*Pan paniscus*) at Wamba. *International Journal of Primatology* 19:1029–1043.

Gangestad, S. W., and R. Thornhill. 1999. Individual differences in developmental precision and fluctuating asymmetry: A model and its implications. *Journal of Evolutionary Biology* 12:402–416.

Garber, P. A. 1997. One for all and breeding for one: Cooperation and competition as a Tamarin reproductive strategy. *Evolutionary Anthropology* 5:187–199.

Gilchrist, J. S. 2006. Reproductive success in a low skew, communal breeding mammal: the banded mongoose, *Mungos mungo. Behavioral Ecology and Sociobiology* 60:854–863.

Gilchrist, J. S., and A. F. Russell. 2007. Who cares? Individual contributions to pup care by breeders vs non-breeders in the cooperatively breeding banded mongoose (*Mungos mungo*). *Behavioral Ecology and Sociobiology* 61:1053–1060.

Gintis, H., E. A. Smith, and S. Bowles. 2001. Costly signaling and cooperation. *Journal of Theoretical Biology* 213:103–119.

Goldstein, A. R., A. R. Linares, L. L. Cavalli-Sforza, and M. W. Feldman. 1995. Genetic absolute dating based on microsatellites and the origin of modern humans. *Proceedings of the National Academy of Sciences* 92:6723–6727.

Goodale, J. C. 1971. *Tiwi wives: A study of the women of Melville Island, North Australia*. Seattle: University of Washington Press.

Goodall, J. 1986. *The chimpanzees of Gombe*. Cambridge, MA: Belknap Press of Harvard University Press.

Goren-Inbar, N., N. Alperson, M. E. Kislev, O. Simchoni, Y. Melamed, A. Ben-Nun, and E. Werker. 2004. Evidence of hominin control of fire at Gesher Benot Ya'aqov, Israel. *Science* 304:725–727.

Grafen, A. 1984. Natural selection, kin selection and group selection. In *Behavioural ecology: An evolutionary approach*, 2nd ed., ed. J. R. Krebs and N. B. Davies, 62–84. Sunderland, MA: Sinauer Associates.

Gray, P. B., and F. Marlowe. 2002. Fluctuating asymmetry of a foraging population: The Hadza of Tanzania. *Annals of Human Biology* 29:495–501.

Grimes, B. F., ed. 2000. *Ethnologue: Languages of the world*. Dallas: SIL International.

Gurven, M. 2004. To give and to give not: The behavioral ecology of human food transfers. *Behavioral and Brain Sciences* 27:543–559.

Gurven, M., K. Hill, H. Kaplan, A. Hurtado, and R. Lyles. 2000. Food transfers among Hiwi foragers of Venezuela: Tests of reciprocity. *Human Ecology* 28:171–218.

Hagen, E. 2003. Genes and culture: Commentary. *Current Anthropology* 44:96–97.

Haldane, J. B. S. 1932. *The causes of evolution*. Princeton, NJ: Princeton University Press.

Hames, R., and W. Vickers. 1982. Optimal diet breadth theory as a model to explain variability in Amazonian hunting. *American Ethnologist* 9:358–378.

Hamilton, A. 1981. *Nature and nurture: Aboriginal child-rearing in North Central Arnhem land*. Canberra: Australian Institute of Aboriginal Studies.

Hamilton, W. D. 1964. The genetical evolution of social behavior. *Journal of Theoretical Biology* 7:1–16.

———. 1966. Moulding of senescence by natural selection. *Journal of Theoretical Biology* 12:12–45.

———. 1967. Extraordinary sex ratios. *Science* 156:477–488.

Hamilton, W. D., and M. Zuk. 1982. Heritable true fitness and bright birds: A role for parasites. *Science* 218:384–387.

Harcourt, A. H., and J. Greenberg. 2001. Do gorilla females join males to avoid infanticide? A quantitative model. *Animal Behaviour* 62:905–915.

Hardy, I. C. W., ed. 2002. *Sex ratios: Concepts and research methods.* Cambridge: Cambridge University Press.

Harpending, H., M. A. Batzer, M. Gurven, L. B. Jorde, A. R. Rogers, and S. T. Sherry. 1998. Genetic traces of ancient demography. *Proceedings of the National Academy of Sciences* 95:1961–1967.

Haselton, M. G., M. Mortezaie, E. G. Pillsworth, A. Bleske-Rechek, and D. A. Frederick. 2007. Ovulatory shifts in human female ornamentation: Near ovulation, women dress to impress. *Hormones and Behavior* 51:40–45.

Hawkes, K. 1991. Showing off: Tests of an hypothesis about men's foraging goals. *Ethology and Sociobiology* 12:29–54.

———. 1992. Sharing and collective action. In *Evolutionary ecology and human behavior*, ed. E. A. Smith and B. Winterhalder, 269–300. New York: Aldine de Gruyter.

———. 2000. Hunting and the evolution of egalitarian societies: Lessons from the Hadza. In *Hierarchies in action: Cui bono*, ed. M. W. Diehl, 59–83. Carbondale: Center for Archeological Investigations, Southern Illinois University.

Hawkes, K., and R. Bliege-Bird. 2002. Showing off, handicap signaling, and the evolution of men's work. *Evolutionary Anthropology* 11:58–67.

Hawkes, K., N. G. B. Jones, and J. F. O'Connell. 1995. Hadza children's foraging: Juvenile dependency, social arrangements, and mobility among hunter-gatherers. *Current Anthropology* 36:688–700.

Hawkes, K., and J. O'Connell. 2005. How old is human longevity? *Journal of Human Evolution* 49:650–653.

Hawkes, K., J. O'Connell, and N. G. B. Jones. 1989. Hardworking Hadza grandmothers. In *Comparative socioecology: The behavioural ecology of humans and other mammals*, ed. V. Standen and R. Foley, 341–366. Oxford: Blackwell.

———. 1991. Hunting income patterns among the Hadza: Big game, common goods, foraging goals and evolution of the human diet. *Philosophical Transactions of the Royal Society of London, Series B* 334:243–251.

———. 1997. Hadza women's time allocation, offspring provisioning, and the evolution of long postmenopausal life spans. *Current Anthropology* 38:551–577.

———. 2001a. Hunting and nuclear families: Some lessons from the Hadza about men's work. *Current Anthropology* 42:681–709.

———. 2001b. Hadza meat sharing. *Evolution and Human Behavior* 22:113–142.

Hawkes, K., J. O'Connell, N. G. B. Jones, H. Alvarez, and E. L. Charnov. 1998. Grandmothering, menopause, and the evolution of human life histories. *Proceedings of the National Academy of Sciences* 95:1336–1339.

Hawkes, K., J. F. O'Connell, and L. Rogers. 1997. The behavioral ecology of modern hunter-gatherers, and human evolution. *Trends in Ecology and Evolution* 12:29–32.

Headland, T. N., and L. A. Reid. 1989. Hunter-gatherers and their neighbors from prehistory to the present. *Current Anthropology* 30:43–66.

Henrich, J. 2000. Does culture matter in economic behavior? Ultimatum game bargaining among the Machiguenga Indians of the Peruvian Amazon. *American Economic Review* 90:973–979.

Henrich, J., R. Boyd, S. Bowles, C. Camerer, E. Fehr, H. Gintis, R. McElreath, M. Alvard, A. Barr, J. Ensminger, N. S. Henrich, K. Hill, F. Gil-White, M. Gurven, F. W. Marlowe, J. Q. Patton, and D. Tracer. 2005. Economic man in cross-cultural perspective: Behavioral experiments in 15 small-scale societies. *Behavioral and Brain Sciences* 28:795–855.

Henrich, J., R. Boyd, S. Bowles, H. Gintis, C. Camerer, and E. Fehr, eds. 2004. *Foundations of human sociality: Economic experiments and ethnographic evidence from fifteen small-scale societies.* Oxford: Oxford University Press.

Henrich, J., R. McElreath, A. Barr, J. Ensminger, C. Barret, A. Bolyanatz, J. Camilo Cardenas, M. Gurven, E. Gwako, N. Henrich, C. Lesorogol, F. Marlowe, D. Tracer, and J. Ziker. 2006. Costly punishment across human societies. *Science* 312:1767–1770.

Henshilwood, C. S., J. C. Sealy, R. Yates, K. Cruz-Uribe, P. Goldberg, F. E. Grine, R. G. Klein, C. Poggenpoel, K. Van Niekerk, and W. I. 2001. Blombos Cave, Southern Cape, South Africa: Preliminary report on the 1992–1999 excavations of the Middle Stone Age Levels. *Journal of Archeological Science* 28:421–448.

Hewlett, B. S. 1988. Sexual selection and paternal investment among Aka pygmies,. In *Human reproductive behavior: A Darwinian perspective*, ed. L. Betzig, M. Borgerhoff Mulder, and P. Turke, 263–276. Cambridge: Cambridge University Press.

———. 1991. *Intimate fathers: The nature and context of Aka Pygmy paternal infant care.* Ann Arbor: University of Michigan Press.

Hiatt, L. R. 1996. *Arguments about aborigines.* Cambridge: Cambridge University Press.

Hiernaux, J., and D. B. Hartono. 1980. Physical measurements of the adult Hadza of Tanzania. *Annals of Human Biology* 4:339–346.

Hill, K. 1987. Foraging decisions among Ache hunter-gatherers: New data and implications for optimal foraging models. *Ethology and Sociobiology* 8:1–36.

———. 2002. Altruistic cooperation during foraging by the Ache, and the evolved human predisposition to cooperate. *Human Nature* 13:105–128.

Hill, K., C. Boesch, J. Goodall, A. E. Pusey, J. Williams, and R. W. Wrangham. 2001. Mortality rates among wild chimpanzees. *Journal of Human Evolution* 40:437–450.

Hill, K., and K. Hawkes. 1983. Neotropical hunting among the Ache of eastern Paraguay. In *Adaptive responses of native Amazonians*, ed. R. B. Hames and W. T. Vickers, 139–188. New York: Academic Press.

Hill, K., and A. M. Hurtado. 1996. *Ache life history: The ecology and demography of a foraging people.* New York: Aldine de Gruyter.

Hirasawa, A. 2005. Infant care among the sedentarized Baka hunter-gatherers in southeastern Cameroon. In *Culture, ecology and psychology of hunter-gatherer children*, ed. B. S. Hewlett and M. E. Lamb, 365–384. New Brunswick, NJ: Transaction.

Hobbes, T. 1651. *Leviathan*, 1968 edition. Baltimore: Penguin.

Howell, N. 1979. *Demography of the Dobe !Kung.* New York: Academic Press.

Hrdy, S. B. 2005. Comes the child before man: How cooperative breeding and prolonged postweaning dependence shaped human potential. In *Hunter-gatherer childhoods: Evolutionary, developmental and cultural perspectives,* ed. B. S. Hewlett and M. E. Lamb, 65–91. New Brunswick, NJ: Aldine Transaction.

Hurtado, A. M., and K. R. Hill. 1992. Paternal effect on offspring survivorship among the Ache and Hiwi hunter-gatherers: Implications for modeling pair-bond stability. In *Father child relations: Cultural and biosocial contexts,* ed. B. Hewlett, 31–55. New York: Aldine de Gruyter.

Iliffe, J. 1973. Tanzania under German and British rule. In *Zamani: A survey of East African history,* ed. B. A. Ogot, 295–313. Nairobi: East African Publishing House/Longman.

Irons, W. 1998. Adaptively relevant environments versus the environment of evolutionary adaptedness. *Evolutionary Anthropology* 6:194–204.

Isaac, G. 1978. The food-sharing behavior of protohuman hominids. *Scientific American* 238:90–108.

Jaeger, F. 1911. *Das Hochland der Riesenkrater und die Umliegenden Hoschlander Deutsch-Ostafrikas.* Berlin: Mittler.

James, W. H. 1971. Distribution of coitus within human intermenstruum. *Journal of Biosocial Science* 3:159–171.

Jasienska, G., A. Ziomkiewicz, P. T. Ellison, S. F. Lipson, and I. Thune. 2004. Large breasts and narrow waist indicate high reproductive potential in women. *Proceedings of the Royal Society of London, Series B* 271:1213–1217.

Jasienska, G., A. Ziomkiewicz, I. Thune, S. F. Lipson, and P. T. Ellison. 2006. Habitual physical activity and estradiol levels in women of reproductive age. *European Journal of Cancer Prevention* 15:439–445.

Jochim, M. A. 1988. Optimal foraging and the division of labor. *American Anthropologist* 90:130–136.

Johnson, A. W., and T. Earle. 1987. *The evolution of human societies.* Palo Alto, CA: Stanford University Press.

Johnson, K., R. Thornhill, J. D. Ligon, and M. Zuk. 1993. The direction of mothers' and daughters' preferences and the heritability of male ornaments in red jungle fowl (*Gallus gallus*). *Behavioral Ecology* 4:254–259.

Johnstone, R. A. 2000. Models of reproductive skew: A review and synthesis. *Ethology* 106:5–26.

Jones, N. G. 1984. Selfish origin for human food-sharing: Tolerated theft. *Ethology and Sociobiology* 5:1–3.

———. 1987. Tolerated theft: Suggestions about the ecology and evolution of sharing, hoarding, and scrounging. *Social Science Information* 26:31–54.

———. 1993. Lives of hunter-gatherer children: Effects of parental behavior and parental reproductive strategy. In *Juvenile primates: Life history, development, and behavior,* ed. Michael E. Pereira, Lynn A. Fairbanks, 309–326. New York: Oxford University Press.

———. 2006. Contemporary hunter-gatherers and human life history evolution. In *The evolution of human life history,* ed. K. Hawkes and R. Paine, 231–266. Santa Fe, NM: School of American Research Press.

———. nd. History and the Hadza: Lost in the bottom of the rift valley. Dept. of Anthropology, UCLA (emeritus).

Jones, N. G., P. Draper, and K. Hawkes. 1994. Foraging returns of !Kung adults and children: Why didn't !Kung children forage? *Journal of Anthropological Research* 50:217–248.

Jones, N. G., K. Hawkes, and J. O'Connell. 1989. Modelling and measuring costs of children in two foraging societies. In *Comparative socioecology: The behavioural ecology of humans and other mammals*, ed. V. Standen and R. Foley, 367–390. London: Basil Blackwell.

———. 1996. The global process and local ecology: How should we explain the differences between the Hadza and !Kung? In *Cultural diversity among twentieth-century foragers: An African perspective*, ed. S. Kent, 159–187. Cambridge: Cambridge University Press.

———. 2002. Antiquity of postreproductive life: Are there modern impacts on hunter-gatherer postreproductive life spans? *American Journal of Human Biology* 14:184–205.

———. 2005a. Hadza grandmothers as helpers: Residence data. In *Grandmotherhood*, ed. E. Voland, A. Chasiotis, and W. Schiefenhovel, 160–176. New Brunswick, NJ: Rutgers University Press.

———. 2005b. Older Hadza men and women as helpers: Residence data. In *Hunter-gatherer childhoods: Evolutionary, developmental and cultural perspectives*, ed. B. S. Hewlett and M. E. Lamb, 214–236. New Brunswick, NJ: Transaction.

Jones, N. G., F. Marlowe, K. Hawkes, and J. O'Connell. 2000a. Paternal investment and hunter-gatherer divorce rates. In *Adaptation and human behavior: An anthropological perspective*, ed. L. Cronk, N. Chagnon, and W. Irons, 69–90. New York: Elsevier.

———. 2000b. Paternal investment and hunter-gatherer divorce rates. In *Adaptation and human behavior: An anthropological perspective*, ed. L. Cronk, N. Chagnon, and W. Irons, 69–90. New York: Elsevier.

Jones, N. G., J. O'Connell, K. Hawkes, C. L. Kamuzora, and L. C. Smith. 1992. Demography of the Hadza, an increasing and high density population of savanna foragers. *American Journal of Physical Anthropology* 89:159–181.

Jones, N. G. B., and F. W. Marlowe. 2002. Selection for delayed maturity: Does it take 20 years to learn to hunt and gather? *Human Nature* 13:199–238.

Kamei, N. 2005. Play activities of the Baka children of Cameroon. In *Culture, ecology and psychology of hunter-gatherer children*, ed. B. S. Hewlett and M. E. Lamb, 343–359. New Brunswick, NJ: Transaction.

Kaplan, H., and K. Hill. 1985. Food sharing among Ache foragers: Tests of explanatory hypotheses. *Current Anthropology* 26:223–246.

Kaplan, H., K. Hill, K. Hawkes, and A. M. Hurtado. 1984. Food-sharing among the Ache hunter-gatherers of eastern Paraguay. *Current Anthropology* 25:113–115.

Kaplan, H., K. Hill, J. Lancaster, and A. Hurtado. 2000. A theory of human life history evolution: Diet, intelligence, and longevity. *Evolutionary Anthropology* 9:156–185.

Kaplan, I., ed. 1978. *Tanzania: A country study*. Washington, DC: American University Press.

Katzmarzyk, P., and C. Davis. 2001. Thinness and body shape of *Playboy* centerfolds from 1978 to 1998. *International Journal of Obesity and Related Metabolic Disorders* 25:590–592.

Kelly, R. C. 2000. *Warless societies and the origin of war*. Ann Arbor: University of Michigan Press.

Kelly, R. L. 1995. *The foraging spectrum*. Washington DC: Smithsonian Institution Press.

Kenrick, D. T., and R. C. Keefe. 1992. Age preferences in mates reflect sex differences in human reproductive strategies. *Behavioral and Brain Sciences* 15:75–133.

Kingdon, J. 1997. *African mammals*. San Diego: Academic Press.

Kitanishi, K. 1998. Food sharing among the Aka hunter-gatherers in northeastern Congo. *African Studies Monographs* 25:3–32.

Kleiman, D. G., and J. R. Malcolm. 1981. The evolution of male parental investment in mammals. In *Parental care in mammals*, ed. D. J. Gubernick and P. H. Klopfer, 347–387. New York: Plenum Press.

Klima, G. J. 1970. *The Barabaig: East African cattle-herders*. New York: Holt, Rinehart and Winston.

Knecht, H. 1997. The history and development of projectile technology research. In *Projectile technology*, ed. H. Knecht, 3–35. New York: Plenum.

Knight, A., P. A. Underhill, H. M. Mortensen, L. A. Zhivotovsky, A. A. Lin, B. M. Henn, D. Louis, M. Ruhlen, and J. L. Mountain. 2003. African Y chromosome and mtDNA divergence provides insight into the history of click languages. *Current Biology* 13:464–473.

Koeslag, J. H. 1990. Koinophilia groups sexual creatures into species, promotes stasis, and stabilizes social behavior. *Journal of Theoretical Biology* 144:15–35.

Koeslag, J. H., and P. D. Koeslag. 1994. Koinophilia. *Journal of Theoretical Biology* 167:55–65.

Kohl-Larsen, L. 1943. *Auf den Spuren des Vormenschen, Bd 1 and 2*. Stuttgart: Kohlhammer Verlag.

———. 1958. *Wildbeuter in Ostafrika: Die Tindiga, ein Jager und Sammlervolk*. Berlin: Dietrich Reimer Verlag.

Kokko, H., R. Brooks, J. M. McNamara, and A. I. Houston. 2002. The sexual selection continuum. *Proceedings of the Royal Society of London, Series B-Biological Sciences* 269:1331–1340.

Konner, M. J. 2005. Hunter-gatherer infancy and childhood: The !Kung and others. In *Hunter-gatherer childhoods: Evolutionary, developmental and cultural perspectives*, ed. B. S. Hewlett and M. E. Lamb, 19–64. New Brunswick, NJ: Transaction.

Krebs, J. R., and N. B. Davies. 1993. *An introduction to behavioural ecology*. Oxford: Blackwell.

Kummer, H. 1995. *In quest of the sacred baboon*. Princeton, NJ: Princeton University Press.

Kutsukake, N., and C. L. Nunn. 2006. Comparative tests of reproductive skew in male primates: The roles of demographic factors and incomplete control. *Behavioral Ecology and Sociobiology* 60:695–706.

Kvarnemo, C., and I. Ahnesjo. 1996. The dynamics of operational sex ratios and competition for mates. *Trends in Ecology and Evolution* 11:404–407.

Lack, D. 1966. *Population studies of birds.* Oxford: Oxford University Press.

Laden, G., and R. Wrangham. 2005. The rise of the hominids as an adaptive shift in fallback foods: Plant underground storage organs (USO's) and australopith origins. *Journal of Human Evolution* 49:482–498.

Laland, K. N., J. Odling-Smee, and M. W. Feldman. 2000. Niche construction, biological evolution, and cultural change. *Behavioral and Brain Sciences* 23:131–175.

Lancaster, J. B., and C. S. Lancaster. 1983. Parental investment: The hominid adaptation. In *How humans evolve*, ed. D. Ortner, 33–58. Washington DC: Smithsonian.

Lee, R. B. 1968. What hunters do for a living, or, how to make out on scarce resources. In *Man the hunter*, ed. R. B. Lee and I. DeVore, 30–48. Chicago: Aldine.

———. 1972. Population growth and the beginnings of sedentary life among the !Kung bushmen. In *Population growth: Anthropological implications*, ed. B. Spooner, 330–342. Cambridge, MA: MIT Press.

———. 1979. *The !Kung San: Men, women, and work in a foraging society.* Cambridge: Cambridge University Press.

———. 1984. *The Dobe !Kung.* New York: Holt Rinehart and Winston.

———. 1988. Reflections on primitive communism. In *Hunters and gatherers v.1: History, evolution and social change.* ed. T. Ingold, D. Riches, and J. Woodburn, 252–268. Oxford: Berg.

———. 1990. Primitive communism and the origin of social inequality. In *Evolution of political systems: Sociopolitics in small-scale sedentary societies*, ed. S. Upham, 225–246. Cambridge: Cambridge University Press.

Lee, R. B., and I. DeVore. 1968. Problems in the study of hunters and gatherers. In *Man the hunter*, ed. R. B. Lee and I. DeVore, 3–12. Chicago: Aldine.

Leonard, W. R., and M. Robertson. 1997. Comparative primate energetics and hominid evolution. *American Journal of Physical Anthropology* 102:265–281.

Lewis, C. S. 1936. *The allegory of love.* Oxford: Oxford Paperbacks.

Li, N. P., J. M. Bailey, D. T. Kenrick, and J. A. W. Linsenmeier. 2002. The necessities and luxuries of mate preferences: Testing the tradeoffs. *Journal of Personality and Social Psychology* 82:947–955.

Lonsdorf, E. V. 2005. Sex differences in the development of termite-fishing skills in the wild chimpanzees, *Pan troglodytes schweinfurthii*, of Gombe National Park, Tanzania. *Animal Behaviour* 70:673–683.

Lonsdorf, E. V., L. E. Eberly, and A. E. Pusey. 2004. Sex differences in learning in chimpanzees. *Nature* 428:715–716.

Lovejoy, O. 1981. The origin of man. *Science* 211:341–350.

Lucas, J. R., S. Creel, and P. M. Waser. 1996. How to measure inclusive fitness, revisited. *Animal Behaviour* 51:225–228.

Mabulla, A. Z. P. 1996. Middle and later stone age land-use and lithic technology in the Eyasi basin, Tanzania. Ph.D. dissertation, University of Florida.

Mallol, C., F. W. Marlowe, B. M. Wood, and C. C. Porter. 2007. Earth, wind, and fire: Ethnoarchaeological signals of Hadza fires. *Journal of Archaeological Science* 34:2035–2052.

Mann, E. H. 1932. *On the aboriginal inhabitants of the Andaman Islands.* London: The Royal Anthropological Institute of Great Britain and Ireland.

Manning, J. T. 1995. Fluctuating asymmetry and body-weight in men and women: Implications for sexual selection. *Ethology and Sociobiology* 16:145–153.

Marlowe, F. W. 1998. The nubility hypothesis. *Human Nature* 9:263–271.

———. 1999a. Male care and mating effort among Hadza foragers. *Behavioral Ecology and Sociobiology* 46:57–64.

———. 1999b. Showoffs or providers? The parenting effort of Hadza men. *Evolution and Human Behavior* 20:391–404.

———. 2000a. Paternal investment and the human mating system. *Behavioural Processes* 51:45–61.

———. 2000b. The patriarch hypothesis. *Human Nature* 11:27–42.

———. 2001. Male contribution to diet and female reproductive success among foragers. *Current Anthropology* 42:755–760.

———. 2002. Why the Hadza are still hunter-gatherers. In *Ethnicity, hunter-gatherers, and the "other": Association or assimilation in Africa,* ed. S. Kent, 247–275. Washington, DC: Smithsonian Institution Press.

———. 2003a. A critical period for provisioning by Hadza men: Implications for pair bonding. *Evolution and Human Behavior* 24:217–229.

———. 2003b. The mating system of foragers in the standard cross-cultural sample. *Cross-Cultural Research* 37:282–306.

———. 2004a. Dictators and ultimatums in an egalitarian society of hunter-gatherers, the Hadza of Tanzania. In *Foundations of human sociality: Economic experiments and ethnographic evidence from fifteen small-scale societies,* ed. J. Henrich, R. Boyd, S. Bowles, H. Gintis, C. Camerer, and E. Fehr, 168–193. Oxford: Oxford University Press.

———. 2004b. Is human ovulation concealed? Evidence from conception beliefs in a hunter-gatherer society. *Archives of Sexual Behavior* 33:427–432.

———. 2004c. Marital residence among foragers. *Current Anthropology* 45:277–284.

———. 2004d. Mate preferences among Hadza hunter-gatherers. *Human Nature* 15:365–376.

———. 2004e. What explains Hadza food sharing? *Research in Economic Anthropology* 23:69–88.

———. 2005a. Hunter-gatherers and human evolution. *Evolutionary Anthropology* 14:54–67.

———. 2005b. Who tends Hadza children? In *Hunter-gatherer childhoods: Evolutionary, developmental and cultural perspectives,* ed. B. S. Hewlett and M. E. Lamb, 177–190. New Brunswick, NJ: Transaction.

———. 2006a. Central place provisioning: The Hadza as an example. In *Feeding ecology in apes and other primates,* ed. G. Hohmann, M. Robbins, and C. Boesch, 359–377. Cambridge: Cambridge University Press.

————. 2006b. The sexual division of foraging labor among Hadza hunter-gatherers. *American Journal of Physical Anthropology* 42 (supplement):125.

————. 2007. Hunting and gathering: The human sexual division of foraging labor. *Cross-Cultural Research* 41:170–195.

————. 2009. Hadza cooperation: Second-party punishment yes, third-party punishment no. *Human Nature* 20:417–430.

————. nd-a. Central place foraging and central place provisioning. Dept. of Anthropology, Florida State University.

————. nd-b. Height is predicted by climate among human foragers. Dept. of Anthropology, Florida State University.

————. nd-c. Sexual dimorphism and polygyny among foragers. Dept. of Anthropology, Florida State University.

————. nd-d. Time Hadza men spend near their wives: Mate-guarding or mate-helping? Dept. of Anthropology, Florida State University.

Marlowe, F. W., C. L. Apicella, and D. Reed. 2005. Men's preferences for women's profile waist-hip-ratio in two societies. *Evolution and Human Behavior* 26:458–468.

Marlowe, F. W., and J. C. Berbesque. 2009. Tubers as fallback foods and their impact on Hadza hunter-gatherers. *American Journal of Physical Anthropology* 140:751–758.

Marlowe, F. W., J. C. Berbesque, A. Barr, C. Barrett, A. Bolyanatz, J. C. Cardenas, J. Ensminger, M. Gurven, E. Gwako, J. Henrich, N. Henrich, C. Lesorogol, R. McElreath, and D. Tracer. 2008. More altruistic punishment in larger societies. *Proceedings of the Royal Society, Series B-Biology* 275:587–590.

Marlowe, F. W., and A. Wetsman. 2001. Preferred waist-to-hip ratio and ecology. *Personality and Individual Differences* 30:481–489.

Marlowe, F. W., and B. M. Wood. 2007. The Hadza male's dilemma: Good father or good citizen. *American Journal of Physical Anthropology.*

————. In prep. The hunter's dilemma: Good father or good citizen.

Marsh, H., and T. Kasuya. 1986. Evidence for reproductive senescence in female cetaceans. *Report International Whaling Commission* 8:57–74.

Marshall, L. 1976. *The !Kung of Nyae Nyae.* Cambridge, MA: Harvard University Press.

Martin, J. A., B. E. Hamilton, P. D. Sutton, S. J. Ventura, et al. 2009. Births: Final data for 2006. *National vital statistics reports*, vol. 57, no. 7. Hyattsville, MD: National Center for Health Statistics.

Masao, F. 1982. The rock art of Kondoa and Singida: A comparative description. Occasional Paper No 5 edition: National Museums of Tanzania, Dar es Salaam.

Matthiessen, P., and E. Porter. 1974. *The tree where man was born.* New York: Avon.

Maynard Smith, J. 1977. Parental investment: A prospective analysis. *Animal Behaviour* 25:1–9.

————. 1982. *Evolution and the theory of games.* Cambridge: Cambridge University Press.

McBrearty, S., and A. S. Brooks. 2000. The revolution that wasn't: A new interpretation of the origin of modern human behavior. *Journal of Human Evolution* 39:453–563.

McClintock, M. K. 1998. Regulation of ovulation by human pheromones. *Nature* 392:177–179.

McDowell, W. 1981. *A brief history of Mangola Hadza.* Mbulu District Development Directorate.

———. 1984. *Hadza ethno-zoology: A hunting people's knowledge of wildlife behavior.* Ministry of Information and Culture Research Division.

McGrew, W. C. 1981. The female chimpanzee as a human evolutionary prototype. In *Woman the gatherer,* ed. F. Dahlberg, 35–73. New Haven, CT: Yale University Press.

———. 1992. *Chimpanzee material culture: Implications for human evolution.* Cambridge: Cambridge University Press.

McGrew, W. C., and T. C. Feistner. 1992. Two nonhuman primate models for the evolution of human food sharing: Chimpanzees and Callitrichids. In *The adapted mind,* ed. J. H. Barkow, L. Cosmides, and J. Tooby, 229–243. Oxford: Oxford University Press.

Mehlman, M. J. 1987. Provenience, age and associations of archaic *Homo sapiens* crania from Lake Eyasi, Tanzania. *Journal of Archeological Science* 14:133–162.

———. 1988. Hominid molars from a middle stone age level at the Mumba rock shelter, Tanzania. *American Journal of Physical Anthropology* 75:69–76.

———. 1991. Context for the emergence of modern man in eastern Africa: Some new Tanzanian evidence. In *Cultural beginnings: Approaches to understanding early hominid life-ways in the African savanna,* ed. D. Clark, 177–196. Bonn: Habelt.

Meindertsma Douwe, J., and J. J. Kessler, eds. 1997. *Towards a better use of environmental resources: A planning document of Mbulu and Karatu districts, Tanzania.* Mbulu, Tanzania.

Metcalfe, D., and K. R. Barlow. 1992. A model for exploring the optimal tradeoff between field processing and transport. *American Anthropologist* 94:340–356.

Michael, R. T., J. H. Gagnon, E. O. Laumann, and G. Kolata. 1994. *Sex in America: A definitive survey.* Boston: Little, Brown and Company.

Milinski, M. 1985. The patch choice model—no alternative to balancing. *American Naturalist* 125:317–320.

Milton, K. 2000. Quo vadis? Tactics of food search and group movement in primates and other animals. In *On the move: How and why animals travel in groups,* ed. S. Boinski and P. A. Garber, 375–417. Chicago: University of Chicago Press.

Minnegal, M. 1997. Consumption and production; Sharing and the social construction of use-value. *Current Anthropology* 38:25–48.

Mitani, J. C., J. Gros-Louis, and A. F. Richards. 1996. Sexual dimorphism, the operational sex-ratio, and the intensity of male competition in polygynous primates. *American Naturalist* 147:966–980.

Mitani, J. C., and P. S. Rodman. 1979. Territoriality: The relation of ranging and home range size to defendability, with an analysis of territoriality among primate species. *Behavioral Ecology and Sociobiology* 5:241–251.

Mitani, J. C., and D. P. Watts. 2000. Why do chimpanzees hunt and share meat? *Animal Behaviour* 61:915–924.

Mitchel, S. R. 1955. Comparison of stone tools of the Tasmanians and Australian aborigines. *Journal of the Royal Anthropological Institute of Great Britain and Ireland* 85:131–139.

Moehlman, P. D., and H. Hofer. 1997. Cooperative breeding, reproductive suppression, and body mass in canids. In *Cooperative breeding in mammals*, ed. N. G. Solomon and J. A. French, 76–128. Cambridge: Cambridge University Press.

Moller, A. P. 2006. A review of developmental instability, parasitism and disease infection, genetics and evolution. *Infection Genetics and Evolution* 6:133–140.

Murdock, G. P. 1949. *Social structure*. New York: Macmillan.

———. 1964. Cultural correlates of the regulation of premarital sex behavior. In *Process and pattern in culture: Essays in honor of Julian H. Steward*, ed. R. A. Manners. Chicago: University of Chicago Press.

———. 1967. The ethnographic atlas: A summary. *Ethnology* 6:109–236.

Murdock, G. P., and C. Provost. 1980. Measurement of cultural complexity. In *Cross-cultural samples and codes*, ed. H. Barry and A. Schlegel, 147–160. Pittsburgh: University of Pittsburgh.

Nash, J. F. 1950. Equilibrium points in n-person games. *Proceedings of the National Academy of Sciences of America* 36:48–49.

Ndagala, D. K., and A. C. Waane. 1982. The effect of research on the Hadzabe, a hunting and gathering group of Tanzania. *Review of Ethnology* 8:94–103.

Newman, J. L. 1995. *The peopling of Africa: A geographic interpretation*. New Haven, CT: Yale University Press.

Newton-Fisher, N. E., V. Reynolds, and A. J. Plumptre. 2000. Food supply and chimpanzee (*Pan troglodytes schweinfurthii*) party size in the Budongo Forest Reserve, Uganda. *International Journal of Primatology* 21:613–628.

Nishida, T., and M. Hiraiwa-Hasegawa. 1987. Chimpanzee and bonobos: Cooperative relationships among males. In *Primate societies*, ed. B. Smuts, D. L. Cheney, R. M. Seyfarth, R. W. Wrangham, and T. T. Struhsaker, 165–177. Chicago: University of Chicago Press.

Nonacs, P. 2007. Tug-of-war has no borders: It is the missing model in reproductive skew theory. *Evolution* 61:1244–1250.

Nowak, M., and K. Sigmund. 1993. A strategy of win-stay, lose-shift that outperforms tit for tat in the prisoner's dilemma game. *Nature* 364:56–58.

Nurse, D. 1982. Bantu expansion into East Africa: Linguistic evidence. In *Archaeological and linguistic reconstruction of African history*, ed. C. Ehret and M. Posnansky, 199–222. Berkeley: University of California Press.

O'Connell, J. F. 1997. On Plio/Pleistocene archeological sites and central places. *Current Anthropology* 38:86–88.

O'Connell, J. F., K. Hawkes, and N. G. B. Jones. 1988. Hadza scavenging: implications for Plio/Pleistocene hominid subsistence. *Current Anthropology* 29:356–363.

———. 1999. Grandmothering and the evolution of *Homo erectus*. *Journal of Human Evolution* 36:461–485.

Obst, E. 1912. Von Mkalama ins land der Wakindiga. *Mitteilungen der Geographischen Gesellschaft in Hamburg* 26:2–27.

Ochieng, W. R. 1975. *An outline history of the Rift Valley of Kenya up to AD 1900*. Kampala, Nairobi, Dar es Salaam: East African Literature Bureau.

Ofek, H. 2001. *Second nature: Economic origins of human evolution*. Cambridge: Cambridge University Press.

Okasha, M., P. McCarron, G. D. Smith, and J. McEwen. 2001. Age at menarche: Secular trends and association with adult anthropometric measures. *Annals of Human Biology* 28:68–78.

Oota, H., W. Settheetham-Ishida, D. Tiwawech, T. Ishida, and M. Stoneking. 2001. Human mtDNA and Y-chromosome variation is correlated with matrilocal versus patrilocal residence. *Nature Genetics* 29:20–21.

Orians, G. H. 1969. On the evolution of mating systems in birds and mammals. *American Naturalist* 103:589–603.

Orians, G. H., and N. E. Pearson. 1979. On the theory of central place foraging. In *Analysis of ecological systems*, ed. D. J. Horn, R. D. Mitchell, and G. R. Stairs, 154–177. Columbus: Ohio State University Press.

Oswalt, W. H. 1973. *Habitat and technology*. New York: Holt, Rinehart and Winston.

Packer, C., and A. E. Pusey. 1997. Divided we fall: Cooperation among lions. *Scientific American* 276:52–59.

Palombit, R. A. 1999. Infanticide and the evolution of pair bonds in nonhuman primates. *Evolutionary Anthropology* 7:117–129.

Pawlowski, B. 1999. Loss of oestrus and concealed ovulation in human evolution: The case against the sexual selection hypothesis. *Current Anthropology* 40:257–275.

Pennington, R. 2001. Hunter-gatherer demography. In *Hunter-gatherers: An interdisciplinary perspective*, ed. C. Panter-Brick, R. H. Layton, and P. Rowley-Conwy, 170–204. Cambridge: Cambridge University Press.

Pennington, R., and H. Harpending. 1988. Fitness and fertility among Kalahari !Kung. *American Journal of Physical Anthropology* 77:303–319.

Peoples, J., and G. Bailey. 1991. *Humanity: An introduction to cultural anthropology*. St Paul, MN: West Publishing Co.

Perrett, D., D. Burt, I. Penton-Voak, K. Lee, D. Rowland, and R. Edwards. 1999. Symmetry and human facial attractiveness. *Evolution and Human Behavior* 20:295–307.

Pertoldi, C., T. N. Kristensen, D. H. Andersen, and V. Loeschcke. 2006. Developmental instability as an estimator of genetic stress. *Heredity* 96:122–127.

Perusse, D. 1994. Mate choice in modern societies: Testing evolutionary hypotheses with behavioral data. *Human Nature* 5:255–278.

Peterson, N. 1976. *Tribes and boundaries in Australia*. Canberra: Australian Institute of Aboriginal Studies.

———. 1993. Demand sharing: reciprocity and the pressure for generosity among foragers. *American Anthropologist* 95:860–874.

Phillips, J., C. M. Worthman, and J. F. Stallings. 1991. New field techniques for detection of female reproductive status (abstract). *American Journal of Physical Anthropology* 85:143.

Phillips, J., C. M. Worthman, J. F. Stallings, N. Blurton Jones, and D. W. Sellen. 1991. New field techniques for detection of female reproductive status.

Pierce, G. J., and J. G. Ollason. 1987. Eight reasons why optimal foraging theory is a complete waste of time. *Oikos* 49:111–117.

Porter, C. C., and F. W. Marlowe. 2007. How marginal are forager habitats? *Journal of Archaeological Science* 38:59–68.

———. nd-a. Foraging party sizes among Hadza women.

———. nd-b. Male and female foraging party sizes among hunter-gatherers.

Potts, R. 1987. Reconstructions of early hominid socioecology: A critique of primate models. In *The evolution of human behavior: Primate models*, ed. W. G. Kinzey, 28–47. Albany: State University of New York Press.

———. 1994. Variables versus models of early Pleistocene hominid land use. *Journal of Human Evolution* 27:7–24.

Price, M. V. 1983. Ecological consequences of body size: A model for patch choice in desert rodents. *Oecologia* 59:384–392.

Price, R. A., and S. G. Vandenberg. 1980. Spouse similarity in American and Swedish couples. *Behavior Genetics* 10:59–71.

Prokosch, M. D., R. G. Coss, J. E. Scheib, and S. A. Blozis. 2009. Intelligence and mate choice: Intelligent men are always appealing. *Evolution and Human Behavior* 30:11–20.

Pulliam, H. R. 1974. Theory of optimal diets. *American Naturalist* 108:59–74.

Pusey, A. E., and C. Packer. 1987. Dispersal and philopatry. In *Primate societies*, ed. B. Smuts, D. L. Cheney, R. M. Seyfarth, R. W. Wrangham, and T. T. Struhsaker, 250–266. Chicago: University of Chicago Press.

Radcliffe-Brown, A. R. 1964. *The Andaman Islanders*. New York: Free Press.

Reeve, H. K., S. T. Emlen, and L. Keller. 1998. Reproductive sharing in animal societies: Reproductive incentives or incomplete control by dominant breeders. *Behavioral Ecology* 9:267–278.

Reichard, U. 1999. Sleeping sites, sleeping places, and presleep behavior of gibbons (*Hylobates lar*). *American Journal of Primatology* 46:35–62.

Reynolds, J. D. 1996. Animal breeding systems. *Trends in Ecology and Evolution* 11:68–72.

Rhodes, G. 2006. The evolutionary psychology of facial beauty. *Annual Review of Psychology* 57:199–226.

Richerson, P. J., and R. Boyd. 2005. *Not by genes alone*. Chicago: University of Chicago Press.

Ridley, M. 1996. *The origins of virtue*. New York: Penguin.

Robson, S. L., C. P. van Schaik, and K. Hawkes. 2006. The derived features of human life history. In *The evolution of human life history*, ed. K. Hawkes and R. R. Paine, 17–44. Santa Fe, NM: School of American Research.

Rodseth, L., R. W. Wrangham, A. M. Harrigan, and B. Smuts. 1991. The human community as a primate society. *Current Anthropology* 12:221–254.

Rose, L., and F. Marshall. 1996. Meat-eating, hominid sociality, and home bases revisited. *Current Anthropology* 37:307–338.

Rotundo, M., E. Fernandez-Duque, and A. F. Dixson. 2005. Infant development and parental care in free-ranging *Aotus azarai azarai* in Argentina. *International Journal of Primatology* 26:1459–1473.

Rousseau, J. J. 1762. *The social contract*, 1954 edition. Chicago: Gateway.

Ruhlen, M. 1991. *A guide to the world's languages, Volume 1: Classification*. Stanford, CA: Stanford University Press.

Sahlins, M. 1968. Notes on the original affluent society. In *Man the hunter*, ed. R. B. Lee and I. DeVore, 85–89. New York: Aldine Publishing Company.

———. 1972. *Stone age economics*. Chicago: Aldine.

Sands, B. 1995. Evaluating claims of distant linguistic relationships: The case of Khoisan. Ph.D. dissertation, University of California, Los Angeles.

Sapolsky, R. M. 2004. Social status and health in humans and other animals. *Annual Review of Anthropology* 33:393–418.

Scarre, C., ed. 1997. *Past worlds: Atlas of archeology*. London: HarperCollins.

Schaller, G. B. 1983. *Golden shadows, flying hooves*. Chicago: University of Chicago.

Schelling, T. C. 1960. *The strategy of conflict*. Cambridge, MA: Harvard University Press.

Schrire, C. 1980. An inquiry into the evolutionary status and apparent identity of San hunter-gatherers. *Human Ecology* 8:9–32.

———. 1984. Wild surmises on savage thoughts. In *Past and present in hunter gatherer studies*, ed. C. Schrire, 1–25. Orlando, FL: Academic Press.

Seielstad, M. T., E. Minch, and L. L. Cavalli-Sforza. 1998. Genetic evidence for a higher female migration rate in humans. *Nature Genetics* 20:278–280.

Semaw, S., P. Renne, J. W. K. Harris, C. S. Feibel, and R. L. Bernor. 1997. 2.5 million-year-old stone tools from Gona, Ethiopia. *Nature* 385:333–336.

Senior, H. S. 1957. Sukuma salt caravans to Lake Eyasi. *Tanganyika Notes and Records* 46:87–90.

Sept, J. 1992. Was there no place like home? New perspective on early hominid archeological sites from the mapping of chimpanzee nests. *Current Anthropology* 33:187–207.

———. 1998. Shadows on a changing landscape: Comparing nesting patterns of hominids and chimpanzees since their last common ancestor. *American Journal of Primatology* 46:85–101.

Sherry, D. S., and F. W. Marlowe. 2007. Anthropometric data indicate nutritional homogeneity in Hadza foragers of Tanzania. *American Journal of Human Biology* 19:107–118.

Shimkin, D. D. 1983. Introduction of the horse. In *Great Basin, Handbook of North American Indians*, Vol. 11, ed. W. L. D'Azevedo, 517–524. Washington, DC: Smithsonian Institution.

Sievert, L. L., and C. A. Dubois. 2005. Validating signals of ovulation: Do women who think they know, really know? *American Journal of Human Biology* 17:310–320.

Silberbauer, G. B. 1981. *Hunter and habitat in the Central Kalahari Desert*. Cambridge: Cambridge University Press.

Singh, D. 1993. Adaptive significance of waist-to-hip ratio and female physical attractiveness. *Journal of Personality and Social Psychology* 65:293–307.

Singh, D., and P. M. Bronstad. 2001. Female body odor is a potential cue to ovulation. *Proceedings of the Royal Society of London, Series B-Biological Sciences* 268:797–801.

Small, M. F. 1996. "Revealed" ovulation in humans? *Journal of Human Evolution* 30:483–488.

Smith, E. A. 1981. The application of optimal foraging theory to the analysis of hunter-gatherer group size. In *Hunter-gatherer foraging strategies*, Ed. B. Winterhalder and E. A. Smith, 36–65. Chicago: University of Chicago Press.

———. 1983. Anthropological applications of optimal foraging theory: A critical review. *Current Anthropology* 24:.625–651.

———. 1985. Inuit foraging groups: Some simple models incorporating conflicts of interest, relatedness, and central-place sharing. *Ethology and Sociobiology* 6:27–47.

———. 1991. *Inujjuamuit hunting strategies: A preliminary report.* Hawthorne, NY: Aldine de Gruyter.

———. 2004. Why do good hunters have higher reproductive success? *Human Nature* 15:343–364.

Smith, E. A., and R. Bliege-Bird. 2000. Turtle hunting and tombstone opening: Public generosity as costly signaling. *Evolution and Human Behavior* 21:245–261.

Smith, E. A., and B. Winterhalder. 1985. On the logic and application of optimal foraging theory: A brief reply to Martin. *American Anthropologist* 87:645–648.

———. 1992. Natural selection and decision making. In *Evolutionary ecology and human behavior*, ed. E. A. Smith and B. Winterhalder, 25–60. New York: Aldine de Gruyter.

Smith, L. 1980. *The status and utilization of wildlife in Arusha Region, Tanzania.* EcoSystems Ltd.

Smuts, B. B., and D. J. Gubernick. 1992. Male-infant relationships in nonhuman primates: Paternal investment or mating effort? In *Father-child relations: Cultural and biosocial contexts*, ed. B. Hewlett, pp. 1–30. New York: Aldine.

Soffer, O., J. M. Adovasio, J. S. Illingworth, H. A. Amirkhanov, N. D. Praslov, and M. Street. 2000. Paleolithic perishables made permanent (fiber artifacts). *Antiquity* 74:812–821.

Solomon, N. G., and J. A. French, eds. 1997. *Cooperative breeding in mammals.* Cambridge: Cambridge University Press.

Somer, E. 2001. *The origin diet: How eating like our stone age ancestors will maximize your health.* New York: Henry Holt.

Soper, R. 1982. Bantu expansion in to eastern Africa: Archeological evidence. In *Archaeological and linguistic reconstruction of African history*, ed. C. Ehret and M. Posnansky, 223–238. Berkeley: University of California Press.

Spencer, B., and F. J. Gillen. 1899. *The native tribes of Central Australia.* London: Macmillan and Company.

————. 1904. *The northern tribes of Central Australia*. London: MacMillan and Company.

Sprecher, S., Q. Sullivan, and E. Hatfield. 1994. Mate selection preferences: Gender differences examined in a national sample. *Journal of Personality and Social Psychology* 66:1074–1080.

Stanford, C. B. 2001. A comparison of social meat-foraging by chimpanzees and human foragers. In *Meat-eating and human evolution*, ed. C. B. Stanford and H. T. Bunn, 122–140. Oxford: Oxford University Press.

Stanford, C. B., and H. T. Bunn, eds. 2001. *Meat-eating and human evolution*. Oxford: Oxford University Press.

Stearns, S. C. 1992. *The evolution of life histories*. Oxford: Oxford University Press.

Stephens, D. W., and J. R. Krebs. 1986. *Foraging theory*. Princeton, NJ: Princeton University Press.

Stevens, A., J. Morissette, J. Woodburn, and F. J. Bennett. 1977. The inbreeding coefficients of the Hadza. *Annals of Human Biology* 4:219–223.

Strassman, B. I. 1997. The biology of menstruation in *Homo sapiens*: Total life-time menses, fecundity, and nonsynchrony in a natural-fertility population. *Current Anthropology* 38:123–129.

Sugiyama, L. 2004. Illness, injury, and disability among Shiwiar forager-horticulturalists: Implications of health-risk buffering for the evolution of human life history. *American Journal of Physical Anthropology* 123:371–389.

Sugiyama, L. S. 2003. Social roles, prestige, and health risk: Social niche specialization as a risk-buffering strategy. *Human Nature* 14:165–190.

Sutton, J. E. G. 1986. The irrigation and manuring of their Engaruka field system. *Azania* 21:27–48.

Sutton, J. E. G. 1989. Toward a history of cultivating the fields. *Azania* 21:27–48.

————. 1992. *A thousand years of East Africa*. Nairobi: British Institute in East Africa.

Symington, M. M. 1988. Food competition and foraging party size in the black spider monkey (*Ateles-paniscus-chamek*). *Behaviour* 105:117–134.

Symons, D. 1987. If we're all Darwinians, what's the fuss about? In *Sociobiology and psychology: Ideas, issues, and applications*, ed. C. B. Crawford, M. F. Smith, and D. L. Krebs, 121–146. Hillsdale, NJ: Lawrence Erlbaum Associates.

Tanner, N., and A. Zihlman. 1976. Women in evolution. 1. Innovation and selection in human origins. *Signs* 1:585–608.

Testart, A. 1985. *Le communisme primitif: Economie et ideologie*. Paris: Maison des Sciences de l'Homme.

————. 1987. Game sharing systems and kinship systems among hunter-gatherers. *Man* 22:287–304.

Thieme, H. 1997. Lower paleolithic hunting spears from Germany. *Nature* 385:807–810.

Thomas, F., F. Renaud, E. Benefice, T. De Meeus, and J. F. Guegan. 2001. International variability of ages at menarche and menopause: Patterns and main determinants. *Human Biology* 73:271–290.

Thornhill, R. 1984. Alternative female choice tactics in the scorpionfly *Hylobittacus-apicalis (Mecoptera)* and their implications. *American Zoologist* 24:367–383.

Tindale, N. 1953. Tribal and intertribal marriages among the Australian aborigines. In *Human biology: A record of research*, Vol. 25, ed. G. W. Lasker, J. Brozek, B. Glass, D. Mainland, J. N. Spuhler, and W. L. Straus, 169–190. Baltimore: John Hopkins Press.

Todd, P. M., L. Penke, B. Fasolo, and A. P. Lenton. 2007. Different cognitive processes underlie human mate choices and mate preferences. *Proceedings of the National Academy of Sciences of the United States of America* 104:15011–15016.

Tomita, K. 1966. The sources of food for the Hadzapi tribe: The life of a hunting tribe in East Africa. *Kyoto University African Studies* 1:157–171.

Tonkinson, R. 1978. *The Mardudjara aborigines: Living the dream in Australia's desert.* New York: Holt, Rhinehart and Winston.

Tooby, J., and L. Cosmides. 1990. The past explains the present: Emotional adaptations and the structure of ancestral environments. *Ethology and Sociobiology* 11:375–424.

Townsend, J. M., and T. Wasserman. 1998. Sexual attractiveness: Sex differences in assessment and criteria. *Evolution and Human Behavior* 19:171–191.

Trivers, R. L. 1971. The evolution of reciprocal altruism. *Quarterly Review of Biology* 46:35–57.

———. 1972. Parental investment and sexual selection. *Sexual Selection and the Descent of Man* 1971:136–179.

———. 1974. Parent-offspring conflict. *American Zoologist* 14:249–264.

Trivers, R. L., and D. E. Willard. 1973. Natural selection of parental ability to vary the sex ratio of offspring. *Science* 179:90–92.

Turnbull, C. M. 1983. *The Mbuti pygmies: Change and adaptation.* New York: Holt, Rinehart and Winston.

Ungar, P. S., ed. 2007. *Evolution of the human diet: The Known, the unknown, and the unknowable.* Oxford: Oxford University Press.

U.S. Census Bureau. 2002. U.S. census data.

———. 2004. *America's families and living arrangements: 2003: Annual social and economic supplement: 2003 current population survey.*

———. 2007. U. S. Census data.

van den Berghe, P. 1979. *Human family systems.* Prospect Heights, IL: Waveland.

Van Schaik, C. P., E. A. Fox, and L. T. Fechtman. 2003. Individual variation in the rate of use of tree-hole tools among wild orang-utans: Implications for hominin evolution. *Journal of Human Evolution* 44:11–23.

Vaughan, R. 1994. *The Arctic: A history.* Dover, NH: Sutton.

Vehrencamp, S. L. 1983a. A model for the evolution of despotic versus egalitarian societies. *Animal Behaviour* 31:667–682.

———. 1983b. Optimal degree of skew in cooperative societies. *American Zoologist* 23:327–335.

Vickery, W. L., L. Giraldeau, J. J. Templeton, D. L. Kramer, and C. A. Chapman. 1991. Producers, scroungers, and group foraging. *American Naturalist* 137:847–863.

Vincent, A. S. 1985a. Plant foods in savanna environments: A preliminary report of tubers eaten by the Hadza of northern Tanzania. *World Archaeology* 17:131–147.

———. 1985b. Wild tubers as a harvestable resource in the East African savannas: Ecological and ethnographic studies. Ph.D. dissertation, University of California, Berkeley.

von Neumann, J., and O. Morgenstern. 1944. *Theory of games and economic behavior*. Princeton, NJ: Princeton University Press.

Waldbaum, J. C. 1978. *From bronze to iron: The transition from the Bronze Age to the Iron Age in eastern Mediterranean*. Goteborg, Sweden: Paul Astroms Forlag.

Walker, R., M. Gurven, K. Hill, H. Migliano, N. Chagnon, R. De Souza, G. Djurovic, R. Hames, A. M. Hurtado, H. Kaplan, K. Kramer, W. J. Oliver, C. Valeggia, and T. Yamauchi. 2006. Growth rates and life histories in twenty-two small-scale societies. *American Journal of Human Biology* 18:295–311.

Walters, J. R., and R. M. Seyfarth. 1987. Conflict and cooperation. In *Primate societies*, ed. B. Smuts, D. L. Cheney, R. M. Seyfarth, R. W. Wrangham, and T. T. Struhsaker, 306–317. Chicago: University of Chicago Press.

Waser, P. M. 1996. Patterns and consequences of dispersal in gregarious carnivores. In *Carnivore behavior, ecology, and evolution*, vol. 2, ed. J. L. Gittleman, 267–295. Ithica, NY: Cornell University Press.

Washburn, S. L., and I. DeVore. 1961. Social behavior of baboons and early man. In *Social life of early man*, ed. S. L. Washburn, 91–105. Chicago: Aldine.

Werther, C. W., ed. 1898. *Die Mittleren Hochlander des Nordilichen Deutsch-Ost-Afrika*. Berlin: Verlag von Hermann Patel.

West, M. M., and M. J. Konner. 1976. The role of father in anthropological perspective. In *The role of the father in child development*, ed. M. E. Lamb, 185–216. New York: John Wiley and Sons.

Westermarck, E. 1929. *Marriage*. New York: Jonathan Cape and Harrison Smith.

White, F. J., and K. D. Wood. 2007. Female feeding priority in bonobos, *Pan paniscus*, and the question of female dominance. *American Journal of Primatology* 69:837–850.

White, T., B. Asfaw, D. DeGusta, H. Gilbert, G. D. Richards, G. Suwa, and F. C. Howell. 2003. Pleistocene *Homo sapiens* from Middle Awash, Ethiopia. *Nature* 423:742–747.

Whiten, A. 1992. Commentary: Was there no place like home? A new perspective on early hominid archeological sites from the mapping of chimpanzee nests. *Current Anthropology* 33:200–201.

Whitfield, J. 2003. Ape populations decimated by hunting and ebola virus. *Nature* 422:551.

Whitten, P. L. 1987. Infants and adult males. In *Primate societies*, ed. B. Smuts, D. L. Cheney, R. M. Seyfarth, R. W. Wrangham, and T. T. Struhsaker, 343–357. Chicago: University of Chicago Press.

Wilcox, A. J., D. D. Baird, D. B. Dunson, D. R. McConnaughey, J. S. Kesner, and C. R. Weinberg. 2004. On the frequency of intercourse around ovulation: Evidence for biological influences. *Human Reproduction* 19:1539–1543.

Wilkins, J. F., and F. W. Marlowe. 2006. Historical changes in marital residence shape global patterns of mitochondrial and Y-chromosome diversity. *BioEssays* 28:290–300.

Williams, G. C. 1957. Pleiotropy, natural-selection, and the evolution of senescence. *Evolution* 11:398–411.

———. 1966. *Adaptation and natural selection*. Princeton, NJ: Princeton University Press.

Wilmsen, E. N. 1989. *Land filled with flies: A political economy of the Kalahari*. Chicago: Chicago University Press.

Winn, S., G. A. Morelli, and E. Z. Tronick. 1990. The infant in the group: A look at Efe caretaking practices. In *The cultural context of infancy*, ed. J. K. Nugent, B. M. Lester, and T. B. Brazelton, 87–109. Norwood, NJ: Ablex.

Winterhalder, B. 1986. Diet choice, risk, and food sharing in a stochastic environment. *Journal of Anthropological Archaeology* 5:369–392.

———. 1996a. Marginal model of tolerated theft. *Ethology and Sociobiology* 17:37–53.

———. 1996b. Social foraging and the behavioral ecology of intragroup resource transfers. *Evolutionary Anthropology* 5:46–57.

———. 2001. Intragroup resource transfers: Comparative evidence, models, and implications for human evolution. In *Meat-eating and human evolution*, ed. C. B. Stanford and H. T. Bunn, 279–301. Oxford: Oxford University Press.

Winterhalder, B., and E. A. Smith. 2000. Analyzing adaptive strategies: Human behavioral ecology at twenty-five. *Evolutionary Anthropology* 9:51–72.

Wolovich, C. K., S. Evans, and J. A. French. 2008. Dads do not pay for sex but do buy the milk: Food sharing and reproduction in owl monkeys (*Aotus spp.*). *Animal Behaviour* 75:1155–1163.

Wood, B. M. 2006. Prestige or provisioning: A test of foraging goals among the Hadza. *Current Anthropology* 47:383–387.

Wood, B. M., and F. M. Marlowe. 2007. Do Hadza children benefit from their father's foraging? Human Behavior and Evolution Society, Williamsburg, VA.

———. In prep. Where do men's foods go? The sharing and eating of male acquired foods among the Hadza.

Wood, J. W. 1994. *Dynamics of human reproduction: Biology, biometry, demography*. New York: Aldine de Gruyter.

Woodburn, J. C. 1959. Hadza conceptions of health and disease. *One day symposium on attitudes to health and disease among some East African tribes, East Africa, 1959*, 89–94.

———. 1962. The future of the Tindiga. *Tanganyika Notes and Records* 59:268–273.

———. 1964. The social organization of the Hadza of north Tanganyika. Ph.D. disseration, Cambridge University.

———. 1968a. An introduction to Hadza ecology. In *Man the hunter*, ed. R. B. Lee and I. DeVore, 49–55. Chicago: Aldine.

———. 1968b. Stability and flexibility in Hadza residential groupings. In *Man the hunter*, ed. R. B. Lee and I. DeVore, 103–110. Chicago: Aldine.

———. 1970. *Hunters and gatherers: The material culture of the nomadic Hadza*. London: Trustees of the British Museum.

———. 1979. Minimal politics: The political organization of the Hadza of north Tanzania. Iin *Politics in leadership*, ed. W. A. Shack and P. S. Cohen, 244–266. Oxford: Clarendon Press.

———. 1980. Hunters and gatherers today and reconstruction of the past. In *Soviet and Western anthropology*, ed. E. Gellner, 95–117. London: Duckworth.

———. 1982a. Egalitarian societies. *Man* 17:431–451.

———. 1982b. Social dimensions of death in four African hunting and gathering societies. In *Death and the regeneration of life*, ed. M. Bloch and J. Barry, 187–210. Cambridge: Cambridge University Press.

———. 1988. African hunter-gatherer social organization: Is it best understood as a product of encapsulation? In *Hunters and Gatherers, Vol. 1: History, evolution, and social change*, ed. T. Ingold, D. Riches, and J. Woodburn, 31–65. Oxford: Berg.

———. 1997. Indigenous discrimination: The ideological basis for local discrimination against hunter-gatherer minorities in sub-Saharan Africa. *Ethnic and Racial Studies* 20:345–361.

———. 1998. Sharing is not a form of exchange: An analysis of property-sharing in immediate-return hunter-gatherer societies. In *Property relations: Renewing the anthropological tradition*, ed. C. M. Hann, 48–63. Cambridge: Cambridge University Press.

——— nd. Explaining paternal authority: A social anthropologist's analysis. Social Anthropology, University College London (retired).

Work, T. H., A. Ifekwunigwe, D. B. Jelliffe, P. Jelliffe, and C. G. Neumann. 1973. Tropical problems in nutrition. *Annals of Internal Medicine* 79:701–711.

World Cultures. 2005. Vol. 15, data file. La Jolla, CA: World Cultures.

Wrangham, R. W. 1975. The behavioral ecology of chimpanzees in Gombe National Park, Tanzania. Ph.D., dissertation, Cambridge University, Cambridge, UK.

Wrangham, R. W., J. H. Jones, G. Laden, D. Pilbeam, and N. Conklin-Brittain. 1999. The raw and the stolen: Cooking and the ecology of human origins. *Current Anthropology* 40:567–594.

Wrangham, R. W., and D. Peterson. 1996. *Demonic males*. Boston: Houghton Mifflin.

Wrangham, R. W., and M. L. Wilson. nd. Intrasexual bonding and the economics of territorial defense in fission-fusion communities of primates.

Wright, S. 1931. Evolution in Mendelian populations. *Genetics* 16:97–159.

Wynne-Edwards, V. C. 1962. *Animal dispersion in relation to social behaviour*. London: Oliver and Boyd.

Yeakel, J. D., N. C. Bennett, P. L. Koch, and N. J. Dominy. 2007. The isotopic ecology of African mole rats informs hypotheses on the evolution of human diet. *Proceedings of the Royal Society, Series B-Biological Sciences* 274:1723–1730.

Yellen, J. E. 1976. Settlement patterns of the !Kung: An archeological perspective. In *Kalahari hunter-gatherers*, ed. R. B. Lee and I. DeVore, 47–72. Cambridge, MA: Harvard University Press.

Zaadstra, B., M., J. C. Seidell, P. A. H. Van Noord, E. R. te Velde, J. D. F. Habbema, and B. Vrieswijk, Karbaat, 1993. Fat and female fecundity: Prospective study of effect of body fat distribution on conception rates. *British Medical Journal* 306:484–487.

Zahavi, A. 1995. Altruism as a handicap: The limitations of kin selection and reciprocity. *Journal of Avian Biology* 26:1–3.

Index

Note: Page numbers followed by f indicate figures, and those followed by t indicate tables.

adaptation, 3
adaptive behavior, 7
Adaptively Relevant Environment
    (ARE), 8
adolescents, 156–158, 168–169
adulthood, 57–60, 158–159
affairs, 169, 171, 176, 179
Africa, 11
African trypanosomiasis, 141
age, 122, 129, 143–148, 151, 154–155,
    182–183, 184–185, 190, 192, 199,
    208, 220f
age estimates, 135–136
agricultural food, 36
agriculture, 11, 32, 48, 135
Aka Pygmies, 207t
alcohol use, 287
Alexander, R. D., 145
allomothers, 200, 201, 204–206
ambush hunting, 118–119
Andamanese, 267
animal skins/skinning. *See* skins/skinning
anthropology, 139
Apicella, Coren, 188
Arabs, 18–19
archaeology, 17–18
Arctic foragers, 258
ARE (Adaptively Relevant Environment), 8
area (foraging), 263–267
arrows, 18, 82t, 86–89, 97
art, 18, 94–95
artifacts, 74, 75t
Australia: agriculture in, 11; foraging in,
    269; male contribution to diet in,
    279

autonomy, 55, 172, 174, 198
avoidance relationships, 53
axes, 83t, 90–91

baalako, 116
baboons, 104, 135
babysitting, 200, 205, 206f
Bagshawe, F. J., 30, 61
Balambala, 55
Bantu people, 18–19, 28
baobab: foraging for, 79, 115–116; as
    honey source, 29; processing of,
    120
baskets, 93
beads, 94–95
beliefs, 63
berries: availability of, 108; foraging
    for, 114–115, 227; in Hadza diet,
    126, 127, 127t; sharing of, 234–235,
    237
bilateral descent, 270
bilocality, 49
bipedalism, 8, 281
bird nest sticks, 83t
birth, 64–65
blindness, 138
Blurton Jones, Nicholas, 31, 35, 48, 80,
    137, 141, 153, 196, 215–217, 220,
    231–232
BMI. *See* body mass index
body adornment, 94
body fat, 142t, 145, 146, 147f
body mass index (BMI), 142t, 145, 146,
    146f
bonobos, 47, 281

bows, 82*t*, 84–86, 97, 157, 278
British colonialism, 32
Burley, Nancy, 196

camps, 39–43, 79, 238–239
cancer, 140, 159
carrying devices, 76, 92–93
central-place foraging (CPF), 104,
    106–107, 273
central-place provisioning (CPP), 103–105;
    and body size, 134; as factor in
    food-sharing, 235–237, 236*t*; in for-
    aging populations, 273
children, 55. *See also* parenting; during
    adolescence, 156–158; clothing of,
    94; death of, 149–150; and food-
    sharing, 239; and foraging, 36,
    104–106, 130; growth of, 134,
    137–139; during infancy, 156; and
    marriage, 178–181; number of,
    182*f*, 183*f*; residential arrangements
    for, 52
chimpanzees: dominance hierarchies of,
    43–44; feed-as-you-go patterns of,
    104; food acquisition by, 125; hunt-
    ing by, 268; sex dispersal of, 47; sur-
    vivorship of, 150, 151*f*; tool use by,
    74, 76, 97, 98
Christianity, 33
climate, 13
clitorectomy, 56–57, 63
clothes, 94, 199
colonialism, 32
competition, 165, 175, 176
concealed ovulation, 176–177
conflict, 248–249, 265
congolobe, 86
conservatism, 33–38
Cooper, B., 31, 172
cooperation, 225–228. *See also* food-
    sharing; in foraging, 131, 227–229;
    and primitive communism, 252–254
cooperative hunting, 268
costly signaling, 231, 232, 243*t*, 249,
    251
CPF. *See* central-place foraging
CPP. *See* central-place provisioning
creation myth, 61–62, 66
crèche, 104–107
Crittenden, Alyssa, 65
cultural complexity, 69–71, 70*t*–71*t*

dancing, 59–60, 67–68
Darwin, C., 3, 4
Datoga people, 28, 31, 56
Dawkins, R., 5
death, 65–66

death pollution, 57
delayed-return foragers, 37
Dempwolff, Otto, 29
DG. *See* dictator game
dictator game (DG), 243–244, 246*f*, 247
diet: and age of menarche, 134; of forag-
    ing populations, 259–260, 262; male
    contributions to, 279–280
diet breadth model, 101
differential allocation hypothesis, 196
digging sticks: dimensions of, 83*t*; early
    uses of, 76, 84; as naturefacts, 74;
    for self-defense, 280; and sexual
    division of labor, 97; types of, 80–81
direct care: in parenting, 199–200;
    providers of, 204*t*
divorce, 178–181, 187
Dobe !Kung, 11
dominance, 43–46
drinking water, 41, 42*f*
dry season: camp sizes during, 40;
    foraging during, 108; hunting
    during, 118, 119; living conditions
    during, 95
Dunduiya region, 13–15

EA (Ethnographic Atlas), 69
East Africa, 1, 2*f*
ecology, 39, 258–259
economic theory, 244
EEA. *See* Environment of Evolutionary
    Adaptedness
Efe Pygmies, 172, 207*t*
effective mating system, 167
egalitarianism, 44–46, 55, 248
//ekwa, 109, 113
elati, 55, 57
elati-ka-eh, 55
elati-nakwete, 55
elderly Hadza, 160–161
encounter hunting, 118
Enderlein, Peter, 61
energy-dense foods, 134
Environment of Evolutionary Adapted-
    ness (EEA), 7–8
environments, 3, 7–9
epeme, 57–60
epeme dance, 59–60, 67–68
epeme meat ritual, 57–59, 62–64, 66, 102
epilepsy, 140
equestrian foragers, 258
ESS (evolutionarily stable strategy), 7
ethnic groups: in foraging populations,
    269–270; influences on Hadza from,
    34*t*–35*t*; in neighboring populations,
    19, 28–29
Ethnographic Atlas (EA), 69

evolutionarily stable strategy (ESS), 7
evolutionary psychology, 7
evolutionary theory, 2–9; adaptive behavior in, 7; and environments, 3, 7–9; natural selection in, 3–4; and optimal foraging theory, 5–6
extramarital affairs, 169, 176, 179

face preferences, 187–189, 188f
family. See kinship
fathers. See also parenting: in large camps, 41; parenting by, 206–212; provisioning by, 220–224
feed-as-you-go foragers, 104, 237
female choice, 165, 166, 170–173
female-female bonding, 54
female-female competition, 165
female genital mutilation, 56–57, 63
fertility: as factor in mating, 168t, 184; in life history, 149, 151–152, 158
fertility sticks, 56, 174
fidelity, 187
fire drills, 83t, 91–92, 97
fires, 92
fish, 63, 254, 260, 262, 262f, 279
Fisher, Ronald, 136
fitness: inclusive, 3–4; and maladaptive behavior, 8–9
Fleming, H. C., 16
fluctuating asymmetry, 147–149
food: and optimal foraging theory, 5–6; and parenting, 213–215, 214t; taboos about, 63; types of, 110f–112f
food processing, 97, 98t; as factor in food-sharing, 235; and foraging, 120
food-sharing, 229–252; factors influencing, 235–239; in foraging populations, 273; frequencies of, 236; and mortality, 163; primary distribution in, 239–242; reasons for, 224–252, 229–232; types of, 232–235
food transfer, 229, 236t
foraging, 101–131; for baobab, 115–116; for berries, 114–115; central-place provisioning in, 103–105; cooperation in, 227–229; daily routine of, 108–109; diet based on returns from, 125–130; and environment, 9; and food processing, 120; for honey, 116–118; by hunting, 118–119; leaving weanlings in camp for, 105–108; and optimal foraging theory, 5–6, 101–103; and parenting, 216–224; parties for, 120–125; and physical growth, 153–156; by scavenging, 119; and seasonality, 108;

sexual division of labor in, 103, 128t, 130–131; for tubers, 109, 113–114; types of food found in, 110–112
foraging parties, 120–125, 237
fossils: hominin, 1; "living," 12, 285–286

gambling, 66
game preserves, 37
gametes, 166
game theory, 6, 195, 225
gender, 53–54. See also sex (biological)
genetics: in evolutionary theory, 3–5, 7; of Hadza, 16; and philopatry, 48
genital mutilation, 56–57, 63
Germany, 19
gerontocracy, 271
Gidgingali, 207t
gonorrhea, 140
gourds, 92–93, 93f
grandmother hypothesis, 162
grandparents, 204–206
grass huts, 95–97, 96f
grip strength, 142t, 146, 147, 148f
grooming, 66, 67f
group size, 263–267
growth, physical, 141–149; anthropometrics for, 142t; and body fat, 142t, 145, 146, 147f; and body mass index, 142t, 145, 146f; and grip strength, 142t, 146, 147, 148f; in height, 142–143, 142t, 143f; and offspring variation, 145; in weight, 142–144, 142t, 144f
growth rates, 133

ha!ako. See hammerstones
habitat, 13–15
habitat variation, 259, 260f, 261t
hach'e'e. See poison
Hadzaland, 2f; archaeology in, 17–18; protection of, 43, 287
Hadzane language, 2, 15–16; gender distinctions in, 53; numbers in, 135
hamadryas baboons, 104
Hamilton, William, 3–4
hammerstones, 74, 76, 79–80, 97
hawk-dove game, 6–7, 6t
Hawkes, Kristen, 31, 36, 44–45, 215–217, 220
health, 137–139
height, 142–143, 142t, 143f
hik!owa, 86
history, of Hadza, 18–28, 20–27t
Hobbes, Thomas, 252, 286
holding, of infants, 200, 201t, 207t, 209f

Holocene epoch, 257
hominins: defined, 1; environments of,
    7–8; horizontal expansion of, 15;
    tools used by, 74, 276, 278; use of
    central places by, 103
Homo erectus, 18, 84, 134, 270
Homo ergaster, 17, 134, 270
Homo habilis, 17
Homo-Pan split, 281
Homo sapiens, 17
homosexuality, 53, 168–169
honey: foraging for, 116–118, 117f, 222,
    223; guide birds for, 31, 117; shar-
    ing of, 233f, 234, 253; use of axes
    for acquiring, 90
houses, 95–97
human niches, 258
hunter-gatherers: defined, 1; egalitarian-
    ism of, 44–45
hunting, 118–119; by foraging popula-
    tions, 268–269; scavenging vs., 276,
    278–279; style of, 36, 123
hunting reputation, 192–193, 211,
    215–216
hypergyny, 172

IBIs. *See* inter-birth intervals
illness, 65, 139–141
immediate-return foragers, 37
inclusive fitness, 3–4
independence: of children, 198; of
    women, 172, 174
India, 152
infant mortality, 150, 271
infants, 79, 156, 200, 201t, 207t, 209f
in-kind delayed-reciprocity, 230–231,
    243t
intelligence, 186
inter-birth intervals (IBIs), 104, 135
intermarriage, 28
inter-sexual selection, 165. *See also* female
    choice
intrasexual selection, 165. *See also* male-
    male competition
Iraqw people, 19, 28, 56–57
iron, 28, 80, 84, 99, 276
Isaac, Glynn, 231
Isanzu people, 16
ivory trade, 19

jealousy, 175, 192
Jelliffe, D. B., 137–138
Jelliffe, P., 137–138
jewelry, 94–95
Ju/'hoansi, 11, 16
juvenile mortality, 150, 163
juveniles, 156–158

Kalahari debate, 12
kalakasy, 89
kangas, 94
kanoa, 116, 117–118
Kaplan, H., 153
Khoisan languages, 15, 16
kinship, 49–52; and food-sharing, 239;
    in foraging populations, 270
kin terms, 49–51, 50t, 51t
Kiswahili language, 2, 16, 135–136
knives, 83t, 84, 85, 97, 140
Kohl-Larsen, L., 17, 66, 172, 175, 196
koinophilia, 189
!Kung, 11–12, 16, 172, 207t, 267

Lack, David, 4
lactose tolerance, 8
Laetoli site, 17
Lake Eyasi, 13
language(s), 15–16; of foraging popula-
    tions, 269–270; Hadzane, 2, 15–16,
    53, 135; Khoisan, 15, 16; and kinship
    terms, 49–51, 50t, 51t; Kiswahili,
    2, 16, 135–136; San, 15–16; Swahili,
    16, 36
leadership, 31, 40
Lee, Richard, 11, 12, 252
leisure, 66–67
levirate, 52, 131, 171
life expectancy, 160
life history, 133–135
life stages, 55
"living fossils," 12, 285–286
lukuchuko, 66

McDowell, W., 32, 35
mai-to-ko ritual, 55–57, 169
maize, 36
maladaptive behavior, 8–9
malaria, 140
male choice, 165
male-male bonding, 54
male-male competition, 165, 175, 176
male provisioning, 171f
Mangola region, 13, 14f
marriage: and mating, 170–176; median
    ages of, 151; and residence, 46–49
marula, 79, 80f
Masai population: expansion of, 28, 38;
    female genital mutilation in, 56;
    wars with, 30
mate-guarding, 191
mate provisioning, 230, 243t, 251
mating, 165–193; and adolescents,
    168–169; and divorce, 178–181,
    187; female choice in, 165, 166,
    170–173; and food-sharing, 239; in

foraging populations, 261, 270–272, 271; hunting reputation as factor in, 192–193; and marriage, 170–176; and polygyny, 168, 172, 176, 178–181; preferences in, 184–189; reproductive effort in, 189–192; selection processing for, 181–184; and sex ratio, 175–178; and sexuality, 174, 175; and sexual selection, 165–166; systems for, 166–168
maturity, 153
mbira, 67
Mbuti Pygmies, 71
meat: *epeme*, 57–59, 62–64, 66, 102; in Hadza diet, 36, 128; and hunting reputation, 217–220; preparation of, 120
medicine, 46, 139–141
men: competition amongst, 165, 175, 176; dominance of, 45–46; *epeme* meat ritual of, 57–59, 62–64, 66, 102
menarche, 55, 134, 151
Mendelian genetics, 3
menopause, 152, 161–163, 178
menstruation, 158–159, 175, 177
midwives, 65
millett, 36
miseko. See fire drills
missionaries, 33, 288
mitochondrial DNA (mtDNA), 48
mobility: and egalitarianism, 45; of foraging populations, 263–267; and social organization, 39–43
Mongo wa Mono, 33
monogamy, 145, 164, 167, 171–172
morbidity, 140–141
mortality, 140–141, 149–151
mothers, 200–203. *See also* allomothers; parenting; and child mortality, 150; nursing by, 76, 196, 198, 199f; provisioning by, 219–220
MtDNA (mitochondrial DNA), 48
multilocality, 48, 49
murder, 141
Murdock, G. P., 69
music, 67–68
mutations, 166, 189
mutualism, 229–230

naming, 52–53
natal groups, 47
nateako, 116
natural fertility societies, 7
natural selection, 3–4
naturefacts, 74, 75t, 76
neolocality, 49
nepotism, 230, 243t, 251

net primary productivity (NPP), 259, 264, 265
night blindness, 138
not-in-kind exchange, 230, 241, 243t
NPP. *See* net primary productivity
nursing, 76, 196, 198, 199f

Obst, Erich, 29–30, 36, 60, 170, 172, 173, 196
O'Connell, James, 31, 36, 84, 119, 215–217, 220
offspring variation, 145
OFT. *See* optimal foraging theory
olako, 55
ola-pe, 55
Oldeani, Mount, 13, 14f
Olduvai Gorge, 17
operational sex ratio (OSR), 137, 167, 176, 210
optimal foraging theory (OFT), 5–6, 101–103
orangutans, 74
Orians, G. H., 103
OSR. *See* operational sex ratio
Oswalt, Wendell, 74
ovulation, 176–177

Pa-nekwete, 55
Pa-nekwete-ka-eh, 55
Pan-Homo split, 281
panjube, 89
Paranthropus boisei, 17
parenting, 195–224; by allomothers, 200, 201, 204–206; direct care in, 199–200; by fathers, 206–212; and foraging, 216–224; and hunting reputations, 215–216; by mothers, 200–203; and provisioning, 212–215, 219–224; in reproductive effort, 195–196; styles of, 196–199
pastoralism, 30, 37, 288
patch-choice model, 101
Pavlov strategy, 226
PD. *See* prisoner's dilemma
peacocks, 165
Pearson, N. E., 103
philopatry, 47
physical growth. *See* growth, physical
plant poison, 89
Pleistocene epoch, 257
poison, 89–90
polyandry, 171–172
polygyny: in foraging populations, 271; frequency of, 55; and mating, 168, 172, 178–181; and operational sex ratio, 176; and sexual dimorphism, 144, 145

population density: growth of, 15; in
    warm-climate sample, 262–263,
    263f
Porter, Claire, 259
potential reproductive rates (PRRs), 167
premarital affairs, 169, 171
primary distribution, 239–242
primitive communism, 252–254
prisoner's dilemma (PD), 225, 226t
private property, 253
property, 253
provisioning, 212–215, 219–224
Provost, C., 69
PRRs (potential reproductive rates),
    167
psychology, evolutionary, 7
puberty, 55–57

Quelea quelea, 139
quivers, 82t

rainy season, 95, 108, 264–265
rape, 174, 187
reciprocity, 226, 230–231, 243t
recreation, 66–67
religion, 8, 60–63
reproduction, 151–153
reproductive cancers, 140
reproductive effort: in mating, 189–192;
    parenting in, 195–196
reproductive skew, 145, 181
reproductive success (RS), 3, 4, 149, 189,
    193, 215
reproductive value (RV), 184
reptiles, 63, 102
residence patterns, 40–43
rituals: epeme dance, 59–60; epeme meat,
    57–59, 62–64, 66, 102; mai-to-ko,
    55–57, 169
rock art, 18
rock shelters, 95, 96f
role specialization, 46
Rousseau, Jean-Jacques, 286
RS. See reproductive success
runaway selection, 166
RV (reproductive value), 184

Sahlins, Marshall, 12, 252
Sandawe people, 15–16
Sands, Bonny, 16, 31
San languages, 15–16
scars, 54
scavenging: foraging by, 119; hunting vs.,
    276, 278–279
SCCS. See Standard Cross-Cultural
    Sample
schooling, 36

scrounging, tolerated. See tolerated
    scrounging
seasonality, 108
selection processing, 181–184
self-reliance, 198
settlement attempts, 32–33
sex (biological), 53–54; and dominance,
    45–46; and marital residence pat-
    terns, 46–49; and tool use, 98
sex play, 168
sex ratio, 136–137, 163, 175–178,
    210
sexual chastity, 8
sexual dimorphism, 143–145, 270
sexual division of labor: in foraging, 103,
    128t, 130–131; of foraging popula-
    tions, 268–269; as role specializa-
    tion, 46; and tools, 97–99
sexuality, 174, 175
sexually transmitted diseases, 149, 152
sexual selection: in evolutionary theory,
    3; in life history, 144; and mating,
    165–166
shanjo, 89
sheaths, 83t
Sipunga region, 13, 14f, 97
skins/skinning, 76, 93–94, 106f
slave trade, 19, 30
sleep, 106
Smith, Eric, 215
Smith, Lars, 31
snakes, 102–103
snaring, 217
socialism, 37
social mating system, 167
social organization: as cultural trait, 256;
    of foraging populations, 269–270; of
    Hadza, 259, 260f, 261t
sororate, 171
spears, 279
Standard Cross-Cultural Sample (SCCS),
    69–71, 70t–71t
status, 43–46
stepparenting, 201, 208–212
sterility, 152
sticks: bird nest, 83t; digging (see digging
    sticks); fertility, 56, 174
stone tools, 74. See also specific tools
storytelling: as form of entertainment, 66;
    frequency of, 37; and mating, 171;
    and religion, 61
stringing, of bows, 85
subsistants, 74, 75t
Sukuma people, 29, 30
Swahili language, 16, 36
Swahili people, 29
syphilis, 140

taboos, 63, 66, 102
Tanzania: European control of, 19; un-
    derdevelopment of, 37
technology: and cultural complexity, 71;
    definitions of, 75*t*; in foraging popu-
    lations, 276, 277*t*–278*t*; in social
    organization, 258–259
techno-units, 75*t*, 76, 97
teeth, 87, 88*f*
termites, 102
territoriality: and food-sharing, 248; of
    foraging populations, 267–268; in
    social organization, 43
TFR. *See* total fertility rate
TFT (tit for tat), 226
theft, 232
theory of mind (TOM), 281
third-party-punishment game (TPPG), 247
tit for tat (TFT), 226
tlakwenakweko, 55
Tli'ika region, 13, 14
tobacco, 175
tolerated scrounging, 231–232, 242,
    243*t*, 250, 251
tolerated theft, 232
TOM (theory of mind), 281
tools, 74–92; arrows, 18, 82*t*, 86–89, 97;
    axes, 83*t*, 90–91; bird nest sticks,
    83*t*; bows, 82*t*, 84–86, 97, 157, 278;
    carrying devices, 76, 92–93; classifi-
    cations of, 75*f*, 77–78*t*; definitions
    of, 75*t*; digging sticks, 74, 76,
    80–81, 83*t*, 84, 97, 280; dimensions
    of, 82–83; fire drills, 83*t*, 91–92, 97;
    hammerstones, 74, 76, 79–80, 97;
    knives, 83*t*, 84, 85, 97, 140; poison,
    89–90; quivers, 82*t*; and sexual divi-
    sion of labor, 97–99; sheaths, 83*t*;
    taxonomy of, 74–75, 75*f*; used by
    hominins, 74, 276, 278
tortoises, 63, 103
total fertility rate (TFR), 149, 271
tourism, 287–288
TPPG (third-party-punishment game), 247
trading, 34*t*, 35*t*, 36, 46, 230
traps, 74, 76

trespassing, 265
ts'apale. *See* digging sticks
tstseya-pe, 55
tubers, 81*f*; availability of, 108; foraging
    for, 109, 113–114, 114*f*

ultimatum game (UG), 243–244,
    246*f*
underground storage units (USOs), 74,
    109. *See also* tubers
undushipi, 114, 115*f*, 139, 254
United States, 142, 158
USOs. *See* underground storage units
uxorilocality, 47–49

Vincent, Anne, 80
virilocality, 47–49
vitamin A deficiency, 138

waist-to-hip (WHR) ratio preferences,
    185–186
walkabouts, 118, 124*f*
war, 264, 268, 269
water-hole ambush hunting, 118–119
water holes, 40, 41
weaning, 156
weapons, 75*t*, 76
weight, 142-144, 142*t*, 144*f*
WHR (waist-to-hip) ratio preferences,
    185–186
Williams, G. C., 4
Wilmsen, E. N., 12
witchcraft, 63–65
women: hierarchies among, 46; independ-
    ence of, 172, 174
Wood, Brian, 218, 240
Woodburn, James, 15, 31, 32, 35, 37, 44,
    60, 91, 137, 253
wooden arrows, 86
Wrangham, Richard, 231
Wynne-Edwards, V. C., 4

Yaeda (Munguli), 33
Y-chromosomes, 48

zeze, 67

Indexer:	Stephen Ingle
Composition:	Westchester Book Group
Text:	10/13 Sabon
Display:	Sabon

Printed in the USA
CPSIA information can be obtained
at www.ICGtesting.com
LVHW021317231223
767295LV00054B/2305